Fodor's 4th Edition

Rome

Fodor's Travel Publications • New York, Toronto, London, Sydney, Auckland
www.fodors.com

CONTENTS

MAPS

Circled letters in text correspond to letters on the photographs. For more information on the sights pictured, turn to the indicated page number Ⓐ⟩ on each photograph.

DESTINATION
ROME

With its statues, lovely fountain, graceful church, and antique ruins, the Piazza Navona embodies the essence of Rome, a vibrant and extraordinary city layered with relics of all the ages of Western civilization. Paintings and sculptures from the Renaissance and Baroque times through the 19th century are at every turn, along with Fascist monoliths and vestiges of ancient times, sometimes inhabited by complacent cats. Take a stroll in a garden pungent with cypress trees. Rub elbows with the politicians and businessmen, the teens and twentysomethings, and the mammas and papas who have the *buona fortuna* to call this place home, and linger over your meals as they do. It won't be long before you beat a path to the legendary Fontana di Trevi to toss in a coin—to make sure you'll return.

ANCIENT ROME

A succession of emperors showed little restraint in ensuring that no one would ever assume their city was anything other than what it was—the center of the civilized world. Most of their extravagant temples, palaces, and monuments are in ruin, but splendidly so, and the ancient city, concentrated around the Campidoglio, the ⒟**Foro Romano,** and the Terme di Caracalla, still conveys might and awe as it was intended to. The city's

Ⓑ 64

Ⓒ 115

most famous ancient monument, the Ⓐ**Colosseo,** still stands proud, and a good thing, too: another legend has it that when this stupendous arena falls, Rome will fall with it. Not all of Imperial Rome's monuments are so grand. The ⒞**Bocca della Verità** (Mouth of Truth), which will allegedly clamp down on the hand of a liar, is actually a drain cover. The Ⓑ**Pantheon,** meanwhile, survives largely intact—probably because this pagan temple became a church, but just maybe because even plunderers had the sense not to tamper with a building of such perfect proportion and harmony.

⒟ 28

THE
HOLY CITY

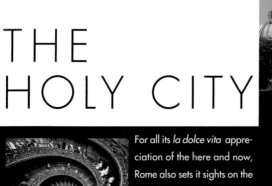

Ⓐ 52

For all its *la dolce vita* appreciation of the here and now, Rome also sets it sights on the hereafter. The city has, after all, been the seat of Christianity for 2,000 years and celebrates this state of enlightenment with no small amount of pomp and circumstance. The Vatican, dominated by the massive dome of the Basilica di San Pietro, may be the spiritual home of 700 million Roman Catholics, but its many splendors, including the lush ©**Vatican Gardens** and the immense collections of the

ⓐ**Vatican Museums,** attract lovers of beauty from all over the world, regardless of religious affiliations. Painters and sculptors have proved themselves particularly adept at lifting Roman churchgoers to heights of ecstasy, and you don't have to walk far before you come upon one of their masterpieces; step into the church of Sant'Agostino, say, and your reward will be Caravaggio's once-scandalous ⓔ*Madonna of the Pilgrims.* The oldest churches in Rome provide a fascinating glimpse of the not-so-heavenly early days of Christianity. The vivid frescoes in 4th-century ⓑ**San Clemente** show harrowing scenes from the lives and deaths of the eponymous saint and other martyrs; the mosaics that light up ⓓ**Santa Maria in Trastevere,** which may be even older, chronicle the life of the Virgin Mary. These uniquely human achievements are striking not because of their grandeur but because, transcending the ages, they embody the sheer power of belief.

9

LA STRADA AND LA PIAZZA

You can explore the Colosseo until your ears ring with the roars of wild beasts, and make the rounds of churches until visions of putti dance in your head. But you won't know Rome until you have paused to appreciate the loveliness and vibrancy of the cityscape, perhaps from a table on the terrace of a bar or caffè. Ⓑ**Trastevere** is particularly well endowed with such ringside seats, but you can enjoy the show from just about anywhere. Chances are you'll eventually want to join the Romans in one of their favorite pastimes, the passeggiata, or stroll. Early Sunday mornings reveal the piazzas free of everyday bustle; most Romans enjoy their walk in late afternoon, and if your ambling then brings you to a place like the Ⓒ**Piazza Navona** or the Ⓐ**Spanish Steps,** you'll savor

Ⓑ 105

Ⓒ 65

this city in all its glory. Be warned, though. Even when you can't imagine coming upon one more stunning scene, you're likely to be drawn into yet another spectacle. This may be the

Ⓓ**Campo dei Fiori** in its nighttime buzz, and if you do find yourself here, who knows? You may just be tempted to wait until the square's market gets into full swing after dawn and the curtain goes up on another performance that in Rome passes for just another daily event.

SHOPPING

Even if you are resolutely determined not to shop in Rome, sooner or later you will probably be seduced into handing over a few euros to the Eternal City's merchants. For one thing, displays in shop windows are almost as arresting as the street life that unfolds in front of them. Along the lanes and byways near the Ⓐ**Piazza di Spagna,** such as the Ⓑ**Via Condotti,** and Via Borgogonona, Via del Corso, you can ricochet from Gucci and Armani to Prada, Valentino, and Versace with less effort than it takes to whip out your platinum card. Then, too, the Italian flair for design seems to be all the more alluring on its home turf, as you'll see at couturiers and antiques dealers, perfumers and stationers. Elegance reigns in leather goods and fashion in all price categories, from hats and gloves to jewelry and knitwear. And traditional markets such as the one in the Ⓒ**Campo dei Fiori** line a street or two of every Roman neighborhood.

DINING

Ⓐ 144

Rome doesn't foment culinary trends or breed star chefs, and some local diners are suspicious of dishes that are not *alla nonna* (as grandma used to make it). Still, Romans are passionate about food and appreciate restaurants such as Ⓐ**Agata e Romeo,** where chefs dig deep to their Roman roots to create delicious variations of old standbys. Here and at other *ristoranti* and *osterie* around town, pasta is always homemade and ingredients are invariably excellent and fresh, even if that means certain vegetables are off menus except when truly in season—*abbacchio* (baby lamb, perhaps roasted with rosemary) shows up on menus only in spring. Look for chops grilled *alla scottadito* (hot off the grill) and *carciofi* (artichokes, heavenly prepared just about any way). Of course, no Roman meal stands solely on the merit of what comes out of the kitchen. There's the wine, to begin with. And conviviality is essential. The fact is, an excellent meal with congenial company is a Roman experience not to be forgotten. So much the better if it comes with a spectacular view, as you'll find at Ⓑ**La Terazza dell'Eden.**

Ⓑ 147

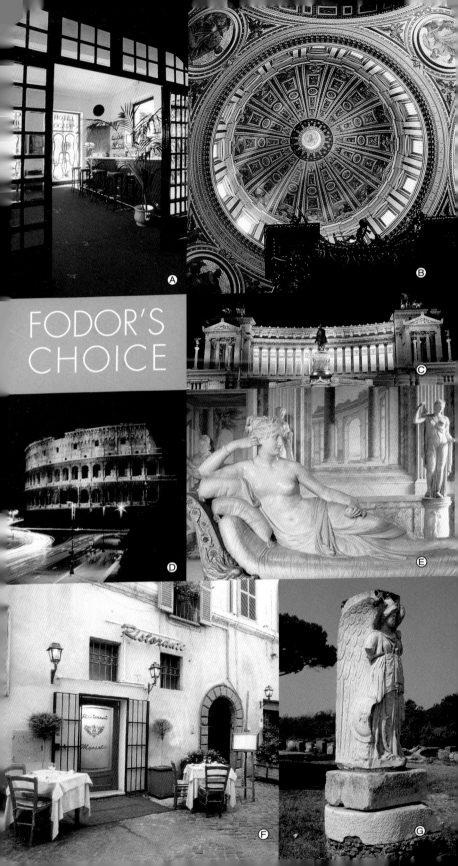

FODOR'S
CHOICE

Even with so many special places in Rome, Fodor's writers and editors have their favorites. Here are a few that stand out.

ANCIENT WONDERS

Ⓓ **Colosseo.** The shouts of gladiators, the cries of the crowd, and wails of pitiless persecutions (though the Christians were probably martyred elsewhere) echo across these ancient stones. ☞ p. 33

Ⓖ **Ostia Antica.** Perhaps even more than Pompeii, the excavated port city of ancient Rome conveys a picture of everyday life in a busy commercial center. ☞ p. 220

The Pantheon. Take time to absorb the harmonious proportions of this pagan temple, later consecrated as a church, and stand under the oculus to look up at the eye of heaven. ☞ p. 64

CHURCHES

Ⓑ **St. Peter's Basilica.** The largest church in the world, built over the tomb of St. Peter, is also the most imposing and breathtaking architectural achievement of the Renaissance. ☞ p. 42

San Clemente. Delve deep into the excavations below this church for an idea of how Rome, and its religions, grew. ☞ p. 120

Santa Maria in Trastevere. Mosaics from the 12th and 13th centuries give a unique glow to what is purportedly Rome's oldest church dedicated to the Virgin Mary. ☞ p. 111

Santi Quattro Coronati. An enclave of peace where nuns chant their prayers, this is one of the most unusual and unexpected corners of Rome, resisting the tide of time and traffic outside its doors. ☞ p. 123

ARTISTIC TREASURES

Ⓔ **Galleria Borghese.** Resplendent with frescoes and stuccos, this museum harbors Canova's *Pauline Borghese* and several Bernini works that define Baroque sculpture. ☞ p. 98

Palazzo Altemps. The restored interior hints at the splendid Roman lifestyle of the 16th through 18th centuries and serves as a stunning showcase for the most illustrious pieces from the Museo Nazionale Romano's collection of ancient Roman sculpture. ☞ p. 63

The ceiling of the Sistine Chapel. No matter how many photos you've seen of Michelangelo's masterpiece, it never fails to amaze. ☞ p. 47

QUINTESSENTIAL ROME

Campo dei Fiori. The "Field of Flowers" has a double identity as a bustling marketplace and a bohemian haunt. The vibrant street life has changed little in 200 years. ☞ p. 59

Gianicolo. The climb to the top of this hill rewards you with a marvelous vista of the entire city and the Castelli Romani. Add a sunset and you have a perfect Roman moment. ☞ p. 107

Ⓒ **Monumento a Vittorio Emanuele II.** For sheer size and conspicuousness, this is Rome's most visible and bombastic landmark, nicknamed "the typewriter." ☞ p. 74

Piazza Navona. The exuberant spirit of the Baroque Age is embodied in Bernini's fantastic Fontana dei Quattro Fiumi (Fountain of the Four Rivers), set off by the curves and steeples of Borromini's church of Sant'Agnese, and admired by colorful crowds devouring gelati. ☞ p. 65

DINING

La Pergola. This is the most celebrated restaurant in Rome, with the fantastic creations of chef Heinz Beck. It's one of the few places in the ancient city that understands modern cuisine. $$$$ ☞ p. 148

La Rosetta. At this elegant, wood-paneled restaurant, first-rate fish is the specialty. Try grilled fish and crustaceans or *vongole veraci* (large sautéed clams). $$$$ ☞ p. 140

Alberto Ciarla. Look past the somewhat gaudy red-and-black interior, and you'll discover one of Rome's most reliable fish restaurants. $$$ ☞ p. 145

Papá Baccus. The city's leading outpost of Tuscan cuisine took the mad-cow scare as an impetus to expand its menu beyond the traditional *bistecca alla fiorentina*, adding nonbeef dishes that make a good restaurant even better. $$$ ☞ p. 147

Ⓕ **Myosotis.** A central location, an extensive menu that treads the delicate line between tradition and innovation, and great value make Myosotis a place to return to. $$–$$$ ☞ p. 140

Tazza d'Oro. Italy's national coffee habit is a key to its character, and there's no better place to take a cup of *caffè* than here. Do as the Romans do: order a glass of water as a chaser. $ ☞ p. 156

LODGING

Forum. This beautiful hotel is set amid the towering ruins of the Imperial Forums, complete with views and a famous rooftop restaurant. $$$$ ☞ p. 167

Grand Hotel Plaza. Serene luxury sits in the very heart of the historic center, an easy stroll from every major sight. $$$$ ☞ p. 168

Raphaël. Perhaps the best location in Rome, just behind Piazza Navona, is combined here with strikingly original decor and exquisite service. $$$$ ☞ p. 171

Ⓐ **Locarno.** The location, near Piazza del Popolo, is convenient, the atmosphere is welcoming, and the rooms have old-world charm. $$$ ☞ p. 170

Palazzo al Velabro. One of Rome's secret treasures is discreetly positioned within the ancient Boario Forum, next to the Arch of Janus. $$$ ☞ p. 161

Albergo del Sole al Biscione. A rambling, multilevel terrace overlooking medieval Campo dei Fiori and the surrounding tile rooftops makes this quaint hotel unforgettable. $$ ☞ p. 165

1 EXPLORING ROME

Rome is a heady blend of artistic and architectural masterpieces, classical ruins, and extravagant Baroque churches and piazzas. The places evoke the people— Roman emperors concerned with outdoing their predecessors in grandeur, powerful prelates enmeshed in intricate scandals, geniuses summoned by popes to add to the Vatican's treasures, a dictator who left his mark on the city before his imperial dreams were shattered, and the contemporary Romans, full of the earthy energy that makes this a city of unique vitality.

Updated by
Valerie
Hamilton

OME'S 2,700 YEARS of history are laid open with every step. Ancient Rome rubs shoulders with the medieval, the modern runs into the Renaissance, and the result is like nothing so much as an open-air museum, a city that glories in its glories and is a monument to itself. Senators, emperors, Vandals, popes and the Borgias, Michelangelo and Bernini, Napoléon, and Mussolini all left their physical, cultural, and spiritual stamps on the city. More than Florence, more than Venice, Rome is Italy's treasure trove, packed as it is with masterpieces from more than two millennia of artistic achievement. It's here that a metropolis once bustled around the carved marble monuments of the Roman Forum, where centuries later Michelangelo Buonarroti painted Christian history in the Sistine Chapel, where Gian Lorenzo Bernini's nymphs and naiads dance in their fountains, and where an empire of gold was worked into the crowns of centuries of rulers.

Today Rome's formidable legacy is upheld by its people, their history knit into the fabric of their everyday lives. Students walk dogs in the park that was once the mausoleum of the family of the Emperor Augustus; Raphaelesque madonnas line up for buses on busy corners; a priest in flowing robes walks through a medieval piazza talking on a cell phone. Modern Rome has one foot in the past, one in the present—a delightful stance that allows you to have an espresso in a square designed by Bernini, then take the Metro back to your hotel room in a renovated Renaissance palace. "When you first come here you assume that you must burrow about in ruins and prowl in museums to get back to the days of Numa Pompilius or Mark Antony," Maud Howe observes in her book *Roma Beata*. "It is not necessary; you only have to live, and the common happenings of daily life—yes, even the trolley car and your bicycle—carry you back in turn to the Dark Ages, to the early Christians, even to prehistoric Rome."

Visitors to Rome often face a conundrum: the more you see of the city, the more you'll realize how little you have time to see. Take heart; Rome wasn't built in a day. The Italian author Silvio Negro said it best: *"Roma, non basta una vita"* (Rome, a lifetime is not enough). It's wise to start out knowing this, and to have a focused but flexible itinerary. A ramble through a picturesque quarter of Old Rome can be just as enchanting as the quiet contemplation of a chapel or a trek through marbled miles of museum corridors.

ANCIENT ROME

Rome, as everyone knows, was built on seven hills—Capitolino (commonly known as Campidoglio), Palatino, Esquilino, Viminale, Celio, Quirinale, and Aventino. Two of these historic hills—the Campidoglio and the Palatine—formed the hub of ancient Rome, the center of the civilized world. The Campidoglio has always been the seat of Rome's government; its Latin name is echoed in the designation of national and state capitol buildings. On the Palatine the earliest recorded inhabitants of Rome lived in modest mud huts; later, its position made it Rome's most exclusive residential zone, site of the emperors' vast and luxurious palaces. Between the hills, in the Forum, the Romans worshipped, discussed politics, and carried on commerce. Between the Palatine and the Tiber were the markets where livestock and produce arrived by boat. Though it remained the heart of monumental and religious Rome, the Forum was later dwarfed by the Imperial Fora, built by a succession of emperors to augment the original, overcrowded

Forum and to make sure that the people would have tangible evidence of their generosity.

More than any other, this part of Rome is a perfect example of that layering of historic eras, the overlapping of ages, of religions, of a past that is very much a part of the present. Christian churches rise on the foundations of ancient pagan temples. An immense marble monument to a 19th-century king of a newly united Italy shares a square with a medieval palace built by a future pope. But it is the history and memory of ancient Rome that dominate the area. After a more than 27-centuries-long parade of pageantry, it is not surprising that Shelley and Gibbon reflected on the sense of *sic transit gloria mundi* (thus pass the glories of the world) they felt here. The ruins and monuments, the Colosseo and the triumphal arches have stood through the centuries as emphatic reminders of the genius and power that made Rome the center of the Western world.

It's worth noting that you can save some money by purchasing an all-in-one ticket for €15.50. It lasts five days and includes access to many of the major sites such as the Colosseo, Palatine Hill, Terme di Cara-calla, Palazzo Massimo, Palazzo Altemps, and the Cripta Balbi.

Numbers in the text and margin correspond to points of interest on the Ancient Rome map.

The Campidoglio

A Good Walk

Begin your walk on the **Campidoglio** ①, or Capitoline Hill, site of Michelangelo's spectacular Piazza del Campidoglio and Rome's cere-monial city hall, **Palazzo Senatorio** ②. Take in the view from the pi-azza, putting your back to the replica of the ancient bronze statue of Marcus Aurelius. In front of you, to the north, stretch the rooftops of central Rome, punctuated by domes and TV antennas, with the heights of Monte Mario in the distance. This is a perfect opportunity to visit the **Musei Capitolini** ③, located on the Piazza del Campidoglio and home to one of the city's finest and most famous collections of ancient sculp-ture and Baroque painting. Off the southeast flank of Palazzo Nuovo, at the head of a formidable flight of steep steps, stands the ancient red-brick church of **Santa Maria di Aracoeli** ④. The vantage points in the Campidoglio gardens, the belvederes on the sides of Palazzo Senato-rio, offer great views of the ruins of the ancient city.

From the southwest flank of Palazzo Senatorio, take Via del Campi-doglio and then Via del Tempio di Giove for a look at the Roman Forum from the **Belvedere Tarpeo** ⑤; imagine what the area looked like when most of these magnificent ruins were covered over by marshy pastureland, and cows grazed beside half-buried columns and trod 2,000-year-old marble paving slabs. From the belvedere on the northeast side of Palazzo Senatorio, descend Via San Pietro in Carcere, actually a flight of stairs, to the gloomy **Carcere Mamertino** ⑥.

TIMING

This walk can be done in about 2 hours, but allow an extra 1½ to 2 hours for a visit to the Musei Capitolini. Take the walk as well as those exploring the Foro Romano and Palatino on one of your first days in Rome in order to get a sense of where and how the city began and how it expanded. Fair weather helps, but it is not essential. Late evening is an option for this walk; though the church is closed, the museums are open until 9 PM, and the views of the city lights and the illuminated Altare della Patria and Foro Romano are striking.

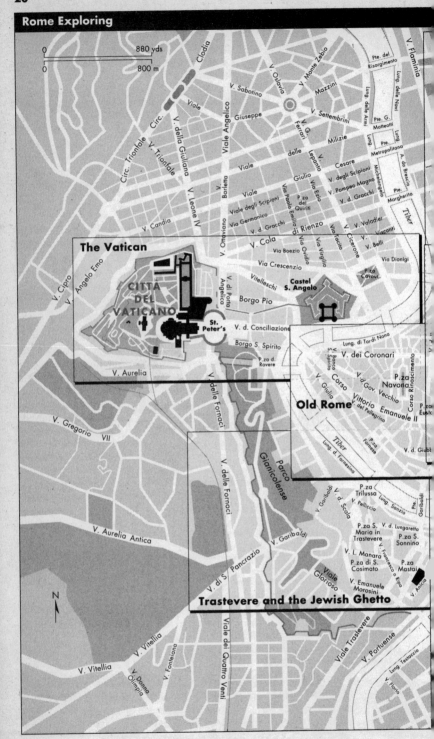

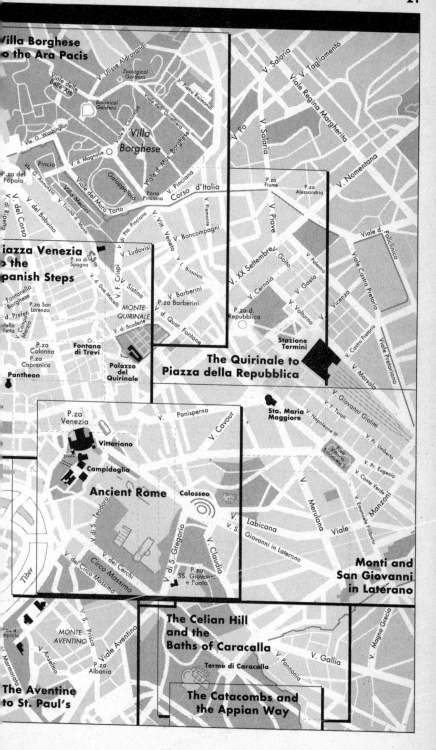

Villa Borghese to the Ara Pacis

Villa Borghese

Piazza Venezia to the Spanish Steps

The Quirinale to Piazza della Repubblica

Ancient Rome

Monti and San Giovanni in Laterano

The Celian Hill and the Baths of Caracalla

The Aventine to St. Paul's

The Catacombs and the Appian Way

PLANNING YOUR ROMAN HOLIDAY

If You Have 4 Days

Day 1: Begin by surveying Rome from atop the Campidoglio. Next, explore the Foro Romano (Roman Forum) and see the Monte Palatino (Palatine Hill) and the Colosseo (Colosseum). In the afternoon, combine sightseeing with shopping and make your way through the neighborhood around the Piazza di Spagna. **Day 2:** Dedicate your day to Vatican City. Visit the Musei Vaticani (Vatican Museums) and the Cappella Sistina (Sistine Chapel), then the Basilica di San Pietro (St. Peter's Basilica). The museums have limited afternoon hours, so make them your first stop. Spend what remains of your afternoon relaxing, perhaps exploring the neighborhood around your hotel. **Day 3:** In the morning explore Old Rome and make your way to Fontana di Trevi (Trevi Fountain). In the afternoon you can visit a museum (such as Castel Sant'Angelo) or watch the passing parade from a sidewalk café in one of the city's beautiful piazzas. You could walk from the Piazza Venezia to the great basilicas of Santa Maria Maggiore and San Giovanni in Laterano. **Day 4:** Choose between a morning of shopping or a visit to more of Rome's sights—Galleria Borghese (Borghese Gallery) or the Colle Oppio and the underground remains of Nero's Domus Aurea (Golden House). Spend your final afternoon and evening exploring the Jewish Ghetto and Trastevere neighborhoods.

If You Have 6 Days

Spend your first four days as above. **Day 5:** In the morning wander through Villa Borghese and, if you haven't done so already, see the Canova and Bernini sculptures in the Galleria Borghese. Alternatively, on the other side of the park you can visit the Villa Giulia with its world-class collection of Etruscan art and artifacts. Explore the Piazza del Popolo area and make your way to the Ara Pacis. In the afternoon see Piazza del Quirinale and stroll on to Piazza della Repubblica. **Day 6:** Make an excursion either to the Appian Way or to the ancient city of Ostia Antica. In the afternoon, stroll on the Aventine or Celian Hill.

If You Have 10 Days

Day 1: Start at the Campidoglio; see the Foro Romano and Monte Palatino and then the Colosseo. In the afternoon visit one of the archaeological museums—Palazzo Altemps or Palazzo Massimo alle Terme. **Day 2:** Give the day over to the Musei Vaticani and the Basilica di San Pietro. **Day 3:** Start the morning at the Campo dei Fiori and devote most of the day to Old Rome, finishing up with a trip across the Tiber to Castel Sant'Angelo. **Day 4:** Set off through Villa Borghese to the Galleria Borghese and then continue westward to the Ara Pacis. In the afternoon explore the shopping streets around Piazza di Spagna and toss a coin into the Fontana di Trevi. **Day 5:** Start from Piazza Venezia and make your way to the basilicas of Santa Maria Maggiore and San Giovanni in Laterano. In the afternoon explore the area between the Quirinale and Piazza della Repubblica. **Day 6:** Take a day for a side trip: head for Ostia Antica. **Day 7:** Walk from the Jewish Ghetto through Trastevere and continue up to the Gianicolo (Janiculum Hill). **Day 8:** Explore the Aventine and make your way to San Paolo fuori le Mura (St. Paul's Outside the Walls). In the afternoon, take in the Celian Hill and the Baths of Caracalla. **Day 9:** Make an excursion to the Appian Way; then spend the afternoon shopping or relaxing. **Day 10:** Take stock—head for any must-see sights you've missed, or return to a favorite. A ramble through Old Rome is a fitting end to your visit.

Sights to See

⑤ Belvedere Tarpeo (Tarpeian Belvedere). This was the infamous Tarpeian Rock from which traitors were dashed to the ground below. In the 18th and 19th centuries it became a popular vantage point for grand tourists because of its view of the Palatine Hill. Here, in the 7th century BC, Tarpeia betrayed the Roman citadel to the besieging Sabines, sworn enemies of the early Romans, asking in return for what they wore on their left arms, thinking of their heavy gold bracelets. The scornful Sabines did indeed shower her with their gold as they passed, but added the crushing weight of their heavy shields, also carried on their left arms. ⊠ *Via del Tempio di Giove.*

① Campidoglio. The Campidoglio has been the seat of civic government since Rome itself began. Though most of the buildings here date from the Renaissance, this hill was once the epicenter of the Roman Empire. Originally, the Capitoline Hill consisted of two peaks: the Capitolium and the Arx. The hollow between them was known as the Asylum; it was here, in the days before the Roman Republic was founded, in 510 BC, that prospective settlers came to acknowledge the protection of Romulus, legendary first king of Rome—hence the term "asylum." Later, during the Republic, temples occupied both peaks, and, later still, in 78 BC, the Tabularium, or Hall of Records, was built here to house the city archives. Throughout the Middle Ages an earlier incarnation of Palazzo Senatorio built over the Tabularium was just about the only building on the Campidoglio, then an unkempt hill strewn with the classical rubble of temples and used mainly as a goat pasture. Nonetheless the fame of the place lingered on. Petrarch, the 14th-century Italian poet, was just one of many to extol its original splendor, though its sumptuous marble palaces and temples had long since crumbled.

In 1537, Michelangelo was charged with restoring the square to its former glory, in preparation for the impending visit of Holy Roman Emperor Charles V, triumphant after the empire's victory over the Moors. In emulation of ancient Roman triumphal processions, it was decided that Charles V should follow what was believed to have been the route of the Roman emperors, through the city to the newly magnificent Campidoglio. Much of Michelangelo's plan was not finished for several centuries, but nearly everything here today follows his original designs, including the distinctive stellate pattern set into the pavement and the equestrian statue of Marcus Aurelius at the center.

⑥ Carcere Mamertino (Mamertine Prison). A minor attraction amid the glories of ancient Rome, the prison consists of two gloomy subterranean cells where Rome's vanquished enemies, most famously the Goth Jugurtha and the indomitable Gaul Vercingetorix, were imprisoned and died of starvation or strangulation. In the lower cell, St. Peter himself is believed to have been held prisoner and to have miraculously brought forth a spring of water in order to baptize his jailers. That explains why a church, San Giuseppe dei Falegnami, was built over the prison. ⊠ *Via del Tulliano.* ▱ *Donations requested.* ☉ *Daily 9–12:30 and 2–5.*

★ ③ Musei Capitolini (Capitoline Museums). The collections in the twin Museo Capitolino and Palazzo dei Conservatori were assembled in the 15th century by Pope Sixtus IV (1414–84), one of the earliest of the great papal art patrons. Although parts of the collection may excite only archaeologists and art historians, others contain some of the most famous pieces of classical sculpture, such as the poignant *Dying Gaul,* the regal *Capitoline Venus* (recently identified as another Mediterranean beauty, Cleopatra herself), and the delicate *Marble Faun* that inspired 19th-century novelist Nathaniel Hawthorne's novel of the same name. Re-

Arco di Costantino . . .**32**
Arco di Settimio Severo **10**
Arco di Tito **23**
Basilica di Massenzio **21**
Basilica Emilia **7**
Basilica Giulia **13**
Belvedere Tarpeo **5**
Campidoglio **1**
Carcere Mamertino . . .**6**
Casa di Livia **30**
Circo Massimo **29**
Colonna di Foca **12**
Colonna di Traiano . .**39**
Colosseo **33**
Comitium **9**
Curia **8**
Domus Augustana . . .**27**
Domus Aurea **34**
Domus Flavia **26**
Fonte di Giuturna **18**
Foro di Augusto **37**
Foro di Cesare **36**
Foro di Traiano **38**
Monte Palatino **25**
Musei Capitolini **3**
Orti Farnesiani **31**
Palazzo Senatorio **2**
Santa Francesca Romana **22**
Santa Maria Antiqua **19**
Santa Maria di Aracoeli **4**
Santi Cosma e Damiano **35**
Stadio Palatino **28**
Tempio di Antonino e Faustina **15**
Tempio di Castore e Polluce **17**
Tempio di Cesare **14**
Tempio di Venere e Roma **24**
Tempio di Vespasiano **11**
Tempio di Vesta **16**
Via Sacra **20**

Ancient Rome

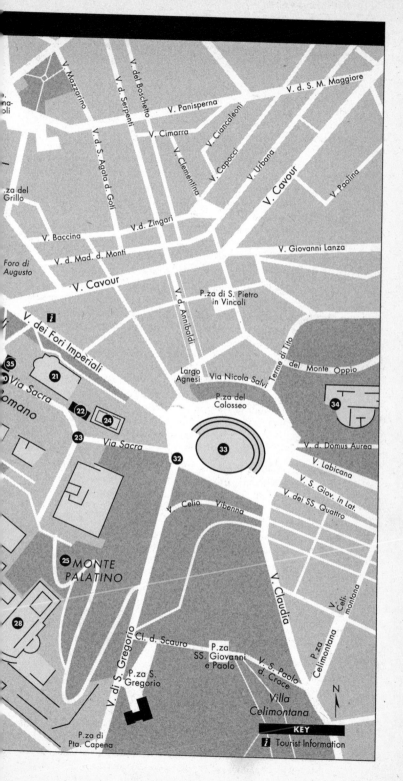

V. Mazzarino

V. del Boschetto

V. d. Serpenti

V. Panisperna

V. d. S. M. Maggiore

V. Cimarra

V. Ciancaleoni

V. d. S. Agata d. Goti

V. Clementina

V. Capocci

V. Urbana

V. Cavour

V. Paolina

.za del
Grillo

V. Baccina

V.d. Zingari

V. d. Mad. d. Monti

V. Giovanni Lanza

Foro di
Augusto

V. Cavour

V. d. Annibaldi

P.za di S. Pietro
in Vincoli

V. dei Fori Imperiali

Terme di Tito

del Monte Oppio

Largo
Agnesi

Via Nicola Salvi

Via Sacra

P.za del
Colosseo

V. d. Domus Aurea

Via Sacra

V. Labicana

omano

V. S. Giov. in Lat.

V. dei SS. Quattro

V. Celio Vibenna

MONTE
PALATINO

V. Claudia

V. Celimontana

Cl. d. Scauro

P.za Celimontana

V. di S. Gregorio

P.za
SS. Giovanni
e Paolo

V. S. Paolo
d. Croce

P.za S.
Gregorio

Villa
Celimontana

N

P.za di
Pta. Capena

KEY

i Tourist Information

member that many of the works here and in Rome's other museums were copied from Greek originals. For hundreds of years, craftsmen of ancient Rome prospered by producing copies of Greek statues using a process called "pointing," by which exact replicas could be created to order.

Portraiture, however, was one area in which the Romans outstripped the Greeks. The hundreds of Roman portrait busts of emperors in the Sala degli Imperatori and of philosophers in the **Museo Capitolino**'s Sala dei Filosofi constitute a Who's Who of the ancient world. Within these serried ranks are 48 Roman emperors, ranging from Augustus to Theodosius (346–95). On one console you'll see the handsomely austere Augustus, who "found Rome a city of brick and left it one of marble." On another rests Claudius "the stutterer," an indefatigable builder brought vividly to life in the novel *I, Claudius,* by Robert Graves (1895–1985). Also in this company is Nero, most notorious of the emperors—though by no means the worst—who built for himself the fabled Domus Aurea. And, of course, the baddies: cruel Caligula (AD 12–41) and Caracalla (AD 186–217), and the dissolute, eerily modern boy-emperor, Heliogabalus (AD 203–22).

Unlike the Greeks, whose portraits are idealized and usually beautiful, the Romans belonged to the "warts and all" school of representation. Many of the busts that have come down to us, notably that of Commodus (AD 161–92), the emperor-gladiator (found in a gallery on the upper level of the museum), are nearly savage in the relentlessness of their portrayals. As you leave the museum, be sure to stop in the courtyard. To the right is the original equestrian statue of Marcus Aurelius, restored and safely kept behind glass. At the center of the courtyard is the gigantic, reclining figure of Oceanus, found in the Roman Forum and later dubbed *Marforio,* one of Rome's famous "talking statues" to which citizens from the 1500s up to the 20th century affixed anonymous notes of political protest and satirical verses. (A talking statue is still in use near Piazza Navona, at Piazza Pasquino.)

The **Palazzo dei Conservatori** is a trove of ancient and Baroque treasures. Lining the courtyard are the colossal fragments of a head, leg, foot, and hand—all that remains of the famous statue of the Emperor Constantine the Great, who believed that Rome's future lay with Christianity. These immense effigies were much in vogue in the later days of the Roman Empire. The resplendent Salone dei Orazi e Curiazi (Salon of Horatii and Curatii) on the first floor is a ceremonial hall with a magnificent gilt ceiling, carved wooden doors, and 16th-century frescoes. At either end of the hall reign statues of the Baroque era's most charismatic popes, a marble Urban VIII (1568–1644) by Bernini (1598–1680) and a bronze likeness of Innocent X (1574–1655) by Bernini's rival Algardi (1595–1654). The renowned symbol of Rome, the *Capitoline Wolf,* a 6th-century-BC Etruscan bronze, holds a place of honor in the museum; the suckling twins were added during the Renaissance to adapt the statue to the legend of Romulus and Remus.

Recently reopened after restorations, the museum's Pinacoteca, or painting gallery, holds some of Baroque painting's great masterpieces, including Caravaggio's *La Buona Ventura* (1595) and *San Giovanni Battista* (1602), Peter Paul Rubens's (1577–1640) *Romulus and Remus* (1614), and Pietro da Cortona's sumptuous portrait of Pope Urban VIII (1627). Admission to the Pinacoteca is included in your ticket. Also included is a look at the ruins of the **Tabularium**, or ancient hall of records, on whose physical and philosophical foundations all successive Roman seats of government have been built. ⊠ *Piazza del Campi-*

doglio, ☎ 06/39967700. ⌨ €6.20, *free last Sun. of month.* ⊙ *Tues.–Fri. and Sun. 9:30–7:30, Sat. 9:30 AM–11 PM.*

❷ **Palazzo Senatorio.** Rome's city hall thrusts its foundations deep into the Tabularium, the ancient city's hall of records. During the Middle Ages it looked like the medieval town halls you see in Tuscan hill towns, part fortress and part assembly hall. The building was entirely rebuilt in the 1500s as part of Michelangelo's revamping of the Campidoglio for Pope Paul III; the master's design was adapted by later architects, who wisely left the front staircase as the focus of the facade. The ancient statue of Minerva in the niche at the center was opportunely renamed the Goddess Rome, and the river gods (the Tiber, right, and the Nile, left) were hauled over from the Terme di Costantino on the Quirinal Hill. ⊠ *Piazza del Campidoglio.*

Piazza del Campidoglio. On the summit of the Campidoglio, this is one of Rome's most classically majestic sites, thanks mainly to Michelangelo's vision of spatial harmony. You approach the Campidoglio up a gently graded ramp, the *cordonata,* designed by Michelangelo to allow a carriage to be pulled up the hill with minimal fuss. As you climb it, the buildings and visual effects of the site gradually reveal themselves. The equestrian **statue of the emperor Marcus Aurelius** that stands in the center of the piazza is a copy of the Roman-era original, which was placed here by Michelangelo as a visual reference to the link between the rank of Charles V and that of the ancient emperor. Statues of emperors were typically melted down after the fall of Rome; it is thought this one survived because it was mistakenly believed to have been a likeness of the Christian Emperor Constantine rather than of the pagan Marcus Aurelius. It's claimed that Michelangelo was so struck by the statue's vivid naturalism that, having placed it in the piazza, he commanded it to walk. A legend holds that the return of the statue's original gold patina (only traces of it are left) will signal the imminent end of the world. ⊠ *Piazza del Campidoglio.*

❹ **Santa Maria di Aracoeli.** On the north slope of the Capitoline Hill, a steep flight of steps topped by a stark, redbrick church parallels the gentler cordonata leading to the Campidoglio. There's been a temple of some sort here since the earliest days of Rome: the ancient Romans came up here to worship at the Temple of Juno Moneta, which also housed the Roman mint (hence the origin of the word *money*). According to legend, it was here that the Sybil predicted to Augustus the coming of a Redeemer. The emperor responded by erecting an altar, the Ara Coeli—the Altar of Heaven. This was in turn replaced by one of Rome's first Christian churches. The church passed to the Benedictines in the 10th century and in 1250 to the Franciscans, who restored and enlarged it in Romanesque-Gothic style. In the Middle Ages, before the present Campidoglio was built, the city elders used to meet here to discuss affairs of state, just as the ancient Romans had met in the Temple of Jupiter.

In true Roman style, the church interior is a historical hodgepodge, with materials and decorations dating from ancient times all the way to the Renaissance. There are classical columns and large marble fragments from pagan buildings and a 13th-century Cosmatesque pavement—so called because, like so many other brilliantly colored mosaics of the period, this was the work of the prolific Cosmati family, who used bits of the precious marbles of ancient Rome in their compositions. The rich Renaissance gilded ceiling commemorates the naval victory at Lepanto in 1571 over the Turks. Among these artistic treasures, the first chapel on the right is noteworthy for Pinturicchio's 16th-century frescoes of San Bernardino of Siena. There's a Byzantine madonna over the altar, where the emperor Augustus and the Sybil are depicted in the apse amid saints and angels (a most unusual position for a pagan emperor). In the third chapel on the left you can admire Benozzo Gozzoli's (1420–97) 15th-century fresco *St. Anthony of Padua*; on the right of the main portal there's a handsome polychrome monument to Cardinal D'Albret by Bregno and next to it a tombstone by Donatello, worn by the passage of time and the hands of the faithful. ⊠ *Via del Teatro di Marcello, on top of steep stairway,* ☏ *06/6798155.*

Foro Romano

The Roman Forum lies in what was once a marshy valley between the Capitoline and Palatine hills, a valley crossed by a mud track and used as a cemetery by the Iron Age settlers on the Palatine. Over the years, a marketplace and some huts were established here, and after the land was drained in the 6th century BC the site eventually became the Forum. It evolved into a symbol of the values that had inspired Republican Rome's conquest of an empire—the stern moral authority of the republic. It was the historic and monumental heart of ancient Rome that had existed long before the emperors and the pleasure-loving, ever-more-corrupt imperial Rome of the 1st to the 4th century AD. The original Roman Forum is only one part of the labyrinthine archaeological complex that goes by that name. Don't confuse it, either, with the later Imperial Forums (or, more properly, Fora), built by Julius Caesar and the emperors as the city's needs grew.

Hundreds of years of plunder and the tendency of later Romans to carry off what was left of the better building materials reduced the Forum to its current desolate state. It is difficult to imagine this enormous area as Rome's pulsating heart, filled with stately and extravagant temples, palaces, and shops and crowded with people from all corners of the empire. Adding to the confusion is the fact that the Forum developed over many centuries; what you see today are not the ruins from just one period but from almost 900 years, from about 500 BC to AD 400. As the original buildings became too small or were thought too old-fashioned for a Rome that grew ever more powerful, they were pulled down and replaced by larger, more lavish structures. But as often as not, the foundations of the older buildings remained, and many have survived to the present, pitted and scarred with age, alongside their later cousins.

Archaeological digs continue to discover more about the site, but for the uninitiated, making sense of these gaunt and craggy ruins isn't easy. It's worth investing in the little booklet that superimposes a plan of the Forum in its heyday onto a photo of the site as it is today. Nonetheless, the enduring romance of the place, with its lonely columns and great, broken fragments of sculptured marble and stone, is such that it makes a lovely, quintessentially Roman walk—whether through its past glories, or its present, splendid ruin. ⊠ *Entrances at Via dei Fori Imperiali and Piazza del Colosseo,* ☏ *06/6990110 or 06/39967700.* 🎫 *Free.* ☉ *Mon.–Sat. 9–2 hrs before sunset, Sun. 9–1.*

A Good Walk

Head for Via dei Fori Imperiali and the entrance to the Foro Romano. Here you can find what remains of the various buildings in the Forum: the **Basilica Emilia** ⑦, not a church but a civic hall; the **Curia** ⑧, where the Senate met; the **Comitium** ⑨, where Mark Antony eulogized Caesar. Although the **Arco di Settimio Severo** ⑩, the remaining columns of the **Tempio di Vespasiano** ⑪, and the **Colonna di Foca** ⑫ rise above the ruins, the **Basilica Giulia** ⑬ is little more than a large raised platform. The **Tempio di Cesare** ⑭, on the spot where Caesar was cremated,

CAPITAL HILLS

ALTHOUGH IT'S BEEN the capital of the Republic of Italy only since 1946, Rome has been the capital of *something* for more than 2,500 years, and it shows. The magnificent ruins of the Palatino, the massive complex of the Forum, the balanced lines of the Campidoglio, the imperial majesty of the Colonna di Marco Aurelio, not to mention St. Peter's Basilica, capital of Catholic Christianity, are all part of Rome's longest-lasting identity—that of seat of government, one of the world's most enduring. The Roman Republic, founded in the 6th century BC, was the philosophical base of modern republics; the Roman Senate the inspiration for modern senates (complete with dynastic rule and seat-buying). Even the language of modern government comes from Rome: the English words "capitol" and "palace" come from the names of the Capitoline (Campidoglio) and Palatine (Palatino) Hills, the ancient sites of, respectively, the government halls and imperial residences.

This is not to say that it's been an easy 2½ millennia: the birth of modern government seems to have brought with it the birth of modern politics. While senators of the Roman Republic contented themselves with buying influence, would-be emperors of later centuries found much more permanent ways of getting their opponents out of office. The end of the Roman Republic and the beginning of the Roman Empire was marked by the ambush and murder of Julius Caesar, while Nero ascended to the throne with the help of his mother, who cleared the way by poisoning Claudius with death's-head mushrooms. Popes elected to rule in medieval times were frequently challenged by anti-popes, rival pontiffs chosen in opposition elections; many anti-popes "ruled" concurrently with official popes, starting with Hippolytus in 217 and continuing until Felix V in 1439. Hundreds of years later, with the advent of the democratic Italian Republic, political methods have become tamer, and, perhaps for this reason, the turnover rate has increased: there's been a new government, on average, every 11 months since 1954.

Much to the world's amusement, Italy's ever-changing leadership often gets its day in court—more frequently, perhaps, than some politicians would like. The *tangentopoli* (literally, kickback city) scandals of 1992 led to the investigation, conviction, and/or resignation of more than 200 of Italy's political elite, including former prime minister Bettino Craxi, who went into exile in Tunisia rather than face imprisonment. In 1999, seven-time PM Giulio Andreotti was acquitted (for lack of evidence) of colluding with and protecting the Mafia—but the seriousness of the accusations shocked the world. And in the spring of 2001, Italy voted itself another try with, Silvio Berlusconi as prime minister, despite the indicted media tycoon's string of legal troubles.

Rome's major sights constitute a tour through the governments of the ages. The Imperial Fora, monuments to the power and wealth of the emperors, nestle up against the monument to Vittorio Emanuele II, the first king of a united Italy; next door is the Campidoglio, home of the municipal records building in Republican times, now the site of modern Rome's City Hall. Across the street on Piazza Venezia is the Palazzo Venezia, from whose balcony Fascist dictator Benito Mussolini gave his most famous addresses, and up the Quirinal Hill is the Palazzo Quirinale, once home to popes, then kings, and now to the Italian president. Modern Italian politics are played right in the center of it all: at Palazzo Madama (the Italian Senate), next to Piazza Navona; Palazzo Chigi (the prime minister's office), on Piazza Colonna; and the Chamber of Deputies, next door at Piazza Montecitorio. After all, if the three-ring circus that is Italy's government is legendary, it only stands to reason that Italy's most legendary city should be its home.

is hardly distinguishable. The **Tempio di Antonino e Faustina** ⑮ met with better luck; incorporated into a church, its column front has been well preserved. Nearby are three columns of the partially reconstructed, round **Tempio di Vesta** ⑯. The **Tempio di Castore e Polluce** ⑰ and the **Fonte di Giuturna** ⑱ have to be imagined, as little is left of them. Off to one side, you can see but not visit the church of **Santa Maria Antiqua** ⑲, built into what was originally a vestibule of the imperial palace on the Palatino.

Stroll east along the **Via Sacra** ⑳, and turn left into the **Basilica di Massenzio** ㉑. The 10th-century church of **Santa Francesca Romana** ㉒ stands atop a rise next to the Basilica di Massenzio. The Via Sacra ends at the **Arco di Tito** ㉓, where a carved menorah recalls Rome's recapture of Jerusalem after the great Jewish revolt. The **Tempio di Venere e Roma** ㉔, one of the projects of the architecturally savvy emperor Hadrian, was begun on the site of the vast vestibule of Nero's grandiose Domus Aurea in AD 121.

TIMING

It takes about one hour to explore the Forum and identify the principal ruins. With the exception of mobile refreshment stands along Via dei Fori Imperiali and cafés on Largo Corrado Ricci, there are few places within easy reach where you can take a break for lunch or a snack. Consider bringing along some sustenance to keep you going. As this walk is almost entirely outdoors, good weather is a must; the beaten-earth paths of the Foro Romano are muddy and slippery in the rain. The route is a magical one for a late-evening stroll, when the site and surrounding monuments are illuminated. In summer, the Forum is sometimes open for midnight (guided) tours—look for signs at the entrances in July and August, or ask at the tourist office or your hotel.

Sights to See

⑩ **Arco di Settimio Severo** (Arch of Septimius Severus). The most richly decorated arch ever seen by the ancient Romans was built in AD 203 to celebrate the emperor Severus's victory over the Parthians. It was topped by a bronze statuary group of a chariot drawn by four or perhaps as many as six life-size horses. The stone reliefs on the arch were probably based on huge painted panels depicting the event, a kind of visual report that the emperor sent home to Rome to make sure his subjects were duly impressed by his foreign campaigns. ⊠ *West end of Foro Romano.*

㉓ **Arco di Tito** (Arch of Titus). This triumphal arch stands at a slightly elevated position at the northern approach to the Palatine Hill. It was erected in AD 81 to celebrate the recapture of Jerusalem 10 years earlier, after the great Jewish revolt. It's famous for a relief representing the seven-branched candelabrum—a menorah—that was part of the spoils of war. ⊠ *East end of Via Sacra.*

㉑ **Basilica di Massenzio** (Basilica of Maxentius). The great arched vaults of this structure dominate the north side of the Via Sacra. Begun under the Emperor Maxentius about AD 306, the edifice was a center of judicial and commercial activity, the last of its kind to be built in Rome. What remains is only one-third of the original. Like so many other Roman monuments, it served as a quarry for building materials and was stripped of its lavish marble and stucco decorations. Its coffered vaults, like the coffering inside the Pantheon's dome, were later copied by many Renaissance artists and architects. ⊠ *Via Sacra.*

⑦ **Basilica Emilia** (Aemilian Basilica). Once a great colonnaded hall, this was a meeting place for merchants and a kind of community center of the 2nd century BC; it was later rebuilt in the 1st century AD by Augustus. The term "basilica" refers not to a church as such, but to a particular architectural form developed by the Romans. A rectangular hall flanked by colonnades, it served as a court of law or a center for business and commerce. Some Roman basilicas were later converted into churches, and the early models proved remarkably enduring in the design of later Roman churches; there are 13th-century churches in the city that are fundamentally no different from many built during the 5th and 6th centuries AD. ⊠ *On the right as you descend into the Roman Forum from the Via dei Fori Imperiali entrance.*

⓭ Basilica Giulia (Basilica Julia). The Basilica Giulia owes its name to Julius Caesar, who had it built. One of several such basilicas in the center of Rome, this one was where the Centumviri, the hundred-or-so judges forming the civil court, met to hear cases. The open space between the Basilica Emilia and this basilica was the heart of the Forum proper, prototype of Italy's famous piazzas, and center of civic and social activity in ancient Rome. ⊠ *Via Sacra.*

⓬ Colonna di Foca (Column of Phocas). The last monument to be added to the Forum was erected in AD 608 in honor of a Byzantine emperor who had donated the Pantheon to Pope Boniface IV. ⊠ *West end of Foro Romano.*

❾ Comitium. The open space in front of the Curia was the political center of ancient Rome. Julius Caesar had rearranged the Comitium, moving the Curia to its present site and transferring the Imperial **Rostra,** the podium from which orators spoke to the people (decorated originally with the prows of captured ships, or *rostra,* hence the term "rostrum"), to a spot just south of the Arch of Septimius Severus. It was from this platform that Mark Antony delivered his funeral address in Caesar's honor. Also here, under protective roofing (visitors are not allowed to enter), is the black pavement that supposedly marks the **burial place of Romulus,** first king of Rome, in the primitive settlement's burial ground near the mud track that gave rise to the Forum. Legend is supported by the fact that the underlying tombstones bear the earliest known Latin inscription in characters somewhat resembling Greek. On the left of the Rostra stands what remains of the **Tempio di Saturno** (Temple of Saturn), which served as ancient Rome's state treasury. ⊠ *West end of Foro Romano.*

❽ Curia (Senate Hall). The large and well-preserved brick building in the northwest part of the Forum was built during the era of Diocletian in the late 3rd century AD. By that time the Senate, which met in the Curia, had lost practically all of the power and prestige that it had possessed during the Republican era, becoming a mere echo chamber for decisions made in other centers of power. ⊠ *Via Sacra, northwest corner of Foro Romano.*

㊽ Fonte di Giuturna (Spring of Juturna). Legend says that as Castor and Pollux carried the news of a great victory to Rome they paused to water their horses at the rectangular, marble-lined pool near what became their temple. ⊠ *Via Sacra.*

㉒ Santa Francesca Romana. This church, a 10th-century edifice with a Renaissance facade, is dedicated to the patron saint of motorists; on her feast day, March 9, cars and taxis crowd the roadway below for a special blessing. Its incomparable setting also makes it a favorite for weddings. ⊠ *Piazza di Santa Francesca Romana, next to Colosseum.*

⓳ Santa Maria Antiqua. The earliest Christian site in the Forum was originally part of an imperial temple, before it was converted into a church some time in the 5th or 6th century. Within are some exceptional but faded 7th- and 8th-century frescoes of the early church fathers, saints, and popes similar to those in the rock churches of Cappadocia in Turkey. It is rarely open to the public. ⊠ *South of the Tempio di Castore and Polluce, at the foot of Palatine Hill.*

⓯ Tempio di Antonino e Faustina (Temple of Antoninus and Faustina). Erected by the Senate in honor of Faustina, deified wife of emperor Antoninus Pius (138–161), Hadrian's successor, this temple was dedicated to the emperor himself upon his death. Because it was transformed into a church, it is one of the best-preserved ancient structures in the Forum. ⊠ *North of Via Sacra.*

⓱ Tempio di Castore e Polluce (Temple of Castor and Pollux). This temple was dedicated in 484 BC to the twin brothers of Helen of Troy who carried to Rome the news of the victory of Lake Regillus, southeast of Rome, the definitive defeat of the deposed Tarquin dynasty. The twins flew on their fabulous white steeds over the 20-km (12-mi) distance between the lake and the city to bring the news to the people before mortal messengers could arrive. ⊠ *West of House of the Vestals.*

⓮ Tempio di Cesare (Temple of Caesar). Built by Augustus, Caesar's successor, the temple stands over the spot where Julius Caesar's body was cremated. A pyre was improvised by grief-crazed citizens who fed the flames with their own possessions. ⊠ *Between 2 forks of Via Sacra.*

㉔ Tempio di Venere e Roma (Temple of Venus and Rome). The truncated columns of this temple, begun by Hadrian in AD 121, frame a view of the Colosseum. ⊠ *East of Arco di Tito.*

⓫ Tempio di Vespasiano (Temple of Vespasian). All that remains of this temple are three graceful Corinthian columns. They marked the site of the Forum through the centuries while the rest was hidden beneath overgrown rubble. Nearby is the ruined platform that was the **Tempio di Concordia** (Temple of Concord). ⊠ *West end of Foro Romano.*

⓰ Tempio di Vesta (Temple of Vesta). The small, circular temple is where the highly privileged vestal virgins kept the sacred flame alive. Next to the temple, the ruins of the **Casa delle Vestali** (House of the Vestals) give no hint of the splendor in which the women lived out their 30-year vows of chastity. Inside was the garden courtyard of their palace, surrounded by airy colonnades, behind which lay at least 50 rooms. Chosen when they were between 6 and 10 years old, the six vestal virgins dedicated their lives for 30 years to keeping the sacred fire, a tradition that dated back to the very earliest days of Rome, when guarding the community's precious fire was essential to its well-being. Their standing in Rome was considerable; indeed, among women, they were second in rank only to the empress. Their intercession could save a condemned man, and they did, in fact, rescue Julius Caesar from the lethal vengeance of his enemy Sulla. The virgins were handsomely maintained by the state, but if they allowed the sacred fire to go out they were scourged by the high priest, and if they broke their vows they were buried alive. The vestal virgins were one of the last of ancient Rome's institutions to die out, enduring to as late as the end of the 4th century AD, even after Rome's emperors had become Christian. They were finally suppressed by Theodosius. ⊠ *South side of Via Sacra.*

㉚ Via Sacra. The basalt-paved road that loops through the Roman Forum, lined with temples and shrines, was also the route of religious and triumphal processions. It is now little more than a dirt track, with occasional patches of the paving stones trod by Caesars and plebs, rutted with the ironclad wheels of Roman wagons. Yet it is one of the most evocative walks in Rome.

Monte Palatino

There are few more atmospheric places to wander in Rome than the Palatino, with its hidden corners and restful, shady lanes. From the Belvedere, there are panoramic views of the Circus Maximus, the green slopes of the Aventine and Celian hills, the bell tower of Santa Maria in Cosmedin, and, less picturesque, the immense white marble block of the United Nations Food and Agriculture Organization head-quarters. This is one of Rome's great picnic sites, with views over the ancient city; unfortunately, alfresco lunching is frowned upon. Eat at your own risk.

A Good Walk

Ticket offices and entrances to **Monte Palatino** ㉕ are inside the Forum at the base of the hill near the Arco di Tito and on Via di San Gregorio. From the former, follow the path known as the Clivus Palatinus, whose worn, original paving stones were trodden by both slaves and emperors, up to the flat hilltop where the ruins of the emperors' palaces stand. The palace complex built by Domitian includes the **Domus Flavia** ㉖ on the west, the **Domus Augustana** ㉗ at the center, and the **Stadio Palatino** ㉘ on the east. Below and south of the Palatino lies the **Circo Massimo** ㉙, and beyond that is the Aventino (Aventine Hill). The **Casa di Livia** ㉚ and the **Orti Farnesiani** ㉛, which are adjacent, on the northwest crest of the Palatino, represent two of the Palatino's golden ages: the first when it was prime real estate covered with ancient Roman patrician residences, and the second when it became the private property of one of Renaissance Rome's most powerful families.

TIMING

A leisurely stroll on the Palatino, with stops for the views and a visit to the Museo Palatino, takes about an hour. Fair weather is a must, as are good walking shoes for dusty slopes that are slippery when damp.

Sights to See

★ ㉚ **Casa di Livia** (House of Livia). Atop the Palatine are the excavations of one of the few remaining examples of a well-to-do Republican family's dwelling. Its delicate, delightful frescoes reflect the sophisticated taste of wealthy Romans, whose love of beauty and theatrical conception of nature was revived, much later, by their descendants in the Renaissance. You'll need to call ahead to visit. ⊠ *Northwest crest of the Palatino,* ☎ *06/4815576.*

㉙ **Circo Massimo** (Circus Maximus). Ancient Rome's oldest and largest racecourse lies in a natural hollow between two hills. From the imperial box in their palace on the Palatine Hill, the emperors could look out over the elongated oval course. Stretching about 650 yards from end to end, the Circus Maximus could hold more than 300,000 spectators. On certain occasions there were as many as 24 races a day, and competitions could last for 15 days. The noise, the color, and the excitement of the crowd must have been astounding. Later, when Rome was ruled by the popes, another kind of spectacle drew crowds to the site—the execution of criminals and transgressors of papal laws. ⊠ *Valley between the Palatine and Aventine hills.*

㉗ **Domus Augustana** (Palace of the Emperors). In the Palazzi Imperiali complex, this building consisted of private apartments for Domitian and his family. ⊠ *Southern crest of the Palatino.*

㉖ **Domus Flavia** (Palace of the Flavians). This palace in the Palazzi Imperiali complex served Domitian for official functions and ceremonies. Also called Palazzo dei Flavi, it included a basilica where the emperor could hold judiciary hearings. There was also a large audience hall, a peristyle (a columned courtyard), and the imperial triclinium (dining room). ⊠ *Southern crest of the Palatino.*

㉕ Monte Palatino. Rising above and to the south of the Forum, Palantine Hill is the oldest inhabited site in Rome. Archaeologists have uncovered remains of an Iron Age settlement here dating as far back as the 9th century BC. In fact, the ancient Romans always believed that Romulus, founder of Rome, lived on the Palatine. During the Republican era it was an exclusive residential area for wealthy families such as the Flacci and the Crassi, and in the Imperial age, the emperors took it over as a suitable site for their huge and splendid palaces. It was believed for years that Augustus, the first emperor to live on the Palatine, had tactfully chosen to keep the modest house he had lived in as a private citizen. Now it seems that he, like his successors, opted for suitably regal quarters. Tiberius was one of the first to build a full-fledged palace here; others followed. ⊠ *Entrances at the Arch of Titus in the Roman Forum and Via S. Gregorio 30,* ☎ *06/39967700.* ☜ *€6.20.* ☉ *Mon.–Sat. 9–2 hrs before sunset, Sun. and holidays 9–2.*

㉛ Orti Farnesiani (Farnese Gardens). Alessandro Farnese, a nephew of Pope Paul III, commissioned the 16th-century architect Vignola to lay out the archetypal Italian garden over the ruins of the Palace of Tiberius, up just a few steps from the House of Livia. The adjacent **Museo Palatino** (⊠ Via di San Gregorio 30, ☎ 06/520726) holds finds from the excavations; also adjacent is the restored **Loggia Mattei**, with early 16th-century frescoes. It's open Monday–Saturday from 9 until two hours before sunset, Sunday 9–2. ⊠ *Monte Palatino.*

Palazzi Imperiali (Imperial Palaces). Late in the 1st century AD, the Palatino underwent an extensive—and expensive—remodeling at the behest of the Emperor Domitian. In keeping with the imperial tradition of outdoing his predecessors to impress his successors, he had his architects put up two separate palaces and a stadium or garden. The lack of undeveloped space on the small hilltop was no problem: the emperor simply had his workers reshape the hill, razing older structures, filling in hollows, and building terraces to make room.

㉘ Stadio Palatino (Palatine Stadium). Next to his palace, Domitian created this vast open space. It may have been his private hippodrome, or it may simply have been an immense sunken garden; alternatively, perhaps it was used to stage games and other amusements for the benefit of the emperor. ⊠ *Southeast crest of Palatino.*

Arco di Costantino and Colosseo

This cobblestoned piazza and the park next to it hold three of the Roman Empire's most magnificent monuments to imperial wealth and power. The Arco di Costantino, a majestic, ornate triumphal arch, was built solely as a tribute to the emperor Constantine; victorious armies purportedly marched under it on their return from war. The Colosseo is the famed ancient sports arena constructed by Vespasian and Titus. Next to the Colosseo, hidden under the Colle Oppio, is Nero's opulent Domus Aurea, a palace that stands as testimony to the lavish lifestyle for which the emperors were known.

A Good Walk

The exit of the Palatino leads to the Arco di Tito, where you turn east toward the Colosseo. To the right is the **Arco di Costantino** ㉜. Next, you can explore the **Colosseo** ㉝, one of antiquity's largest and most famous monuments. Cross Piazza del Colosseo and stroll through the park on the Colle Oppio (Oppian Hill), where most of Nero's fabulous palace, the **Domus Aurea** ㉞, is hidden under the remains of the monumental baths that were built over it. The park has some good views over the Colosseum; one of the best vantage points is from Via Nicola Salvi, which climbs uphill from the Colosseum.

TIMING

A look at the Arco di Costantino won't take up more than 15 minutes of your time, but the Colosseo deserves more. You can give it a cursory look in 30 minutes, but if you want to climb to the upper tiers, allow another 20 minutes or so.

Sights to See

32 **Arco di Costantino** (Arch of Constantine). This majestic arch was erected in AD 315 to commemorate Constantine's victory over Maxentius at the Milvian Bridge. It was just before this battle, in AD 312, that Constantine—the emperor who converted Rome to Christianity—had a vision of a cross in the heavens and heard the words "In this sign thou shalt conquer." The economy-minded Senate ordered that many of the rich marble decorations for the arch be taken from earlier monuments. It is easy to picture ranks of Roman legionnaires marching under the great barrel vault. ⌧ *Piazza del Colosseo.*

★ **33** **Colosseo** (Colosseum). The most spectacular extant edifice of ancient Rome, this sports arena was designed to hold more than 50,000 spectators for gory entertainments such as combats between wild beasts and gladiators. It has a circumference of 573 yards and was faced with stone from nearby Tivoli. Its construction was a remarkable feat of engineering, for it stands on marshy terrain reclaimed by draining an artificial lake on the grounds of Nero's Domus Aurea, done to make amends to the Roman people for Nero's earlier confiscation of the land. Originally known as the Flavian amphitheater, it came to be called the Colosseum by later Romans who identified it with the site of the Colossus of Nero, a 115-ft-tall gilded bronze statue of the emperor in the guise of the sun god that stood at the entrance to what is now Via dei Fori Imperiali. Twelve pairs of elephants were needed to transport the statue here from its original site at the entrance to the Domus Aurea; it was pulled down and destroyed by order of Pope Gregory the Great at the end of the 6th century.

Designed by the Flavian emperor Vespasian in AD 72, the Colosseum was inaugurated by Titus eight years later with a program of games and shows lasting 100 days. On the opening day alone, 5,000 wild beasts perished. Among the stadium's many wonders was a velarium, an ingenious system of sail-like awnings—rigged on ropes maneuvered by sailors culled from the imperial fleet—that could be unfurled to protect the arena's occupants from sun or rain.

In one of the arches on the Metro station side, look for the traces of ancient Roman stucco decoration that once adorned most of the arena. Explore the upper levels, where behind glass you can see a scale model of the Colosseum as it was, sheathed with marble and studded with statues. From the upper tiers you can get a good view of the labyrinthine passageways on the subterranean level of the arena. Take the new wooden walkway across the arena floor for a gladiator's-eye view.

Legend has it that as long as the Colosseum stands, Rome will stand; and when Rome falls, so will the world. This prophecy didn't deter Renaissance princes from using the Colosseum as a quarry for building materials for such noble dwellings as Palazzo Barberini and Palazzo Farnese. Earlier, the Colosseum had been seriously damaged by earthquakes and, during the Middle Ages, had been transformed into a fortress. Some experts maintain that it was in Rome's circuses, and not here, that thousands of early Christians were martyred. Still, tradition

Close-Up

AN EMPEROR CHEAT SHEET

OCTAVIAN, later known as **CAESAR AUGUSTUS**, was Rome's first emperor (27 BC–AD 14), and his rule began a 200-year period of peace known as the Pax Romana.

The name of **NERO** (AD 54–68) lives in infamy as a violent persecutor of Christians, and as the murderer of his wife, his mother, and countless others; while it's not certain whether he actually fiddled as Rome burned in AD 64, he was well known as a singer and a composer of music.

TRAJAN (AD 98–117), the first Roman emperor to be born outside Italy (in southern Spain), enlarged the Empire's boundaries to include modern-day Romania, Armenia, and Upper Mesopotamia.

HADRIAN (AD 117–138), Trajan's younger cousin once removed, expanded the empire in Asia and the Middle East. Best known in Rome for having designed and rebuilt the Pantheon, he was also the author of the famed wall across Britain.

MARCUS AURELIUS (AD 161–180) is remembered as a humanitarian emperor, a Stoic philosopher whose *Meditations* are still read today. Nonetheless, he was devoted to expansion and an aggressive leader of the empire.

CONSTANTINE I (AD 306–337) was the empire's first Christian emperor. His conversion to Christianity changed the course of history, legitimizing the once-banned religion and paving the way for the papacy in Rome.

has reserved a special place for the Colosseum in the story of Christianity, and it was Pope Benedict XIV who stopped the use of the building as a quarry when, in 1749, he declared it sanctified by the blood of the martyrs. A tiny chapel built in the 6th century under one of the Colosseum's arches was restored and reconsecrated for the 1983 Holy Year. A guided tour in English is available. ⊠ *Piazza del Colosseo,* ☎ 06/39967700 or 06/7004261. ☉ *Daily 9–2 hrs before sunset.*

NEED A BREAK? About half a block east of the Colosseum is **Pasqualino** (⊠ Via dei Santi Quattro 66, ☎ 06/67004576), a neighborhood trattoria with sidewalk tables providing a view of the arena's marble arches. For delicious *gelato* try **Ristoro della Salute** (⊠ Piazza del Colosseo 2/a, ☎ 06/77590465), on the east side of the Piazza del Colosseo, one of Rome's best gelaterias (ice cream parlors).

34 Domus Aurea (Nero's Golden House). This ridge of the Esquiline Hill was the site of Nero's fabulous Domus Aurea. To build this extravagant palace after the catastrophic fire of AD 64, the capricious emperor confiscated a vast tract of land right in the center of Rome, earning the animosity of most of his subjects. The palace was huge and sumptuous, with a facade of pure gold, seawater piped into the baths, decorations of mother-of-pearl and other precious materials, and vast gardens. Not much has survived of all this; a good portion of the buildings and grounds were buried under the public works with which subsequent emperors sought to make reparation to the Roman people for Nero's phenomenal greed.

The largest of the buildings put up by later emperors over the Domus Aurea was the great complex of baths built by Trajan. As a result, the site of the Domus Aurea itself remained unknown for many centuries; indeed, when a few of Nero's original halls were discovered underground at the end of the 15th century, no one realized that they actually were part of the palace. Raphael was one of the artists who had themselves lowered into the rubble-filled rooms, which resembled grottoes. The artists copied the original painted Roman decorations, barely visible by torchlight, and, like modern, ill-mannered tourists, scratched their names on the ceilings. Raphael later used these models—known as *grotesques* because they were found in the so-called grottoes—in his decorative motifs for the Vatican Loggia. Keep in mind that the temperature underground is about 50°F all year round. Reservations are strongly recommended. (In May 2001 a portion of the Domus Aurea roof collapsed, causing it to be closed temporarily. Call ahead to find out the current status.) ⊠ *Via della Domus Aurea,* ☎ *06/6990110 information; 06/39967700 reservations.* ⊡ *€5.15, plus €1.05 reservation fee.* ☉ *Wed.–Mon. 9–7:45.*

Fori Imperiali

A complex of five grandly conceived squares flanked with colonnades and temples, the Imperial Fora formed the magnificent monumental core of ancient Rome, together with the original Roman Forum. Recent excavations have revealed more of the Imperial Fora than has been seen in nearly a thousand years.

A Good Walk

From Piazza del Colosseo, head northwest on Via dei Fori Imperiali toward Piazza Venezia. On the walls to your left, maps in marble and bronze put up by Mussolini show the extent of the Roman Republic and Empire. The dictator's own dreams of empire led him to construct this avenue, cutting brutally through the Imperial Fora area, so that he would have a suitable venue for parades celebrating his own military triumphs. Beyond the ancient brick walls behind the Imperial Fora lay the Suburra, the mean streets of ancient Rome, where the plebs lived in crowded tenements. The church of **Santi Cosma e Damiano** ㉟, a little gem, started life as a library in the Forum of Vespasian, and it holds a marvelous early Christian mosaic. Among the Fori Imperiali along the avenue you can see the **Foro di Cesare** ㊱ and the **Foro di Augusto** ㊲. The grandest of all the Imperial Fora was the **Foro di Traiano** ㊳, with its huge semicircular Mercati Traianei and the **Colonna di Traiano** ㊴.

TIMING

The walk along Via dei Fori Imperiali, with a stop at the church of Santi Cosma e Damiano and a look at the Fori Imperiali from sidewalk level, takes only about 30 minutes. To explore the emperors' fora more closely, allow another 30 minutes or so. The fora are lit up at night and on rare occasion are open for evening visits, when guided tours in English may also be offered (check with the tourist office).

Sights to See

㊴ **Colonna di Traiano** (Trajan's Column). The remarkable series of reliefs spiraling up this column celebrate the emperor's victories over the Dacians in what is today Romania. It has stood in this spot since AD 113. The scenes on the column are an important primary source for information on the Roman army and its tactics. An inscription on the base declares that the column was erected in Trajan's honor and that its height corresponds to the height of the hill that was razed to create a level area for the grandiose Foro di Traiano. The emperor's ashes, no longer here, were kept in a golden urn in a chamber at the column's base, and his statue stood atop the column until 1587, when the pope had it replaced with a statue of St. Peter. ☒ *Via del Foro di Traiano.*

㊲ Foro di Augusto (Forum of Augustus). These ruins, along with those of the **Foro di Nerva** (Forum of Nerva), on the northeast side of Via dei Fori Imperiali, give only a hint of what must have been impressive edifices. ☒ *Via dei Fori Imperiali.*

㊱ Foro di Cesare (Caesar's Forum). The first forum to be built, Caesar's, appeared in the middle of the 1st century BC. Without fail, on the Ides of March, an unknown hand lays a bouquet at the foot of Caesar's statue. Call several days in advance to arrange a visit. ☒ *Via dei Fori Imperiali,* ☎ *06/69780532.*

★ **㊳ Foro di Traiano** (Trajan's Forum). Of all the Imperial Fora complexes, Trajan's was the grandest and most imposing, a veritable city unto itself. Designed by architect Apollodorus of Damascus, it comprised a vast basilica, two libraries, and a temple laid out around the square, all once housed in rich marble ornament. Adjoining the forum were the **Mercati Traianei** (Trajan's markets), a huge, multilevel brick complex of shops, walkways, and terraces that was one of the marvels of the ancient world.

The market stands on the site of what was originally a low hill running between the Quirinal Hill to the northeast and the Capitoline Hill to the west, razed by Trajan to make room for his forum. It speaks volumes for the confidence of Apollodorus and his patron—not to mention the almost unlimited slave labor at their disposal—that they could so blithely remove this great quantity of earth just to build a market, even one as splendid as this. In fact the architectural centerpiece of the market is the enormous curved wall—technically known as an exedra, a form of apse—that shores up the side of the Quirinal Hill that had been exposed by Apollodorus's gangs of laborers. Here the Romans would come to meet and to gossip, sitting on the seats Apollodorus thoughtfully provided, which extend the length of the exedra.

Enter the large, vaulted hall in front of you. Two stories of shops rise up on either side. It's thought that they were probably a bazaar or a similar sort of specialty market. Head for the flight of steps at the far end that leads down to Via Biberatica (*bibere* is the Latin for "to drink" and the shops that open onto the street were taverns). Then head back to the three tiers of shops that line the upper levels of the great exedra and look out over the remains of the forum. Though empty and bare today, the cubicles were once ancient Rome's busiest market stalls. Wine, oils, flowers, perfumes, shoes, clothing, and household goods were all sold in this thriving market—everything a burgeoning and sophisticated population desired. There is evidence that the market was equipped with fresh- and saltwater tanks so the Romans could buy their fish live. Though it seems to be part of the market, the **Torre delle Milizie** (Tower of the Militia), the tall brick tower that is a prominent feature of Rome's skyscape, was built in the early 1200s. In those times wealthy families vied with one another to build the strongest, highest defensive towers. Pope Boniface VIII bought this one from the Conti family so that he could use it as a stronghold to defend his Roman territory against his arch enemies, the Colonnas. ☒ *Entrance at Via IV Novembre 94,* ☎ *06/6790048.* ▭ *€6.20.* ☉ *Tues.–Sun. 10–1 hr before sunset.*

㉟ Santi Cosma e Damiano. This church was adapted in the 6th century from two ancient buildings: the library in Vespasian's Forum of Peace and a hall of the Temple of Romulus (dedicated to the son of Maxentius). It was restored in the 17th century by the Barberini Pope Urban

VIII, who added a few bees from his family's coat of arms to the lower left-hand side of the mosaic in the apse. Note in the mosaic the dark-skinned Jesus flanked by light-skinned popes—this is an eastern Mediterranean representation rarely seen in Rome. There's also a Neapolitan *presepio,* or Christmas crèche, on permanent display. ⊠ *Off Via Sacra, opposite Tempio di Antonino e Faustina,* ☎ *06/6991540.* ☉ *Daily 9– 1 and 3–6:30.*

THE VATICAN

The Basilica di San Pietro and the Vatican are the heart and headquarters of the Roman Catholic Church. The massive walls surrounding Vatican City strongly underscore the fact that this is an independent, sovereign state, established by the Lateran Treaty of 1929 between the Holy See—the pope—and the Italian government. Vatican City covers 108 acres on a hill west of the Tiber and is separated from the city on all sides by high walls, except at Piazza di San Pietro. Inside the walls, about 1,000 people live as residents. The Vatican has its own daily newspaper (*L'Osservatore Romano*), issues its own stamps, mints its own coins, and has its own postal system. Within its territory are administrative and foreign offices, a pharmacy, banks, an astronomical observatory, a print shop, a mosaic school and art restoration institute, a tiny train station, a supermarket, a small department store, and several gas stations. Radio Vaticana broadcasts in 35 languages to six different continents.

The sovereign of this little state is Pope John Paul II, who, until his election on October 16, 1978, was Karol Cardinal Wojtyla, archbishop of Kraków. He is the 264th pope of the Roman Catholic Church, the first non-Italian in 456 years, and the first-ever Pole to hold the office. He has full legislative, judicial, and executive powers, with complete freedom under the Lateran Treaty to organize armed forces within his state (the Swiss Guards and the Vatican police) and to live in or move through Italian territory whenever he so desires. The pope reigns over 700 million Roman Catholics throughout the world. The intricate rules of etiquette that were once characteristic of the Vatican have been greatly relaxed by the last few popes, and much of the Apostolic Palace has been redecorated in severely simple style. But the colorful dress uniforms of the Swiss Guards and the pomp and circumstance of Vatican ceremonies are reminders of past ostentation and worldly power.

The Basilica di San Pietro, the world's largest and most splendid Christian church, is the expression of an age when the popes wielded considerable temporal power together with enormous religious authority. Few consider a visit to Rome complete without seeing it—and without visiting the Musei Vaticani's collections, of staggering richness and diversity, and the Sistine Chapel, Michelangelo's masterpiece.

Numbers in the text and margin correspond to numbers on the Vatican map.

A Good Walk

To enter the Musei Vaticani, the Sistine Chapel, and the Basilica di San Pietro you must comply with the Vatican's dress code, or you will be turned away by the implacable custodians at the doors. For both men and women, shorts and tank tops are taboo, as are miniskirts and otherwise revealing clothing. Wear a jacket or shawl over sleeveless tops, and avoid T-shirts with writing or pictures that could give offense. Start at the **Musei Vaticani** ①. The entrance on Viale Vaticano (there is a separate exit on the same street) can be reached by bus 49 from Piazza

CHURCH AND STATE

IN ADDITION TO THE COLOSSEUM, the Forum, and the other sights that make the city unique, another institution makes Rome different from any other city in the world: it is the only Catholic diocese with an elected bishop. He's not just any bishop, of course; the Bishop of Rome is none other than the pope, chosen for life by the members of the College of Cardinals in an election that arguably affects more of the world's people than any other. Although his primary role is as the leader of the Catholic Church, this job title brings with it sovereignty over Vatican City and ecclesiastical responsibility for the city of Rome from Rome's cathedral, San Giovanni in Laterano (St. John in Lateran).

The complicated accord between Rome and the Vatican was laid down in 1929 in the terms of the Lateran Concordat and Treaty, signed by Fascist strongman Benito Mussolini and Cardinal Gasparri, on behalf of Pope Pius XI. Under Italian unification in 1870, the land controlled by the Church, the Papal States, had been annexed by the Kingdom of Italy, giving rise to complaints that dependence on a political body compromised the pope's ability to direct the Church. Nearly 60 years later, a compromise was reached, establishing the Vatican's autonomy but requiring its sworn political neutrality and establishing Catholicism as the Italian state religion. This is the agreement that exists today (although the Italian Republic no longer has a state religion), and it's responsible for the delicate, often awkward, unquestionably unique relationship between Italy and the world's smallest country, tucked away in the center of Rome.

Vatican City is completely surrounded by the city of Rome, and although it's possible to pass through without ever knowing you've left the sovereignty of the Italian state, closer inspection reveals a number of differences more striking than the low brick walls that mark the city limits. The Vatican is an autonomous political body, with independent leadership and diplomatic relationships like any other nation. The country is ruled by the pope and the various papally appointed Pontifical Councils that advise him; although technically the pope is an elected official, the electorate is not the population of Vatican City but the College of Cardinals, who have chosen a leader from among their number in every election since 1378. Toss a soda can inside the Vatican walls, and it's the Vatican police who'll give you a ticket; anything more serious and you might make headlines in L'Osservatore Romano, the Vatican's own newspaper. Although its population is just over 1,000 (including the pope, who lives in the Apostolic Palace), the Vatican has its own postal system, reputedly more reliable than the Posta Italiana (look for blue or yellow boxes marked Posta Vaticana). To use the Vatican Post, you'll have to buy special stamps at the Posta Vaticana, with offices at both sides of St. Peter's Square.

With two autonomous nations so closely linked, it can get messy when they disagree. In recent years, Italy has clashed with the Vatican over such diverse issues as a Gay Pride march in Rome, a visit of Austrian rightist Joerg Haider to the pope, electronic pollution from Vatican Radio transmission towers, and the eternally thorny issue of the Vatican's tax-exempt status, established in the Lateran Concordat and the subject of heated debate ever since. It's an uneasy balance between the two states, but the Vatican's sovereignty (and wealth) and Italy's secularity (and wealth) mean that, at least on paper, neither has much leverage over the other. In Rome, church and state are at a standoff and look to remain that way for many years to come.

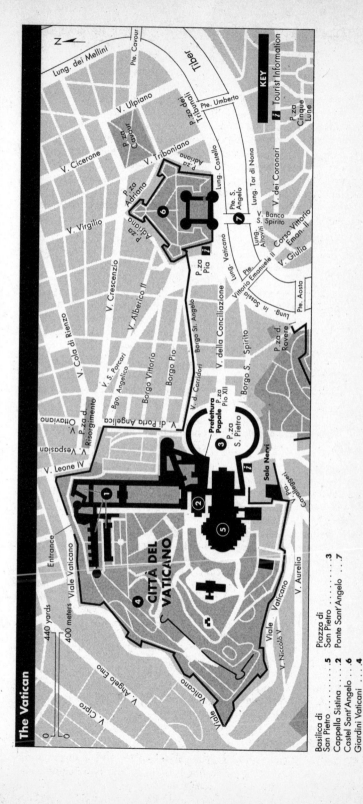

The Vatican

KEY

i Tourist Information

Basilica di
San Pietro **5**
Cappella Sistina **2**
Castel Sant'Angelo . . **6**
Giardini Vaticani **4**
Musei Vaticani **1**

Piazza di
San Pietro **3**
Ponte Sant'Angelo . . **7**

CITTÀ DEL VATICANO

Prefettura Papale

P.za S. Pietro

Sala Nervi

Entrance

Cavour, which stops right in front; or on foot from Piazza del Risorgimento (bus 81 or tram 19) or a brief walk from the Via Cipro–Musei Vaticani stop on Metro line A. The collections of the museums are immense, covering about 7 km (4½ mi) of displays. You can rent a taped commentary in English explaining the Sistine Chapel and the Raphael Rooms. You're free to photograph what you like, barring use of flash, tripod, or other special equipment, for which permission must be obtained. To economize on time and effort, once you've seen the frescoes in the Borgia rooms, you can skip the collections of modern religious art in good conscience and get on with your tour. Lines at the entrance to the **Cappella Sistina** ② can move slowly as custodians block further entrance when the room becomes crowded. Keep in mind that sometimes it's possible to exit the museums from the Sistine Chapel into St. Peter's, saving time and legwork. A sign at the entrance to the museums indicates whether the exit is open.

Piazza di San Pietro ③ is at the west end of Via della Conciliazione. If you have the stamina, take the tour of the **Giardini Vaticani** ④; then enter the **Basilica di San Pietro** ⑤, visiting the Museo Storico-Artistico e Tesoro and the Grotte Vaticane. Take the elevator to the roof of the basilica, a strange fairy-tale landscape of little cupolas and towers. Climb the short staircase to the gallery inside the base of the huge dome for a dove's-eye view of the papal altar below. If you can't handle a steep, claustrophobic, one-way-only climb, don't attempt the ascent to the lantern, the small topmost cupola of the dome.

You can continue your walk to **Castel Sant'Angelo** ⑥, on Borgo Pio, where there are a number of trattorias and cafés. The huge medieval fortress, built over the tomb of emperor Hadrian, saved at least one pope's life, when Clement VII took refuge here during the Sack of Rome in 1527. From Castel Sant'Angelo's terraces you get a bird's-eye view of **Ponte Sant'Angelo** ⑦, the graceful bridge adorned with statues designed by Bernini, and the rooftops of central Rome.

TIMING

If possible, break up this itinerary into two half days. Keep in mind that tours of the Giardini Vaticani start at 10 AM; it's possible to visit St. Peter's Basilica beforehand, but you won't have time for the Vatican Museums. You could do St. Peter's Basilica and Castel Sant'Angelo one day and devote another day to the museums. To do all three on the same day takes stamina and dedication; even if you rush through to the Sistine Chapel, you run the risk of cultural indigestion. As the Vatican is close to the Via Cola di Rienzo and Via Ottaviano shopping areas, you might want to combine sightseeing with shopping. Another option would be to add Castel Sant'Angelo to the end of the Old Rome tour.

The crowds at the museums, and especially the Sistine Chapel, can be overwhelming; a good strategy to get there either very early, before the pressure builds up, or late, as the crowds thin out. Plan on about 90 minutes for even the most cursory visit to the Vatican Museums and the Sistine Chapel. Allow an hour for St. Peter's Basilica and an hour for Castel Sant'Angelo. To do all three sights, including a lot of walking from one to another, would take from five to six hours, not counting breaks.

Sights to See

★ ⑤ **Basilica di San Pietro** (St. Peter's Basilica). The largest church in the world, built over the tomb of St. Peter, is also the most imposing and breathtaking architectural achievement of the Renaissance (although much of the lavish interior dates to the Baroque). Its history goes back

St. Peter's Basilica

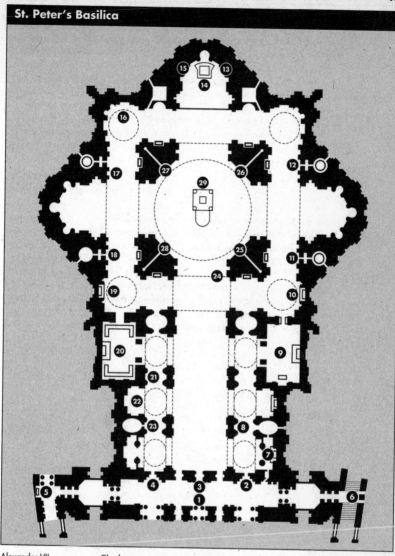

to AD 319, when the emperor Constantine built a basilica over the site of the tomb of St. Peter, the Church's first pope. The original church stood for more than 1,000 years, undergoing a number of restorations and alterations, until it was in danger of collapse toward the middle of the 15th century. In 1452 a reconstruction job began but was quickly abandoned for lack of cash. In 1506 Pope Julius II instructed the architect Bramante to raze all the existing buildings and to build a new basilica, one that would surpass even Constantine's for grandeur. But it wasn't until 1626 that the basilica was completed and dedicated. Five of Italy's greatest Renaissance artists died during the time of their work on the new and greater St. Peter's—Bramante, Raphael, Peruzzi, Antonio Sangallo the Younger, and Michelangelo.

Though Bramante made little progress in rebuilding St. Peter's, he succeeded nonetheless in outlining a basic plan for the church, and, crucially, he built the piers of the crossings—the massive pillars supporting the dome. After Bramante's death in 1514, Raphael, the Sangallos, and Peruzzi all proposed variations on the original plan at one time or another. Again, however, lack of finances, rivalries between the architects, and, above all, the turmoil caused by the Sack of Rome in 1527 and the mounting crisis of the Reformation conspired to ensure that little serious progress was made. In 1546, however, Pope Paul III turned to Michelangelo and more or less forced the aging artist to complete the building. Michelangelo, in turn, insisted on having carte blanche to do as he thought best. He returned to Bramante's first idea of having a centralized Greek-cross plan—that is, with the "arms" of the church all the same length—and completed most of the exterior architecture except for the dome and the facade. His design for the dome, however, was modified after his death by Giacomo della Porta. The nave, too, was altered after Michelangelo's death. Pope Paul V wanted a Latin-cross church (a church with one "arm" longer than the rest), so Carlo Maderno lengthened one of the arms to create a longer central nave. He was also responsible for the facade. This was much criticized at the time because it hides the dome from observers below. It is also wider than it is high.

As you climb the shallow steps up to the great church, flanked by the statues of Sts. Peter and Paul, you'll see the **Loggia delle Benedizioni** (Benediction Loggia) over the central portal. This is the balcony where newly elected popes are proclaimed and where they stand to give their apostolic blessing on solemn feast days. The vault above you is encrusted with rich stuccowork, and the mosaic above the central entrance to the portico is a much-restored work by the 14th-century painter Giotto that was in the original basilica. The bronze doors of the main entrance also were salvaged from the old basilica. The sculptor Filarete worked on them for 12 years; they show scenes from the Council of Florence and the Life of Pope Eugene IV (1431–47), his patron. The large central figures are Sts. Peter and Paul. In the basilica, look at the inside of these doors for the amusing "signature" at the bottom in which Filarete shows himself and his assistant dancing with joy, tools in hand, at having completed their task. To the left are two modern bronze doors, the so-called Doors of Death, in both of which you'll see Pope John XXIII. On the right of the main entrance are the Door of the Sacraments and the Holy Door, opened only during Holy Years.

Pause a moment to judge the size of the great building. The people near the main altar seem dwarfed by the incredible dimensions of this immense temple. The statues, the pillars, and the holy-water stoups borne by colossal cherubs are all imposing. Brass inscriptions in the marble pavement down the center of the nave indicate the approximate lengths of the world's other principal Christian churches, all of which fall far short of St. Peter's Basilica's 186-m span.

Immediately to your right is Michelangelo's *Pietà,* one of the world's most famous statues. It was safely screened behind shatterproof glass after being damaged in 1972 and masterfully restored in the Vatican's workshops.

Exquisite bronze grilles and doors by Borromini open into the third chapel in the right aisle, the **Cappella del Santissimo Sacramento** (Chapel of the Most Holy Sacrament), with a Baroque fresco of the Trinity by Pietro da Cortona and carved angels by Bernini. At the last pillar on the right (the pier of St. Longinus) is a bronze statue of St. Peter, whose big toe is kissed by the faithful. In the right transept, over the door to the **Cappella di San Michele** (Chapel of St. Michael), usually closed, Canova created a brooding neoclassical monument to Pope Clement XIII.

In the central crossing, Bernini's great bronze *baldacchino*—a huge, spiral-columned canopy—rises high over the *altare papale* (papal altar). Bernini's Barberini patron, Pope Urban VIII, had no qualms about stripping the bronze from the Pantheon in order to provide Bernini with the material to create this curious structure. The Romans reacted with the famous quip, *"Quod non fecerunt barbari, fecerunt Barberini."* ("What the barbarians didn't do, the Barberini did.") A curious legend connected with the baldacchino, which swarms with Barberini bees (the bee was the Barberini family symbol), relates that the pope commissioned it in thanks for the recovery of a favorite niece who had almost died in childbirth. The story is borne out by the marble reliefs on the bases of the columns: the Barberini coat of arms is surmounted by a series of heads, all but two of which seem to represent a woman in what might be the pain of labor, while a smiling baby's face appears on the base at the right front.

The antique casket in the niche under the papal altar contains the *pallia,* bands of white wool that are conferred by the pope on archbishops as a sign of authority. These pallia are made by nuns from the wool of two lambs blessed every year in the Church of Sant'Agnese on her feast day, January 21. When completed, they are blessed by the pope during the rites of the feast of Sts. Peter and Paul on June 29 and are stored in the casket that you see.

The splendid gilt-bronze **Cattedra di San Pietro** (throne of St. Peter) in the apse above the main altar was designed by Bernini to contain a wooden and ivory chair that St. Peter himself is said to have used, though in fact it doesn't date from further than medieval times. (You can see a copy of the chair in the treasury.) Above it, Bernini placed a window of thin alabaster sheets that diffuses a golden light around the dove, symbol of the Holy Spirit, in the center.

Two of the major papal funeral monuments in St. Peter's Basilica are on either side of the apse and unfortunately are usually dimly lit. To the right is the **tomb of Pope Urban VIII;** to the left is the **tomb of Pope Paul III.** Paul's tomb is the earlier, designed between 1551 and 1575 by della Porta, the architect who completed the dome of St. Peter's Basilica after Michelangelo's death. The nude figure of Justice was widely believed to be a portrait of the pope's beautiful sister, Giulia. The charms of this alluring figure were such that in the 19th century, it was thought that she should no longer be allowed to distract worshipers from their prayers and she was swathed in marble drapery. It was in emulation of this splendid late-Renaissance work that Urban VIII ordered Bernini to design his tomb. Notice the skeleton figure of Death writing the pope's name on a marble slab. The **tomb of Pope Alexander VII**, also designed by Bernini, stands to the left of the altar as you look up the nave, behind the farthest pier of the crossing.

With advance notice you can take a guided tour in English (€7.75); about 1¼ hours) of the **Vatican Necropolis** under the basilica, which gives a rare glimpse of early Christian Roman burial customs. Apply by fax (FAX 06/69885518) or e-mail () at least 20 days in advance, specifying the number of people in the group (all must be age 15 or older), preferred language, preferred time, available dates, and your contact information in Rome.

Under the Pope Pius V monument, the entrance to the sacristy also leads to the **Museo Storico-Artistico e Tesoro** (Historical-Artistic Museum and Treasury; €4.15; Apr.–Sept., daily 9–6; Oct.–Mar., daily 9–5), a small collection of Vatican treasures. They range from the massive and beautifully sculptured 15th-century tomb of Pope Sixtus IV by Pollaiuolo, which you can view from above, to a jeweled cross dating from the 6th century and a marble tabernacle by the Florentine mid-15th-century sculptor Donatello. Among the other priceless objects are a platinum chalice presented to Pope Pius VI by Charles III of Spain in the middle of the 18th century and an array of sacred vessels in gold, silver, and precious stones.

Continue on down the left nave past Algardi's **tomb of St. Leo** (Pope Leo XI). The handsome bronze grilles in the **Capella del Coro** (Chapel of the Choir) were designed by Borromini to complement those opposite in the Cappella del Santissimo Sacramento. The next pillar holds a rearrangement of the Pollaiuolo brothers' austere monument to Pope Innocent VIII, the only major tomb to have been transferred from the old basilica. The next chapel contains the handsome bronze monument to Pope John XXIII by contemporary sculptor Emilio Greco. On the last pier in this nave stands a monument by the late-18th-century Venetian sculptor Canova marking the spot in the crypt below where the last of the ill-fated Stuarts—the 18th-century Roman Catholic claimants to the British throne, who were long exiled in Rome—were buried.

Between the Gregorian Chapel and the right crossing, take the elevator or climb the long flight of shallow stairs to the **roof** of the church (€4.15 stairs, €6.20 elevator; Apr.–Aug., daily 8–6; Sept.–Mar., daily 8–5; closed to tourists during ceremonies in the basilica), a surreal landscape of vast sloping terraces punctuated by cupolas that serve as skylights over the various chapels. The roof affords unusual perspectives on the dome above and the piazza below. The terrace is equipped with the inevitable souvenir shop and with rest rooms. A short flight of stairs leads to the entrance of the *tamburo* (drum)—the base of the dome—where, appropriately enough, there's a bust of Michelangelo, the dome's principal designer. Within the drum, another short ramp and staircase give access to the **gallery** encircling the base of the dome. From here you have a dove's-eye view of the interior of the church. It's well worth the slight effort to make your way up here—unless you suffer from vertigo.

Only if you're of stout heart and strong lungs should you then make the taxing climb from the drum of the dome up to the *lanterna* (lantern) at the very apex of the dome. A narrow, seemingly interminable staircase follows the curve of the dome between inner and outer shells, finally releasing you into the cramped space of the lantern balcony for an absolutely gorgeous panorama of Rome and the countryside on a clear day. There's also a nearly complete view of the palaces, courtyards, and gardens of the Vatican. Be aware, however, that it's a tiring, slightly claustrophobic climb. There's one stairway for going up and a different one for coming down, so you can't change your mind halfway and turn back.

The entrance to **Le Sacre Grotte Vaticane** (Tombs of the Popes; ⊠ free; ☉ Apr.–Sept., daily 7–6; Oct.–Mar., daily 7–5) is at the base of the pier dedicated to St. Longinus. As the only exit from the crypt leads outside St. Peter's Basilica, it is best to leave this visit for last. The crypt is lined with marble-faced chapels and simple tombs occupying the area of Constantine's basilica and standing over the cemetery in which recent excavations have brought to light what is believed to be the tomb of St. Peter himself.

⊠ *Piazza di San Pietro.* ⊠ *Free.* ☉ *Apr.–Sept., daily 7–7; Oct.–Mar., daily 7–6. Free 1-hr guided tours in English available; inquire at Centro Servizi (information office) as times vary.*

NEED A BREAK? **Insalata Ricca** (⊠ Piazza Risorgimento 6, ☎ 06/39730387), about halfway between the Vatican Museums and St. Peter's Basilica, offers light meals, chiefly pasta, salads, and pizza.

★ ❷ **Cappella Sistina** (Sistine Chapel). In 1508, the redoubtable Pope Julius II commissioned Michelangelo to fresco the more than 10,000 square ft of the Sistine Chapel's ceiling. (*Sistine,* by the way, is simply the adjective from *Sixtus,* in reference to Pope Sixtus IV, who commissioned the chapel.) The task took four years, and it's said that for many years afterward Michelangelo couldn't read anything without holding it up over his head. The result, however, was the masterpiece that you see. A pair of binoculars helps greatly, as does a small mirror—hold the mirror facing the ceiling and look down to study the reflection.

Before the chapel was consecrated in 1483, its lower walls had been decorated by a group of artists including Botticelli, Ghirlandaio, Perugino, and Signorelli, all working under the direction of Pinturicchio. They had painted scenes from the life of Moses on one wall and episodes from the life of Christ on the other. Later, Julius II, dissatisfied with the simple vault decoration—it consisted of no more than stars painted on the ceiling—decided to call in Michelangelo. At the time, Michelangelo was carving Julius II's gargantuan tomb—a project that never came near completion. He had no desire to give the project up in order to paint a ceiling, considering painting a task unworthy of him. Julius was not, however, a man to be trifled with, and Michelangelo reluctantly began work. The project proceeded fitfully until Michelangelo, dismissing his assistants, decided that he would paint the ceiling himself. (By contrast, substantial sections of Raphael's *Stanze* were the work of assistants; Raphael himself probably painted only the principal figures.)

Michelangelo's subject was the story of humanity before the coming of Christ. It is told principally by means of the scenes depicted in nine central panels. These show, working from the altar: the *Separation of Light from Darkness,* the *Creation of the Heavenly Bodies,* the *Separation of Land and Sea,* the *Creation of Adam,* the *Creation of Eve,* the *Fall of Man and the Expulsion from Paradise,* the *Sacrifice of Noah,* the *Flood,* and the *Drunkenness of Noah.* These focal scenes appear in an architectural framework, further embellished with Old Testament figures, prophets, sybils, and 20 *ignudi,* or nude youths. In the lunettes below, the spaces between the windows, Michelangelo painted the ancestors of Christ.

The ceiling, cleaned and restored in the early 1990s, is vibrantly colored, a startling contrast to the dark and veiled tones known for so many years. The cleaning, which was not without controversy, has led art historians to reevaluate Michelangelo's influence on the Mannerist style, which favored similarly vivid colors. What remains unchanged, however, is the remarkable power and imagination of the ceiling. Notice the way that the later scenes—the *Creation of Adam* is a good example—are larger and more simply painted than the earlier scenes. As the work advanced, Michelangelo became progressively bolder in his treatment, using larger forms and simpler colors.

More than 20 years later, Michelangelo was called on again, this time by the Farnese Pope Paul III, to add to the chapel's decoration by painting the *Last Judgment* on the wall over the altar. The subject was well suited to the aging and embittered artist, who had been deeply moved by the horrendous Sack of Rome in 1527 and the confusions and disturbances of the Reformation. The painting stirred up controversy even before it was unveiled in 1541, shocking many Vatican officials, especially one Biagio di Cesena, who criticized its "indecent" nudes. Michelangelo retaliated by painting Biagio's face on the figure with donkey's ears in Hades, in the lower right-hand corner of the work. Biagio pleaded with Pope Paul to have Michelangelo erase his portrait, but the pontiff replied that he could intercede for those in purgatory but had no power over hell. Michelangelo painted his own face on the wrinkled human skin in the hand of St. Bartholomew. ⊠ *Vatican Palace; entry only through the Musei Vaticani.*

❻ **Castel Sant'Angelo** (Holy Angel Castle). This great circular building—with one of the most distinctive silhouettes of any structure in Rome—stands between the Tiber and the Vatican. Castel Sant'Angelo's loggias and terraces have wonderful views. The structure was in fact built as a mausoleum for the emperor Hadrian. Work began in AD 135 and was completed by the emperor's successor, Antoninus Pius, about five years later. When first finished, it consisted of a great square base topped by a marble-clad cylinder on which was planted a ring of cypress trees. Above them towered a gigantic statue of Hadrian. From about the middle of the 6th century AD the building became a fortress, the military key to Rome for almost 1,000 years and the place of refuge for numerous popes during wars and sieges. Its name dates from 590, when Pope Gregory the Great, returning to the Vatican during a terrible plague, saw an angel standing on the summit of the castle in the act of sheathing its sword. Taking this as a heavenly sign that the plague was at an end, the pope built a chapel on the spot where he had seen the angel. Next to it he had a statue of the angel placed. Henceforth, it became known as Castel Sant'Angelo. Later, Puccini set the final scene of *Tosca* here; on the upper terrace is the rampart off of which the tempestuous diva throws herself to end the opera.

Enter the building from the former moat, and through the original Roman door of Hadrian's tomb. From here you pass through a courtyard that was enclosed in the base of the classical monument. You enter a vaulted brick corridor that hints at grim punishments in dank cells. On the right, a spiral ramp leads up to the chamber in which Hadrian's ashes were kept. Where the ramp ends, the Borgia Pope Alexander VI's staircase begins. Part of it consisted of a wooden drawbridge, which could isolate the upper part of the castle completely. The staircase ends at the Cortile dell'Angelo, a courtyard that has become the resting place of the marble angel that stood above the castle. (It was replaced by a bronze sculpture in 1753.) The stone cannonballs piled in the courtyard look like oversize marble snowballs. In the rooms off the Cortile dell'An-

HOW TO USE THIS GUIDE

Great trips begin with great planning, and this guide makes planning easy. It's packed with everything you need—insider advice on hotels and restaurants, cool tools, practical tips, essential maps, and much more.

COOL TOOLS

Fodor's Choice Top picks are marked throughout with a star.

Great Itineraries These tours, planned by Fodor's experts, give you the skinny on what you can see and do in the time you have.

Smart Travel Tips A to Z This special section is packed with important contacts and advice on everything from how to get around to what to pack.

Good Walks You won't miss a thing if you follow the numbered bullets on our maps.

Need a Break? Looking for a quick bite to eat or a spot to rest? These sure bets are along the way.

Off the Beaten Path Some lesser-known sights are worth a detour. We've marked those you should make time for.

POST-IT® FLAGS
Dog-ear no more!

"Post-it" is a registered trademark of 3M.

Favorite restaurants • Essential maps • Frequently used numbers • Walking tours • Can't-miss sights • Smart Travel Tips • Web sites • Top shops • Hot nightclubs • Addresses • Smart contacts • Events • Off-the-beaten-path spots • Favorite restaurants • Essential maps • Frequently used numbers • Walking tours • Can't-miss sights • Smart Travel Tips • Web sites • Top shops • Hot nightclubs • Addresses • Smart contacts • Events • Off-the-beaten-path spots • Favorite restaurants • Essential maps • Frequently used numbers • Walking tours •

ICONS AND SYMBOLS

Watch for these symbols throughout:

★   Our special recommendations

✕   Restaurant

🏠   Lodging establishment

✕🏠   Lodging establishment whose restaurant warrants a special trip

🖱   Good for kids

☞   Sends you to another section of the guide for more information

⊠   Address

☎   Telephone number

FAX   Fax number

WEB   Web site

🎟   Admission price

☉   Opening hours

$-$$$$ Lodging and dining price categories, keyed to strategically sited price charts. Check the index for locations.

①❶   Numbers in white and black circles on the maps, in the margins, and within tours correspond to one another.

ON THE WEB

Continue your planning with these useful tools found at **www.fodors.com**, the Web's best source for travel information.

"Rich with resources." —*New York Times*

"Navigation is a cinch." —*Forbes* "Best of the Web" list

"Put together by people bursting with know-how."
—*Sunday Times* (London)

Create a Miniguide Pinpoint hotels, restaurants, and attractions that have what you want at the price you want to pay.

Rants and Raves Find out what readers say about Fodor's picks—or write your own reviews of hotels and restaurants you've just visited.

Travel Talk Post your questions and get answers from fellow travelers, or share your own experiences.

On-Line Booking Find the best prices on airline tickets, rental cars, cruises, or vacations, and book them on the spot.

About our Books Learn about other Fodor's guides to your destination and many others.

Expert Advice and Trip Ideas From what to tip to how to take great photos, from the national parks to Nepal, Fodors.com has suggestions that'll make your trip a breeze. Log on and get informed and inspired.

Smart Resources Check the weather in your destination or convert your currency. Learn the local language or link to the latest event listings. Or consult hundreds of detailed maps—all in one place.

gelo, there's a small collection of arms and armor; on the left are some frescoed halls, which are used for temporary exhibitions, and the **Cappella di Papa Leone X** (Chapel of Pope Leo X), with a facade by Michelangelo.

In the courtyard named for Pope Alexander VI, a wellhead bears the Borgia coat of arms. The courtyard is surrounded by gloomy cells and huge storerooms that could hold great quantities of oil and grain in case of siege. Benvenuto Cellini, the rowdy 16th-century Florentine goldsmith, sculptor, and boastful autobiographer, spent some time in Castel Sant'Angelo's foul prisons; so did Giordano Bruno, a heretical monk who was later burned at the stake in Campo dei Fiori, and Beatrice Cenci, accused of patricide and incest and executed just across Ponte Sant'Angelo. (Beatrice's story forms the lurid plot of Shelley's verse drama *The Cenci*.)

Take the stairs at the far end of the courtyard to the open terrace. From here, you have some wonderful views of the city's rooftops and of the lower portions of the castle. You can also see the Passetto, the fortified corridor connecting Castel Sant'Angelo with the Vatican. Pope Clement VII used it to make his way safely to the castle during the Sack of Rome in 1527. Opening off the terrace are more rooms containing arms and military uniforms. There's also a café where you can pause for refreshments.

Continue your walk along the perimeter of the tower and climb the few stairs to the *appartamento papale* (papal apartment). Though used by the popes mainly in times of crisis, these splendid rooms are far from spartan. The sumptuous Sale Paoline (Pauline Room), the first you enter, was decorated in the 16th century by Pierino del Vaga and his assistants with lavish frescoes of scenes from the Old Testament and the lives of St. Paul and Alexander the Great. Look for the trompe l'oeil door with a figure climbing the stairs. From another false door, a black-clad figure peers into the room. This is believed to be a portrait of an illegitimate son of the powerful Orsini family. The Camera del Perseo (Perseus Room), next door, is named for a frieze in which del Vaga represents Perseus with damsels and unicorns. The classical theme is continued in the next room, the Camera d'Amore e Psiche (Cupid and Psyche Room), used by the popes as a bedroom. From the Pauline Room a curving corridor covered with grotesques (based on ancient Roman wall paintings seen by the artists of the time in the grottolike ruins of Nero's palace) leads to the library, some smaller rooms, and the treasury. Here the immense wealth of the Vatican was brought for safekeeping during times of strife; it was stored in the large 16th-century strongboxes you see today. You can continue on to the upper terrace at the feet of the bronze angel for a magnificent view. ✉ *Lungotevere Castello 50,* ☎ *06/6819111.* ⏰ *Tues.–Sun. 9–8 (ticket office 9–7); longer hrs in summer.*

| NEED A BREAK? | A tiny take-out pastry shop, **Dolceborgo** (✉ Borgo Pio 162, ☎ no phone) is one of the area's best. Walk three blocks down Borgo Pio from Via Porta Angelica; it's on the left. |

❹ **Giardini Vaticani** (Vatican Gardens). Extending over the hill behind St. Peter's Basilica is Vatican City's enclave of neatly trimmed lawns and flower beds dotted with some interesting constructions and other, duller ones that serve as office buildings. The Vatican Gardens occupy almost 40 acres of land on the Vatican hill, behind St. Peter's Basilica. The mandatory tour begins in front of the Centro Servizi on Piazza San Pietro. It takes about two hours and includes a visit to the little-

Vatican Museums

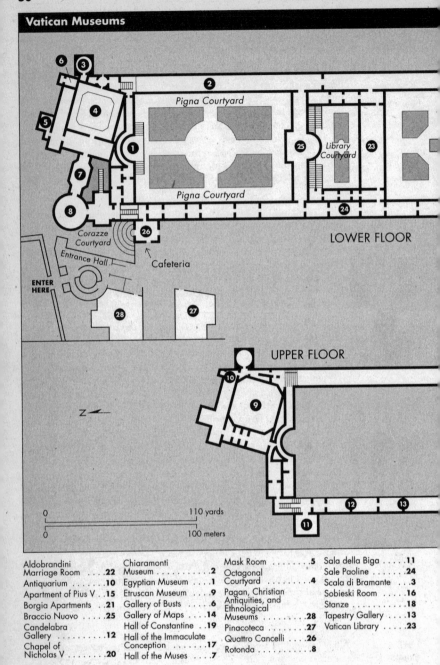

Pigna Courtyard

Library Courtyard

Pigna Courtyard

LOWER FLOOR

Corazze Courtyard

Entrance Hall

Cafeteria

ENTER HERE

UPPER FLOOR

0   110 yards
0   100 meters

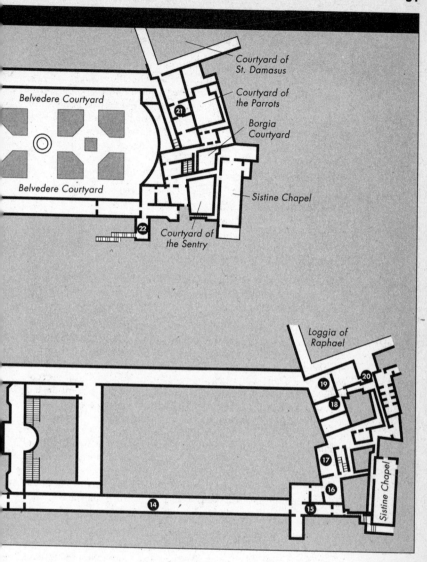

Courtyard of
St. Damasus

Courtyard of
the Parrots

Belvedere Courtyard

Borgia
Courtyard

21

Belvedere Courtyard

Sistine Chapel

22

Courtyard of
the Sentry

Loggia of
Raphael

19   **20**

18

17

Sistine Chapel

16

14

15

used Vatican railroad station, which now houses a museum of coins and stamps made in the Vatican, and the Torre di San Giovanni (Tower of St. John), restored by Pope John XXIII as a place where he could retreat to work in peace and now used as a residence for distinguished guests. The tower is at the top of the hill, which you explore on foot. The plantings include a formal Italian garden, a flowered French garden, a romantic English landscape, and a small forest. Photography is not allowed, but souvenir snapshots can be purchased. The visit includes considerable walking and climbing of stairs and slopes. Wear suitable shoes and observe the Vatican dress code. Reservations are required. ⊠ *Centro Servizi, south side of Piazza San Pietro,* ☎ *06/ 69884466,* FAX *06/69885100.* 🖃 *€8.80.* ⊘ *Apr.–Oct., Mon.–Tues. and Thurs.–Sat. tour 10 AM; Nov.–Mar., Sat. tour 10 AM.*

★ ➊ **Musei Vaticani** (Vatican Museums). This vast museum complex is part of the **Vatican Palace,** residence of the popes since 1377. The palace consists of a number of individual buildings containing an estimated 1,400 rooms, chapels, and galleries. The pope and his household occupy only a small part of the palace, most of the rest of which is given over to the Vatican Library and Museums.

The collection is extraordinarily rich (even more so when one considers that a great deal of it is not on display), but the museums' crowning jewel is the Sistine Chapel.

Among the collections on the way to the chapel, the **Egyptian Museum** (in which Room II reproduces an underground chamber tomb of the Valley of Kings) is well worth a stop. The **Chiaramonti Museum** was organized by the neoclassical sculptor Canova and contains almost 1,000 copies of classical sculpture. The gems of the Vatican's sculpture collection are in the **Pio-Clementino Museum,** however. Just off the hall in Room X, you'll find the *Apoxyomenos* (Scraper), a beautiful 1st-century AD copy of a bronze statue of an athlete. There are other even more famous pieces in the **Octagonal Courtyard,** where Pope Julius II installed the greatest pieces from his private collection: in the left-hand corner stands the celebrated *Apollo Belvedere.* In the far corner, on the same side of the courtyard, is the *Laocoön* group, found on Rome's Esquiline Hill in 1506, held to be possibly the single most important antique sculpture group in terms of its influence on Renaissance artists.

An adjacent hall dedicated to animals is filled with sculpture and mosaics done in colored marble, some of them very charming. There is a gallery of classical statues and a **Gallery of Busts;** the smallish **Mask Room** displays a lively mosaic pavement from the emperor Hadrian's Villa at Tivoli just outside Rome, and a copy of the 4th-century BC Greek sculptor Praxiteles' *Cnidian Venus.* In the **Hall of the Muses,** the *Belvedere Torso* occupies center stage: this is a fragment of a 1st-century BC statue, probably of Hercules, all rippling muscles and classical dignity, much admired by Michelangelo. The lovely neoclassical room of the **Rotonda** has an ancient mosaic pavement and a huge porphyry basin from Nero's palace, as well as several colossal statues. The room on the Greek-cross plan contains two fine porphyry sarcophagi (great marble burial caskets), one of Costantia and one of St. Helena, mother of the Emperor Constantine.

Upstairs, the **Etruscan Museum** holds many objects from the Regolini-Galassi find near Cerveteri, and a wealth of other material as well. Adjacent are three sections of limited interest: the **Antiquarium,** with Roman originals; three small rooms of Greek originals (followed by a broad staircase lined with Assyrian reliefs); and a vase collection. The domed **Sala della Biga** comes next. The *biga* (chariot) group at the center was extensively reconstructed in 1780. The chariot itself is original and was used in the church of San Marco as an episcopal throne.

In the **Candelabra Gallery**, the tall candelabra—immense candlesticks—under the arches are, like the sarcophagi and vases, of ancient origin. The walls facing the windows of the **Tapestry Gallery** are hung with magnificent tapestries executed in Brussels in the 16th century from designs by Raphael. On the window walls are tapestries illustrating the life of Pope Urban VIII. They were done in a workshop that the Barberini family set up in Rome in the 17th century expressly for this purpose.

The long **Gallery of Maps** is frescoed with 40 topographical maps of Italy and the papal territories, commissioned by Pope Gregory XIII in 1580. On each map is a detailed plan of the region's principal city. The ceiling is decorated with episodes from the history of the regions.

In the **Apartment of Pius V** is a small hall hung with tapestries. Facing the windows are the precious 15th-century *Passion* and *Baptism of Christ* from Tournai, in Belgium. The **Sobieski Room** gets its name from a huge painting by the Polish artist Matejko. It shows the *Victory of Vienna,* a decisive defeat of the invading Ottoman forces in the late 17th century. A massive display case in the **Hall of the Immaculate Conception** shows some preciously bound volumes containing the text of the papal bull promulgating that particular dogma.

Rivaling the Sistine Chapel for artistic interest are the **Stanze** (Raphael Rooms), which are directly over the Borgia apartments. Pope Julius II moved into this suite of rooms in 1507, four years after his election. Reluctant to continue living in the Borgia apartments with their memories of his ill-famed predecessor, Alexander VI, he called in Raphael to decorate his new quarters. The first in the series is the Incendio Room; it was the last to be painted in Raphael's lifetime, and was executed mainly by Giulio Romano, who worked from Raphael's drawings for the new pope, Leo X. It served as the pope's dining room. The frescoes depict stories of previous popes called Leo, the best of them showing the great fire in the Borgo (the neighborhood between the Vatican and Castel Sant'Angelo), which threatened to destroy the original St. Peter's Basilica in AD 847. Miraculously, Pope Leo IV extinguished it with the sign of the cross. The other frescoes show the coronation of Charlemagne by Leo III in St. Peter's Basilica, the *Oath of Leo III,* and a naval battle with the Saracens at Ostia in AD 849, after which Pope Leo IV showed clemency to the defeated.

The Segnatura Room, the first to be frescoed, was painted almost entirely by Raphael himself (as opposed to the others, which were painted in large part by his assistants). The theme of the room—which may broadly be said to be "learning"—reflects the fact that this was Julius's private library. Theology triumphs in the fresco known as the *Disputa,* or *Debate on the Holy Sacrament,* on the wall behind you as you enter. Opposite, the *School of Athens* glorifies philosophy in its greatest exponents. Plato (perhaps a portrait of Leonardo da Vinci), in the center, is debating a point with Aristotle. The pensive figure on the stairs is sometimes thought to be Raphael's rival, Michelangelo, who was painting the Sistine Chapel at the same time that Raphael was working here. In the foreground on the right are Euclid, the architect Bramante, and, on the far right, the handsome youth just behind the white-clad older man is Raphael himself. Over the window on the left are Parnassus, who represents poetry, and Apollo, the Muses, and famous poets, many of whom are likenesses of Raphael's contemporaries. In the lunette over the window opposite, Raphael painted figures representing and alluding to the Cardinal and Theological Virtues, and subjects showing the establishment of written codes of law. Beautiful personifications of the four subject areas, Theology, Poetry, Philosophy, and Jurisprudence, are painted in circular pictures on the ceiling above.

The Eliodoro (Heliodorus) Room is a private antechamber. Working on the theme of Divine Providence's miraculous intervention in defense of endangered faith, Raphael depicted Leo the Great's encounter with Attila; it's on the wall to your left as you enter. The *Expulsion of Heliodorus from the Temple of Jerusalem,* opposite the entrance, refers to Pope Julius II's insistence on the Church's right to temporal possessions. He appears on the left, watching the scene. On the left window wall, the *Liberation of St. Peter* is one of Raphael's best-known and most effective works.

Adjacent to the Raphael Rooms, the **Hall of Constantine** was decorated by Giulio Romano and other assistants of Raphael after the latter's untimely death in 1520. The frescoes represent various scenes from the life of the Emperor Constantine. The tiny **Chapel of Nicholas V,** aglow with Fra Angelico (1395–1455) frescoes of episodes from the life of St. Stephen (above) and St. Lawrence (below), is a gem of Renaissance art. If it were not under the same roof (or roofs) as Raphael's and Michelangelo's works, it would undoubtedly draw the attention it deserves.

Returning downstairs, you enter the **Borgia apartments,** where some intriguing historic figures are depicted in the elaborately painted ceilings, designed but only partially executed by Pinturicchio at the end of the 15th century and greatly retouched in later centuries. It's generally believed that Cesare Borgia murdered his sister Lucrezia's husband, Alphonse of Aragon, in the Room of the Sybil. In the Room of the Saints, Pinturicchio painted his self-portrait in the figure to the left of the possible portrait of the architect Antonio da Sangallo (his profession is made clear by the fact that he holds a T-square). The lovely picture of St. Catherine of Alexandria is said to be a representation of Lucrezia Borgia herself. The Resurrection scene in the next room, the Room of the Mysteries, offers excellent portraits of the kneeling Borgia pope, of Cesare Borgia (the soldier with a lance at the center), and of the young Francesco Borgia (the Roman at the soldier's side), who also was probably assassinated by Cesare. These and the other rooms of the Borgia apartments have been given over to exhibits of the Vatican's collection of modern religious art, which continues interminably on lower levels of the building.

In the frescoed exhibition halls that are part of the Vatican Museums, the **Vatican Library** displays precious illuminated manuscripts and documents from its vast collections. The **Aldobrandini Marriage Room** contains beautiful ancient frescoes of a Roman nuptial rite, named for their subsequent owner, Cardinal Aldobrandini.

The **Braccio Nuovo** (New Wing) holds an additional collection of ancient Greek and Roman statues, the most famous of which is the *Augustus of Prima Porta,* in the fourth niche from the end on the left. It's considered a faithful likeness of the emperor Augustus, 40 years old at the time. Note the workmanship in the reliefs on his armor. The two gilt bronze peacocks in the gallery were in the courtyard of the original basilica of St. Peter's. Before that it's likely that they stood in the emperor Hadrian's mausoleum, today Castel Sant'Angelo. To the ancient Romans the peacock was a symbol of immortality.

The paintings in the **Pinacoteca** (Picture Gallery) are almost exclusively of religious subjects and are arranged in chronological order, beginning with what in the 19th century were called the "primitives" of the 11th and 12th century. Room II has a marvelous Giotto triptych, painted on both sides, which stood on the high altar in the old St. Peter's. In Room III you'll see Madonnas by the Florentine 15th-century painters Fra Angelico and Filippo Lippi. The Raphael Room contains the exceptional *Transfiguration*, the *Coronation of the Virgin*, and the *Foligno Madonna* as well as the tapestries that Raphael designed to hang in the Sistine Chapel. The next room contains Leonardo's *St. Jerome* and a Bellini *Pietà*. In the courtyard outside the Pinacoteca you can admire the reliefs from the base of the Colonna di Marco Aurelio, the column in Piazza Colonna.

The **Museo Gregoriano Profano** (Museum of Pagan Antiquities) contains classical statues and other objects found in the territory of the Papal States (much of antiquity-rich central Italy) over the centuries. Up-to-date display techniques here heighten interest in this extensive collection of Roman and Greek sculptures.

In the **Museo Pio Cristiano** (Museum of Christian Antiquities), the most famous piece is the 3rd-century AD statue, the *Good Shepherd*, much reproduced as a devotional image. The **Museo Missionario-Etnologico** (Ethnological-Missionary Museum), usually open only Wednesday and Saturday, has artifacts from exotic places all over the world. There are some precious Asian statuettes and vases, scale models of temples, and full-scale Melanesian spirit huts. The **Museo Storico** (Historical Museum) displays a collection of state carriages—including an early version of the Popemobile, an ordinary car adapted to take an armchair in the back—uniforms, arms, and banners. ⊠ *Vatican Museums: Viale Vaticano,* ☎ *06/69884947.* ⊑ *€9.30, free last Sun. of month; audio guide €5.15.* ☉ *Easter week and mid-Mar.–Oct., weekdays 8:45–4:45 (no admission after 3:45), Sat. and last Sun. of month 8:45–1:45 (no admission after 12:30); Nov.–mid-Mar. (except Easter week), Mon.–Sat. and last Sun. of month 8:45–1:45 (no admission after 12:30).*

NEED A BREAK?	About five minutes from the Vatican Museums exit are two good neighborhood trattorias that are far less touristy than those opposite the museums. At **Dino e Toni** (⊠ Via Leone IV 60, ☎ 06/39733284) you can dine on typical Roman fare, fresh from the nearby outdoor market on Via Andrea Doria, and pizza. **La Caravella** (⊠ Via degli Scipioni 32 at Via Vespasiano, off Piazza Risorgimento, ☎ 06/39726161) serves classic Roman food and pizza.

★ ❸ **Piazza di San Pietro** (St. Peter's Square). This square (actually an oval) is the vast main entrance into Vatican territory. It's one of Bernini's most spectacular masterpieces, completed in 1667 after 11 years' work—a relatively short time in those days, considering the vastness of the task—and capable of holding 400,000 people. It is surrounded by a curving pair of quadruple colonnades, which are topped by a balustrade and statues of 140 saints. Look for the two disks set into the pavement on either side of the obelisk. If you stand on either disk, a trick of perspective makes the colonnades seem to consist of a single row of columns. Bernini had an even grander visual effect in mind when he designed the square. By opening up this immense, airy, and luminous space in a neighborhood of narrow, shadowy streets, he created a contrast that would surprise and impress anyone who emerged from the darkness into the light, in a characteristically Baroque metaphor. But in the 1930s, Mussolini ruined the effect. To celebrate the "conciliation" between the Vatican and the Italian government under the Lateran Pact of 1929, he conceived of the Via della Conciliazione, the broad, rather soulless avenue that now forms the main approach to St. Peter's and gives the eye time to adjust to the enormous dimensions of the square and church, nullifying Bernini's grand Baroque intentions.

The 85-ft-high Egyptian **obelisk** was brought to Rome by Caligula in AD 38 and was probably placed in his circus, believed to have been near here. It was moved to its present site in 1586 by Pope Sixtus V. According to legend, the monumental task of raising it almost ended in disaster when the ropes started to give way. In the absolute silence—the spectators had been threatened with death if they made a sound—a voice called "Water on the ropes!" Thus a Genoese sailor saved the day and was rewarded with the papal promise that thereafter the palms used in St. Peter's Basilica on Palm Sunday should come from Bordighera, the sailor's hometown.

The emblem at the top of the obelisk is the Chigi star, placed here in honor of Alexander VII, the Chigi pope under whom the piazza was built. Alexander had been categorical in dictating to Bernini his requirements for the design of the piazza. It had to make the pope visible to as many people as possible from the Benediction Loggia and from his Vatican apartments; it had to provide a covered passageway for papal processions; and it had to skirt the various existing buildings of the Vatican, while incorporating the obelisk and the fountain already there. (This fountain was moved to its present position, and a twin fountain was installed to balance it.)

Piazza San Pietro is the scene of mass papal audiences as well as special commemorations, masses, and beatification ceremonies. When he is in Rome, the pope makes an appearance every Sunday around 11 AM (call the Vatican Information office to find out if the pope is in town and the exact hour) at the window of the Vatican Palace. He addresses the crowd and blesses all present. The pope holds mass audiences on Wednesday morning at about 10 (at 9 in the hotter months). Whether or not they are held in the square depends on the weather and sometimes on the pope's health. There is an indoor audience hall adjacent to the basilica. While the pope is vacationing at Castel Gandolfo in the Castelli Romani hills outside of Rome, he gives a talk and blessing from a balcony of the papal palace there. For admission to an audience, apply for tickets, which are free, in advance (by mail, Prefettura della Casa Pontefice, 00120 Vatican City, or by fax, FAX 06/69885863), indicating the date you prefer, the language you speak, and the hotel in which you will stay. Or apply for tickets on the Monday or Tuesday before the Wednesday audience at the Prefettura della Casa Pontificia (Papal Prefecture; ☎ 06/69883273, ☉ Mon. and Tues. 9–1), which you reach through the **Portone di Bronzo** (Bronze Door) at the end of the right-hand colonnade. For a fee that includes transportation from your hotel and some sketchy sightseeing along the way, some travel agencies will arrange tickets for an audience. The American Church of Santa Susanna often has free tickets to give away on Tuesdays.

On the south side of the square are the **Centro Servizi Vaticani (Vatican Information Office)** (☎ 06/69881662; ☉ Mon.–Sat. 8:30–7), and the **Vatican Bookshop** (☉ weekdays 8:30–7, Sat. 8:30–2). There are Vatican post offices (known for fast handling of outgoing mail) on both sides of St. Peter's Square and inside the Vatican Museum complex. You can also buy Vatican stamps and coins at the shop annexed to the information office. Although postage rates are the same at the Vatican as elsewhere in Italy, the stamps are not interchangeable, so any post stamped with Vatican stamps must go in a blue or yellow Posta Vaticana box. Public toilets are near the Information Office, under the colonnade opposite, and outside the exit of the crypt. Religious objects and souvenirs are sold at shops in the surrounding neighborhood. ⊠ *West end of Via della Conciliazione.*

❼ **Ponte Sant'Angelo** (Sant'Angelo Bridge). One of the most beautiful of central Rome's 20 or so bridges is lined with Baroque angels designed by Bernini, Baroque Rome's most prolific architect and sculptor. Bernini himself carved only two of the angels, both of which were moved to the church of Sant'Andrea delle Fratte shortly afterward for safekeeping. Though copies, the angels on the bridge today convey forcefully the grace and characteristic sense of movement—a key element of Baroque sculpture—of Bernini's best work. ⊠ *Between Lungotevere Castello and Lungotevere Altoviti.*

OLD ROME

A district of narrow streets with curious names, airy Baroque piazzas, and picturesque courtyards, Old Rome (Vecchia Roma) occupies the horn of land that pushes the Tiber westward toward the Vatican. During the Renaissance, when the popes ruled both from the palaces in the Vatican and the Lateran, this area in between became the commercial hub of the city. Artisans and shopkeepers toiled in the shadow of the huge palaces built to consolidate the power and prestige of the leading figures in the papal court. Writers and artists, such as the satirist Aretino and the goldsmith-sculptor Cellini, made sarcastic comments on the alternate fortunes of the courtiers and courtesans who populated the area. Artisans and artists still live in Old Rome, but their numbers are diminishing as the district becomes gentrified. Two of the liveliest piazzas in Rome, Piazza Navona and Piazza del Pantheon, are the lodestars in a constellation of cafés, trendy stores, eating places, clubs, and wineshops.

Old Rome is an area to be seen on foot, both on weekdays, when the little shops are open and it hums with activity, and on Sunday, when there's much less traffic and noise and you can take a leisurely look at the old palaces and churches to appreciate their scale and harmonious forms. The walk here is a long one and could well be divided into two or even three sections, to include other sights on the fringes, such as Castel Sant'Angelo, the Palazzo Doria Pamphilj, or the Ghetto. You can give free rein to your curiosity, poking into corners, peeking into courtyards, stepping into esoteric shops, and finding eye-catching vistas at every turn.

Numbers in the text and margin correspond to points of interest on the Old Rome map.

A Good Walk

Start at **Il Gesù** ①, the grandmother of all Rome's Baroque churches, with its spiraling ceiling frescoes. Cross Corso Vittorio and take Via del Gesù, turning left onto Via Piè di Marmo (literally, Street of the Marble Foot, named for the broken-off foot of what must have been a very large classical statue that was found here; the foot is at the corner of Via Santo Stefano del Cacco). Via Piè di Marmo leads into Piazza Santa Caterina di Siena and into Piazza della Minerva. On the right is the church of **Santa Maria sopra Minerva** ②, the only major church in Rome built in Gothic style.

Straight ahead is the curving, brick-bound mass of the **Pantheon** ③. What you see is the side and rear of the building, where you can observe how the Romans built a series of weight-carrying arches into the walls of the building to support the huge dome, a technique later taken up by Renaissance architects. Follow Via della Minerva to Piazza della Rotonda and go to the north end of the square to get an overall view of the temple's columned portico. The piazza is the focus of a busy café scene that starts in the late morning and continues until late at night. Streets throughout this area are lined with gelaterias, pubs, pizzerias, restaurants, clubs, and discos.

Take Via degli Orfani north to Piazza Capranica and follow Via della Guglia into Piazza Montecitorio. Off the west side of the piazza, head into Via Uffizi del Vicario. Continue west on Via della Stelletta. Ahead of you, across Via della Scrofa, is Via dei Portoghesi and the **Torre della Scimmia** ④. More a piazza than a street, Via dei Portoghesi leads almost immediately into Via dell'Orso, lined with the shops of artisans, cabinetmakers, and antiques restorers. It ends at Via dei Soldati; climb the short flight of street stairs in front of the Hostaria dell'Orso, which has been serving guests since the 15th century, to see the **Museo Napoleonico** ⑤. Highly conspicuous across the Tiber is the huge Palazzo di Giustizia (Court Building), a bombastic late-19th-century travertine marble monster.

Instead of heading south on heavily trafficked Via Zanardelli, go back down the street stairs and follow Via dei Soldati to **Palazzo Altemps** ⑥, which houses a fine collection of classical antiquities. Piazza Navona is just across Piazza Sant'Apollonia, but you can save it for later. Instead, head east, under the arch, to the church of **Sant'Agostino** ⑦, which harbors a Caravaggio masterpiece. To see more Caravaggios, turn right on Via della Scrofa to reach Via della Dogana Vecchia and the church of **San Luigi dei Francesi** ⑧. Continue south on Via della Dogana Vecchia to Piazza Sant'Eustachio, pausing to admire the bizarre pinnacle crowning the dome of Sant'Ivo alla Sapienza, which you can see from the piazza (the church's rear entrance is on the west side of Piazza Sant'Eustachio). Via del Salvatore skirts the flank of **Palazzo Madama** ⑨, Italy's Senate building, and leads to Corso Rinascimento. Go left on Corso Rinascimento to number 40, where you can get a frontal view of the church of **Sant'Ivo alla Sapienza** ⑩. The huge church looming at the end of Corso Rinascimento is **Sant'Andrea della Valle** ⑪, setting of the first act of *Tosca*. The slightly curved, columned facade on the north side of Corso Vittorio Emanuele is that of **Palazzo Massimo alle Colonne** ⑫, one of Rome's oldest patrician homes and still residence of the Colonna family. On the south side of this major traffic artery is the **Museo Barracco** ⑬.

From Piazza San Pantaleo, Via della Cuccagna (Street of the Greased Pole, site of a favorite game in Piazza Navona) gives access to **Piazza Navona** ⑭, a celebrated 17th-century example of Baroque exuberance, with Bernini's **Fontana dei Quattro Fiumi** ⑮ as its centerpiece. Flanking the Piazza are **Palazzo Pamphili** ⑯ and the church of **Sant'Agnese in Agone** ⑰.

From the west side of Piazza Navona, enter Via di Tor Millina and turn right at pretty Piazza della Pace. Narrow alleys curve around either side of the church of **Santa Maria della Pace** ⑱. They lead to Via dei Coronari (Street of the Crown Makers, where craftsmen fashioned crowns and wreaths for sacred images, a flourishing business in papal Rome). This attractive street is lined with art galleries and antiques shops. About halfway along Via dei Coronari is large Piazza San Salvatore in Lauro and on it the church of **San Salvatore in Lauro** ⑲. Continue west along Via dei Coronari to Via di Panico. Turn right and follow Via di Panico to Ponte Sant'Angelo and a good frontal view of Castel Sant'Angelo.

Next, turn left, away from the river, onto Via del Banco di Santo Spirito. On the right-hand side of this byway is an arched passageway, the Arco dei Banchi, entrance to Renaissance financier Agostino Chigi's counting rooms. A marble inscription on the left pillar of the arch states that the street was often flooded by the Tiber, a problem finally solved in the late 1800s when embankments were put up along the course of the river. In the pretty little edifice on the corner of Via dei Banchi Nuovi, Rome's oldest bank, the Banco di Santo Spirito (Bank of the Holy Spirit, now Banca di Roma), has operated since the early 1600s.

Cross Largo Tassoni to the west side of Corso Vittorio, where both Via del Consolato and Via dei Cimatori lead to the graceful church of **San Giovanni dei Fiorentini** ⑳, on Piazza dell'Oro (Gold Square), heart of Renaissance Rome's gold district. One of Old Rome's most stately and historic streets, **Via Giulia** ㉑ begins at the south end of Piazza dell'-Oro.

Stroll down Via Giulia, almost to the end, and take a left onto Via dei Farnese, which flanks **Palazzo Farnese** ㉒ and leads to the piazza of the same name. On the south side of Piazza Farnese, Via Capo di Ferro leads to **Palazzo Spada** ㉓. From Piazza della Quercia take Via dei Balestrari or Vicolo delle Grotte east to **Campo dei Fiori** ㉔, one of Rome's most picturesque piazzas and home to the historic center's open-air market. North of Campo dei Fiori is the immense **Palazzo della Cancelleria** ㉕, headquarters of the Vatican's high court. Head northwest on Via del Pellegrino (the route pilgrims took to reach St. Peter's Basilica). Turn right onto Via Larga to reach busy Corso Vittorio Emanuele, dominated here by the huge **Santa Maria in Vallicella** ㉖ and the **Oratorio dei Filippini** ㉗. To return to Piazza Navona, go east on Via del Governo Vecchio. The street takes its name from the 15th-century Palazzo Nardini, at number 39, once seat of Rome's papal governors and later a law court.

TIMING

Not a walk for a rainy day, this tour can, however, be broken up and resumed again to suit your program and energy. To do the entire walk, spending about 40 minutes in Palazzo Altemps, would take about five hours, not counting breaks. But taking breaks is what this walk is all about: the route takes you past a plethora of piazzas to linger in and cafés where you can sit and take in the sights over coffee or a gelato. Campo dei Fiori is best seen on mornings Monday–Saturday, while it hosts a lively outdoor market.

Sights to See

★ ㉔ **Campo dei Fiori** (Field of Flowers). A bustling marketplace in the morning (Monday–Saturday 8 AM–1 PM) and bohemian haunt the rest of the day (and night), this piazza has plenty of earthy charm. Except for the pizzerias and gelaterias, it looks much as it did in the early 1800s. Brooding over the piazza is a hooded statue of the philosopher Giordano Bruno, who was burned at the stake here in 1600 for heresy. His was the first of the executions that drew Roman crowds to Campo dei Fiori in the 17th century. Now the area is crowded with shops selling crafts and secondhand furniture. ⊠ *Junction of Via dei Baullari, Via Giubbonari, Via del Pellegrino, and Piazza della Cancelleria.*

⑮ **Fontana dei Quattro Fiumi** (Fountain of the Four Rivers). Piazza Navona's most famous work of art, planted right in the center, was created for Pope Innocent X by Bernini in 1651. The obelisk rising out of the fountain, a Roman copy, had stood in the Circo di Massenzio on Via Appia Antica. Bernini's powerful figures of the four rivers represent the four corners of the world: the Nile, with its face covered in

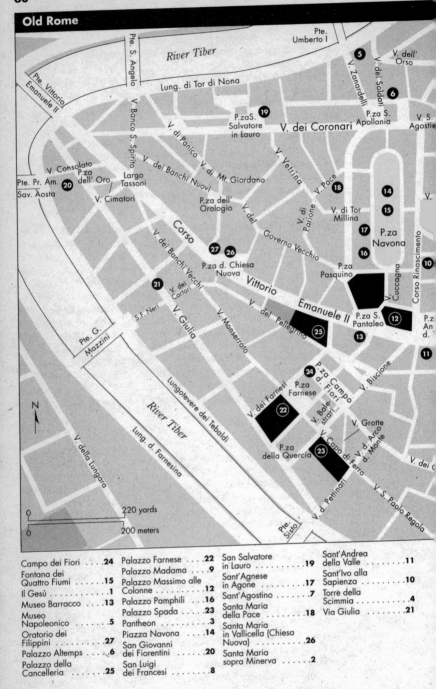

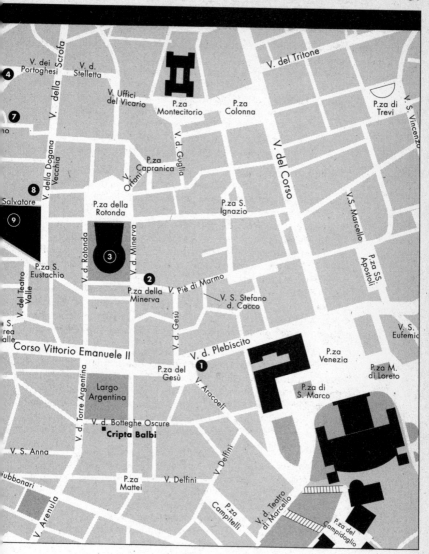

V. dei Portoghesi

V. della Scrofa

V. d. Stelletta

V. Uffici del Vicario

P.za Montecitorio

P.za Colonna

V. del Tritone

P.za di Trevi

V. S. Vincenzo

V. della Dogana Vecchia

V. d. Guglia

P.za Capranica

V. Orfani

P.za della Rotonda

P.za S. Ignazio

V. del Corso

V. S. Marcello

Salvatore

P.za SS. Apostoli

V. d. Rotonda

V. d. Minerva

P.za della Minerva

V. Piè di Marmo

V. S. Stefano d. Cacco

V. S. Eufemia

P.za S. Eustachio

V. del Teatro Valle

S. rea alle

Corso Vittorio Emanuele II

V. d. Gesù

V. d. Plebiscito

P.za Venezia

P.za M. di Loreto

P.za del Gesù

V. Aracoeli

P.za di S. Marco

V. d. Torre Argentina

Largo Argentina

V. d. Botteghe Oscure

Cripta Balbi

V. S. Anna

V. Delfini

ubbonari

P.za Mattei

V. Delfini

P.za Campitelli

V. d. Teatro di Marcello

P.za del Campidoglio

V. Arenula

allusion to its unknown source; the Ganges; the Danube; and the Plata, with its hand raised. ☒ *Piazza Navona.*

❶ Il Gesù. The mother church of the Jesuits in Rome is the grandmother of all Baroque churches. Its architecture (the overall design was by Vignola, the facade by della Porta) influenced ecclesiastical building in Rome for more than a century and was exported by the Jesuits throughout Europe. Though consecrated in 1584, the church wasn't decorated inside for 100 years or more. It had been intended originally that the interior be left plain to the point of austerity—but, when it was finally embellished, no expense was spared. For sheer, unadulterated grandeur, no church in Rome, save perhaps St. Peter's Basilica, compares with it.

The most striking element is the ceiling, covered with frescoes swirling down from on high and merging with the painted stucco figures at their base, the illusion of space in the two-dimensional painting becoming the reality of three dimensions in the sculpted figures. Baciccia, their painter, achieved extraordinary effects in these frescoes, especially in the *Triumph of the Holy Name of Jesus,* over the nave. Here, the heretics cast out of heaven seem to be hurtling down onto the observer. Further grandeur is represented in the altar in the Chapel of St. Ignatius in the left-hand transept. This is surely the most sumptuous Baroque altar in Rome; as is typical, the enormous globe of lapis lazuli that crowns it is really only a shell of lapis over a stucco base—after all, Baroque decoration prizes effects and illusions. The heavy bronze altar rail by architect Carlo Fontana is in keeping with the surrounding opulence.

The architectural significance of Il Gesù extends far beyond the splendid interior. The first of the great Counter-Reformation churches, it was put up after the Council of Trent (1545–63) had signaled the determination of the Roman Catholic Church to fight back against the Reformed Protestant heretics of northern Europe. Il Gesù spawned imitations throughout Italy and the other Catholic countries of Europe. ☒ *Piazza del Gesù, off Via del Plebiscito,* ☎ *06/697001.* ☉ *Daily 7–noon and 4–7.*

⓭ Museo Barracco (Barracco Museum). This small but select museum offers a compact overview of sculpture from the ancient civilizations of the Mediterranean area, including Egyptian, Assyrian, and Greek works. The chronologically ordered collection is housed in a Renaissance building commissioned by a French prelate, a member of the papal court. Lilies—symbols of France—are prominent in the frieze circling the exterior. ☒ *Corso Vittorio Emanuele II 166,* ☎ *06/68806848.* ☎ *€2.50.* ☉ *Tues.–Sat. 9–7, Sun. 9–1.*

❺ Museo Napoleonico (Napoleonic Museum). This small museum in 16th-century Palazzo Primoli contains a specialized and rich collection of Napoléon memorabilia, including a bust by Canova of the general's sister, Pauline Borghese. On the top floor of the same building (separate entrance) the unusual **Museo Mario Praz** (Mario Praz Museum; ☒ *Via Zanardelli 1,* ☎ *06/6861089;* ☎ *€2.05;* ☉ *Mon. 2:30–7:30, Tues.–Sun. 9–7:30)* preserves the apartment in which a noted Italian art historian and collector lived and accumulated an astounding collection of neoclassical art and antiques. ☒ *Museo Napoleonico: Palazzo Primoli, Piazza di Ponte Umberto I,* ☎ *06/68806286.* ☎ *€2.50.* ☉ *Tues.–Sat. 9–7, Sun. 9–1:30.*

㉗ Oratorio dei Filippini (Oratory of the Philippines). This religious residence is named for Rome's favorite saint, Philip Neri, founder in 1551 of the Congregation of the Oratorians. Like the Jesuits, the Oratorians—or Filippini, as they were known—were one of the new religious orders established in the mid-16th century as part of the Counter-Reformation. Under Neri's benign leadership, the Oratorians lived by a code of humility and good works. Neri, a man of rare charm and wit, insisted that the members of the order—most of them young noblemen whom he had recruited personally—not only renounce their worldly goods and declare their good intentions by acts such as parading the streets dressed in rags, but also work as common laborers in the building of Neri's great church of Santa Maria in Vallicella. The Oratory itself, headquarters of the order, was built by Borromini between 1637 and 1662. Its gently curving facade is typical of Borromini's near obsession with introducing movement into everything he designed. The church is open most days before noon. ⊠ *Piazza della Chiesa Nuova (Corso Vittorio Emanuele),* ☎ *06/6869374.*

★ ❻ **Palazzo Altemps.** The palace's sober exterior belies a magnificence that appears as soon as you walk into the majestic courtyard, studded with statues and covered in part by a retractable awning. It's a reconstruction of a nicety used in many a patrician abode, a throwback to the type of awning that shaded the ancient Romans in the Colosseum. The restored interior hints at the splendid Roman lifestyle of the 16th through 18th centuries and serves as a stunning showcase for the most illustrious pieces from the Museo Nazionale Romano's collection of ancient Roman sculpture, which includes famous pieces from the Ludovisi family collection. In the frescoed salons you can see the *Galata,* a poignant work portraying a barbarian warrior who chooses death for himself and his wife rather than humiliation by the enemy. Another highlight is the so-called Ludovisi sarcophagus, large and magnificently carved of marble. In a place of honor is the Ludovisi throne, which at least one authoritative art historian considers a colossally overrated fake. Look for the framed explanations of the exhibits that detail (in English) how and exactly where Renaissance sculptors, Bernini among them, added missing pieces to the classical works. In the lavishly frescoed Loggia stand busts of the Caesars. ⊠ *Piazza Sant'-Apollinare 46,* ☎ *06/6833566.* ☒ *€5.15.* ⊙ *Tues.–Sun. 9–7:45.*

❷❺ **Palazzo della Cancelleria** (Chancery Palace). Occupying a massive site in a neighborhood of splendid palazzos, this is the largest and one of the most beautiful of the city's Renaissance palaces. It was built for a nephew of the Riario Pope Sixtus IV toward the end of the 15th century and reputedly paid for by the winnings of a single night's gambling by another nephew. The Riario family symbol of the rose appears on the windows of the main floor and in the pillars and pavement of the courtyard. The palace houses the offices of the Papal Chancery and is part of the Vatican's extraterritorial possessions. You can step inside to see the courtyard; some salons are occasionally open to the public as concert venues.

Inconspicuously tucked into a corner of the palace, the church of **San Lorenzo in Damaso** was probably added by Bramante during the construction of the Cancelleria at the beginning of the 16th century. The original church of that name, on another part of the site, was one of the oldest churches of Rome, founded in the 4th century. When Napoléon occupied Rome, the 16th-century church was used as a law court and later had to be reconsecrated. ⊠ *Piazza della Cancelleria, off Corso Vittorio Emanuele II.*

❷❷ **Palazzo Farnese.** This is considered the most beautiful of all of Rome's Renaissance palaces, the result of the combined talents of architects Sangallo the Younger, Michelangelo, and Giacomo della Porta, in that order. The imposing building was commissioned by Alessandro Farnese, later Pope Paul III, while he was still cardinal. In the piazza, twin fountains fall into massive Egyptian granite basins found in the ruins of the Terme di Caracalla. The palace is now the French Embassy. The main gallery, with its magnificent ceiling fresco painted between 1597 and 1604 by Annibale Carracci, is open to the public the last Sunday in September. ✉ *Piazza Farnese.*

⑨ Palazzo Madama. The handsome 17th-century palace is a onetime Medici residence, now seat of the Italian Senate. It is most admired for its Baroque facade, with exotic cornice and roof detail. ✉ *Corso Rinascimento.*

⑫ Palazzo Massimo alle Colonne. A curving, columned portico identifies this otherwise inconspicuous palace on a traffic-swept bend of busy Corso Vittorio Emanuele. In the 1530s architect Baldassare Peruzzi adapted the structure of an earlier palace belonging to the Massimo family, transforming it to suit the clan's high rank in the papal aristocracy and its status as the oldest of Rome's noble families, older than even the Colonna and Orsini clans. If you're here on March 16, you'll be able to go upstairs in the palace, seeing the antique livery on the servants, and the courtyard and loggias on your way to the family chapel. On this day the public is invited inside to take part in commemorations of a prodigious miracle performed here in 1583 by Philip Neri, who is said to have recalled a young member of the family, one Paolo Massimo, from the dead. ✉ *Corso Vittorio Emanuele II 141.*

⑯ Palazzo Pamphili. Sometimes in the evening you can get a tantalizing glimpse of Pietro da Cortona's magnificent frescoes through the great illuminated windows of this palace. It is now the Brazilian Embassy. ✉ *Piazza Navona 14.*

㉓ Palazzo Spada. In this neighborhood of huge, austere palaces, Palazzo Spada strikes an almost frivolous note, with its upper stories covered with stuccos and statues and its pretty ornament-encrusted courtyard. The little garden gallery is a delightful example of the sort of architectural games rich Romans of the 17th century found irresistible. Even if you don't go into the gallery, step into the courtyard and look through the glass window of the library to the colonnaded corridor in the adjacent courtyard, which appears to stretch for a great distance with a large statue at the end. In fact the distance is an illusion: the corridor grows progressively narrower and the columns progressively smaller as they near the statue, which is just 2 ft tall. The illusion of depth multiplies the space by a factor of four. It was long thought that Borromini was responsible for this ruse; in fact it's now known that it was designed by an Augustinian priest, Giovanni Maria da Bitonto. The picture gallery in the palace has some outstanding works. Among them are Brueghel's *Landscape with Windmills*, Titian's *Musician*, and Andrea del Sarto's *Visitation*. ✉ *Vicolo del Polverone 15/b,* ☎ *06/6861158,* WEB *www.galleriaborghese.it.* 🎫 €5.15. ⏰ *Tues.–Sat. 8:30–7:30, Sun. 8:30–6:30.*

★ ③ Pantheon. This onetime pagan temple, a marvel of architectural harmony and proportion, is the best-preserved monument of Imperial Rome. It was entirely rebuilt by the emperor Hadrian around AD 120 on the site of an earlier pantheon (from the Greek *pan,* all, and *theon,* gods) erected in 27 BC by Augustus's general Agrippa. The majestic circular building was actually designed *by* Hadrian, as were many of the temples, palaces, and lakes of his enormous villa outside the city at Tivoli. Hadrian nonetheless retained the inscription over the entrance from the original building that named Agrippa as the builder, in the process causing enormous confusion among historians until, in 1892, archaeologists discovered that all the bricks used in the Pantheon were stamped AD 120.

The most striking thing about the Pantheon is not its size, immense though it is (until 1960 the dome was the largest ever built), nor even the phenomenal technical difficulties posed by so vast a construction; rather, it is the remarkable unity of the building. You don't have to look far to find the reason for this harmony: the diameter of the dome is exactly equal to the height of the walls. It is the use of such simple mathematical balance that gives classical architecture its characteristic sense of proportion and its nobility and timeless appeal.

Why, alone among the major monuments of Imperial Rome, did the Pantheon survive intact? The answer is that it became a church, in AD 608. No building, church or not, escaped some degree of plundering through the turbulent centuries of Rome's history after the fall of the empire. In 655, for example, the gilded bronze covering the dome was stripped. Similarly, in the early 17th century, Pope Urban VIII removed the bronze that covered the wooden beams of the portico, using the metal to produce the baldacchino (canopy) that covers the high altar at St. Peter's Basilica. Nonetheless, the Pantheon suffered less than many other structures from ancient Rome that can now only be imagined. Inside, the coffered vault was once faced with ornamental stuccos, now lost, but the pavement has been restored in the style of the original. The Pantheon also serves as one of the city's important burial places. Its most famous tomb is that of Raphael (between the second and third chapels on the left as you enter). The inscription reads "Here lies Raphael; while he lived, mother Nature feared to be outdone; and when he died, she feared to die with him." Two of Italy's 19th-century kings are buried here, too: Vittorio Emanuele II and Umberto I. The tomb of the former was partly made from bronze taken from the Pantheon by Urban VIII, cast as cannons by him, and then symbolically remelted and returned here. The great opening at the apex of the dome, the oculus, is nearly 30 ft in diameter and was the temple's only source of light. It was intended as a symbol of the "all-seeing eye of heaven." ⊠ *Piazza della Rotonda,* ☎ *06/68300230.* 🎟 *Free.* 🕙 *Mon.–Sat. 9–6:30, Sun. 9–1.*

....

NEED A BREAK?   On Via degli Orfani, on the east side of Piazza del Pantheon, the **Tazza d'Oro** coffee bar (no tables, no frills) is the place for serious coffee drinkers, who also indulge in *granita di caffè con panna* (coffee ice with whipped cream). This area is ice-cream heaven, with some of Rome's best gelaterias within a few steps of each other. Romans consider **Giolitti** (⊠ Via Uffizi del Vicario 40, ☎ 06/6991243) superlative; the scene at the counter often looks like the storming of the Bastille. Remember to pay the cashier first, and hand the stub to the counterperson when you order your cone. Giolitti has a good snack counter, also.

....

★ ⑭ **Piazza Navona.** Here everything that makes Rome unique is compressed into one beautiful Baroque piazza. It has antiquity, Bernini sculptures, a gorgeous fountain (Fontana dei Quattro Fiumi), a graceful church (Sant'Agnese in Agone) and, above all, the excitement of people out to enjoy themselves—strolling, café-sitting, seeing, and being seen. Piazza Navona has been an entertainment venue for Romans down through the centuries. It stands over the ruins of Domitian's circus; you can see a section of the ancient arena's walls by walking out of the long end of the piazza (toward Piazza Sant'Apollinare) and taking a quick left. The square still has the carefree air of the days when it was the scene of Roman circus games, medieval jousts, and 17th-century carnivals. Even now it's the site of a lively Christmas fair and the place where revelers gather for many other entertainment events throughout the year.

Glamorous televised fashion events are occasionally staged in this fabulous setting, but most of the time the square is simply Rome's most popular place to meet, have ice cream and coffee, take the children and dogs for a walk, and watch the passing parade. The piazza still looks much as it did during the 17th and 18th centuries.

The piazza dozes in the morning, when small groups of pensioners sun themselves on stone benches and children pedal tricycles around the big fountain. In the late afternoon, the sidewalk cafés fill up for the aperitif hour. In the evening, especially in good weather, Piazza Navona comes to life with a colorful throng of vendors, street artists, tourists, and Romans out for their evening *passeggiata* (promenade). ⊠ *Junction of Via della Cuccagna, Corsia Agonale, Via di Sant'Agnese, and Via Agonale.*

NEED A BREAK?

The sidewalk tables of the **Tre Scalini** (⊠ Piazza Navona 30, ☎ 06/6879148) café offer a grandstand view of the piazza and the action. This is the place that invented the *tartufo,* a luscious chocolate ice-cream specialty. The restaurant-pizzeria annex (the menu features Pizza Navona) has the same view.

㉑ San Giovanni dei Fiorentini. This graceful church dedicated to Florence's patron saint, John the Baptist, stands in what was the heart of the Florentine colony in Old Rome. Many of these Florentines were goldsmiths who contributed to the building of the church. Talented goldsmith and sculptor Benvenuto Cellini of Florence, known for his vindictive nature as much as for his genius, lived nearby. Inside the church, Borromini executed a splendid altar for the Falconieri family chapel in the choir. The animal-loving pastor allows well-behaved pets to keep their owners company at services. ⊠ *Via Accaioli (Piazza dell'Oro),* ☎ *06/68892059.* ☉ *Daily 9–1 and 4–7.*

㉘ San Luigi dei Francesi. The church is famous for its three magnificent Caravaggios, painted at the beginning of the 17th century. It is also the official church of Rome's French colony (San Luigi is St. Louis, patron of France). The Caravaggios are in the Chapel of St. Matthew (at the altar end of the left nave). Put some coins in the machine to illuminate these canvases, revealing Caravaggio's mastery of light and shadow. The works are, from the left, the *Calling of St. Matthew, Matthew and the Angel,* and *Matthew's Martyrdom.* When painted, they caused considerable consternation to the clergy of San Luigi, who thought the artist's dramatically realistic approach was scandalously disrespectful. A first version of the altarpiece was rejected; the priests were not particularly happy with the other two either. Time has fully vindicated Caravaggio's patron, Cardinal Francesco del Monte, who commissioned these works and stoutly defended them. They're recognized to be among the artist's greatest paintings. ⊠ *Piazza San Luigi dei Francesi,* ☎ *06/688271.* ☉ *Daily 8:30–12:30, Fri.–Wed. also 3:30–5.*

㉙ San Salvatore in Lauro. Outside and in, this church looks more Venetian than Roman. It was designed along the lines of models by the Venetian architect Palladio. If the church is not open, ring the bell at number 15 for admission to the interior and to the charming little 15th-century cloister that is used by a civic association. ⊠ *Piazza San Salvatore in Lauro 15,* ☎ *06/6875187.* ☉ *Daily 9–1 and 5–7.*

㉗ Sant'Agnese in Agone. The church's name comes from *agona,* the source of the word *navona* and a corruption of the Latin *agonalis,* describing the type of games held there in Roman times. The saint associated with the church is Agnes, who was martyred here in the piazza's forerunner, the Stadium of Domitian. As she was stripped nude before the crowd, hair miraculously grew to maintain her modesty before she was killed. The graceful Baroque facade is by Borromini. ✉ *Piazza Navona.*

❼ Sant'Agostino. Caravaggio's celebrated *Madonna of the Pilgrims*—which scandalized all Rome because a kneeling pilgrim is pictured, all too realistically for the taste of the time, with dirt on the soles of his feet, and the Madonna stands in a less than majestic pose in a dilapidated doorway—is in the first chapel on the left. In a niche just inside the door of the church is Sansovino's sculpted *Madonna and Child*, known to the Romans as the Madonna del Parto (of Childbirth) and piled high with ex-votos. ✉ *Piazza Sant'Agostino,* ☎ *06/68801962.* ◷ *Daily 8–noon and 4–7:30.*

❶❽ Santa Maria della Pace. A semicircular portico stands in front of the 15th-century church. It was an architectural solution devised by Pietro da Cortona (1596–1669), who was commissioned in 1656 to restore the church and design its facade. He demolished a few buildings here and there to create the relatively spacious approach to the church. Then he added arches to give architectural unity to the piazza, which has become the core of a trendy café scene. The church is usually closed, but if it happens to be open when you pass by, stop in to see Raphael's fresco of the Sybils above the first altar on your right, and the fine decorations of the Cesi Chapel, second on the right, designed in the mid-16th century by Sangallo. ✉ *Via Arco della Pace 5 (near Piazza Navona),* ☎ *06/6861156.*

❷❻ Santa Maria in Vallicella. This church, also known as Chiesa Nuova (New Church), was built toward the end of the 16th century at the urging of St. Philip Neri, and like Il Gesù is a product of the fervor of the Counter-Reformation. It has a sturdy Baroque interior, all white and gold, with ceiling frescoes by Pietro da Cortona and three magnificent altarpieces by Rubens. An enormous statue of the saint is in the sacristy. ✉ *Piazza della Chiesa Nuova, Corso Vittorio Emanuele II,* ☎ *06/6875289.* ◷ *Daily 8–noon and 4:30–7.*

❷ Santa Maria sopra Minerva. The name of the church reveals that it was built *sopra* (over) the ruins of a temple of Minerva, ancient goddess of wisdom. Erected in 1280 by the Dominicans on severe Italian Gothic lines, it has undergone a number of more or less happy restorations to the interior. Certainly, as the city's major Gothic church, it provides a refreshing contrast to Baroque flamboyance. Have some coins handy to illuminate the **Cappella Carafa** in the right transept, where Filippino Lippi's (1457–1504) glowing 15th-century frescoes are well worth the small investment. Under the main altar is the tomb of St. Catherine of Siena, one of Italy's patron saints. Left of the altar you'll find Michelangelo's *Risen Christ* and the tomb of the gentle artist Fra Angelico, behind a modern sculptured bronze screen. Bernini's unusual and little-known monument to the Blessed Maria Raggi is on the fifth pier from the door on the left as you leave the church. In front of the church, the little obelisk-bearing elephant carved by Bernini is perhaps the city's most charming sculpture. An inscription on the base makes reference to the church's ancient patroness, reading something to the effect that it takes a strong mind to sustain solid wisdom. ✉ *Piazza della Minerva,* ☎ *06/6793926.* ◷ *Daily 7:30–7.*

❶❶ Sant'Andrea della Valle. This huge 17th-century church has the highest dome (by Maderno) in Rome after St. Peter's Basilica. Imposing though its dimensions are, the church is remarkably balanced in design. Inside, where Puccini set the first act of *Tosca*, note the early 17th-century frescoes in the choir vault by Domenichino and those by Lanfranco in the dome, one of the earliest ceilings in full Baroque style. Richly marbled and decorated chapels flank the nave. ⊠ *Piazza Vidoni 6 (Corso Vittorio Emanuele II),* ☎ *06/6861339.* ⊙ *Daily 7:30–12:30 and 4:30–8.*

⑩ Sant'Ivo alla Sapienza. The main facade of this eccentric Baroque church, probably Borromini's best, is on the stately courtyard of an austere building that once housed Rome's university. Sant'Ivo has what must surely be one of the most delightful domes in all Rome—a golden spiral said to have been inspired by a bee's stinger. The bee symbol is a reminder that Borromini built the church on commission from the Barberini Pope Urban VIII. The geometrically conceived interior is worth a look, especially if you share a taste for Borromini's complex mathematical architectural idiosyncrasies. ⊠ *Corso Rinascimento 40 (another entrance off Piazza Sant'Eustachio),* ☎ *06/6864987.* ⊙ *Sun. 10–noon.*

❹ Torre della Scimmia (Monkey Tower). The medieval tower atop the building that stands at the junction of Via dei Portoghesi with Via dei Pianellari figures in a chapter in the lore of Old Rome. In the building, so the story goes, a pet monkey ran amok one day, seizing a baby and carrying it to the top of the tower. Here the crazed animal seemed about to dash the child to the street below. A crowd of neighbors and bystanders invoked the Madonna's intercession, and the monkey carefully descended with the baby, carrying it to safety. In gratitude, the father placed a statue of the Madonna on the tower, along with a vigil light, both of them still neighborhood landmarks. (One version of the story relates that the monkey was sold to pay for the statue.) ⊠ *Via dei Portoghesi.*

㉑ Via Giulia. The street was named for Pope Julius II, who commissioned it in the early 1500s as part of a scheme to open up a grandiose approach to St. Peter's Basilica. Though the pope's plans to change the face of the city were only partially completed, Via Giulia became an important thoroughfare in Renaissance Rome. It was the first street since ancient times to be laid out in a straight line, and it was flanked with elegant churches and palaces. It has again become one of Rome's most exclusive addresses, with antiques shops at street level and fabulous rooftop penthouses overlooking the Tiber.

Among the buildings that should attract your attention are **Palazzo Sacchetti** (⊠ Via Giulia 66), with an imposing stone portal, and the forbidding brick building that housed the **Carceri Nuove** (New Prison; ⊠ Via Giulia 52), Rome's prison for more than two centuries. Now it contains judiciary offices and a small criminology museum. Near the bridge that arches over the southern end of Via Giulia is the church of **Santa Maria dell'Orazione e Morte** (Holy Mary of Prayer and Death), with stone skulls on its door. These are a symbol of a confraternity that was charged with burying the bodies of the unidentified dead found in the city streets. There are several other curious old churches along this route, but most of them are closed except on special occasions. The **Palazzo Falconieri** (⊠ Via Giulia 1), adjacent to Santa Maria dell'Orazione e Morte, was designed by Bramante. The arch over the street was meant to link Palazzo Farnese, on the east side of Via Giulia, with the building across the street and a bridge to the Villa Farnesina, directly across the river. Ponte Sisto, the bridge just down river, was built by Pope Sixtus IV. ⊠ *Between Piazza dell'Oro and Piazza San Vincenzo Pallotti.*

TOWARD THE SPANISH STEPS AND THE TREVI FOUNTAIN

The Corso and Piazza di Spagna area is more than a shopper's paradise. Major attractions include a series of imposing Renaissance and Baroque palaces—among them Palazzo Borghese, the luxurious home of one of Rome's most talked-about families—and a number of striking churches. Sumptuously theatrical Roman ecclesiastical architecture, in particular heroic illusionistic ceiling painting, is in ample supply here. The highlights of this area are the Scalinata di Trinità dei Monti (a.k.a. the Spanish Steps), 18th-century Rome's most famous example of city planning, and the Fontana di Trevi, the most ornate and thrilling of the city's great fountains.

Numbers in the text and margin correspond to points of interest on the Piazza Venezia to the Spanish Steps map.

A Good Walk

Begin at **Piazza Venezia** ①, the square in front of the elaborate marble mountain that is the **Monumento a Vittorio Emanuele II** ②. On the west side of the piazza is **Palazzo Venezia** ③, built in the 15th century for the Venetian Cardinal Pietro Barbo, who became Pope Paul II and who totally renovated the adjacent church of **San Marco** ④, on Piazza San Marco on the south side of the palace. From Piazza Venezia, head north on Via del Corso, making sure to walk on the right-hand side of the street so that you can get a good view of the attractive facade of **Palazzo Doria Pamphilj** ⑤, one of Rome's grandest palaces. The entrance to its sumptuous art gallery and state apartments is on Piazza del Collegio Romano, until 1870 home to Rome's most famous and enormously influential Jesuit school. After a look at how an aristocratic family lives, take Via di Sant'Ignazio to the enchanting 18th-century rococo Piazza di Sant'Ignazio, designed by architect Raguzzini as if it were a stage set. But then, of course, theatricality was a key element of almost all the best Baroque and rococo art. Nowhere is this more evident than in the church of **Sant'Ignazio** ⑥, where the ceiling frescoes hold a surprise or two.

Behind the "stage set," Via del Burrò leads to Piazza di Pietra, where the Rome Stock Exchange is set inside the columns of an ancient temple. From here it's just a few steps along Via dei Bergamaschi to Piazza Colonna, named for the celebrated **Colonna di Marco Aurelio** ⑦ at its center. North of the column, Palazzo Chigi, a 16th- and 17th-century building, serves as the seat of the prime minister. Next door is **Palazzo Montecitorio** ⑧, where the Chamber of Deputies (lower house) of the Italian parliament meets.

Just off Via del Tritone is little **Santa Maria in Via** ⑨, where you can have a sip of some very special water. Across Via del Tritone, a busy thoroughfare that climbs to Piazza Barberini and Via Veneto, Piazza San Silvestro is a hub of public transportation and location of the main post office. It is also on the edge of a shopping district that has few equals elsewhere in the world. From Via del Tritone on the south to Piazza del Popolo on the north, from the Tiber on the west to Villa Borghese on the east, this is a fabulous trove of specialty shops and boutiques offering all types of fashions, jewelry, household goods, and anything else you might want—including the well-maintained rest-room facilities in the Rinascente department store, which occupies the block at the corner of Via del Corso and Largo Chigi. You can detour in and out of the area's narrow byways as your fancy takes you, attracted by stunning window displays.

THREE COINS AND A TRITON

ANYONE WHO'S THROWN a coin backward over his or her shoulder into the Fontana di Trevi to ensure a return to Rome appreciates the magic of the city's fountains. From the magnificence of the Fontana dei Quattro Fiumi in Piazza Navona to the graceful caprice of the Fontana delle Tartarughe in the Ghetto, the ever-flowing sculptures seem as essential to the *piazze* they inhabit as the cobblestones and ocher buildings that surround them. In fact, much of central Rome was established well before most of its fountains were put in place, and it was more than a hundred years after this that the creations came to be regarded as anything more than public services.

In the late 16th century, after the running-water heyday of the Roman Empire and before the 20th century's municipal pipelines, the primary purpose of the Roman fountain was simply to provide water. To mark the completion of the Virgin Aqueduct, architect Giacomo della Porta designed 18 unassuming, functional fountains, all consisting of a large basin with two or three levels of smaller basins in the center, which were built and placed throughout the city at points along the water line (or, as in the case of the Fontana delle Tartarughe in Piazza Mattei, at points where the locals wanted the water line to be; the residents of this part of the Ghetto convinced the city to install the fountain despite the lack of water and then engineered a deviation from the aqueduct line to supply it). Although nearly all of della Porta's fountains remain, their spare Renaissance design is virtually unrecognizable, as most were elaborately redecorated with dolphins, obelisks, and sea monsters, in the flamboyant style of the Baroque.

Of this next generation of Baroque fountaineers, the most famous is Gian Lorenzo Bernini (who is thought, incidentally, to be responsible for the delicate turtles in della Porta's fountain in Piazza Mattei). Bernini's writhing, muscular creatures of myth adorn most of Rome's most visible fountains, including the Fontana di Trevi (so named for the three streets—*tre vie*—that converge at its piazza); the Fontana del Nettuno, with its tritons, in Piazza Barberini; and, in Piazza Navona, the Fontana dei Quattro Fiumi, whose hulking figures represent the four great rivers of the known world: the Nile, the Ganges, the Danube, and the Rio de la Plata.

The most common type of fountain in Rome is also the noted by visitors: the small, inconspicuous drinking fountains that burble away from side-street walls, old stone niches, and fire hydrant–like installations on street corners. You can drink this water—many of these *fontanelle* even have pipes fitted with a little hole that water shoots up from when you hold your hand under the main spout. To combine the glorious Roman fountain with a drink of water, head to Piazza di Spagna, where the Barcaccia fountain (designed by Pietro Bernini, Gian Lorenzo's father) is outfitted with spouts from which you can wet your whistle.

Anita Ekberg and Marcello Mastroianni made cinematic history with their midnight dip in the Fontana di Trevi in the Fellini classic *La Dolce Vita*. On hot summer nights—and days—the temptation to follow in their soggy footsteps can be almost unbearable. Be forewarned: police guard the fountain 24 hours a day to keep out movie buffs and lovebirds alike, and transgressors risk a fine of up to €500. Far safer, and cheaper, to emulate Dorothy McGuire, Jean Peters, and Maggie McNamara in *Three Coins in the Fountain* —your Roman fountain fantasy will cost no more than the change in your pocket, and who knows? Your wish might come true.

At some point, head north on Via del Corso again to Piazza San Lorenzo in Lucina to see the Bernini works in **San Lorenzo in Lucina** ⑩ and perhaps linger in one of the fashionable cafés on this pretty square. At the west end of the piazza, take Via del Leone to Largo Fontanella Borghese to see the portal of **Palazzo Borghese** ⑪ and browse at the stalls selling old books and prints around the corner in airy Piazza della Fontanella Borghese, where you can get an even better idea of the palace's size. Follow Via della Fontanella Borghese, lined with smart shops, to Largo Goldoni, site of an information kiosk.

From Largo Goldoni you enter Via Condotti and get a head-on view of the **Scalinata di Trinità dei Monti** ⑫ and the church of **Trinità dei Monti** ⑬. On Via Condotti you can get from Bulgari to Gucci to Valentino to Ferragamo with no effort at all, except perhaps that of pushing through the crowds. On weekend and holiday afternoons the square, along with Via del Corso and neighboring streets, is packed with teenagers out for a mass stroll. They perch on the steps and around the low-lying **Fontana della Barcaccia** ⑭ in the middle of the piazza. To the right of the Spanish Steps, the **Keats and Shelley Memorial House** ⑮ gives you an idea of how England's Romantic poets lived in what was then Rome's bohemian quarter. The column at the far end of the piazza, adjacent to the American Express office, supports a statue dedicated to the Immaculate Conception. Each December 8, a crack unit of the Rome Fire Department sends one of its best men up a ladder to replace the garland crowning the Madonna, and the pope usually stops by in the afternoon to pay his respects. Just in front of the column stands **Palazzo di Propaganda Fide** ⑯, brain center of the far-flung missionary activities of the Jesuits.

Follow Via di Propaganda to the church of **Sant'Andrea delle Fratte** ⑰, where you can pause under the orange trees in the cloister. From Via Sant'Andrea delle Fratte, turn left onto Via del Nazareno and cross busy Via del Tritone to Via della Stamperia. On the right-hand side of Via della Stamperia is **Palazzo Poli** ⑱, which houses the Calcografia dello Stato. A few paces beyond is the old building in which the **Accademia di San Luca** ⑲, with a gallery of old masters, is located. As you near the end of Via della Stamperia you can probably hear the sound of **Fontana di Trevi** ⑳, a Baroque extravaganza of sculpture and cascading waters. From the Fontana di Trevi, Via Lucchesi leads you to Piazza della Pilotta and Via della Pilotta, where ornate bridges overhead connect **Palazzo Colonna** ㉑ with the Colonna family's gardens on the slope of the Quirinal Hill. The west side of the palace is flanked by the church of **Santi Apostoli** ㉒. On the ceiling, the early 18th-century artist Baciccia painted one of his swooping, swirling illusionist frescoes. Opposite the church is another of Rome's splendid patrician palaces, 17th-century Palazzo Odescalchi, used as a model for aristocratic palaces throughout Europe.

TIMING

Not counting shopping, this walk could take from 3½ to 5 hours, allowing for visits to the galleries and for a few coffee or ice-cream breaks. It certainly should be done on days when the shops are open, even if you're only window-shopping. Though the Palazzo Doria Pamphilj is open most days of the week, the Galleria in Palazzo Colonna is open only on Saturday morning.

Sights to See

⑲ **Accademia di San Luca.** This private academy of the arts, founded by a group of painters in the 1400s, is housed in 16th-century Palazzo Carpegna. Its gallery is open to the public (though currently closed for restoration) and contains some fine Renaissance paintings, including

72

Piazza Venezia to the Spanish Steps

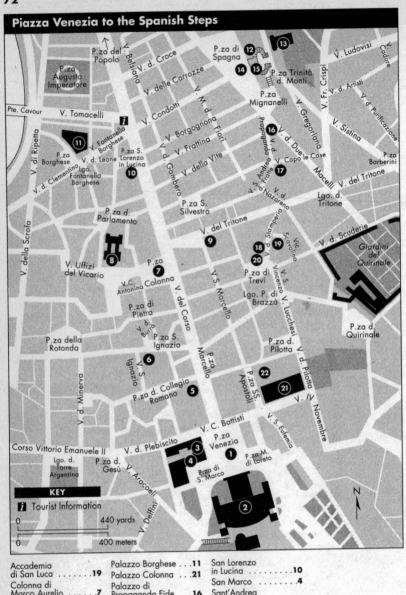

a charming putto by Raphael as well as his *Madonna of St. Luke.* ⊠ *Piazza dell'Accademia di San Luca 77,* ☎ *06/6798850.* ☜ *Free. Closed indefinitely for restoration.*

❼ Colonna di Marco Aurelio (Column of Marcus Aurelius). Inspired by Trajan's Column, this 2nd-century AD column is composed of 27 blocks of marble covered with a series of reliefs recording Marcus Aurelius's victory over the Germans. At the top is a bronze statue of St. Paul, which replaced the effigy of Marcus Aurelius in the 16th century. The column is the centerpiece of Piazza Colonna. ⊠ *Piazza Colonna.*

⓮ Fontana della Barcaccia (Leaky Boat Fountain). At the center of Piazza di Spagna and at the bottom of the Spanish Steps, this curious, half-sunken boat gently spills out water rather than cascading it dramatically into the air; it may have been designed that way to make the most of the area's low water pressure. It was thanks to the Barberini Pope Urban VIII, who commissioned the fountain, that there was any water at all in this area, which was becoming increasingly built up during the 17th century. He restored one of the ancient Roman aqueducts that once channeled water here. The bees and suns on the boat constitute the Barberini trademark. Some insist that the Berninis (Pietro and his more famous son Gian Lorenzo) intended the fountain to be a reminder that this part of town was often flooded by the Tiber; others that it represents the Ship of the Church; and still others that it marks the presumed site of the emperor Domitian's water stadium in which sea battles were reenacted in the glory days of the Roman Empire. ⊠ *Piazza di Spagna.*

⓴ Fontana di Trevi (Trevi Fountain). Alive with rushing waters and marble sea creatures commanded by an imperious Oceanus, this aquatic marvel is one of the city's most exciting sights. The work of Nicola Salvi—though it's thought that Bernini may have been responsible for parts of the design—it was completed in 1762 and is a perfect example of the rococo taste for dramatic theatrical effects. The water comes from the Acqua Vergine aqueduct, and is so called because of the legend that it was a young girl, a *vergine,* who showed its source to thirsty Roman soldiers. The story is pictured in the relief on the right of the figure of Oceanus. Usually thickly fringed with tourists tossing coins into the basin to ensure their return to Rome (the fountain grosses about €120,000 a year, most of it donated to charity), the fountain took center stage for Anita Ekberg's famous dip in *La Dolce Vita.* (Unfortunately, the water is turned off during the wee hours and occasionally at other times for cleaning; if that's the case when you arrive, make a point of returning another day to see it in full gush.) ⊠ *Piazza di Trevi.*

NEED A BREAK?

Gelateria San Crispino (⊠ Via della Panetteria 42, ☎ 06/6793924), closed Tuesday, has become a mecca for gelato aficionados. Flavors are pure and balanced, thanks to the use of only natural ingredients.

⓯ Keats and Shelley Memorial House. The English Romantic poet Keats lived here, in what was the colorful bohemian quarter of 18th- and 19th-century Rome, especially favored by the English. You can visit his rooms, which have been preserved as they were when he died here in 1821. They contain a rather quaint collection of memorabilia of English literary figures of the period—Byron, Shelley, Joseph Severn, and Leigh Hunt as well as Keats—and an exhaustive library of works on the Romantics. ⊠ *Piazza di Spagna 26, next to the Spanish Steps,* ☎ *06/6784235,* WEB *www.Keats-Shelley-House.org.* ☜ *€2.50.* ⊙ *Weekdays 9–1 and 3–6, Sat. 11–2 and 3–6.*

② **Monumento a Vittorio Emanuele II,** or **Altare della Patria** (Victor Emmanuel Monument, or Altar of the Nation). Romans say you can avoid seeing it only if you're standing on it. The huge white mass of the "Vittoriano" is an inescapable and handy Roman landmark. Some have likened it to a huge wedding cake; others, to an immense typewriter. However modern eyes may look at it, it was the splendid focus of civic pride to turn-of-the-20th-century Romans. In order to create this elaborate marble monster and the vast piazza in which it stands, its architects blithely destroyed many ancient and medieval buildings and altered the slope of the Capitoline Hill, which abuts it. Built to honor the unification of Italy and the nation's first king, Victor Emmanuel II, it also shelters the eternal flame at the tomb of Italy's Unknown Soldier, guarded day and night by sentinels, and the (rather dry) Institute of the History of the Risorgimento—relics of the struggle for the unification of Italy in the 19th century.

The steps of the monument reopened to the public in 2000 after 30 years, and the views from the top are unforgettable—some of Rome's best. Before you climb up, be sure to stop into the museum entrance to get a pamphlet identifying the sculpture groups on the monument and the landmarks you see from the top. Opposite the monument, note the enclosed wooden veranda fronting the palace on the corner of Via del Plebiscito and Via Corso. For the many years that she lived in Rome, Napoléon's mother had a fine view from here of the local goings-on. ✉ *Piazza Venezia; museum entrance at Piazza Ara Coeli,* ☎ *06/6781848,* 🌐 *www.ambienterm.arti.beniculturali.it/vittoriano/index. html.* ☉ *Tues.–Sun. 10:30–1 hr before sunset.*

⓫ **Palazzo Borghese.** One of the princely palaces of Rome's aristocratic families, this is a huge, rambling Renaissance building that goes on for blocks and has several portals. The palace was begun in 1590 for a Spanish cardinal by architect Martino Longhi, who designed the sturdy facade facing Largo Fontanella Borghese. In 1605 Cardinal Borghese celebrated his election as Pope Paul V by purchasing the palace; it later passed to his nephew, Cardinal Scipione Borghese, who assembled his magnificent art collection here. Still used by the Borghese family, though part of it is rented out, the palace is closed to the public. You can get as far as the gate inside the main portal on Largo Fontanella Borghese to take a peek at the double courtyard. ✉ *Largo Fontanella Borghese.*

㉑ **Palazzo Colonna.** This immense palace faces Piazza Santi Apostoli on one side and the Quirinal Hill on the other. A little bridge over Via della Pilotta links the palace with the gardens on the hill. Palazzo Colonna is home to one of Rome's oldest and most patrician families, whose picture gallery is open to the public one day a week. The galleria is itself a setting of aristocratic grandeur; the centerpiece of one of the salons is the ancient red marble column (*colonna* in Italian) that is the family's emblem. Adding redundant luster to the opulently stuccoed and frescoed salons are works by Poussin, Tintoretto, and Veronese, and a number of portraits of illustrious members of the family such as Vittoria Colonna—Michelangelo's muse and longtime friend—and Marcantonio Colonna, who led the papal forces in the great naval victory at Lepanto in 1577. Cinema buffs may recognize the **Sala Grande** as the site where Audrey Hepburn met the press in *Roman Holiday.* ✉ *Via della Pilotta 17,* ☎ *06/6794362,* 🌐 *web.tin.it/galleriacolonna.* 🎟 *€5.15.* ☉ *Sept.–July, Sat. 9–1.*

⓰ **Palazzo di Propaganda Fide** (Palace of the Propagation of the Faith). Jesuit missionary activity is headquartered here. Bernini created the simpler facade on the piazza in 1644, while his arch rival Borromini designed the more elaborate one on Via di Propaganda not long before his death in 1667. ⊠ *Piazza di Spagna 48.*

⑤ Palazzo Doria Pamphilj. The beauty of the graceful 18th-century facade of this patrician palace may escape you unless you take time to step to the opposite side of the street for a good view. The foundations of the immense complex of buildings probably date from classical times. The present building dates from the 15th century, with the exception of the facade. It passed through several hands before it became the property of the famous seafaring Doria family of Genoa, who had married into the Roman Pamphilj (also spelled Pamphili) clan. As in most of Rome's older patrician residences, the family still lives in part of the palace but rents out some of its 1,000 rooms, five courtyards, and four monumental staircases to various public and private enterprises.

The incredibly rich family art collection is open to the public, along with part of the private apartments. Set like the family jewels that they are in an alcove off the galleria are the famous Velázquez portrait and the Bernini bust of the Pamphili Pope Innocent X. Of the three Caravaggios in the collection, the *Rest on the Flight to Egypt* is the finest. You'll also find a Titian and some splendid 17th-century landscapes by Claude Lorrain and Gaspar Dughet. The guided tour of the private apartments includes a Baroque chapel, a ballroom, and three authentically furnished 18th-century salons. In the private apartments are an *Annunciation* by Filippo Lippi, a family portrait by Lotto, and a stately portrait of Andrea Doria by Sebastiano del Piombo. It's the glimpse of an aristocratic lifestyle that makes this tour special. ⊠ *Piazza del Collegio Romano 2,* ☎ *06/6797323,* WEB *www.doriapamphilj.it.* ⊠ *Galleria Doria Pamphilj 6.70 (includes audio guide); private-apartments tours €3.05.* ☉ *Fri.–Wed. 10–5; private-apartments tours 10:30, 11, 11:30, noon only.*

⑧ Palazzo Montecitorio. The Chamber of Deputies, the lower house of the Italian parliament, meets here. The huge palace occupies two city blocks and has two facades, one facing Piazza del Parlamento. The facade on Piazza Montecitorio was designed by Bernini and is adorned with a 6th-century BC Egyptian obelisk. The obelisk once served as the pointer of an immense sundial traced in the pavement of the Campo Marzio, a vast open area set aside under the emperor Augustus in the 1st century AD. Embellished with gardens and promenades, it extended as far as the Tiber and included the Augusteo (the emperor's family mausoleum) and the Ara Pacis. Almost entirely hidden by subsequent constructions, parts of the area's original pavement, with symbols of the planets, lie under the buildings on Piazza San Lorenzo in Lucina. ⊠ *Piazza Montecitorio,* ☎ *06/67601.* ⊠ *Free.* ☉ *1st Sun. of month 10–5:30.*

⑱ Palazzo Poli. The palazzo is home to the Calcografia dello Stato (National Graphics Institute). Together with similar institutes in Paris and Madrid, the Calcografia preserves the world's most important collections of copper engraving plates by artists from the 1500s up to the present. There is an exhibition space on the ground floor, where samples of its historic treasures and contemporary work may be on display. The collection includes invaluable antique presses and more than 1,400 engraving plates by 18th-century Roman artist Piranesi. ⊠ *Via della Stamperia 6,* ☎ *06/699801.* ⊠ *Free.* ☉ *Daily 9–1 and 3–4.*

③ Palazzo Venezia. The palace was originally built for Venetian Cardinal Pietro Barbo, who became Pope Paul II. It was also the backdrop used by Mussolini to harangue crowds with dreams of empire from the balcony over the main portal. The palace shows a mixture of Renaissance grace and heavy medieval lines, and it houses an eclectic collection of decorative objects, paintings, sculptures, and ceramics in handsome salons, some of which Mussolini used as his offices. Lights were left on all night long during Mussolini's reign, to suggest that the Fascist regime worked without pause. The café on the loggia has a pleasant view over the garden courtyard. ⊠ *Piazza San Marco 49,* ☎ *06/6798865.* 🖼 *€4.15.* ⊘ *Tues.–Sat. 9–2.*

① **Piazza Venezia.** The geographic heart of Rome, this is the spot from which all distances from Rome are calculated and it is the principal crossroads of city traffic. Piazza Venezia stands at what was the beginning of Via Flaminia, the ancient Roman road that leads east across Italy to Fano on the Adriatic Sea. Via Flaminia was, and still is, a vital artery. The initial tract of Via Flaminia, from Piazza Venezia to Piazza del Popolo, is now known as the Corso (Via del Corso, one of the busiest shopping streets in the city), after the horse races (*corse*) that were run here during the wild Roman carnival celebrations of the 17th and 18th centuries. The podium near the beginning of the Corso is the sometime domain of Rome's most practiced traffic policemen, whose imperious gestures and imperative whistles are a spectacle not to be missed. The massive female bust, a fragment of antiquity near the church of San Marco in the corner of the piazza, is known to the Romans as Madama Lucrezia; it was one of the "talking statues" on which anonymous poets hung verses pungent with political satire, a practice that has not entirely disappeared. ⊠ *Junction of Via del Corso, Via Plebiscito, and Via Cesare Battisti.*

⑩ **San Lorenzo in Lucina.** The church was probably founded on the site of an early Christian meeting place under the aegis of a Roman matron named Lucina, whose name was added to that of St. Lorenzo (Lawrence) to distinguish it from other churches dedicated to him. Behind its 12th-century portico and campanile (bell tower), the interior is not especially interesting. There's one exception, however: the **Cappella Fonseca** (Fonseca Chapel), the fourth on the right, was designed by Bernini. His bust of Fonseca, Innocent X's physician, represents the doctor in moving contemplation. On the chapel's right wall, a 17th-century painting shows Elisha pouring salt into the waters of Jericho in order to purify them; it's a clear reference to Fonseca's concern with purifying the malarial waters of Rome and its *campagna,* the area surrounding the city. The 17th-century *Crucifixion* over the main altar is by Guido Reni. The church guards relics of the grill on which the early Christian martyr St. Lawrence was roasted alive. ⊠ *Piazza San Lorenzo in Lucina,* ☎ *06/6871494.*

④ **San Marco.** The ancient church was used for official ceremonies by Venetian Pope Paul II, who resided in the palace he built next door. Tradition relates that St. Mark wrote his gospel in Rome, and the church is dedicated to the evangelist, as well as to the 4th-century Pope Mark, whose relics are under the main altar. One of many Roman churches built as a basilica, the original edifice was destroyed by fire and replaced in the 6th century. The third church, the one you see today, was built in the 9th century by Pope Gregory IV, as the dedication in the Byzantine apse mosaics testifies.

The church is a perfect example of Rome's layering of history, of periods and styles built up one upon another. From the early Christian architectural motifs to the Romanesque bell tower, from the Byzantine mosaics to the windows in the nave, nearly 1,500 years of architectural styles are represented here. Then there's the full flowering of Renaissance style in the magnificent gilt ceiling and the ample portico that Pope Paul II built to provide shelter for himself and his retinue during outdoor rites in bad weather. On the right wall of the portico is the tomb of Vannozza Cattanei. The mistress of the Borgia Pope Alexander VI, she bore him three children, including the infamous Lucrezia and Cesare. Originally in the Church of Santa Maria del Popolo, the tomb was moved here under mysterious circumstances. No one has ever been able to discover why, when, or by whom. ⊠ *Piazza San Marco, off Piazza Venezia,* ☎ *06/6795205.* ☉ *Daily 7:30–1 and 4–7.*

⑰ Sant'Andrea delle Fratte. On either side of the choir are the two original angels that Bernini himself carved for the Ponte Sant'Angelo, where copies now stand. The door in the right aisle leads into one of Rome's hidden gardens, where orange trees bloom in the cloister. Borromini's contributions—the dome and a curious bell tower—are best seen from Via Capo le Case, across Via Due Macelli. ⊠ *Via Sant'Andrea delle Fratte 1 (Via della Mercede),* ☎ *06/6793191.* ☉ *Daily 6:15–12:30 and 4–7.*

❻ Sant'Ignazio. This 17th-century church harbors some of the magnificent illusions typical of the Baroque style. To get the full effect of the marvelous illusionistic ceiling by priest-artist Andrea del Pozzo, stand on the small disk set into the floor of the nave. The heavenly vision above you, seemingly extending upward almost indefinitely, represents the *Glory of St. Ignatius Loyola* and is part of Del Pozzo's cycle of works in this church exalting the early history of the Jesuit Order, whose founder was the mystic Ignatius of Loyola. The artist repeated this illusionist technique, so popular in the late 17th century, in the false dome, which is actually a flat canvas. The overall effect of the frescoes is dazzling (be sure to have coins handy for the machine that switches on the lights) and was fully intended to rival that produced by Baciccia in the nearby church of Il Gesù. The church is often host to concerts of sacred music performed by choirs from all over the world; look for posters at the church doors for more information. ⊠ *Piazza Sant'-Ignazio,* ☎ *06/6794406.* ☉ *Daily 7:30–12:30 and 4–7:15.*

❾ Santa Maria in Via. This small 16th-century church is like many others, except for one well-kept secret—under the foundations hides a bona fide natural spring, out of which bubbles purportedly curative water you can imbibe in the chapel on the right. In addition to mineral water, it's claimed the spring once brought forth the icon of the Madonna that's now over the altar. ⊠ *Via di Santa Maria in Via (Via del Tritone),* ☎ *06/6796760.* ☉ *Daily 8–1 and 4–8.*

㉒ Santi Apostoli (Holy Apostles). The Basilica of Santi Apostoli is a mixture of architectural styles, the result of successive restorations of an ancient church. The grandiose ceiling fresco by Baciccia, who did an even grander one for the Jesuits at Il Gesù, celebrates the founding of the Franciscan Order. One of the church's best features is the lovely double portico on the facade, dating from the 15th century. The church is often the scene of the weddings and funerals of Rome's aristocracy, and the piazza frequently serves as a gathering place for heated political rallies and demonstrations. ⊠ *Piazza SS. Apostoli,* ☎ *06/59602716.* ☉ *Open only for mass: Mon.–Sat. 8 AM, 9 AM, and 6 PM; Sun. 8:30 AM, 11 AM, and 6 PM.*

NEED A
BREAK?

The **L'Osteria dell'Ingegno** (⊠ Piazza di Pietra 45, ☎ 06/6780662), closed Saturday lunch and all day Sunday, off Piazza Colonna, is an ideal stop for a light lunch or supper, with an ample choice of wines.

★ ⑫ **Scalinata di Trinità dei Monti** (Spanish Steps). This spectacular staircase takes its nickname from the Spanish Embassy to the Holy See—the Vatican—which has occupied the historic palace facing what is now the American Express office since the 17th century. However, the idea for a monumental staircase connecting the piazza with the French Church of Trinità dei Monti at the top of the hill originated with the French minister Mazarin. Its construction in 1723 was partially financed by French funds. Perfect for lounging and for photographing from all angles, the steps have always attracted a lively crowd, from 19th-century artists' models in folk costumes to present-day tourists from the four corners of the earth. Romans don't linger here; they leave the steps and square to the tourists. But they don't fail to stop by between Easter and early May, when the Spanish Steps are gloriously blanketed with huge pots of azaleas in bloom. ⊠ *Piazza di Spagna, junction of Via Condotti, Via del Babuino, and Via Due Macelli.*

NEED A BREAK?
You may prefer to limit your shopping here to the window variety, but there's one thing on Via Condotti that everybody can afford, and that's a stand-up coffee at the bar at the **Antico Caffè Greco** (⊠ Via Condotti 86, ☎ 06/6791700), a 200-year-old institution, the haunt of artists and literati; it's closed Sunday. With its tiny, marble-top tables and velour settees, it's a nostalgic old place. Goethe, Byron, and Liszt were habitués; Buffalo Bill stopped in when his road show hit Rome. It's still a haven for writers and artists, and for ladies carrying Gucci shopping bags. Remember, table service is very pricey here.

⓭ **Trinità dei Monti.** Standing high above the Spanish Steps, this church is beautiful not so much in itself but for its dramatic location and magnificent views. It is occasionally used as a concert venue. ⊠ *Piazza Trinità dei Monti* ☎ 06/6794179. ☉ *Daily 8–8.*

MONTI AND SAN GIOVANNI IN LATERANO

In ancient times, the Suburra (the present-day Monti neighborhood) was one of Rome's most populous areas. The dark, warrenlike sector of multistory dwellings, a notorious slum that lived by its own rules, was the cramped home of a substantial portion of ancient Rome's more than one million citizens in the 1st century AD. So infamous were the Suburra's mean streets that it's thought the great fire of 64 BC, which all but destroyed the neighborhood, may have been intentionally set to wipe out a troublesome population that could be subdued no other way. A high stone wall separating the Suburra from the Imperial Fora acted as a barrier, keeping the flames from endangering Rome's most august monuments—and citizens.

The neighborhood is clearly different from that of Old Rome, near the Vatican to the west. Here you'll find the stamp of a much more remote past—with the Colosseum's marble-clad walls looming at the end of narrow, shadowy streets with Latin-sounding names: Panisperna, Baccina, Fagutale. Other walls, built for the Caesars, shore up medieval tower-houses; streets dip and climb, hugging the curves of two of the seven hills on which Romulus founded his city. Emerging from antiquity, the great churches of the Christian era stand out like islands connected by broad avenues. The new streets laid out by the popes or, later, by the planners of the capital of the new Italy slice through the meandering byways, providing a shorter, surer route for pilgrims and commerce. Majestic Santa Maria Maggiore, its interior gleaming with gold from the New World, and San Giovanni in Laterano, with its grand, echoing vastness, are among the oldest of the city's churches, though restored and remodeled through the centuries. They are also major pilgrimage sites, the focus of Holy Year rites for Roman Catholics, and a magnet for anyone interested in art and architecture. Another lodestone is the smaller, hard-to-find church of San Pietro in Vincoli, with its hidden treasure—Michelangelo's statue of *Moses*.

Numbers in the text and in the margin correspond to numbers on the Monti and San Giovanni in Laterano map.

A Good Walk

Start at the Colosseum and walk up the stairs through the Metro station to reach Largo Agnesi, a scenic overlook with views of the Colosseum and the columns of the Tempio di Venere e Roma. Facing away from the Colosseum, walk right, then turn left on Via Fagutale, which runs along and above the sunken main road. Turn right at Via della Polveriera, then left at Via Eudosiana to the piazza home to the church of **San Pietro in Vincoli** ①, to which Michelangelo's *Moses* attracts throngs of tourists. Walk down the staircase, called Salita dei Borgia, passing under Palazzo Borgia, home of the notorious family and hotbed of Renaissance intrigue.

Returning to Via Cavour, turn right onto it and head northeast (or take the quieter Via Urbana, which runs parallel). Make a brief detour to the left, or west, to see the mosaics in the church of **Santa Pudenziana** ②. Both Via Urbana and Via Cavour lead straight to Piazza dell'Esquilino and the sweeping staircase at the rear of **Santa Maria Maggiore** ③. Walk around the enormous church to Piazza Santa Maria Maggiore, taking a moment to admire the full effect of facade, loggia, and bell tower. Narrow Via di Santa Prassede, which is at the southwest corner of the Piazza, leads to the little church of **Santa Prassede** ④, with a tiny porch marking the portal and 9th-century mosaics inside. Returning to Via Merulana, you reach Largo Brancaccio. On your right is the large **Museo Nazionale d'Arte Orientale** ⑤, Italy's main collection of art and artifacts from the East and Middle East. The area between Via Merulana and Stazione Termini, to the east, with Piazza Vittorio as its fulcrum, is as multiethnic as Rome gets. Asian, Indian, and African grocery stores and restaurants abound.

Via Merulana was laid out as a pilgrimage route in the 1500s and runs straight as an arrow between the basilicas of Santa Maria Maggiore and **San Giovanni in Laterano** ⑥, with its medieval cloister. Attached to the north flank of the church is the **Palazzo Apostolico Lateranense** ⑦. The **Scala Santa** ⑧ is in the churchlike edifice diagonally across from the Lateran Palace. Turn south into **Piazza San Giovanni in Laterano** ⑨. On the square is the octagonal **Battistero** ⑩.

From Piazza di Porta San Giovanni and the ancient city walls, follow Viale Carlo Felice east to the church of **Santa Croce in Gerusalemme** ⑪. Behind the church is the **Museo Nazionale degli Strumenti Musicali** ⑫. Then you can head back to San Giovanni's Metro stop and bus lines, or continue northeast to see **Porta Maggiore** ⑬, a part of the Acqua Claudia aqueduct.

TIMING

The walk takes about three hours, including visits to the basilicas. They're open through lunch hour, but if you want to see Michelangelo's *Moses* in San Pietro in Vincoli, you have to get there before 12:30 or after 3:30. Santa Pudenziana and Santa Prassede also close from about noon to 3 or 4. Allow an additional 30 minutes for a visit to the Museo d'Arte Orientale and 20–30 minutes for a cursory look at the Museo Nazionale degli Strumenti Musicali.

Sights to See

⑩ **Battistero** (Baptistry). Though much altered through the centuries, the Baptistry of San Giovanni is the forerunner of all such buildings where baptisms take place, a ritual of key importance in the Christian faith. It was built by Constantine in the 4th century and enlarged by Pope Sixtus III about 100 years later. It stands on the site of the baths attached to the home of Constantine's second wife, Fausta, who, emperor's wife or not, was suffocated in the hot room of the baths after having falsely accused Constantine's son by his first wife of having tried to rape her. This exceedingly unpleasant death is an example of one of the accepted Roman methods of dealing with members of the ruling classes who were implicated in scandals of this type. Of the four chapels arranged around the walls of the baptistry, the most interesting is the first on the right (as you enter). It has a set of ancient bronze doors whose hinges send out a musical sound when the doors are opened and closed. They probably came from the Terme di Caracalla. Notice also the splendid porphyry columns that support the entire structure, typical of the Romans' love of luxurious and exotic materials. ⊠ *Piazza San Giovanni in Laterano.* ☉ *Daily 9–1 and 3–1 hr before sunset.*

⑤ **Museo Nazionale d'Arte Orientale** (National Museum of Oriental Art). The museum's extensive collection of Middle Eastern and East Asian art is being continually enriched by the finds of Italian archaeological expeditions. Italian archaeologists have been in on some of the most important finds of recent decades, such as Ebla in Syria. ⊠ *Via Merulana 248,* ☎ 06/4874415. ☙ €4.15. ☉ *Mon., Wed., Fri., Sat. 8:30–2; Tues., Thurs., Sun. 9–7:30; closed 1st and 3rd Mon. of month.*

⑫ **Museo Nazionale degli Strumenti Musicali** (National Museum of Musical Instruments). Just behind Santa Croce is this museum housing a sizable collection of instruments from prehistory to the present, arranged by type, including folk instruments, mechanical instruments, a 16th-century clavichord, and the richly carved 17th-century Barberini Harp. ⊠ *Piazza Santa Croce in Gerusalemme 9/a,* ☎ 06/7014796. ☙ €2.05. ☉ *Tues.–Sun. 9–1:30.*

⑦ **Palazzo Apostolico Lateranense** (Lateran Apostolic Palace). The building flanking the basilica of San Giovanni was the popes' official residence until their exile to Avignon in the south of France in the 14th century. The present palace was built by Domenico Fontana in 1586. Still technically part of the Vatican, it now houses the offices of the Rome Diocese and the Vatican Historical Museum. On the (required) tour you'll see the historic Papal Apartment, with antique furnishings, medieval sculptures, and Renaissance tapestries, and the Sala della Conciliazione, with a magnificent 16th-century carved and painted wood ceiling. ⊠ *Entrance outside at atrium of San Giovanni in Laterano,* ☎ 06/69886386. ☙ €3.10. ☉ *Sat. tours at 9:30, 11, and 12:15; Sun. tours at 8:45 and 1.*

⑨ **Piazza San Giovanni in Laterano.** At the center of this square stands Rome's oldest and tallest obelisk, which originally stood in front of the Temple of Ammon in Thebes, Egypt, in the 15th century BC. It was brought to Rome by Constantine in AD 357 to stand in the Circus Maximus and finally was set up here in 1588. Adjoining the square is the rambling city hospital of San Giovanni, founded in the Middle Ages as a kind of infirmary for the Lateran Palace. ⊠ *Via Merulana at Via Amba Aradam.*

⑬ **Porta Maggiore.** The massive 1st-century AD monument is not really a *porta* (city gate) but part of the Acqua Claudia aqueduct. It gives you an idea of the scale of Roman public works, and also of the level of

Monti and San Giovanni in Laterano

110 yards
100 meters

KEY

7 Tourist Information

Battistero **10**	Porta Maggiore **13**
Museo Nazionale d'Arte Orientale **5**	San Giovanni in Laterano **6**
Museo Nazionale degli Strumenti Musicali **12**	San Pietro in Vincoli **1**
Palazzo Apostolico Lateranense **7**	Santa Croce in Gerusalemme . . . **11**
Piazza San Giovanni in Laterano **9**	Santa Maria Maggiore **3**
Santa Prassede **4**	
Santa Pudenziana . . . **2**	
Scala Santa **8**	

the ancient city—you have to look down from the present sidewalk to see the gate. On the Piazzale Labicano side of the portal, to the east, is the curious **Baker's Tomb**, erected in the 1st century BC by the grieving wife of a prosperous baker. Look closely—the tomb is decorated with stone ovens and charming friezes with scenes of the deceased's trade. ⊠ *Junction of Via Eleniana, Via di Porta Maggiore, and Via Casilina.*

❻ San Giovanni in Laterano (St. John Lateran). This is one of Rome's four patriarchal basilicas, and the city's cathedral; it is the Pope's official seat in his capacity as Bishop of Rome. The towering facade dates from 1736 and was modeled on that of St. Peter's Basilica. The 15 colossal statues (Christ, John the Baptist, John the Evangelist, and the 12 Apostles of the church) look out on the sea of dreary suburbs that have spread from Porta San Giovanni to the lower slopes of the Alban Hills.

San Giovanni was founded in the 4th century on land donated by the emperor Constantine, who had obtained it from the wealthy patrician family of the Laterani. Vandals, earthquakes, and fire damaged the original and successive constructions. Finally, in 1646, Pope Innocent X commissioned Borromini to rebuild the church, and it's Borromini's rather cool, tense Baroque interior that you see today.

Under the portico on the left stands an ancient statue of Constantine. Another link with Rome's past is the central portal's ancient bronze doors, brought here from the Curia building in the Forum. Inside, little is left of the early decorations. The fragment of a fresco on the first pillar in the double aisle on the right depicts Pope Boniface VIII proclaiming the first Holy Year in 1300; it is attributed to the 14th-century Florentine painter Giotto. The mosaic in the apse was reconstructed from a 12th-century original by Torriti, the same Franciscan friar who executed the apse mosaic in Santa Maria Maggiore. The papal altar at the center of the church contains a wooden table believed to have been used by St. Peter to celebrate the Eucharist. The altar's rich Gothic tabernacle dates from 1367 and, somewhat gruesomely, contains what are believed to be the heads of Sts. Peter and Paul.

You shouldn't miss the church **cloister**, with its twin columns encrusted with 13th-century Cosmatesque mosaics by the Vassallettos, a father-and-son team. Enter the cloister from the last chapel at the end of the left aisle. ⊠ *Piazza di Porta San Giovanni,* ☎ *06/69886452.* ☒ *Cloister €2.05.* ☉ *Basilica daily 7–6 (until 7 in summer), cloister daily 9–½ hr before church closing.*

❶ San Pietro in Vincoli (St. Peter in Chains). What has put this otherwise unprepossessing church on the map is the monumental statue of Moses carved by Michelangelo in the early 16th century for the never-completed tomb of his patron, Pope Julius II, which was to include dozens of statues and stand nearly 40 ft tall when installed in St. Peter's Basilica. Only three statues—*Moses* and the two that flank it here, *Leah* and *Rachel*—had been completed when Julius died. His successor as pope, from a rival family, had other plans for Michelangelo, and Julius's tomb was abandoned unfinished and ultimately installed here. The fierce power of this remarkable sculpture dominates its setting. People say that you can see the sculptor's profile in the lock of Moses's beard right under his lip, and that the pope's profile is also there somewhere. But don't let the search distract you from the overall effect of this marvelously energetic work. As for the rest of the church, St. Peter, after whom the church is named, takes second billing to Moses. What are reputed to be the chains that bound St. Peter during his imprisonment by the Romans in Jerusalem are in a bronze and crystal

San Giovanni in Laterano

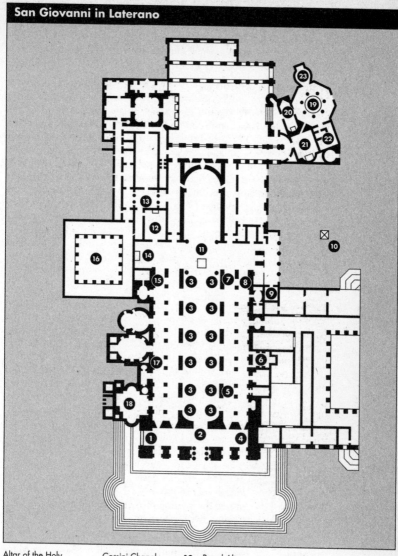

urn under the main altar. Other treasures in the church include a 7th-century mosaic of St. Sebastian, in front of the second altar on the left of the main altar, and, by the door, the tomb of the Pollaiuolo brothers, two lesser 15th-century Florentine artists. ⊠ *Piazza San Pietro in Vincoli,* ☎ *06/4882865.* ⊙ *Daily 7–12:30 and 3:30–6 (7 in summer).*

⓫ **Santa Croce in Gerusalemme** (Holy Cross of Jerusalem). Like Santa Maria Maggiore and San Giovanni in Laterano, the outward appearance of this church doesn't give away its ancient origins. The Romanesque bell tower off to one side was put up in the 12th century, the facade was rebuilt in the 18th century, and the interior was extensively remodeled in the 17th and 18th centuries. But the church foundations were once part of the 4th-century AD palace of St. Helena, mother of the emperor Constantine. She was an indefatigable collector of holy relics, and her most precious discovery was fragments of the Holy Cross—the cross on which Christ was crucified—which she had unearthed during one of many forays through the Holy Land. The relics of the cross are in the modern chapel at the end of the left aisle. The chapel dedicated to St. Helena, in the lower level of the building, was redecorated in the 15th century with a dazzling gold-and-blue version of an earlier mosaic. ⊠ *Piazza Santa Croce in Gerusalemme,* ☎ *06/7014769.* ⊙ *Daily 7–7.*

★ ❸ **Santa Maria Maggiore** (St. Mary Major). The exterior of the church, from the broad sweep of steps on Via Cavour to the more elaborate facade on Piazza Santa Maria Maggiore, is that of a gracefully curving 18th-century building, the very model of Baroque architecture of the period. But in fact Santa Maria Maggiore is one of the oldest churches in Rome, built around 440 by Pope Sixtus III. One of the four great pilgrimage churches of Rome, it is by far the most complete example of an early Christian basilica in the city—one of the immense, hall-like structures derived from ancient Roman civic buildings and divided into thirds by two great rows of columns marching up the nave. The other six basilicas—San Giovanni in Laterano and St. Peter's Basilica are the most famous—have been entirely transformed, or even rebuilt. Paradoxically, the major reason why this church is such a striking example of early Christian design is that the same man who built the incongruous exteriors about 1740—Ferdinando Fuga—also conscientiously restored the interior, throwing out later additions and, crucially, replacing a number of the great columns.

Every August 5, a special mass in the Cappella Sistina commemorates the miracle that led to the founding of the basilica: the Virgin Mary appeared in a dream to Pope Liberio and ordered him to build a church in her honor on the spot where snow would fall on the night of August 5 (an event about as likely in a Roman August as snow in the Sahara). The Madonna of the Snows is celebrated with a shower of white rose petals from the ceiling.

Precious 5th-century mosaics high on the nave walls and on the triumphal arch in front of the main altar are splendid testimony to the basilica's venerable age. Those along the nave show 36 scenes from the Old Testament (unfortunately, they are hard to see clearly without binoculars), while those on the arch illustrate the Annunciation and the Youth of Christ. The majestic mosaic in the apse was created by a Franciscan monk named Torriti in 1275. The resplendent carved wood ceiling dates from the early 16th century; it's supposed to have been gilded with the first gold brought from the New World. The inlaid marble pavement (called Cosmatesque after the family of master artisans who developed the technique) in the central nave is even older, dating from the 12th century.

Santa Maria Maggiore

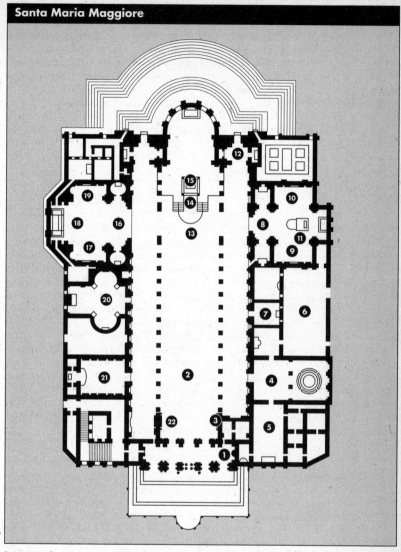

The **Cappella Sistina** (Sistine Chapel), which opens onto the right-hand nave, was created by architect Domenico Fontana for Pope Sixtus V in 1585. Elaborately and heavily decorated with precious marbles "liberated" from the monuments of ancient Rome, the chapel includes a lower level in which some 13th-century sculptures by Arnolfo da Cambio are all that's left of what was once the incredibly richly endowed chapel of the presepio, the Christmas crèche, looted during the Sack of Rome in 1527. Directly opposite, on the other side of the church, stands the **Cappella Paoline** (Pauline Chapel), a rich Baroque setting for the tombs of the Borghese popes Paul V—who commissioned the chapel in 1611 with the declared intention of outdoing Sixtus's chapel across the nave—and Clement VIII. The *Madonna* above its altar is a precious Byzantine image painted perhaps as early as the 8th century. The **Cappella Sforza** (Sforza Chapel) next door was designed by Michelangelo and completed by della Porta (the same partnership that was responsible for the dome of St. Peter's Basilica). ⊠ *Piazza Santa Maria Maggiore,* ☎ *06/4881094.* ⊙ *Daily 7–7.*

❹ **Santa Prassede** (St. Praxedes). This small and inconspicuous 9th-century church is known above all for the exquisite little **Cappella di San Zenone.** It's just to the left of the entrance, and it gleams with vivid mosaics that reflect their Byzantine inspiration. Though much less classical and naturalistic than the earlier mosaics of Santa Pudenziana, they are no less splendid. Note the square halo over the head of Theodora, mother of St. Pasquale I, the pope who built this church. It indicates that she was still alive when she was depicted by the artist. The chapel also contains one curious relic: a miniature pillar, supposedly part of the column at which Christ was flogged during the Passion. It was brought to Rome in the 13th century. Next to the entrance to the chapel is an early work of Bernini, a bust of Bishop Santoni, executed when the sculptor was in his mid-teens. Over the main altar, the magnificent mosaics on the arch and apse are also in rigid Byzantine style; in them Pope Pasquale I wears the square halo of the living and holds a model of his church. ⊠ *Via di Santa Prassede 9/a,* ☎ *06/4882456.* ⊙ *Daily 7:30–noon and 4–6:30.*

❷ **Santa Pudenziana** (St. Pudentia). This much-restored early Christian church is well worth a visit for its strikingly colored 5th-century apse mosaic representing Christ and the Apostles, in which Sts. Praxides and Pudenziana hold wreaths over the heads of Sts. Peter and Paul. ⊠ *Via Urbana 160,* ☎ *06/4814622.* ⊙ *Mon.–Sat. 8–6:30.*

❽ **Scala Santa** (Holy Steps). A 16th-century building encloses the Holy Steps, which tradition holds to be the staircase from Pilate's palace in Jerusalem, brought to Rome by St. Helena, mother of the Emperor Constantine. Wood protects the 28 marble steps worn smooth by the knees of pilgrims through the centuries. There are two other staircases that you can ascend to see the **Sancta Sanctorum,** the private chapel of the popes. The chapel is richly decorated with well-preserved Cosmatesque mosaics and a famous portrait of Jesus, attributed to St. Luke. ⊠ *Piazza San Giovanni in Laterano,* ☎ *06/70494489.* ⊙ *Apr.–Oct., daily 6:15–12:15 and 3:30–7; Nov.–Mar., daily 3:30–6.*

THE QUIRINALE TO PIAZZA DELLA REPUBBLICA

The area east of Old Rome and northeast of the Roman Forum owes its broad streets and dignified palazzi to the city's transformation after 1870, when it became the capital of a newly unified Italy. The influx of ministries and new businesses set off a frenzied building boom and a rush to modernize the city's infrastructure. Vast tracts of gardens and vineyards, once part of the parks of patrician villas, were divided and developed, particularly in the area around Via Veneto and the Quirinale. Distinguished turn-of-the-20th-century architecture became the neighborhood's hallmark. Broad avenues were laid out and given the patriotic names of Via Nazionale and Via XX Settembre (September 20, 1870, was the date when Italian troops breached Porta Pia to claim Rome as the kingdom's new capital). A new railroad station was built where Pope Pius IX had established a terminal for the various rail lines entering Rome. Its name, Stazione Termini, was chosen because of the nearby Roman-era baths (*terme* in Italian). Piazza della Repubblica was laid out to serve as a monumental foyer between the station and the rest of the city. After World War II the old Termini Station was replaced with a then-daring modern structure, and the huge Piazza dei Cinquecento was laid out in front of it.

After its 1950s and early '60s heyday as the focus of dolce vita excitement, Via Veneto declined into dullness as the "in" crowd headed elsewhere. Though the area immediately adjacent to Termini station slid more dramatically downhill, current urban renewal projects and increased policing are pulling it up again. Basically unchanging, the Quirinale and Via Veneto neighborhoods have preserved their solid, bourgeois palaces and enormous ministries. And Via Veneto keeps trying to woo back the mainstream of Roman sidewalk café society from the lively scenes at Piazza del Pantheon and Piazza Navona—as yet to no avail.

Numbers in the text and margin correspond to points of interest on the Quirinale to Piazza della Repubblica map.

A Good Walk

The Quirinal Hill has some of the key Baroque buildings of Rome, notably the two churches of Sant'Andrea al Quirinale and San Carlo alle Quattro Fontane. On the hill's lower slopes is the imposing Palazzo Barberini. Begin your walk at **Piazza del Quirinale** ①. The square marks the summit of the Quirinal Hill, highest of the seven hills of Rome. The front of the largest palace on the plaza, **Palazzo del Quirinale** ② (easily identified by the sentinels at the portal), is quite plain, though it houses the president of Italy. Make a brief detour onto Via XXIV Maggio, which links Piazza del Quirinale with Via Nazionale. On the right, a double ramp of stairs and an ornate stone portal mark the entrance to the gardens of Villa Colonna (closed to the public), domain of the Colonna family, whose palazzo is at the foot of the hill, on Piazza Santi Apostoli. Opposite, on the east side of Via XXIV Maggio, **Palazzo Pallavicini Rospigliosi** ③ belongs to another of Rome's aristocratic clans.

Take Via del Quirinale, on the right of the presidential palace. The featureless, 1,188-ft-long wing of the palace on the left side of the street hides the Quirinale gardens (open to the public on June 2 only). On the right is Bernini's favorite architectural creation, the church of **Sant'Andrea al Quirinale** ④. Borromini's perfectly proportioned church of **San Carlo alle Quattro Fontane** ⑤ stands at the end of Via del Quirinale, at the **Quattro Fontane** ⑥ intersection.

Turn northwest, or left, onto Via Quattro Fontane, where the **Galleria Nazionale d'Arte Antica** ⑦, housed in the Palazzo Barberini, stands about halfway down the hill. The grandest of 17th-century Rome's stately palaces, it was decorated with illusionist frescoes by Pietro da Cortona. Downhill from the palace (turn right when you leave) you'll come upon **Piazza Barberini** ⑧, a handy starting point for exploring the 19th-century Ludovisi district and Via Veneto. On the east corner of Via Veneto, the tree-lined, uphill avenue at the north end of the piazza, is the

Fontana delle Api ⑨, attributed in part to Bernini. Walk uphill into the sedate lower reaches of Via Veneto. At the church of **Santa Maria della Concezione** ⑩, thousands of bones are on morbidly artistic display, a reminder of the impermanence of earthly life. The broad avenue curves up the hill past travel agencies and hotels, with a sidewalk café or two where the only clients seem to be tired tourists and bank employees. At the intersection with Via Bissolati, the pace picks up. The big white palace on the right is **Palazzo Margherita** ⑪, built in 1890 as the residence of Italy's Queen Margherita. It's now the U.S. Embassy.

Turn right and follow Via Bissolati to the end and cross Largo Santa Susanna to the intersection with Via XX Settembre. On Piazza San Bernardo, the Baroque church of **Santa Susanna** ⑫ is Rome's American Catholic church. On the northeast corner of Via XX Settembre, the **Fontanone dell'Acqua Felice** ⑬ features smugly spouting lions. On the northwest corner, the church of **Santa Maria della Vittoria** ⑭ harbors Bernini's surprisingly earthy interpretation of a mystical vision. At this point you can elect to make a detour to the early Christian churches of Sant'Agnese and Santa Costanza, 3 km (2 mi) northeast of here, beyond the old city walls. You can either walk—head straight up Via XX Settembre, past **Porta Pia** ⑮—or take a taxi or the bus: bus 60 stops on the southwest side of Largo Santa Susanna. As you walk or ride northeast along Via Nomentana, you pass through some of Rome's older residential suburbs and **Villa Torlonia** ⑯, a public park, on the right; inside the park is the Casina delle Civette, decorated with art nouveau stained glass.

Return to Piazza della Repubblica (bus 60 stops near the church of Santa Maria della Vittoria) by way of Via Vittorio Emanuele Orlando, passing the historic Grand Hotel and the **Aula Ottagona** ⑰, on the corner of Via Parigi. In **Piazza della Repubblica** ⑱, two neoclassical exedrae (hemicycles) stand over similar, ancient exedrae that were part of the Baths of Diocletian. A simple cross high on stark brick walls identifies the church of **Santa Maria degli Angeli** ⑲, once the great hall of the Roman baths. You can see how parts of the ancient bath complex were adapted to serve as a monastery as you visit the halls and cloister of the **Terme di Diocleziano** ⑳, a section of the Museo Nazionale Romano. Off the southeast end of Piazza della Repubblica, Via delle Terme di Diocleziano leads to **Palazzo Massimo alle Terme** ㉑, where you'll see more of the antiquities that make up the Museo Nazionale Romano's collections.

TIMING

This is a long walk, involving some major museums and a lengthy detour to the church of Sant'Agnese. If the length of your stay in Rome permits, break it up into two shorter walks. The walk from Piazza del Quirinale to Piazza della Repubblica, not counting the detour to Sant'-Agnese, takes about 90 minutes, plus 10–15 minutes for every church visited, and at least 90 minutes each for visits to the Galleria Nazionale d'Arte Antica in Palazzo Barberini and the section of the Museo Nazionale Romano in Palazzo Massimo alle Terme.

Sights to See

⑰ **Aula Ottagona** (Octagon Hall). Once part of the Terme di Diocleziano, this octagonal hall had a twin on what is now the middle of Viale Einaudi, the street leading toward Termini Station. The hall was once used as a planetarium and now serves as a display space for several well-preserved Roman-era bronze sculptures. ⊠ *Via Romita (Piazza della Repubblica)*, ☎ 06/39967700, WEB *www.archeorm.arti.beniculturali. it/sar2000/diocleziano/default.htm.* ☞ *Free.* ☉ *Daily 10–7.*

The Quirinale to Piazza della Repubblica

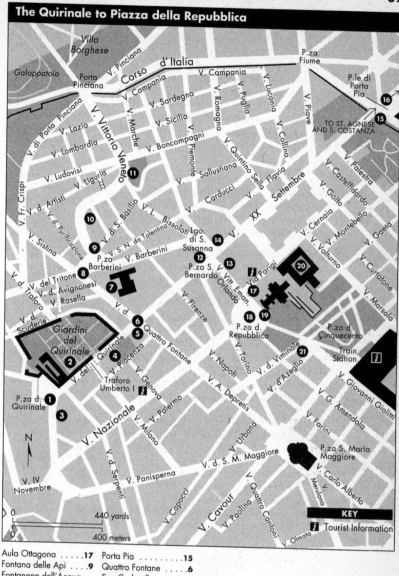

9 **Fontana delle Api** (Fountain of the Bees). The upper shell and the inscription are from a fountain that Bernini designed for Urban VIII; the rest was lost when the fountain had to be moved to make way for a new street. This inscription was the cause of a considerable scandal when the fountain was first put up in 1644. It stated that the fountain had been erected in the 22nd year of the pontiff's reign, while in fact the 21st anniversary of Urban's election to the papacy was still some weeks away. The last numeral was hurriedly erased, but to no avail— Urban died eight days before the beginning of his 22nd year as pope. The superstitious Romans, who had immediately recognized the inscription as a foolhardy tempting of fate, were vindicated. ⊠ *Via Vittorio Veneto at Piazza Barberini.*

NEED A
BREAK?   Along Via degli Avignonesi and Via Rasella (both narrow streets off Via delle Quattro Fontane, opposite Palazzo Barberini) there are some good, moderately priced trattorias. One of the most popular with Romans is **Gioia Mia** (⊠ Via degli Avignonesi 34, ☎ 06/4882784); it's closed Wednesday.

13 **Fontanone dell'Acqua Felice** (Acqua Felice Fountain). When Pope Sixtus V completed the restoration of the Acqua Felice aqueduct toward the end of the 16th century, Domenico Fontana was commissioned to design this commemorative fountain. As the story goes, a sculptor named Prospero da Brescia had the unhappy task of executing the central figure, which was to represent Moses (Sixtus liked to think of himself as, like Moses, having provided water for his thirsting population). The comparison with Michelangelo's magnificent *Moses* in the church of San Pietro in Vincoli was inevitable, and the largely disparaging criticism of Prospero's work is said to have driven him to his grave. Perhaps the most charming aspects of the fountain are the smug little lions spewing water in the foreground. ⊠ *Piazza San Bernardo.*

7 **Galleria Nazionale d'Arte Antica** (National Gallery of Art of Antiquity). The city's finest collection of paintings from the 13th to the 18th century is installed in Palazzo Barberini. Both Bernini and Borromini worked on this massive building, but the overall plan of Rome's most splendid 17th-century palace was produced by Carlo Maderno. Pope Urban VIII had acquired the property and given it to a nephew, who was determined to build an edifice worthy of his generous uncle and the ever-more-powerful Barberini clan. You'll get an idea of the grandeur of the place as you visit the museum.

Entering the palace, you climb a broad marble staircase designed by Bernini. On the main floor (keep your ticket handy, as you'll have to show it again upstairs) you'll find several magnificent paintings, including Raphael's *Fornarina*, a luminous portrait of the artist's lover, cleaned and restored to reveal a jeweled ring and a bracelet on her upper arm bearing Raphael's name. A dramatic Caravaggio depicts a lovely young Judith regarding with some horror the neatly severed head of Holofernes. There's a Holbein portrait of Henry VIII in the finery he donned for his wedding to Anne of Cleves in 1540, and two small but striking El Grecos. The palace's large main salon is part of the gallery. It was decorated in the 1630s by Pietro da Cortona and is a spectacular and surprisingly early example of the Baroque practice of glorifying patrons by depicting them on the ceiling as part of the heavenly host. In this case, Pope Urban VIII appears as the agent of Divine Providence. Also prominent in this glowing vault are some huge Barberini bees, the heraldic symbol of the family. Upstairs you'll find an array of 17th- and 18th-century paintings, including some pretty little views of Rome by Vanvitelli, and four handsome Canalettos. Don't miss the stunning suite of rooms redecorated in 1728 for the marriage of a Barberini heiress to a scion of the Colonna family.

✉ *Via Barberini 18,* ☎ *06/4824184,* WEB *www.galleriaborghese.it.* 🎫 *€6.20.* ◷ *Tues.–Sat. 9–7:30, Sun. 9–1.*

② **Palazzo del Quirinale** (Quirinal Palace). Now official residence of the president of Italy, the palace was begun in 1574 by Pope Gregory XIII, who planned to use it as a summer residence, choosing the hilltop site mainly for the superb view. However, as early as 1592 Pope Clement VIII decided to make the palace the permanent home of the papacy, at a safe elevation above the malarial miasmas shrouding the low-lying Vatican. It remained the official papal residence until 1870, in the process undergoing a series of enlargements and alterations by a succession of architects. When Italian troops under Garibaldi stormed the city in 1870, making it the capital of the newly united Italy, the popes moved back to the Vatican and the Quirinale became the official residence of the kings of Italy. When the Italian people voted out the monarchy in 1946, the Quirinal Palace passed to the presidency of the Italian Republic.

You get a fair idea of the palace's splendor from the size of the building, especially the interminable flank of the palace on Via del Quirinale. Behind this wall are the palace gardens, which, like the gardens of Villa d'Este in Tivoli, were laid out by Cardinal Ippolito d'Este when he summered here. At 4 PM daily you can see the changing of the military guard, and occasionally you can glimpse the *corazzieri* (presidential guard). All extra-tall, they are a stirring sight in their magnificent crimson and blue uniforms, their knee-high boots glistening, and their embossed steel helmets adorned with flowing manes. ✉ *Piazza del Quirinale,* ☎ *06/ 46991,* WEB *www.quirinale.it.* 🎫 *€5.15.* ◷ *Sept.–July, Sun. 8:30–12:30.*

⑪ **Palazzo Margherita.** Built in 1890 as the residence of Italy's Queen Margherita, the white building is now the U.S. Embassy. American citizens on routine business (including replacing lost passports) are directed to the consulate building next door. The embassy and consulate are part of a carefully guarded complex that includes U.S. Information Service offices and the American Library. ✉ *Via Veneto 119,* ☎ *06/46741.*

㉑ **Palazzo Massimo alle Terme** (Museo Nazionale Romano). The enormous collections of the Roman National Museum—which range from stunning classical Roman sculptures and paintings to marble bric-a-brac and fragments picked up in excavations over the centuries—have been organized in four locations: Palazzo Massimo alle Terme, Palazzo Altemps, Aula Ottagona, and the Terme di Diocleziano. Palazzo Massimo alle Terme holds the archaeological collection and the coin collection, as well as decorative stuccos and wall paintings found in the area of the Villa della Farnesina (in Trastevere) and the frescoes from Empress Livia's villa at Prima Porta, delightful depictions of a garden in bloom and an orchard alive with birds. Their colors are remarkably well preserved. These delicate decorations covered the walls of cool, sunken rooms in Livia's summer house outside the city. ✉ *Largo Villa Peretti 2,* ☎ *06/48903501,* WEB *www.archeorm.arti.beniculturali.it/ sar2000/museo_romano/Pal_massimo.htm.* 🎫 *€6.20 (includes Museo delle Terme di Diocleziano).* ◷ *Tues.–Sun. 9–7:45.*

⑤ **Palazzo Pallavicini Rospigliosi.** A patrician palace built for Cardinal Scipione Borghese, this is now the residence of another of Rome's aristocratic families. In the large garden enclosed by the wings of the palace, a summer pavilion has a famous ceiling fresco of Aurora painted by 17th-century artist Guido Reni. Once a month, when the family admits visitors to see the fresco, you can get a peek at the garden. ✉ *Via XXIV Maggio 43,* ☎ *06/4744019.* 🎫 *Free.* ◷ *First day of month, 10–noon and 3–5.*

8 **Piazza Barberini.** One of Rome's more modern quarters, the district was built during the late-19th-century construction boom on the site of the lush gardens of Villa Ludovisi, a patrician family's estate that had in turn been built over the celebrated ancient Roman gardens of Sallust. The piazza, a picturesque marketplace during the 17th and 18th centuries, has lost its original charm in the rush of progress. Undistinguished modern buildings overshadow the older ones, and traffic circles the Bernini **Fontana del Tritone** (Triton Fountain). Bernini's Baroque centerpiece in Piazza Barberini was created in 1637 for Pope Urban VIII, whose Barberini coat of arms is at the base of the large shell. The fountain's triton blows into his conch shell with gusto, sending an arc of water into the air. In a city of beautiful fountains, this is one of the most vivacious. ⊠ *Junction of Via del Tritone, Via Veneto, Via Quattro Fontane, and Via Sistina.*

1 **Piazza del Quirinale.** This strategic location atop the Quirinal Hill has long been of great importance. It served as home of the Sabines in the 7th century BC; then deadly enemies of the Romans, who lived on the Capitoline and Palatine Hills (all of 1 km/½ mi away). Today it's the foreground for the presidential residence, Palazzo del Quirinale, and home to **Palazzo della Consulta**, where Italy's Constitutional Court sits. The open side of the piazza has an impressive vista of the rooftops and domes of central Rome and St. Peter's in the distance. The **Fontana di Montecavallo** (Montecavallo Fountain), or Fontana dei Dioscuri (Fountain of the Dioscuri), is composed of a huge Roman statuary group and an obelisk from the tomb of the Emperor Augustus. The group of the Dioscuri trying to tame two massive marble steeds was found in the Baths of Constantine, which occupied part of the summit of the Quirinal Hill. Unlike just about every other ancient statue in Rome, this group survived the Dark Ages intact and accordingly became one of the city's great sights, especially during the Middle Ages. Next to the figures, the ancient obelisk from the Mausoleo di Augusto (Tomb of Augustus) was put here by Pope Pius VI at the end of the 18th century. ⊠ *Junction of Via del Quirinale and Via XXIV Aprile.*

18 **Piazza della Repubblica.** This broad square was laid out in the late 1800s, and some suggested that the monument to Victor Emmanuel II be built here rather than in Piazza Venezia. The piazza owes its curved lines to the structures of the Terme di Diocleziano; the curving, colonnaded neoclassic buildings on the southwest side trace the underlying form of the ancient baths. The exuberant **Fontana delle Naiadi** (Fountain of the Naiads), the pièce de résistance of Piazza della Repubblica, is draped with voluptuous bronze ladies wrestling happily with marine monsters. The nudes weren't there when the pope unveiled the fountain in 1870, sparing him any embarrassment. But when the figures were added in 1901 they caused a scandal, for it's said that the sculptor, Rutelli, modeled them on the ample figures of two musical comedy stars of the day. ⊠ *Junction of Via Nazionale, Via Vittorio Emanuele Orlando, and Via delle Terme di Diocleziano.*

15 **Porta Pia.** Named for Pope Pius IV, this is one of the principal city gates in the Aurelian walls. The emperor Aurelianus ordered the walls built in the 3rd century, and they owe their survival for 16 centuries to the fact that the popes had to maintain them in good order to defend the city from invaders. Porta Pia is also Michelangelo's last piece of architecture, completed in 1564. Nearby, a monument marks the breach in the walls created by Italian troops when they stormed into Rome in 1870 to claim the city from the pope for the new Italian state. ⊠ *Northeast end of Via XX Settembre.*

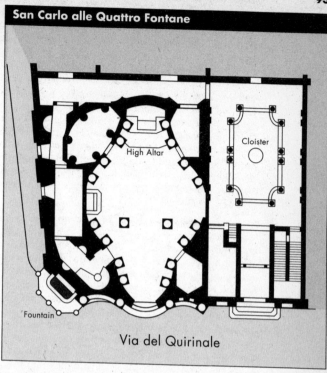

San Carlo alle Quattro Fontane

High Altar

Cloister

Fountain

Via del Quirinale

6 Quattro Fontane (Four Fountains). The intersection takes its name from its four Baroque fountains, representing the Tiber (on the San Carlo corner), the Nile, Juno, and Diana. The fumes from constant heavy traffic have managed to deface them to the point where they're unrecognizable. Despite the traffic, it's worthwhile to take in the views from this point in all four directions: to the southwest as far as the obelisk in Piazza del Quirinale; to the northeast along Via XX Settembre to the Porta Pia; to the northwest across Piazza Barberini to the obelisk of Trinità dei Monti; and to the southeast as far as the obelisk and apse of Santa Maria Maggiore. This extraordinary prospect is a highlight of Pope Sixtus V's campaign of urban beautification and a typical example of the Baroque influence on city planning. ⊠ *Junction of Via delle Quattro Fontane, Via Quirinale, and Via XX Settembre.*

★ **5 San Carlo alle Quattro Fontane.** San Carlo (sometimes identified by the diminutive San Carlino because of its tiny size) is one of Borromini's masterpieces. In a space no larger than the base of one of the piers of St. Peter's Basilica, he created a church that is an intricate exercise in geometric perfection, with a coffered dome that seems to float above the curves of the walls. Borromini's work is often bizarre, definitely intellectual, and intensely concerned with pure form. In San Carlo, he invented an original treatment of space that creates an effect of rippling movement, especially evident in the double-S curves of the facade. Characteristically, the interior decoration is subdued, in white stucco with no more than a few touches of gilding, so as not to distract from the form. Don't miss the **cloister**, a tiny, understated Baroque jewel, with a graceful portico and loggia above echoing the lines of the church. ⊠ *Via del Quirinale 23,* ☎ *06/4883261.* ☉ *Daily 9–noon and 3–7.*

19 Santa Maria degli Angeli. The curving brick facade on the northeast side of Piazza della Repubblica is one small remaining part of the colossal Terme di Diocleziano, erected about AD 300 and the largest and most impressive of the baths of ancient Rome. The baths extended over what is now Piazza della Repubblica and covered much of this entire area. In 1561, Michelangelo was commissioned to convert the vast *tepidarium*, the central hall of the baths, into a church. His work was altered by Vanvitelli in the 18th century, but the huge transept, which formed the nave in Michelangelo's plan, has remained as he adapted it. The eight enormous monolithic columns of red granite that support the great beams are the original columns of the tepidarium, 45 ft high and more than 5 ft in diameter. The great hall is 92 ft high. Though the interior of the church is small in comparison with the vast baths Diocletian built here, it gives a better impression of the remarkable grandeur of ancient Rome's most imposing public buildings than any other edifice in the city. ⊠ *Piazza della Repubblica,* ☎ *06/4880812.* ⊙ *Daily 7–7.*

🔟 **Santa Maria della Concezione.** In the crypt under the main Capuchin church, the bones of some 4,000 dead Capuchin monks are arranged in odd decorative designs around the shriveled and decayed skeletons of their kinsmen, a macabre reminder of the impermanence of earthly life. Signs declare, "What you are, we once were. What we are, you someday will be." Although not for the easily spooked, the crypt is touching and oddly beautiful. Upstairs in the church, the first chapel on the right contains Guido Reni's mid-17th-century *St. Michael Trampling the Devil.* The painting caused great scandal after an astute contemporary observer remarked that the face of the devil bore a surprising resemblance to the Pamphili Pope Innocent X, archenemy of Reni's Barberini patrons. Compare the devil with the bust of the pope that you saw in the Palazzo Doria Pamphilj and judge for yourself. ⊠ *Via Veneto 27,* ☎ *06/4871185.* ▨ *Modest donation expected.* ⊙ *Church daily 6:30–noon and 3–7, crypt daily 9–noon and 3–6.*

🔢 **Santa Maria della Vittoria.** Like the church of Santa Susanna across Piazza San Bernardo, this church was designed by Carlo Maderno, but it's best known for Bernini's sumptuous Baroque decoration of the **Cappella Cornaro** (Cornaro Chapel), on the left as you face the altar, and for his interpretation of heavenly ecstasy in the statue of St. Theresa. In this chapel, Bernini produced an extraordinary fusion of architecture, painting, and sculpture, with the *Ecstasy of St. Theresa* as the focal point of the chapel. Your eye is drawn effortlessly from the frescoes on the ceiling down to the marble figures of the angel and the swooning saint, to the earthly figures of the Cornaro family (which commissioned the chapel), to the two inlays of marble skeletons in the pavement, representing the hope and despair of souls in purgatory.

As evidenced in other works of the period, the theatricality of the chapel is the result of Bernini's masterly fusion of elements. This is one of the key examples of the mature Roman high Baroque. The members of the Cornaro family witnessing the scene are placed in what are, in effect, theater boxes, and they are turned to see the great moment of divine love being played out before them. The swooning saint's robes appear to be on fire, quivering with life, and the white marble group seems suspended in the heavens as golden rays illuminate the scene. An angel assists at the mystical moment of Theresa's vision as the saint abandons herself to the joys of divine love. Bernini represented this mystical experience in what, to modern eyes, may seem very earthly terms. No matter what your reaction, you'll have to admit it's great theater. ⊠ *Via XX Settembre 17 (Largo Santa Susanna),* ☎ *06/4826195.* ⊙ *Mon.–Sat. 8:30–11 and 3:30–6, Sun. 3:30–6.*

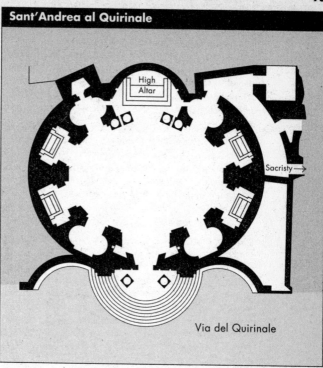

Sant'Andrea al Quirinale

High Altar

Sacristy →

Via del Quirinale

OFF THE
BEATEN PATH

MAUSOLEO DI COSTANZA and **SANT'AGNESE** – The histories of these early Christian sites are intertwined. Sant'Agnese (St. Agnes) was martyred around AD 304, and her catacomb became an important prayer site for Rome's early Christians. After the conversion of Rome to Christianity under Constantine, the emperor's family built a church over the catacomb, and later an adjoining tomb (now used as a church) was erected for Constantine's daughter Constantia (Costanza) over the burial site of St. Agnes herself. St. Agnes's church is of interest for its antique columns, 7th-century mosaics, and murky catacombs underneath (entrance to the left of church, 🎫 €4.15). On January 21 each year, two flower-bedecked lambs are blessed before Agnes's altar (*agnes* means lamb). They are then carried to the pope, who blesses them again before they're sent to the nuns of St. Cecilia in Trastevere. The nuns use the lambs' wool to make the episcopal *pallia* kept in the casket in the niche of the *confessio* in St. Peter's Basilica.

Uphill from the catacomb, the mausoleum's main attraction are the 4th-century mosaics on the vault of the unusual circular nave, among the oldest and best preserved in Rome. The figures on either side of the entrance probably represent Constantia and her husband. Opposite the entrance is a copy of the original heavy porphyry sarcophagus that is in the Vatican Museums. Its carved decorations are an adaptation of pagan symbols to Christian use, as in the sheep and the peacock, whose flesh was held to be incorruptible. From Largo Santa Susanna, allow 40 minutes each way by bus, 20 minutes by taxi. ✉ *Via Nomentana 349,* ☎ *06/8610840. From Largo Santa Susanna, take bus 60 up Via Nomentana; get off immediately after Via Carlo Fea and follow signs.* ☉ *Mon. 9–noon, Tues.–Sat. 9–noon and 4–6, Sun. 4–6.*

❹ **Sant'Andrea al Quirinale.** This small but oddly imposing Baroque church was designed by Bernini. His son wrote that Bernini considered it one of his best works and that he used to come here occasionally just to sit and enjoy it. Bernini's simple oval plan, a classic of Baroque architecture, is given drama and movement by the church's decoration, which carry the story of St. Andrew's martyrdom and ascension into heaven, starting with the painting over the high altar, up past the figure of the saint over the chancel door, to the angels at the base of the lantern and the dove of the Holy Spirit that awaits on high. ⊠ *Via del Quirinale 29,* ☎ *06/48903187.* ⊙ *Wed.–Sun. 10–noon and 4–7.*

⑫ Santa Susanna. This is Rome's American Catholic church. The building's foundations incorporate parts of a Roman house where Susanna was martyred, but the frescoes, carved ceiling, and stucco decorations all date from the late 16th century. Maderno's 1603 facade masterfully heralded the beginning of the Baroque era in Roman architecture. To the left of the main door is the entrance to Santa Susanna's English-language lending library. ⊠ *Via XX Settembre 14,* ☎ *06/42013734.* ⊙ *Daily 7–noon and 4–6*

⑳ Terme di Diocleziano (Baths of Diocletian). Though part of the ancient structure is now the church of Santa Maria degli Angeli, and other parts were transformed into a Carthusian monastery or razed to make room for later urban development, a visit gives you an idea of the scale and grandeur of this ancient bathing establishment. The monastery cloister is strewn with classical serendipity, the lapidary collection of the Museo Nazionale Romano. The baths were closed for restoration at press time with no definite date for reopening. ⊠ *Viale E. De Nicola 79,* ☎ *06/39967700.* ⊠ *€6.20.* ⊙ *Tues.–Sun. 9–7:45.*

⑯ Villa Torlonia. Mussolini's residence as prime minister under Italy's king is now a public park. Long neglected, the park's vegetation and edifices are gradually being refurbished. The first of the buildings to be fully restored is now open to the public as a charming example of the art nouveau style of the early 1900s. In a gabled, fairy-tale-like cottage, the **Museo della Casina delle Civette** (Museum of the Little House of Owls) displays majolica and stained-glass decorations, including windows with owl motifs. ⊠ *Villa Torlonia, Via Nomentana 70,* ☎ *06/ 44250072.* ⊠ *Museum €2.50, free last Sun. of the month.* ⊙ *Villa daily 8–dusk. Museum Oct.–Mar., Tues.–Sun. 9–5; Apr.–Sept., Tues.– Sun. 9–7.*

VILLA BORGHESE TO THE ARA PACIS

Touring Rome's artistic masterpieces while staying clear of its hustle and bustle can be, quite literally, a walk in the park. Some of the city's finest sights are tucked away in or next to green lawns and pedestrian piazzas, offering a breath of fresh air for weary sightseers. As you make your way toward the Tiber, you'll walk through the ages of Rome. In ancient times, the city's most lavish host, Lucullus, staged fabulous alfresco banquets in his terraced villa on the heights of the Pincian Hill. On the plain below, called the Campus Martius, by the banks of the Tiber, Augustus laid out a vast public garden, celebrating his own glory in his mausoleum and the Ara Pacis, and setting up an Egyptian obelisk that served as pointer in a huge sundial. Villa Borghese itself, the 17th-century pleasure gardens created by Cardinal Scipione Borghese, holds several treasures, none so precious as the Galleria Borghese, one of the finest and most beautiful museums in the city.

On the other side of the park are Villa Giulia, a late-Renaissance papal summerhouse now containing a stunning collection of Etruscan art, and the Museo Nazionale d'Arte Moderna, with intriguingly varied collections of modern art in a vast neoclassical palace that has a fashionable terrace café. These are the three major museums in the area, but the past is also palpably preserved in the triangle that has its apex at Piazza del Popolo and extends to the Mausoleum of Augustus and the Spanish Steps. Here 17th-century buildings and churches are interspersed with art and antiques galleries and a plethora of boutiques. Together with the Via Condotti shopping area, this constitutes Rome's most vibrant shopping district.

Numbers in the text and margin correspond to points of interest on the Villa Borghese to the Ara Pacis map.

A Good Walk

If you're staying on Via Veneto, this walk begins at your front door. Start if you want with a cappuccino in one of this famous street's famous cafés. Via Veneto snakes upward from Piazza Barberini to the Porta Pinciana through the Ludovisi neighborhood, known for palatial hotels and stately residences that transformed patrician estates into commercial real estate in the 1880s. In the upper reaches of Via Veneto, near the flower vendors and big newsstands at the corner of Via Ludovisi, is the Café de Paris, erstwhile hub of la dolce vita.

Past the big cafés, Via Veneto continues in a succession of more newsstands, boutiques, expensive shops, and a snack bar or two. If you intend to picnic in the Villa Borghese park (the entrance is at the top of the street), this is your chance to pick up some supplies, whether ready-to-go from the snack bars or do-it-yourself from the *alimentari* (grocery stores) on the side streets. (There are some expensive mobile snack carts in the park and a café in the Galleria Borghese.)

Porta Pinciana ① is one of the historic city gates in the Aurelian walls, built by Emperor Aurelianus late in the 3rd century AD to protect Rome. Take care crossing the thoroughfares on either side of the gate: the traffic here comes hurtling in from all directions. Inside **Villa Borghese** ② park, first look to the left, across the Galoppatoio (riding ring). The handsome 16th-century palace that you can see across the lawns is **Villa Medici** ③, since 1804 the seat of the French Academy, where many great French artists—from Ingres and David to Balthus—found inspiration. Head north on Viale del Museo Borghese to reach the Casino Borghese, which houses the **Galleria Borghese** ④. Once you've torn yourself away from Cardinal Scipione's collections, you can enjoy the vast park to your heart's content. On the right, as you leave the casino, you can continue along Viale dell'Uccelliera to Rome's once-forlorn zoo, recently transformed into a "biopark." Alternatively, turn left, or south, onto Viale dei Pupazzi and head toward Piazza dei Cavalli Marini, with its sea-horse fountain. Continue straight ahead on Viale dei Pupazzi or turn right: either way you'll come upon the **Piazza di Siena** ⑤, a grassy hippodrome shaded by tall pines. At the northwest end of Piazza di Siena, turn left onto Viale Canonica and you'll come to the entrance of the delightful Giardino del Lago (Lake Garden).

If you want to take in one or both of the other museums on this walk, head northwest from the Giardino del Lago to Piazzale Paolina Borghese, at the head of a broad, monumental staircase that descends to Viale della Belle Arti and the **Galleria Nazionale d'Arte Moderna** ⑥. About ¼ km (⅛ mi) northwest on Viale delle Belle Arti is the **Museo Etrusco di Villa Giulia** ⑦. The entrance is at the far end of the building, on Piazza di Villa Giulia. Returning to the staircase, climb it to enter Villa Borghese again. Follow Via Bernadotte to Piazza del Fiocco and turn left onto Viale La Guardia, named for the celebrated New York mayor.

At circular Piazza delle Canestre head west on Viale delle Magnolie. A bridge over heavily trafficked Viale del Muro Torto leads to the **Pin-**

cio ⑧ gardens. After admiring its layout from the Pincio terrace, which offers one of Rome's finest panoramas, descend the ramps and stairs to **Piazza del Popolo** ⑨ and **Porta del Popolo** ⑩. Stop in at the church of **Santa Maria del Popolo** ⑪ to see the art treasures inside, including two paintings by Caravaggio. The churches of **Santa Maria in Montesanto** ⑫ and **Santa Maria dei Miracoli** ⑬ were part of a grand project carried out in the 1500s under several popes that urbanized this triangular area, previously uninhabited. Take Via di Ripetta, the most westerly of the three streets fanning out from Piazza del Popolo. On the left you pass the San Giacomo Hospital, and on the right is the horseshoe-shape, neoclassical building of the Academy of Fine Arts, usually covered with not-so-fine-art student graffiti. The **Ara Pacis** ⑭ and the **Mausoleo di Augusto** ⑮ are on huge Piazza Augusto Imperatore, renovated and redesigned by American architect Richard Meier.

TIMING

This is a fair-weather walk, much of it in Villa Borghese park. The walk alone takes about two hours, plus at least 90 minutes for a visit to the Galleria Borghese. Advance reservations are mandatory for your visit to the Galleria. In addition to the Galleria Borghese, the walk includes two other major museums. If you intend to do justice to all three, it is advisable to skip the two on Viale delle Belle Arti during this walk, saving them for another day (or days). Both the Museo Nazionale Etrusco di Villa Giulia and the Galleria Nazionale di Arte Moderna are easily accessible from Via Flaminia. They are about 1 km (½ mi) from Piazza del Popolo. The 19 tram stops in front of both museums, and the 225 tram that runs along Via Flaminia stops at Piazza delle Belle Arti, about ⅔ km (⅓ mi) from Villa Giulia's entrance. Allow about an hour each for visits to the Museo Nazionale Etrusco di Villa Giulia and the Galleria Nazionale di Arte Moderna.

Sights to See

⑭ **Ara Pacis** (Altar of Augustan Peace). A simple classical altar, the Ara Pacis is noteworthy for the beautifully sculptured marble enclosure that surrounds it. The altar was erected in 13 BC by order of the Senate to celebrate the epoch of peace heralded by Augustus's victories in Gaul and Spain. It was painstakingly reassembled and reconstructed here in 1938 after scholars spent years hunting for the dispersed fragments, some of them as far away as the Louvre. The marble altar enclosure bears magnificent reliefs. Most notable is *Aeneas's Sacrifice,* on the right of the main entrance, and the procession of historical figures, among them members of Augustus's family, on the sides. Famed American architect Richard Meier has been charged with designing a new museum around this monument; reopening is scheduled for early 2003. ⊠ *Via Ripetta,* ☎ *06/68806848,* WEB *www.comune.roma.it/cultura/italiano/ musei_spazi_espositivi/musei/museo_ara_pacis/index.htm.* ▣ *€1.95. Closed for restoration.*

★ ④ **Galleria Borghese** (Borghese Gallery). The Casino Borghese, as the building is known, was erected (from 1613) partly to house Cardinal Scipione Borghese's rich collections of painting and sculpture, partly to provide an elegant venue for summer parties and musical evenings. It was never intended to be, nor was it ever, lived in. Now the building is less celebrated than the collections housed inside—including one of the finest collections of Baroque sculpture anywhere.

Like the gardens, the casino and its collections have undergone many changes since the 17th century. Camillo Borghese, the husband of Napoléon's sister Pauline, was responsible for most of them. He sold off a substantial number of the paintings to Napoléon and swapped 200 of the classical sculptures for an estate in Piedmont, in northern

Villa Borghese to the Ara Pacis

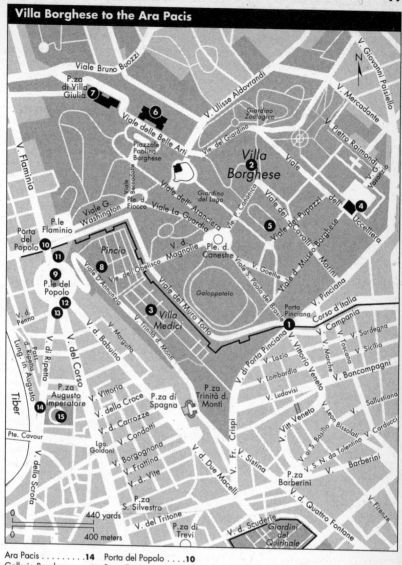

Italy, also courtesy of Napoléon. These paintings and sculptures are all still in the Louvre in Paris. At the end of the 19th century a later member of the family, Francesco Borghese, replaced some of the gaps in the collections and also transferred to the casino the remaining works of art housed in Palazzo Borghese. In 1902 the casino, its contents, and the park were sold to the Italian government.

The most famous work in the collection is Canova's sculpture of Pauline Borghese. It's technically known as *Venus Vincitrix,* but there has never been any doubt as to its real subject. Pauline reclines on a Roman sofa, bare-bosomed, her hips swathed in classical drapery, the very model of haughty detachment and sly come-hither. Surprisingly, Camillo Borghese seems to have been remarkably unconcerned that his wife had posed for this erotic masterpiece. Pauline, on the other hand, is known to have been shocked that her husband took such evident pleasure in showing off the work to guests. This coyness seems all the more curious given the reply Pauline is supposed to have made to a lady who asked her how she could have posed for the sculpture: "Oh, but the studio was heated." Much to the dismay of Canova, following Camillo and Pauline's divorce, the statue was locked away for many years, though the artist was occasionally allowed to show it to a handpicked few. This he would do at night by the light of a single candle.

The next two rooms hold two key early Baroque sculptures: Bernini's *David* and *Apollo and Daphne.* Both illustrate the extraordinary technical facility of Bernini. As important, both also demonstrate the Baroque desire to invest sculpture with a living quality, to transform inert marble into living flesh. Where Renaissance sculptors wanted to capture the idealized beauty of the human form that they had discovered in ancient Greek and Roman sculptures, Baroque sculptors such as Bernini wanted movement and drama as well, capturing not an essence but an instant, infused with theatricality and emotion. The *Apollo and Daphne* shows the moment when, to escape the pursuing Apollo, Daphne is turned into a laurel tree. Leaves and twigs sprout from her fingertips as she stretches agonizingly away from Apollo, who instinctively recoils in terror and amazement. This is the stuff that makes the Baroque exciting. There are more Berninis to see in the collection, notably a very uncharacteristic work, a large unfinished figure called *Verità,* or Truth. Bernini had started work on this brooding figure after the death of his principal patron, Pope Urban VIII. His successor as pope, Innocent X, had little love for the ebullient Urban, and, as was the way in Rome, this meant that Bernini, too, was excluded from the new pope's favors. Bernini's towering genius was such, however, as to gain him the patronage of the new pope with almost indecent haste. The *Verità* was accordingly left incomplete.

The Caravaggio Room holds works by this hotheaded genius who died of malaria at age 37. The disquieting *Sick Bacchus* and charming *Boy with a Basket of Fruit* are naturalistic early works, bright and fresh compared with a dark *Madonna* and the *David and Goliath,* in which Goliath is believed to be a self-portrait of the artist.

In the Pinacoteca (Picture Gallery) on the first floor of the casino, three Raphaels, a Botticelli, and a Pinturicchio are only a few of the paintings that the cardinal chose for his collection, which includes an incisive Cranach *Venus* and a shadowy Del Sarto *Madonna.* Probably the most famous painting in the gallery is Titian's allegorical *Sacred and Profane Love,* with a nude figure representing sacred love. ⊠ *Piazza Scipione Borghese 5, off Via Pinciana,* ☎ *06/8548577 for information; 06/328102 for reservations (press 2 for English),* WEB *www.galleriaborghese.it.*

✉ €6.20, plus €1.05 reservation fee. ☉ Winter, Tues.–Sun. 9–7; summer, Tues.–Fri. 9–9, Sat. 9–midnight, Sun. 9–8; reservations required.

6 Galleria Nazionale d'Arte Moderna (National Gallery of Modern Art). This massive white beaux arts building looks anything but modern, yet it contains one of Italy's leading collections of 19th- and 20th-century works. It's primarily dedicated to the history of Italian modernism, examining the movement's development over the last two centuries, but crowd-pleasers Degas, Monet, Courbet, van Gogh, and Cézanne put in appearances. A recent addition is an outstanding Dadaist collection. ✉ Via delle Belle Arti 131, ☎ 06/322981. ✉ €6.20. ☉ Tues.–Sun. 8:30–7:30; later in summer.

NEED A BREAK?
> The **Caffè delle Arti** (✉ Via Gramsci 73, ☎ 06/32298223), attached to the Galleria d'Arte Moderna, has a pretty terrace and is a favorite all-day rendezvous for Romans and visitors to Villa Borghese park and its museums. This is the place to break up your walk with a gelato or lunch.

15 Mausoleo di Augusto (Mausoleum of Augustus). The Etruscan inspiration is evident in this mausoleum built by Augustus for himself and his family; it is similar to the marble-girded tumulus tombs at Cerveteri. Inside, a series of concentric corridors leads to the central crypt, where the funerary urns were kept. But the tomb itself has had a checkered past. Like the emperor Hadrian's tomb across the Tiber, it was transformed into a fortress during the Middle Ages. At various times it was plundered for building material, planted with a vineyard, used as a hanging garden, and employed as an arena for such rousing public spectacles as bullfights and fireworks displays. In the early 1900s the large crypt at its core served as a concert hall (and was acclaimed for its perfect acoustics). The mausoleum was restored to its original form in 1936 but is usually closed to the public; phone for information about guided tours. ✉ Piazza Augusto Imperatore, ☎ 06/67103819.

7 Museo Etrusco di Villa Giulia (Etruscan Museum of Villa Giulia). Even if you know nothing of the Etruscans, an ancient people who preceded the Romans and taught them a thing or two about refined living, visit this 16th-century villa to see just how gracious the Renaissance lifestyle could be. The world's outstanding collection of Etruscan art and artifacts is housed in Villa Giulia, built around 1551 for Pope Julius III (hence its name). Among the team called in to plan and construct the villa were Michelangelo and his fellow Florentine Vasari. Most of the actual work, however, was done by Vignola and Ammanati. Though large enough to put up a sizable party of guests, the villa was never intended to be lived in, at least not by the pope. He came here for a day's distraction from the cares and intrigues of the Vatican, arriving by boat up the Tiber. The villa's nymphaeum—or sunken sculpture garden—is a superb example of a refined late-Renaissance setting for princely pleasures. The building was set in a park planted with some 36,000 trees.

Today, the Villa Giulia houses one of the world's most important and extensive collections of Etruscan art. Most of the exhibits come from sites in Etruria, the area north of Rome between the Tiber and the Arno that was once the Etruscan heartland. However, you'll also see fascinating objects from other parts of central Italy that were dominated by the Etruscans before the rise of Rome.

No one knows precisely where the Etruscans originated. Many scholars maintain that they came from Asia Minor, appearing in Italy about

1000 BC. Like the Egyptians, they buried their dead with everything that might be needed in the afterlife and painted their tombs with happy scenes of everyday activities. Thus, in death they have provided the present day with precious information about their life. There are countless artistic treasures in the Villa Giulia, and you'll find that even the tiniest gold earrings and brooches and the humblest bronze household implements display marvelous workmanship and inventiveness. Among the most striking pieces are the terra-cotta statues. Some, such as the *Apollo of Veio*, still retain traces of their original multicolor decoration; others, such as the serenely beautiful *Sarcophagus of the Sposi*, are worn to a warm, glowing golden patina. There are rooms full of vases (most of them Greek); it's thought the Etruscans prided themselves on their refined taste for these handsome objects. In the garden in back of the museum building, a reconstruction of an Etruscan temple shows how this people used color in architecture, a model that was also followed in ancient Rome. ⊠ *Piazzale di Villa Giulia 9,* ☎ *06/3226571.* ⊠ *€4.15.* ⏱ *Tues.–Sat. 9–7; Sun. 9–2.*

❾ Piazza del Popolo. Decorative and immense, this square, with its obelisk and twin churches, is a Rome landmark. It owes its present appearance to architect Giuseppe Valadier, who designed it about 1820, also laying out the terraced approach to the Pincio and the Pincio's gardens. It marks what was for centuries the northern entrance to the city, where all roads from the north converge and where visitors, many of them pilgrims, would get their first impression of the Eternal City. The desire to make this entrance to Rome something special had been a pet project of popes and their architects over three centuries. The piazza takes its name from the 15th-century church of Santa Maria del Popolo, huddled on the right side of the Porta del Popolo, or city gate. In the late 17th century, the twin churches of Santa Maria in Montesanto (on the left as you face them) and Santa Maria dei Miracoli (on the right) were added to the piazza at the point where Via del Babuino, Via del Corso, and Via di Ripetta converge. The piazza has always served as a meeting place, crowded with fashionable carriages and carnival revelers in the past. In 1999 it was made a pedestrian zone and serves as a magnet for youngsters on flashy scooters and their elders at café tables. At election time, it's the scene of huge political rallies, and on New Year's Eve Rome stages a mammoth alfresco party in the piazza. ⊠ *Junction of Via del Babuino, Via del Corso, and Via di Ripetta.*

NEED A BREAK? A café that has never gone out of style, **Rosati** (⊠ Piazza del Popolo 5, ☎ 06/3225859) is a rendezvous of literati, artists, and actors. There's a sidewalk café, a tearoom, and an upstairs dining room for a more upscale lunch. Off Piazza del Popolo on Via di Ripetta you'll find places where you can stop for sustenance. **Cose Fritte** (⊠ Via di Ripetta 3) specializes in rice croquettes, batter-fried vegetables, and other tasty snacks to take out. **PizzaRé** (⊠ Via di Ripetta 14, ☎ 06/3211468) offers a wide choice of toppings for pizza cooked in a wood-burning oven. **Buccone** (⊠ Via di Ripetta 19, ☎ 06/3612154) is a wineshop serving light snacks at lunchtime and wine by the glass all day long.

❺ Piazza di Siena. The piazza, actually an 18th-century replica of an ancient Roman amphitheater, was built for the Borghese family's games and named after the Tuscan city from which the family originated. In May, the arena hosts an international horse show. ⊠ *Viale Canonica at Via dei Pupazzi.*

❽ Pincio (Pincian Hill and gardens). The Pincio gardens occupy a corner of the Pincian Hill, one of the seven hills of ancient Rome, and they are separated from the southwest corner of Villa Borghese by a stretch of ancient walls. The view from the Pincio terrace is one of Rome's most celebrated, and the gardens are a favorite spot for strolling. Their rather formal, early 19th-century style contrasts with the far more elaborate terraced gardens of Lucullus that once adorned the site. Lucullus, the Roman gourmand, held lush banquets here that were legendary. Pathways are lined with white marble busts of Italian heroes and artists. Along with the similar busts on the Gianicolo, their noses have been victims of vandalism. Depending on the date of the last nose-knocking wave, you'll see the Pincio's busts forlornly noseless or in the throes of obvious plastic surgery.

From the balustraded Pincio terrace you can look down at Piazza del Popolo and beyond, surveying much of Rome. Across the Tiber, Via Cola di Rienzo goes through the Prati district toward the heights of Monte Mario. That low, brownish building on top of the hill is the Rome Hilton. Off to the left are Castel Sant'Angelo and the dome of St. Peter's Basilica. In the foreground is the curve of the Tiber, embracing Old Rome, where the low-slung dome of the Pantheon emerges from a sea of russet-tile rooftops and graceful cupolas. Southeast of the Pincio terrace is the **Casina Valadier,** a pretty neoclassic building perennially due for renovation and reopening as a restaurant. ✉ *Piazzale Napoleone I and Viale dell'Obelisco.*

❿ **Porta del Popolo** (City Gate). The medieval gate in the Aurelian walls was replaced in 1561 by the present one, which was further embellished by Bernini in 1655 for the much-heralded arrival of Queen Christina of Sweden, who had abdicated her throne to become a Roman Catholic. ✉ *Piazza del Popolo and Piazzale Flaminio.*

❶ **Porta Pinciana** (Pincian Gate). Framed by two squat, circular towers, the gate was constructed in the 6th century. Here you can see just how well the Aurelian walls have been preserved and imagine hordes of Visigoths trying to break through them. Sturdy as the walls look, they couldn't keep out the barbarians, and Rome was sacked three times during the 5th century alone. ✉ *Piazzale Basile, Via Veneto and Corso d'Italia.*

❸ **Santa Maria dei Miracoli.** A twin to the church of Santa Maria in Montesanto, this church was built in the 1670s by Carlo Fontana as an elegant frame for the entrance to Via del Corso from Piazza del Popolo. ✉ *Via del Corso 528 (Piazza del Popolo),* ☎ *06/3610250.* ☼ *Daily 6–1 and 4–7:30.*

★ ⓫ **Santa Maria del Popolo.** Standing inconspicuously in a corner of the vast piazza, this church often goes unnoticed, but the artistic treasures inside make it well worth a stop. Bramante enlarged the apse of the church, which had been rebuilt in the 15th century on the site of a much older place of worship. About 1513, the banker Agostino Chigi commissioned Raphael to build a chapel, known as the **Chigi Chapel** (the second on the left) after the donor, and in the mid-17th century another Chigi, Pope Alexander VII, commissioned Bernini to restore and decorate the building.

Inside, in the first chapel on the right, you'll see some frescoes by Pinturicchio; the adjacent **Cybo Chapel** is a 17th-century exercise in marble decoration. The organ case of Bernini in the right transept bears the Della Rovere family oak tree, part of the Chigi family's coat of arms. The **choir,** with vault frescoes by Pinturicchio, contains the handsome tombs of Ascanio Sforza and Girolamo delle Rovere, both designed by Andrea Sansovino. The **Cerasi Chapel,** to the left of the high altar on the side walls, has two stunning Caravaggios, both key early Baroque works. Compare their earthy realism and harshly dramatic lighting with the much more restrained and classically "pure" *Assumption of the Virgin* by Caravaggio's contemporary and rival, Annibale Carracci; it hangs over the altar of the chapel. Raphael provided the cartoons for the vault mosaic and the designs for the statues of Jonah and Elijah. More than a century later, Bernini added the oval medallions on the tombs and the statues of Daniel and Habakkuk. ⊠ *Piazza del Popolo 12, near Porta Pinciana,* ☎ *06/3610836.* ☉ *Daily 7–noon and 4–7.*

⑫ Santa Maria in Montesanto. Bernini supervised the construction of this church by his brilliant assistant, Carlo Fontana, and he may even have designed the saints' statues topping the facade. ⊠ *Via del Babuino 197 (Piazza del Popolo),* ☎ *06/3610594.*

❷ Villa Borghese. The word "villa" means suburban estate, of the type developed by the ancient Romans and adopted by Renaissance nobles. Villa Borghese is in fact a park that was originally part of the pleasure gardens laid out in the early 17th century by Cardinal Scipione Borghese, a worldly and cultivated cleric and nephew of Pope Paul V. Today's gardens bear little resemblance to the originals. Not only do they cover a much smaller area—by 1630, the perimeter wall was almost 5 km (3 mi) long—but they have also been almost entirely remodeled. This occurred at the end of the 18th century, when a Scottish painter, Jacob More, was employed to transform them into the style of the "cunningly natural" park so popular in 18th-century England. Hitherto, the park was probably the finest example of an Italian-style garden in the entire country.

In contrast to the formal and rigidly symmetrical gardens of 17th-century France—those at Versailles are the best example—these Italian gardens had no overall symmetrical plan. Rather, they consisted of a series of small, interlinked formal gardens attached by paths and divided by meticulously trimmed hedges. Flowers—the Romans were particularly fond of tulips—statues, ponds, and small enclosures for animals (the more exotic the better; lions and peacocks were favorites) were scattered artfully around. Here, the cardinal and his friends strolled and discussed poetry, music, painting, and philosophy. Today the area immediately in front of the casino and the sunken open-air "dining room," a small stone pavilion close to the low wall along the Via di Porta Pinciana side of the park, are all that remain from the cardinal's original grounds. Now the gardens are studded with neoclassical temples and statuary added to suit early 19th-century tastes.

In addition to the gloriously restored Galleria Borghese museum, the highlights of the park are Piazza di Siena, a graceful amphitheater; the botanical garden on Via Canonica, where there is a pretty little lake, a neoclassical faux–Temple of Aesculapius, and a café under the trees. The park has bike, in-line skating, and electric scooter rental concessions and a children's movie theater (showing films for adults in the evening). ⊠ *Main entrances at Porta Pinciana, the Pincio, Piazzale Flaminio (Piazza del Popolo), Viale delle Belle Arti, and Via Mercadante.*

❸ Villa Medici. Purchased by Napoléon and today the home of the French Academy, the Villa Medici, otherwise closed to the public, stages prestigious art exhibits and music festivals, advertised on posters around its gates. The gardens are occasionally open for guided tours on Sunday mornings; call the Academy directly or check with the tourist office for details. ⊠ *Viale Trinità dei Monti,* ☎ *06/69921653.*

TRASTEVERE AND THE JEWISH GHETTO

The two separate communities of this route are both staunchly resisting the tides of change. The old Ghetto, on the banks of the Tiber, is a neighborhood that has proudly retained its Jewish heritage. Right up to the end of the 19th century, this really was a ghetto, its dark buildings clinging to the sides of ancient ruins for support. Next to it is Tiberina Island, and beyond, Trastevere. Despite creeping gentrification, Trastevere remains about the most tightly knit community in Rome, its inhabitants proudly proclaiming descent—whether real or imagined—from the ancient Romans. As far back as the Roman Republic, Trastevere had a large foreign colony. Jews who came to Rome also settled here in the 2nd century BC. Raphael's model and mistress, the dark-eyed Fornarina (literally, "the baker's daughter"), is believed to have been a Trasteverina. The artist reportedly took time off from painting the Vatican Stanze and the *Galatea* in Villa Farnesina to romance—and perhaps marry—the winsome girl.

Literally translated, Trastevere means "across the Tiber"; the Trasteverini have always been proud and combative, a breed apart. In the Middle Ages, Trastevere wasn't considered part of Rome, and the "foreigners" who populated its maze of alleys and piazzas fought bitterly to obtain recognition for the neighborhood as a *rione,* or official district of the city. In the 14th century the Trasteverini won out and became full-fledged Romans. Since then, though, they have stoutly maintained their separate identity. They may be hard to find at first amid the gentrification, but the real Trasteverini are still here, hearty and uninhibited, and justly galled by the immense popularity of their neighborhood among the invading hordes. Trastevere is still romantic and evocative, with crumbling medieval buildings lining sunny piazzas and lines of laundry strung out over narrow, cobbled streets. Come nighttime, though, the trappings of trendiness are everywhere: countless boutiques, cafés, pizzerias, music clubs, and discos draw lively crowds, especially on weekends. For Romans and foreigners alike, Piazza Santa Maria in Trastevere is the center of the action, a sort of outdoor living room, open to all comers. The Gianicolo (Janiculum Hill) affords an overview of the neighborhood below and a marvelous vista of the entire city and the Castelli Romani.

Numbers in the text and margin correspond to points of interest on the Trastevere and the Jewish Ghetto map.

A Good Walk

Piazza Venezia is the starting point for touring the ancient ghetto quarter of the city. From the piazza, walk to the base of the Campidoglio, take Via del Teatro Marcello, and turn right across the street onto Via Montanara and enter Piazza Campitelli, with its Baroque church and fountain. Take Via dei Funari at the northwest end of the piazza and follow it into Piazza Mattei, where one of Rome's loveliest fountains, the 16th-century **Fontana delle Tartarughe** ①, is tucked away. A few steps down Via Caetani, off the north side of Piazza Mattei, you'll find a doorway into the public part of the old Palazzo Mattei, worth a peek for its sculpture-rich courtyard and staircase.

From Piazza Mattei go south on Via della Reginella onto Via Portico d'Ottavia, heart of the Jewish Ghetto. On the buildings, medieval inscriptions, ancient friezes, and half-buried classical columns attest to the venerable history of this area, a lively commercial quarter of old buildings and palaces. Visit at dusk in the summertime for the flavor of an old Roman neighborhood. Tables and chairs are set outside doorways as evening falls, and friends and neighbors gather to enjoy an alfresco card game or chat.

After the church of **Sant'Angelo in Pescheria** ②, set within the remaining columns of the Portico d'Ottavia, you come to the **Teatro di Marcello** ③ on the left side of Via Portico d'Ottavia and the **Sinagoga** ④ on the right. Cross Ponte Fabricio, built in 62 BC and the oldest bridge in the city, onto the **Isola Tiberina** ⑤; then cross Ponte Cestio and head into Trastevere.

Begin your exploration of Trastevere at **Piazza in Piscinula** ⑥ (you will need a detailed street map to make your way around this intricate maze of winding side streets). Explore the little streets and piazzas around the piazza. This was the site of Trastevere's port, Ripa Grande, the largest in Rome until it was destroyed early in the 20th century to make way for the modern embankments. Via del Porto gives you a fine view of the Aventine Hill across the Tiber. Piazza dei Mercanti is especially noted for its colorful, picturesque, if somewhat touristy, restaurants.

Take Via dell'Arco dei Tolomei, one of the city's most elegant byways, and cross Via dei Salumi, where the sausage makers stored their goods, onto tiny Vicolo dell'Atleta. It was in this minuscule alley, in 1849, that excavators discovered the statue *Apoxyomenos* (the athlete holding a *strigil*, or scraper) that is now in the Vatican Museums. Turn left onto Via dei Genovesi, then right into the piazza in front of the church of **Santa Cecilia in Trastevere** ⑦. Behind Santa Cecilia in Trastevere, on Via Anicia, the **Chiostro San Giovanni dei Genovesi** ⑧ is open on Tuesday and Thursday afternoons. Several blocks down Via Anicia at **San Francesco a Ripa** ⑨ is a famous Bernini sculpture. Go west on Via San Francesco a Ripa to Viale Trastevere. Take a detour east on Viale Trastevere to see the 13th-century mosaic pavements in the church of **San Crisogono** ⑩ on Piazza Sonnino. On the adjacent Piazza Belli the medieval Torre degli Anguillara (Anguillara Tower) is a typical fortified residence dating from the Middle Ages. Piazza Belli is named for the top-hatted 19th-century dialect poet whose bronze statue watches jauntily over the square.

Follow Via San Francesco a Ripa or Via della Lungaretta west to the very heart of Trastevere. Piazza San Cosimato hosts the neighborhood's busy outdoor marketplace on weekday mornings, but **Piazza Santa Maria in Trastevere** ⑪ is the place where the neighborhood is at its best, embellished with the glimmering mosaics on the church of **Santa Maria in Trastevere** ⑫ and with an octagonal fountain, as well as inviting cafés.

Via Fonte dell'Olio, on the north side of the piazza, leads to Piazza dei Renzi. Bear right onto Via della Pelliccia or Vicolo dei Renzi to Via del Moro and then proceed to Piazza Trilussa. Ponte Sisto links this part of Trastevere with Old Rome, across the Tiber. The bridge was built in the 15th century by Pope Sixtus IV to expedite commercial traffic in view of the upcoming Holy Year of 1475. On the north side of Piazza Trilussa stands a monument to the beloved, racy dialect poet Trilussa. Both Via Benedetta and Via S. Dorotea lead north to Porta Settimiana (from here Via della Lungara heads straight down toward the Vatican). At the end of Via Corsini, off Via della Lungara, is the **Orto Botanico** ⑬.

Walk north on Via della Lungara to visit **Villa Farnesina** ⑭, on the right, and, opposite, the section of the Galleria Nazionale d'Arte Antica that is housed in **Palazzo Corsini** ⑮. Return to Porta Settimiana, and turn right onto Via Garibaldi, which climbs to the Gianicolo. Continue up Via Garibaldi to the church of **San Pietro in Montorio** ⑯ to see Bramante's architectural gem, the Tempietto. Stairs provide shortcuts up and down the Gianicolo from various points in Trastevere; they save a lot of walking. As you continue your ascent of the Gianicolo, you come upon the huge **Fontana dell'Acqua Paola** ⑰, an early 17th-century creation with a vast pool that can be tempting on a hot day. The fountain is near the entrance to the park at the summit of the **Gianicolo** ⑱. Take in the views and then, if you're tired or pressed for time, ride the 870 bus north toward Corso Vittorio Emanuele, across the Tiber. You will pass a curious lighthouse, a gift of the Argentines in recognition of Garibaldi's efforts on behalf of their independence.

TIMING

This walk could take from four to five hours, but it is easily broken up into two parts—the Ghetto and Isola Tiberina, and Trastevere and the Gianicolo—the first taking about an hour, and the second three to four hours, allowing time for detours into Trastevere's interesting shops and eating places. If you time your visit to Santa Cecilia in Trastevere for Tuesday or Thursday morning between 10 and noon, you can see a famous fresco. If it is not a clear day, end your walk at San Pietro in Montorio; the vistas are the rewards for the effort of making your way to the top of the Gianicolo, so save this part of the walk for a day when visibility is good.

Sights to See

⑧ Chiostro San Giovanni dei Genovesi. You have to ring for the custodian, who will show you the 15th-century cloister of San Giovanni dei Genovesi, emanating the serene Renaissance architectural harmony usually found in Florence and rarely in Rome. In fact, it is attributed to Florentine architect Bacio Pontelli. ⊠ *Via Anicia 12,* ☎ *06/5812644.* 🎫 *Donation.* ☼ *May–Sept., Tues. and Thurs. 3–6; Oct.–Apr., Tues. and Thurs. 2–4.*

⑰ Fontana dell'Acqua Paola (Acqua Paola Fountain). With a facade inspired by ancient Rome's triumphal arches and worthy of an important church, this 17th-century fountain was commissioned by Pope Paul V to celebrate his renovation of Trajan's 1st-century AD aqueduct. This fountain has a namesake in the large but less imposing fountain that is the centerpiece in Piazza Trilussa, which was moved across the river from Via Giulia in 1898 when the Tiber's embankments were constructed. It, too, was built by Paul V. ⊠ *Via Garibaldi.*

❶ Fontana delle Tartarughe (Fountain of the Turtles). This 16th-century fountain is one of Rome's most charming, designed by Giacomo della Porta in 1581 and sculpted by Taddeo Landini. The focus of the fountain is four bronze boys, each grasping a dolphin that spouts water into marble shells. Bronze tortoises held in the boys' hands drink from the upper basin. The tortoises are thought to have been added in the 17th century by Bernini. ⊠ *Piazza Mattei.*

☾ ⑱ Gianicolo (Janiculum Hill). The Gianicolo is famous for splendid views of the city, a noontime cannon, statues of Giuseppe and Anita Garibaldi (Garibaldi was the guiding spirit behind the unification of Italy in the 19th century; Anita was his long-suffering wife), and, like on the Pincio, noseless and bedaubed busts. At the plaza here there's a daily, free **puppet show** (in Italian, ☼ daily 4–7, weekends 10:30–1). ⊠ *Via Garibaldi and Passeggiata del Gianicolo.*

❺ Isola Tiberina (Tiber Island). On the little island in the Tiber River is the hospital of **Fatebenefratelli** (literally, "Do good, brothers"); though a city hospital, it belongs to the Franciscan Order. It continues a tradition that began in 291 BC when a temple to Aesculapius, with annexed infirmary, was erected here. Aesculapius—Asclepius to the

Trastevere and the Jewish Ghetto

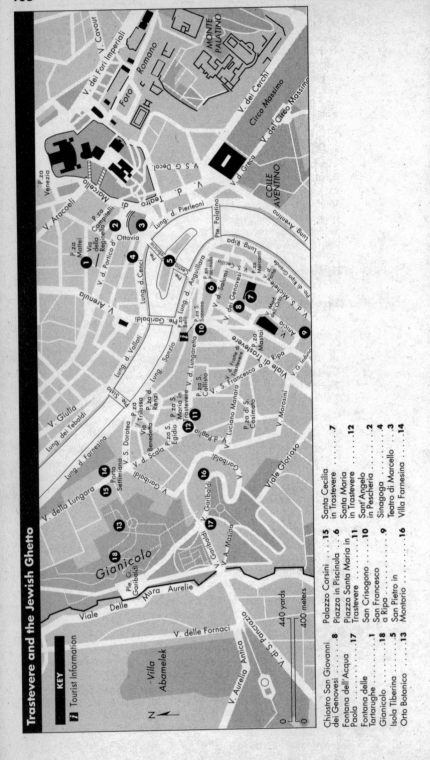

KEY

ℹ Tourist Information

Greeks—was the ancient god of healing and the son of the god Apollo. His symbol was the snake. The Romans adopted him as their god of healing in 293 BC during a terrible plague. A ship was sent to Epidaurus in Greece—heart of the cult of Aesculapius and a sort of Greek Lourdes—to obtain a statue of the god. As the ship sailed back up the Tiber, a great serpent was seen escaping from it and swimming to the island. This was taken as a sign that a temple to Aesculapius should be built here. Here the sick would come to bathe in the island's spring waters and to sleep in the temple, hoping that Aesculapius would visit them in their dreams to cure them. There's no trace of the temple now, but the island has been associated with medicine ever since—the present hospital was built on the site of a medieval hospital.

On the other end of the island is the church of **San Bartolomeo,** built at the end of the 10th century by the Holy Roman Emperor Otto III. Restorations and rebuilding down through the years have left precious little of Otto's original church. It's thought, however, that the small wellhead on the chancel steps—the steps leading to the choir—is original and that it stands on the site of the spring in the temple.

Seasonally, when the Tiber is in flood, the level of the river rises to within a few yards of the level of the piazza, and the island is half submerged. If the waters are low, descend the steps from the piazza and explore the embankment, where Romans like to stroll on fair days and take the sun while listening to the rushing waters of the rapids. The Romans built a wall around the entire island and sheathed it with marble to make the island look like a ship, with the prow pointed downstream. Look for the few remnants of the travertine facing, with a figure of Aesculapius, on the downstream end opposite the left bank. ⊠ *Ponte Fabricio, Lungotevere dei Pierleoni to Via Ponte Quattro Capi; Ponte Cestio, Lungotevere degli Anguillara to Piazza San Bartolomeo all'Isola.*

⑬ Orto Botanico (Botanical Garden). Behind Palazzo Corsini is an attractive oasis of greenery that was once part of the palace's extensive grounds. The garden is known for an impressive collection of orchids, ferns, and cacti. Don't miss the **scents garden for the blind,** with a variety of aromatic flowers and plants unusual to the touch. ⊠ *Largo Cristina di Svezia at the end of Via Corsini,* ☎ *06/6864193.* ▣ *€2.05.* ☉ *Mon.– Sat. 9–1 hr before sunset.*

⑮ Palazzo Corsini. A refined example of Baroque style, the palace houses part of the 16th- and 17th-century sections of the collection of the Galleria Nazionale d'Arte Antica. Among the most famous paintings in this large, dark collection is Guido Reni's *Beatrice Cenci.* Stop in, if only to climb the 17th-century stone staircase, itself a drama of architectural shadows and sculptural voids. ⊠ *Via della Lungara 10,* ☎ *06/68802323,* WEB *www.galleriaborghese.it.* ▣ *€4.15.* ☉ *Tues.–Sun. 8:30–7:30.*

❻ Piazza in Piscinula. The square takes its name from some ancient Roman baths on the site (*piscina* means *pool*). The tiny church of **San Benedetto** on the piazza is the smallest church in the city and, despite its 18th-century facade, is much older than it looks, probably dating back to the 4th century AD. Opposite is the medieval **Casa dei Mattei** (Mattei House). Rich and powerful, the Mattei family lived here until the 16th century, when, after a series of murders on the premises, they decided to move out of the district entirely, crossing the river to build their magnificent palace in the Ghetto. ⊠ *Via della Lungaretta, Piazza della Gensola, Via in Piscinula, and Via Lungarina.*

★ ⓫ **Piazza Santa Maria in Trastevere.** This piazza has seen the comings and goings of innumerable generations of tourists and travelers, intellectuals and artists, who all come to lounge on the steps of the fountain or sip an espresso at a table in the sun. Here the paths of Trastevere's residents intersect repeatedly during the day; they pause, gathering in clusters to talk animatedly in the broad accent of Rome or in a score of foreign languages. At night, this is the center of Trastevere's action, with street festivals, musicians, and gamboling dogs vying for attention from the throngs of people taking the evening air. ⊠ *Via della Lungaretta, Via della Paglia, and Via San Cosimato.*

⑩ **San Crisogono.** Eagles and dragons, symbols of the Borghese family, crown the portico of this pretty church, an early Christian basilica that was done over in the Middle Ages and again in the 17th century. The medieval bell tower can best be seen from the little piazza flanking the church or from the other side of Viale Trastevere. Inside the church are a fine mosaic pavement by the medieval craftsmen of the Cosmati family and an imposing coffered wood ceiling. You can ask the custodian to show you the excavations of the early Christian church beneath the present one. San Crisogono is the religious focus of a lively festival honoring Trastevere's patron, the Madonna of Noantri, with a procession on July 15. ⊠ *Piazza Sonnino 44,* ☎ *06/5818225.*

NEED A BREAK?   The specialty is in the name of the **Casa del Tramezzino** (House of Sandwiches; ⊠ Viale Trastevere 81, ☎ no phone) which offers a tantalizing variety of choices over the counter.

⑨ **San Francesco a Ripa.** This Baroque church attached to a 13th-century Franciscan monastery is noted for one of Bernini's last works, a dramatically lighted statue of Blessed Ludovica Albertoni. ⊠ *Piazza San Francesco d'Assisi 88,* ☎ *06/5819020.* ☉ *Daily 7–noon and 4–7.*

★ ⓰ **San Pietro in Montorio.** This church was built by order of Ferdinand and Isabella of Spain in 1481 over the spot where, tradition says, St. Peter was crucified. A handsome and dignified edifice, the church contains a number of well-known works, including the *Flagellation* in the first chapel on the right, painted by the Venetian Sebastiano del Piombo from a design by Michelangelo, and *St. Francis in Ecstasy,* in the next-to-last chapel on the left, in which Bernini made one of his earliest experiments with concealed lighting effects.

However, the most famous work here is the circular **Tempietto** (Little Temple) in the monastery cloister next door. This sober little building—though tiny, holding only 10 people, it is actually a church in its own right—is one of the key Renaissance buildings in Rome. It was designed by Bramante, the original architect of the new St. Peter's Basilica, in 1502 and represents one of the earliest and most successful attempts to reproduce an entirely classical building with the lessons of ancient Greek and Roman architecture fully evident. The basic design was derived from a circular temple on the grounds of the Emperor Hadrian's great villa at Tivoli outside Rome. ⊠ *Piazza San Pietro in Montorio 2 (Via Garibaldi); entrance to cloister and Tempietto at the portal next to the church,* ☎ *06/5813940.* ☉ *Daily 9–12:30 and 4–6 (ring bell for entry other times); Tempietto closed Mon.*

❼ **Santa Cecilia in Trastevere.** This church commemorates one of ancient Rome's most celebrated early Christian martyrs, the aristocratic St. Cecilia, put to death by the emperor Diocletian around the year AD 300. After an abortive attempt to suffocate her in the baths of her own house (a favorite means of quietly disposing of aristocrats in Roman days), she was brought before the executioner. But not even three blows of the executioner's sword could dispatch the young girl. She lingered for several days, converting others to the Christian cause, before finally dying. A striking white marble statue of the saint languishing in martyrdom lies below the main altar. If you time your visit to the church for Tuesday or Thursday morning between 10 and noon, you can enter the cloistered convent to see what remains of Pietro Cavallini's powerful and rich fresco *Last Judgment,* dating from 1293. It is the only major fresco in existence known to have been painted by Cavallini, a forerunner of Giotto. ⊠ *Piazza Santa Cecilia in Trastevere 22,* ☎ *05/5899289.* ⊠ *Frescoes €1.55.* ⊙ *Daily 9:30–12:30 and 3:45–6:30.*

★ ⓬ **Santa Maria in Trastevere.** Dazzling mosaics and a long history are the draws of this church. It is supposedly the first church in Rome to have been dedicated to the Virgin Mary. Originally built sometime before the 4th century, it certainly is one of the oldest churches in the city. It was rebuilt in the 12th century, and the portico, which was added in the 19th century, seems to focus attention on the 800-year-old mosaics on the facade. The piazza is enhanced by their glow, especially at night, when the front of the church and its bell tower are illuminated. Additional mosaics of the 12th and 13th century light up the interior. In the representation of the *Life of the Virgin,* note the little building labeled "Taberna Meritoria" just under the figure of the Virgin in the Nativity scene, with a stream of oil flowing from it. It recalls the legend that on the day Christ was born, a stream of pure oil flowed from the earth on the site of the piazza, signifying the coming of the grace of God. Off the north side of the piazza, there's a little street called Via delle Fonte dell'Olio in honor of this miracle. ⊠ *Piazza Santa Maria in Trastevere,* ☎ *06/5819443.* ⊙ *Daily 9–noon and 4–9.*

➋ **Sant'Angelo in Pescheria.** This church was built right into the ruins of the Portico d'Ottavia, whose few surviving columns now frame it. The huge porticoed enclosure, named by Augustus in honor of his sister Octavia, was 390 ft wide and 433 ft long. It encompassed two temples, a meeting hall, and a library and served as a kind of grandiose entrance foyer for the adjacent Teatro di Marcello. The ruins of the portico became Rome's *pescheria* (fish market) during the Middle Ages. A stone plaque on a pillar, a relic of that time, admonishes in Latin that the head of any fish surpassing the length of the plaque was to be cut off "up to the first fin" and given to the city fathers or else the vendor was to pay a fine of 10 gold florins. The heads were used to make fish soup and were considered a great delicacy. The church is not usually open to the public, but ring the bell in back and the friendly priest may let you have a look. ⊠ *Via Tribuna di Campitelli 6,* ☎ *06/68801819.*

NEED A BREAK? Stop in at the bakery **Dolceroma** (⊠ Via Portico d'Ottavia 20/b, ☎ 06/6892196) and indulge in American and Austrian baked treats. **Franco e Cristina** (⊠ Via Portico d'Ottavia 5) is a stand-up pizza joint with the thinnest, crispiest pizza in town.

➍ **Sinagoga** (Synagogue). This big, bronze-roof synagogue is the city's largest temple and a Roman landmark. It contains a museum of precious ritual objects and other exhibits documenting the history of Rome's Jewish community. Until the 13th century the Jews were esteemed citizens of Rome. Among them were the bankers and physicians to the popes, who had themselves given permission for the construction of synagogues. But later popes of the Renaissance and Counter-Reformation revoked this tolerance, confining the Jews to the Ghetto and imposing a series of restrictions, some of which were enforced as late as 1870. The main synagogue was built in 1904; earlier, five smaller synagogues for communities of different national origin had existed on nearby Piazza delle Cinque Scole. ⊠ *Lungotevere Cenci*

15, ☎ 06/68400661. ✉ €5.15. ⊙ *Mon.–Thurs. 9–6, Fri. 9–2, Sun. 9–12:30.*

❸ Teatro di Marcello (Theater of Marcellus). Hardly recognizable as a theater today, this place was begun by Julius Caesar and completed by the emperor Augustus in AD 13. It was Rome's first permanent building dedicated to theater, and it held 20,000 spectators. Like other Roman monuments, it was transformed into a fortress during the Middle Ages. Later, during the Renaissance, it was converted into a residence by the Savelli, one of the city's noble families. The small archaeological zone is used as a summer venue for open-air classical music and lyrical concerts. ✉ *Via del Teatro di Marcello.*

⑭ Villa Farnesina. Money was no object to extravagant host Agostino Chigi, a banker from Siena who financed many a papal project. His munificence is evident in this elegant villa, built for him about 1511. He was especially proud of the delicate fresco decorations in the airy loggias, now glassed in to protect their artistic treasures. When Raphael could steal a little time from his work on the Vatican Stanze, he came over to execute some of the frescoes himself, notably a luminous *Galatea*. In his villa, host Agostino entertained the popes and princes of 16th-century Rome. He delighted in impressing his guests at alfresco suppers held in riverside pavilions by having his servants clear the table by casting the precious silver and gold dinnerware into the Tiber. His extravagance was not quite so boundless as he wished to make it appear, however: he had nets unfurled a foot or two under the water's surface to catch the valuable ware as it was flung into the river.

In the **Loggia of Psyche** on the ground floor, Giulio Romano and others worked from Raphael's designs. Raphael's lovely *Galatea* is in the adjacent room. On the floor above you can see the trompe l'oeil effects in the aptly named **Hall of Perspectives** by Peruzzi. Agostino Chigi's bedroom, next door, was frescoed by Il Sodoma with scenes from the life of Alexander the Great, notably the *Wedding of Alexander and Roxanne,* which is considered to be the artist's best work. The palace also houses the **Gabinetto Nazionale delle Stampe,** a treasure house of old prints and drawings. When the Tiber embankments were built in 1879, the remains of a classical villa were discovered under the Farnesina gardens, and their decorations are now in the Museo Nazionale Romano's collections in Palazzo Massimo alle Terme. ✉ *Via della Lungara 230,* ☎ *06/68801767,* 🕸 *www.lincei.it.* ✉ €4.15. ⊙ *Mon.–Sat. 9–1.*

THE AVENTINE TO ST. PAUL'S

The Aventine Hill, one of the seven hills on which the city was founded, enjoys a serenity hard to find elsewhere in Rome. It is one of the city's quietest and greenest neighborhoods, an island on which ancient churches and gardens rise above streams of heavy traffic and the mundane goings-on in the Trastevere and Testaccio neighborhoods below. The approach from the Circus Maximus is worthy of the Aventine's august atmosphere. On the Aventine are a number of Rome's oldest and least-visited churches as well as one of the city's most surprising delights: the keyhole in the gate to the garden of the Knights of Malta. Beyond lies Testaccio, for traditional and inexpensive Roman food and an animated after-hours scene, and the Piramide di Caio Cestio, one of Rome's most distinctive and idiosyncratic landmarks: it's a tomb, built by an ancient Roman with more than half an eye on posterity. Not far away is one of the greatest pilgrimage churches in Italy, the medieval basilica of San Paolo fuori le Mura (St. Paul's Outside the Walls).

Numbers in the text and margin correspond to points of interest on the Aventine to St. Paul's map.

A Good Walk

Start your walk at the southern end of Via del Teatro Marcello at the little church of **San Nicola in Carcere** ①. Follow Via Petroselli south, passing the Casa dei Crescenzi (Crescenzi House), on your right. This is one of only a handful of medieval houses in Rome to have survived almost intact. The inscription on its facade announces that the house was built by Nicolò di Crescenzio, and that in building it he wished—and you must at least admire his ambition—to re-create the glory of ancient Rome. To this end he incorporated various classical fragments in the facade. Far more important are the two small temples in front of you on Piazza Bocca della Verità, both about 2,000 years old and remarkably well preserved for their age. The rectangular **Tempio della Fortuna Virilis** ② and the circular **Tempio di Vesta** ③ (also known as the Temple of Hercules) were both built about 100 BC. **Piazza della Bocca della Verità** ④ was the site of ancient Rome's cattle market; across the street is the church of **Santa Maria in Cosmedin** ⑤, famous for the Bocca della Verità.

Next, head up the Aventine Hill. Take care crossing broad Via Greca—where cars pick up speed—and walk along the street, turning into the first street on the right, Clivo dei Publici. This skirts Valle Murcia, the city's rose garden, open in May and June. Where Clivo dei Publici veers off to the left, continue on Via di Santa Sabina. You'll see the church of Santa Sabina ahead, but just before you reach it, you can take a turn around the delightful walled park, known as the Giardino degli Aranci, famous for its orange trees and wonderful view of the Tiber and St. Peter's Basilica. Regrettably, women alone should take extra care here, as the quiet streets around Giardino degli Aranci have been known to attract the occasional seamy character, and episodes of harassment have been reported. Three of the Aventine's main attractions are lined up, one after another, on the right side of Via di Santa Sabina: the churches of **Santa Sabina** ⑥ and **Sant'Alessio** ⑦, and the famous keyhole on **Piazza Cavalieri di Malta** ⑧, the Square of the Knights of Malta. Via di Sant'Anselmo winds through the district's quiet residential streets. Cross busy Viale Aventino at Piazza Albania and climb the so-called Piccolo Aventino (Little Aventine) on Via di San Saba to the church of **San Saba** ⑨.

To explore the Testaccio neighborhood, return to Viale Aventino and head west, cutting across the park to Via Marmorata. The neighborhood has plain early 1900s housing, a down-to-earth working-class atmosphere, plenty of good trattorias where you can find traditional Roman food—and, of course, Monte Testaccio, a grassy knoll about 150 ft high. What makes this otherwise unremarkable-looking hill special is the fact that it's made from pottery shards—pieces of amphorae, large jars used in ancient times to transport oil, wheat, wine, and other goods. What began as a dump for the broken earthenware jars seemed in time to have taken on a life of its own, until by the Middle Ages the hill, growing even larger, had become a place of pilgrimage. Now clusters of converted warehouses around its base set the latest trends in Roman nightlife. Make your way to Piazza Testaccio, the marketplace, and prettier Piazza di Santa Maria Liberatrice. There are some quintessential Roman trattorias along Via Marmorata and near the Mattatoio, the former slaughterhouse.

Viale Aventino and Via Marmorata converge at **Porta San Paolo** ⑩, one of the ancient city gates in the 3rd-century AD Aurelian walls. You can't miss the big white **Piramide di Caio Cestio** ⑪. Behind it is the

114

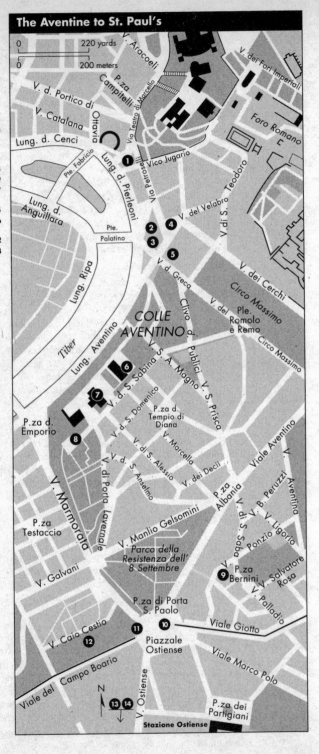

The Aventine to St. Paul's

COLLE AVENTINO

Cimitero Acattolico/Cimitero Protestante ⑫. To reach the Church of **San Paolo fuori le Mura** ⑬, literally St. Paul Outside the Walls, take a taxi or Metro line B (it's the second stop in the Laurentina direction) or bus 23. The **Centrale Montemartini** ⑭, where classical sculpture is juxtaposed with 20th-century machinery, lies in the same direction.

TIMING

The walk takes about 3½ hours, allowing 10–15 minutes for each church and the Protestant cemetery; 30 minutes for the visit to San Paolo fuori le Mura; and 40 minutes to see the ancient sculpture in the Centrale Montemartini on Via Ostiense.

Sights to See

⑭ **Centrale Montemartini.** The 1912 Montemartini power plant serves as an unusual setting for the display of classical sculpture. Life-size statues are juxtaposed with the plant's massive machinery. Many of the sculptures have never been on permanent public display before. Discovered throughout the city, they span the early Republican through the late Imperial periods. In addition to the sculptures, there is a large mosaic of a hunting scene that once made up the floor of an imperial residence. ⊠ *Viale Ostiense 106,* ☎ *06/5748038.* 🎟 *€4.15.* ☾ *Tues.– Fri. 10–6, weekends 10–7.*

⑫ **Cimitero Acattolico/Cimitero Protestante** (Non-Catholic Cemetery/Protestant Cemetery). In a city whose great and not-so-great personages have taken such pride in their tombs over the centuries, the historic cemetery in the shadow of the Piramide is a tranquil understatement; the older sections are much like a country churchyard. The romantic melancholy of tall cypresses and ancient ruins among the headstones makes it a fitting resting place for poets John Keats and Percy Shelley. The oldest tombstones date from 1738. ⊠ *Via Caio Cestio 6,* ☎ *06/ 5741900.* 🎟 *Free.* ☾ *Tues.–Sat. 9–noon and 1–5.*

⑧ **Piazza Cavalieri di Malta.** Peek through the keyhole of the walled compound of the Knights of Malta and you'll get a surprising eyeful: a picture-perfect view of the dome of St. Peter's Basilica, far across the city. The Order of the Knights of Malta is the world's oldest and most exclusive order of chivalry, founded in the Holy Land during the Crusades. Though nominally tenders of the sick in those early days, a role that has since become the order's raison d'être, the knights amassed huge tracts of land in the Middle East and established themselves as a fearsome mercenary force. From 1530 they were based on the Mediterranean island of Malta, having been expelled from another Mediterranean stronghold, Rhodes, by the Turks in 1522. In 1798 Napoléon expelled them from Malta, and in 1834 they established themselves in Rome, with headquarters on Via Condotti. The compound here is the headquarters of the Italian branch of the order. The square itself, and the church and gardens inside the compound, was designed around 1765 by Piranesi, 18th-century Rome's foremost engraver—you have him to thank for the view. ⊠ *Via Santa Sabina and Via Porta Lavernale.*

④ **Piazza della Bocca della Verità** (Mouth of Truth Square). Originally the site of the Forum Boarium, ancient Rome's cattle market, it was later used for public executions. ⊠ *Via L. Petroselli, Via dei Cerchi, and Lungotevere Aventino.*

⑪ **Piramide di Caio Cestio** (Pyramid of Gaius Cestius). An immensely wealthy praetor (magistrate) in Imperial Rome, Gaius Cestius had this monumental tomb built for himself in the form of a 120-ft-tall pyramid in 12 BC. Though little else is known about him, he clearly had a taste for grandeur and money to burn. The structure was completed in just over a month, an extraordinary feat even for the ancient Romans. ✉ *Piazzale Ostiense*.

⑩ Porta San Paolo. This gate marked the beginning of the Via Ostiense, the city's vital overland link with the port city of Ostia, 16 km (10 mi) away. Porta San Paolo, one of some 13 gates in the Aurelian walls, defended Rome's vital market area, including the Emporium—the riverside docks and warehouses through which supplies brought in by barge were funneled into the city. ✉ *Viale Piramide Cestia, Via Marmorata, and Via Ostiense*.

❶ San Nicola in Carcere. The exterior of this church illustrates to perfection the Roman habit of building and rebuilding ancient sites, incorporating parts of existing buildings in new buildings, adding to them, and then adding to them again. The church stands on the site of a temple built around 250 BC; some of the temple's columns are visible to the right of the church as you face it, beside the remains of the medieval campanile, or bell tower. The facade, dating from the mid-16th century, is thought to have been designed by Giacomo della Porta, the architect who completed the dome of St. Peter's Basilica after Michelangelo's death. ✉ *Via Teatro di Marcello 46,* ☎ *06/68307198*.

⑬ San Paolo fuori le Mura (St. Paul's Outside the Walls). For all the dreariness of its location—and, indeed, for all of its exterior's dullness (19th-century British writer Augustus Hare said the church looked like "a very ugly railway station")—St. Paul's is one of the most historic and important churches in Rome, second in size only to St. Peter's Basilica and one of the city's four pilgrimage churches, together with St. Peter's, San Giovanni in Laterano, and Santa Maria Maggiore.

Built in the 4th century AD by Constantine over the site where St. Paul had been buried, St. Paul's was then rebuilt and considerably enlarged about a century later. At the time it was the largest church in Europe, but its location outside the city walls left it especially vulnerable to attack, and it was sacked by the rampaging Saracens in 846. Although fortified in the 9th century, the church gradually declined in importance, especially as the surrounding marshland became malarial swamps. Sheep wandered through the Basilica, undisturbed by the few remaining monks.

This sorry state of affairs came to a sudden end in the middle of the 11th century with the arrival of a new abbot, Hildebrandt. He restored the building, recruited new monks, and made St. Paul's a revered center of pilgrimage once more. And so it remained until July 1823, when a fire burned the church to the ground. All that remained, apart from a few mosaics, the sculptured ciborium (tabernacle), and other decorations, were the cloisters. Although the rebuilt St. Paul's has a sort of monumental grandeur, with its columns stretching up the dusky nave and its 19th-century mosaics glinting dully, it's only in the cloisters that you get a real sense of what must have been the magnificence of the original building. The little columns supporting the arcades of the cloisters are remarkable for their variety and richness. Some are slim and straight, others corkscrew violently; some are carved in creamy marble, others are encrusted with mosaics. Look for the little animals carved in the spaces between the columns. The entrance to the cloisters is from the right transept, the "arm" of the church to your right as you face the altar. ✉ *Piazzale San Paolo (Via Ostiense 190),* ☎ *06/ 5410178.* ☉ *Daily 7:30–6:30*.

❾ San Saba. A medieval church with an almost rustic interior and Cosmatesque mosaic pavement, San Saba harbors a hodgepodge of ancient marble pieces and, on the aisle on the left-hand side of the church, a curious fresco cycle painted by an unknown 13th-century artist. The most famous scene shows three young girls lying naked on a bed. Unlikely as it may seem, this is actually an illustration of the good works of St. Nicholas—the girls are naked because their impoverished father (at right) sees no future for them but prostitution. Outside the window, however, St. Nick is about to save the day, by tossing a bag of gold coins in the window to keep the family from a life of shame. ✉ *Piazza Gianlorenzo Bernini 20 (Via San Saba),* ☎ *06/5743352.* ◷ *Daily 7–noon and 4–6.*

❼ Sant'Alessio. The church's entrance and Romanesque bell tower are on a medieval courtyard. As a whole, the church is the result of reconstructions and restorations over the centuries. Look for the curious marble sculpture at the head of the left nave commemorating St. Alexis, son of a wealthy patrician family in early Christian times. Alexis disdained the luxury to which he had been born and endured years of penitence and prayer before returning home so emaciated that no one recognized him. Ever humble and self-effacing, he elected to live anonymously, as a servant in his family's household, sleeping under the stairs for 17 years until his death. ✉ *Via Sant'Alessio 23,* ☎ *06/5743446.* ◷ *Daily 8:30–6:30 (until 7 in summer).*

❺ Santa Maria in Cosmedin. Though this is one of Rome's oldest churches, with an interesting, almost exotic interior, it plays second fiddle to the renowned artifact installed in the church portico, on the left as you enter. The **Bocca della Verità** (Mouth of Truth) is in reality nothing more than an ancient drain cover, unearthed during the Middle Ages. Legend has it, however, that the teeth will clamp down on a liar's hand, and to tell a lie with your hand in the fearsome mouth is to risk losing it. Hordes of tourists line up to take the test every day, cameras in hand to bring the proof to the folks back home.

The church was built in the 6th century for the city's burgeoning Greek population. Heavily restored at the end of the 19th century, it has the typical basilica form, but it also has an altar screen, an element characteristic of Eastern churches. ✉ *Piazza Santa Maria in Cosmedin,* ☎ *06/6781419.* ◷ *Daily 9–5 (until 7 or 8 in summer).*

❻ Santa Sabina. This early Christian basilica demonstrates the severe simplicity common to churches of its era. Here alterations and later decorations have been peeled away, leaving the essential form as Rome's Christians knew it in the 5th century. Once the church was bright with mosaics and frescoes, now lost. The beautifully carved and preserved wooden doors are the oldest of their kind in existence; they, too, date from the 5th century. ✉ *Piazza Pietro d'Illiria 1 (Via di Santa Sabina),* ☎ *06/57941.* ◷ *Daily 6:30–12:30 and 4–6 (until 7 in summer).*

❷ Tempio della Fortuna Virilis (Temple of Portunus). This rectangular temple from the 2nd century BC is built in the Greek style, as was the norm in Rome's early years. It owes its fine state of preservation, considering its venerable age, to the fact that it was consecrated and used as a Christian church. ✉ *Piazza Bocca della Verità.*

❸ Tempio di Vesta (Temple of Hercules Victor). Long called the Temple of Vesta because of its similarity in shape to the building of that name in the Roman Forum, it is now recognized as a temple to Hercules Victor. All but one of the 20 Corinthian columns of this evocative ruin remain intact. Like the Tempio della Fortuna Virilis, it was built in the 2nd century BC. ✉ *Piazza Bocca della Verità.*

THE CELIAN HILL
AND THE BATHS OF CARACALLA

Like the Aventine, Monte Celio (Celian Hill) seems aloof from the bustle of central Rome. On the slopes of the hill, paths and narrow streets wind through a public park and past walled gardens. Here are some of Rome's earliest churches, such as Santa Maria in Domnica, Santo Stefano Rotondo, and Santi Quattro Coronati. Close by are the Terme di Caracalla, towering ruins of what must have been a spectacular bathing complex, though it does take some imagination to picture what they must have looked like in their prime. In contrast to the busier and noisier districts of the city, the Celio is pervaded by a quiet charm that encourages relaxation and reflection about some of the elements that make Rome so special: the grandeur of antiquity, the mystic power of religion, and the gentle blessings of nature.

Numbers in the text and margin correspond to points of interest on the Celian Hill and the Baths of Caracalla map.

A Good Walk

Start your walk at the Arco di Costantino—it's right by the Colosseum—and walk south along Via di San Gregorio. To your right, on the slopes of the Palatine Hill, are all that remains of the great aqueduct built by the consul Appius Claudius in about 300 BC. Stairs on the left lead to the **Antiquario Comunale** ①, with archaeological exhibits. At the end of Via di San Gregorio, climb the shallow flight of stairs to visit the church of **San Gregorio Magno** ②. Then head up the hill on the Clivo di Scauro to the ancient church of **Santi Giovanni e Paolo** ③. The square in which it stands has been described as one of the few spots in Rome that a medieval pilgrim would easily recognize (if there are no cars parked there, that is). Opposite the church is the gated entrance to private television studios. Just up from there is a tiny door in the wall that opens onto a corner of Villa Celimontana, a park still largely unknown to most visitors to the city. The gate is sometimes locked; if so, there's another entrance on Via San Paolo della Croce just around the corner. Keep to the left as you wander through the park to reach the main entrance on Via della Navicella, where there's a whimsical fountain topped with a Renaissance model in marble of an ancient Roman ship, in front of the church of **Santa Maria in Domnica** ④. This little church packs lavish decoration, including some vibrant mosaics, into a small space. Opposite, the round church of **Santo Stefano Rotondo** ⑤ is unusual for its circular plan and beam ceiling.

Then head north into the large Piazza Celimontana. Passing the entrance to the military hospital, continue straight ahead into Via Celimontana. Turn right onto Via San Giovanni in Laterano, the route of papal processions between the basilicas of San Giovanni in Laterano and St. Peter's. The church of **San Clemente** ⑥ is sandwiched between Via San Giovanni in Laterano and Via Labicana. The 12th-century church is built on the site of even more ancient Roman buildings. From San Clemente walk uphill on Via Santi Quattro Coronati to the 12th-century church of **Santi Quattro Coronati** ⑦, part of a fortified abbey that provided refuge to early popes and emperors. Next, retrace your steps, returning to Piazza Celimontana. From Via della Navicella, follow Via Druso to huge Piazza Numa Pompilio, a busy crossroads. On the northwest side of the piazza, the little church of **Santi Nereo e Achilleo** ⑧ is worth a visit. The tall brick ruins of the **Terme di Caracalla** ⑨ dominate this side of the piazza. The present entrance to the baths is at the northwest end.

The Celian Hill and the Baths of Caracalla

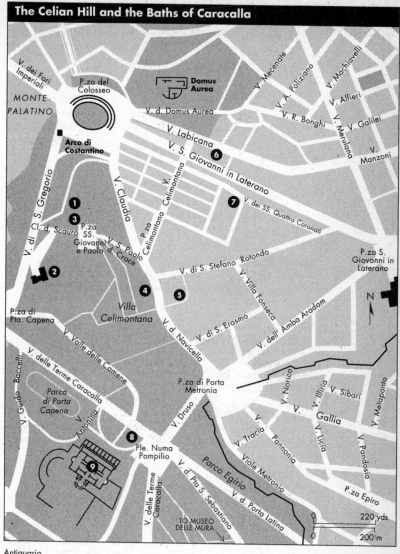

V. dei Fori Imperiali

MONTE PALATINO

P.za del Colosseo

Arco di Costantino

⬜ Domus Aurea

V. d. Domus Aurea

V. Mecenate

V. A. Poliziano

V. Machiavelli

V. Alfieri

V. R. Bonghi

V. Galilei

V. Merulana

V. Manzoni

V. Labicana

V. S. Giovanni in Laterano ❻

V. di S. Gregorio

❶

❸

Cl. d. Scauro

P.za SS. Giovanni e Paolo

V. di Pta. Capena

❷

V. Claudia

V. S. Paolo d' Croce

P.za d' Croce

V. Celimontana

V. Celimontana

V. Celimontana

❼ V. dei SS. Quattro Coronati

V. di S. Stefano Rotondo

P.za S. Giovanni in Laterano

N

❹

❺

Villa Celimontana

V. di Villa Fonseca

V. d. Navicella

V. di S. Erasmo

V. dell' Amba Aradam

P.za di Pta. Capena

V. Guido Baccelli

V. delle Terme Caracalla

V. Valle delle Camene

Parco di Porta Capena

V. Antonina

❽

❾

Ple. Numa Pompilio

P.za di Porta Metronia

V. Druso

V. Norico

V. Illiria

V. Sibari

Gallia

V. Metaponto

V. Tracia

V. Licia

V. Pandosia

V. Pannonia

P.za Epiro

Viale Metronio

V. delle Terme Caracalla

V. d. Pta S. Sebastiano

Parco Egirio

V. d. Porta Latina

TO MUSEO DELLE MURA

220 yds

200 m

On the south side of Piazza Numa Pompilio, Viale delle Terme di Caracalla leads to Via Cristoforo Colombo, a multilane thoroughfare leading south toward the EUR quarter and to the sea at Castelfusano. Via Porta di San Sebastiano is a walled lane that channels fairly heavy city traffic southeast to Porta San Sebastiano and the beginning of the Via Appia Antica. To get an inside view of Porta San Sebastiano, one of the most imposing of the city gates in the Aurelian walls, and to stroll along the battlements, make a detour to the Museo delle Mura. Passing cars can make the walk along Via Porta di San Sebastiano less than pleasant, but the sole bus, number 760, operates only on Sunday and holidays and returns toward the center of Rome on Via di Porta Latina; at other times, the alternative is to walk.

TIMING

The walk takes about 2½ hours, allowing about 10 minutes in each church. Save an additional 45 minutes for a visit to San Clemente's subterranean levels, and about the same to explore the Terme di Caracalla. Add another hour for a detour to the Museo delle Mura and the walk inside the Aurelian walls.

Sights to See

❶ Antiquario Comunale (Municipal Antiquarium). The collection displays marble fragments and artifacts of daily life in ancient Rome. One exhibit has poignant appeal—an ivory doll, with delicate features and jointed limbs, that was buried with its owner, a young girl of Imperial Rome, and was found in her sarcophagus. ⊠ *Via del Parco del Celio 22,* ☎ *06/7001569.* ⊙ *Scheduled to reopen to public at the end of 2001.*

★ **❻ San Clemente.** This church is one of the most extraordinary archaeological sites in Rome. San Clemente as it stands today is the third church built on this location. The first was a 2nd-century AD temple to the god Mithras, built within a private home that itself dated from the 1st century AD. Little remains of it, but the second church, built in the 4th century, and over which today's church stands, has survived almost intact, perhaps because it was rediscovered only in the 19th century.

San Clemente has one of the few complete medieval interiors in Rome. The most interesting features are near the altar. The marble panels in the choir were originally in the 4th-century church and were moved here when the present church was built in 1108. They are decorated with early Christian symbols: doves, vines, and fish. In front of the altar is a sunken tomb containing the relics of St. Clement. The 16th-century canopy over the tomb is decorated with a large anchor, a reference to the martyrdom of St. Clement or, at any rate, to the legend of his martyrdom. St. Clement was the fourth pope and was reputedly banished to the Crimea in Russia by the emperor Trajan around the year 100. Here, chiefly as a result of his success in converting his fellow exiles, he was tied to an anchor and thrown into the sea. When, miraculously, the waters receded, his body was found in a tomb built by angels.

At the beginning of the left nave, be sure to see the frescoes illustrating the life of St. Catherine of Alexandria, another early Christian martyr, born in Alexandria, in Egypt. Her story is memorable even by the extreme standards of early Christian martyrdom. After she publicly protested the worship of idols, the Emperor sent 50 pagan philosophers to talk her out of her beliefs. As each failed, he was condemned to death by fire. The last straw was Catherine's refusal to marry the local governor; she was sentenced to torture and tied to a spiked wheel, henceforth known as the Catherine Wheel. To the amazement of onlookers, the wheel disintegrated under her, so impressing 200 watching Roman soldiers that they converted to Christianity on the spot. Her luck wasn't limitless, however, and eventually she was beheaded, whereupon angels carried her soul to Mt. Sinai in the Holy Land. The frescoes were painted around 1400 by the Florentine artist Masolino, a key figure in the development of Italian painting from the two-dimensional decorative styles of the 14th century to the naturalism of the Renaissance.

The church is in the care of Irish Dominican priests, who sell tickets to the excavations in the vestibule off the right side of the nave. Stairs lead down into the remains of the church. A series of walls built along the nave of the 4th-century structure to support the newer church above make it hard to form a coherent picture of the layout. Though the gloomy interior is confusing, there are a number of areas that bring the building vividly to life.

The most notable—not to mention colorful—are the frescoes on the left wall of the nave illustrating scenes from the life of St. Clement, probably painted in the 11th century. Here in two panels, one above the other, Clement is shown getting the better of a wealthy Roman called Sisinius. In the top panel, Sisinius is struck deaf and blind after having interrupted St. Clement's mass in order to drag his wife, Theodora, a Christian convert, back home. In the lower panel, the enraged Sisinius orders his servants to tie up St. Clement and carry him away. But divine intervention causes them to mistake a column lying on the ground for Clement, and they struggle furiously with ropes to strap it up. Perhaps the most unusual element of this farcical scene is the inscription under the lower panel in which Sisinius bellows at his hapless slaves, "Go on, you sons of harlots, pull!"—one of the earliest examples of the Italian vernacular in print.

From the apse at the end of the church, narrow and slippery steps lead down to the remains of the 1st-century AD house over which the 4th-century church stands. Of particular interest are the remains of a "mithraeum," a shrine dedicated to the god Mithras. The shrine was installed on the first floor of a 2nd-century AD Roman apartment building (almost all ancient Romans, except the super-rich, lived in apartments, or *insulae*).

The cult of Mithras—which spread from Persia and gained a hold in Rome at about the time of the collapse of the Roman Republic, around 50 BC—was the only major pagan religion that offered the possibility of life after death. It was one of the few serious rivals to Christianity, which was then spreading rapidly across the Roman Empire. Moreover, it was the only pagan cult to continue to be practiced widely after the official "disestablishment" of paganism in favor of Christianity by the Romans in AD 382. Its rituals were always held in secret, generally in cavelike grottoes. Interestingly, the most complete part of the shrine left is the triclinium, a room used for religious banquets, the roof of which is studded with small rocks in imitation of a cave. Your visit is made all the more eerie by the sound of running water, evidence of the springs that have been diverted around the excavations. ✉ *Via San Giovanni in Laterano 95,* ☎ *06/70451018.* ✆ *€2.05.* ⊙ *Mon.–Sat. 9–12:30 and 3–6, Sun. 10–12:30 and 3–6.*

❷ **San Gregorio Magno.** This church, dedicated to St. Gregory the Great (who served as pope 590–604), was built about 750 by Pope Gregory II to commemorate his predecessor and namesake. It was from the monastery on this site that Pope Gregory the Great dispatched St. Augustine to Britain in 596 to convert the heathens there. The church of San Gregorio itself appears to all intents and purposes to be a typical Baroque structure, the result of remodeling in the 17th and 18th cen-

turies. But you can still see what's said to be the stone slab on which
the pious Gregory the Great slept; it's in the far right-hand chapel. Outside are three chapels. The right chapel is dedicated to Gregory's
mother, St. Sylvia, and contains a Guido Reni fresco of the *Concert of
Angels.* The one on the left contains the simple table at which Gregory
fed 12 poor men every day. A 13th appeared one day—an angel. The
chapel in the center, dedicated to St. Andrew, contains two monumental
frescoes showing scenes from St. Andrew's life. They were painted at
the beginning of the 17th century by Domenichino (*The Flagellation
of St. Andrew*) and Guido Reni (*The Execution of St. Andrew*). It's a
striking juxtaposition of the sturdy, if sometimes stiff, classicism of
Domenichino with the more flamboyant and heroic Baroque manner
of Guido Reni. ⊠ *Piazza San Gregorio,* ☎ *06/7008827.* ☼ *Daily 8–
12:30 and 1:30–7.*

④ Santa Maria in Domnica. This early Christian structure was built over
the house of a Roman martyr, St. Cyriaca, about whom little seems to
be known other than that she was wealthy. The vibrantly colored 9th-
century mosaics in the apse behind the altar are worth seeing. Notice
the handkerchief carried by the Virgin Mary: it is a *mappa,* a fashionable
accoutrement in 9th-century Byzantium. ⊠ *Via della Navicella 10,* ☎
06/7001519. ☼ *Daily 9–noon and 3:30–6:30.*

❸ Santi Giovanni e Paolo. Built on the site of two ancient Roman houses
in 398 by a Roman senator called Pammachius, the church you see today
is fundamentally unchanged. The houses over which it was built belonged to Sts. John and Paul, not the Apostles of those names, but a
pair of aristocratic early Christian martyrs who had served as officers
at the court of the Christian Emperor Constantine. Constantine's successor, Julian the Apostate, tried vainly to stem the rising tide of Christianity and to restore to Rome her pagan gods. John and Paul were
early victims of his paganizing fervor; they were beheaded in 362 after
having refused to serve as officers in Julian's court. A steep staircase
in the far right-hand corner of the church leads down to the remains
of their houses and their burial place. Frescoes, almost certainly dating from the same period, depict the beheading of two men and a woman;
they are thought to have been early worshipers at the graves of John
and Paul, who, for their pains, received the same treatment at the hands
of Julian. On a happier note, the lovely and incongruous chandeliers
were a hand-me-down from New York's Waldorf-Astoria hotel, a gift
arranged by the late Cardinal Archbishop Spellman of New York,
whose titular church this was. It is one of Rome's most popular wedding spots. ⊠ *Piazza Santi Giovanni e Paolo 13,* ☎ *06/772711.* ☼ *Daily
9–11 and 3:30–6.*

❽ Santi Nereo e Achilleo. One of Rome's oldest churches, probably dating from the 4th century, Sts. Nereus and Achilleus has accumulated
treasures such as 8th-century mosaics, a medieval pulpit on a multicolor marble base from the Terme di Caracalla, a 13th-century mosaic choir, and a fine, 16th-century episcopal—or bishop's—throne. ⊠
Viale delle Terme di Caracalla 28, ☎ *06/5757996. Closed indefinitely
for restoration.*

OFF THE
BEATEN PATH

MUSEO DELLE MURA (Museum of the Walls)– This museum is housed in
the twin towers of Porta San Sebastiano, the largest, most important,
and best-preserved city gate in the walls built by the Emperor Aurelianus
to defend Rome from the barbarians. Begun in the 3rd century AD, the
wall stretched for about 19 km (12 mi) around the city, encompassing
the much earlier Servian wall. A century later, after a new wave of inva-
sions, the walls were restored and doubled in height. The museum has

some interesting displays on how the walls were built and added to over the centuries, but the main attraction is the chance to walk along a section of the wall comprising nine towers and a covered gallery that protected defenders. It has some unexpected views of the gardens and greenery that still exist within the walls. ⊠ *Via di Porta San Sebastiano 18,* ☎ *06/70475284.* ▣ *€2.50.* ⊙ *Tues.–Sun. 9–7.*

★ **⑦ Santi Quattro Coronati.** The original 9th-century church was twice as large as the present one. The abbey was partially destroyed during the Normans' sack of Rome about 1085, but it was reconstructed about 30 years later. This explains the inordinate size of the apse in relation to the small nave. The apse frescoes are clearly Baroque, but the rest of the church is redolent of the Middle Ages. It's one of the most unusual and unexpected corners of Rome, a quiet citadel that has resisted the tide of time and traffic flowing below its ramparts. Don't miss the **cloister,** with its well-tended gardens and 12th-century fountain. The entrance is the door in the left nave; ring if it's not open.

There's another medieval gem hidden away off the courtyard at the church entrance: the **Chapel of San Silvestro.** (Enter the door marked "Monache Agostiniane" and ring the bell at the left for the nun; she will pass the key to the chapel through the wheel beside the grille.) The chapel has remained, for the most part, as it was when consecrated in 1246, decorated with marbles and frescoes. These tell the story of the Christian Emperor Constantine's recovery from leprosy thanks to Pope Sylvester I. Note, too, the delightful *Last Judgment* fresco above the door, in which the angel on the left neatly rolls up sky and stars like a backdrop, signaling the end of the world. When you leave, lock the door and return the key to the nun. A donation is appropriate. ⊠ *Via Santi Quattro Coronati 20,* ☎ *06/70475427.* ⊙ *Church and chapel daily 9:30–noon and 3:30–6; cloister 9:30–noon and 4:30–6; ring bell to visit at other times.*

⑤ Santo Stefano Rotondo. This 5th-century church was inspired perhaps by the design of the church of the Holy Sepulchre in Jerusalem. Its unusual round plan and timbered ceiling set it apart from most other Roman churches. ⊠ *Via Santo Stefano Rotondo 7,* ☎ *06/421191.* ⊙ *Tues.–Sat. 9–1 and 1:50–4:20, Mon. 1:50–4:20, 2nd Sun. of month 9–noon.*

★ **⑨ Terme di Caracalla** (Baths of Caracalla). Although not the largest in ancient Rome, these public baths seem to have been by far the most opulent. Begun in AD 206 by the emperor Septimius Severus and completed by his son, Caracalla, they could accommodate 1,600 bathers at a time.

Taking a bath was a long and complex process, which is eminently understandable if you see it as a social activity first and foremost. Remember, too, that for all their sophistication, the Romans didn't have soap. You began in the *sudatoria,* a series of small rooms resembling saunas. Here you sat and sweated. From these you moved to the *calidarium,* a large circular room that was humid rather than simply hot. This was where the actual business of washing went on. You used a *strigil,* or scraper, to get the dirt off; if you were rich your slave did this for you. Next you moved to the *tepidarium,* a warmish room, the purpose of which was to allow you to begin gradually to cool down. Finally, you splashed around in the *frigidarium,* the only actual "bath" in the place, in essence a shallow swimming pool filled with cold water. The rich might like to complete the process with a brisk rubdown with a scented towel. It was not unusual for a member of the opposite sex to perform this favor for you (the baths were open to men and women, though the times when they could use them were different). There was a nominal admission fee, often waived by officials and emperors wishing to curry favor with the plebeians.

For the Romans, the baths were much more than places to wash. Although providing bathing facilities was their main purpose, there were also recital halls, art galleries, and libraries to improve the mind, and massage and exercise rooms as well as sports grounds to improve the body, in addition to halls and gardens just for talking and strolling. Even the smallest public baths had at least some of these amenities, and in the capital of the Roman Empire, they were provided on a lavish scale. But their functioning depended on the slaves who cared for the clients, checking their robes, rubbing them down, and seeing to their needs. Under the magnificent marble pavement of the stately halls, other slaves toiled in a warren of tiny rooms and passages, stoking the fires that heated the water. ⊠ *Via delle Terme di Caracalla 52,* ☎ *06/ 39967700,* WEB *www.archeorm.arti.beniculturali.it/sar2000/cra-calla/caracalla.htm.* ▣ *€4.15.* ⊙ *Oct.–Mar., Tues.–Sun. 9–3:30, Mon. 9–1; Apr.–Sept., Tues.–Sun. 9–6, Mon. 9–1.*

THE CATACOMBS AND THE APPIAN WAY

In the swelling tide of urban development, a greenbelt of pastures and villas along Via Appia Antica has survived as an evocative remnant of the Roman *campagna* (countryside). Strewn with classical ruins and dotted with grazing sheep, the Via Appia stirs images of chariots and legionnaires returning from imperial conquests, of barrel-shape Roman carts transporting produce from the farms of Campania to the south, and of tearful families mourning at the tombs of their dead. Though time and vandals have taken their toll on the tombs along the Via Appia, what remains of them gives you an idea of how Rome's important families made sure that their deceased members, and the family name, would be remembered by posterity. Known as the "Queen of Roads," the Via Appia was completed in 312 BC by Appius Claudius, who also built Rome's first aqueduct. He had it laid out to connect Rome with settlements in the south, in the direction of Naples: it was later extended to Brindisi, the port on the Adriatic. The dark, gloomy catacombs, the underground cemeteries that early Christians turned into places of worship, contrast with the fresh air, lush greenery, and classical ruins along the ancient road.

The catacombs aren't Rome's oldest cemeteries. Even before Christianity reached Rome, those citizens who couldn't afford a fine funeral monument along one of the consular roads were either cremated or buried in necropoli outside the city gates. An imperial law prohibited burial within the city—except for deified emperors. During the 1st and 2nd centuries AD, Rome's Christians were buried together with their pagan brothers in these common burial grounds. Because the Christians had adopted the Jewish tradition of burying their dead rather than cremating them, they soon required more space. They began to build cemeteries of their own, in which they performed their religious rites. With the approval of the city fathers, they dug their cemeteries in the hilly slopes that lined the consular roads, usually on private land that the owner—often a Christian himself—granted for this purpose. As the need for space became more pressing, the cemeteries were extended in a series of galleries, often on two or more levels.

The general belief that the catacombs served as secret hiding places for the Christians during the persecutions that broke out during early Christian times is romantic but unrealistic. The catacombs were well known to the Romans. Between persecutions, the bodies of the martyrs who had fallen under the sword or had met death by fire, water, or wild beasts were interred in the catacombs. Their remains were given a place of honor, and their presence conferred great prestige on the underground cemetery in which they lay, attracting a stream of devout pilgrims. Little by little the catacombs were embellished with frescoes, and existing staircases and galleries were enlarged to accommodate the faithful. Sometimes older parts of the cemetery were dug out to make room for underground basilicas.

You'll see a great variety of tombs and decorations here. They range from a simple rectangular niche in the wall that was closed by bricks or marble slabs to a sarcophagus carved out of the wall and surmounted by a niche, to a freestanding sarcophagus in terra-cotta, marble, or lead. Off some of the galleries you'll see rooms lined with niches, where members of the same family or community were buried. Later, when space became scarce, tombs were dug in the pavement. Each tomb was distinguished by a particular mark or sign so that the deceased's relatives could recognize it among the rows of niches. Sometimes this was an object, such as a coin or oil lamp; sometimes it was an inscription. The wealthier families called in painters to decorate their tombs with frescoes and ordered sculptured sarcophagi from artisans' workshops.

After AD 313, when Constantine's edict put an end to the persecutions and granted full privileges to the Christians, the construction of the catacombs flourished; they were increasingly frequented by those who wished to honor their own dead and to venerate the tombs of the early martyrs. During the Dark Ages, invading armies made a habit of showing up at the gates of the city, devastating the countryside, and plundering from the living and the dead. When this part of the Campagna Romana became a malaria-infested wasteland, the popes prudently decreed that the remains of the martyrs be removed from the catacombs and laid to rest in the relative security of Rome's churches. With the loss of these holy relics and the appearance of the first cemeteries within the city walls, the catacombs fell into disuse and were abandoned and forgotten, with the sole exception of the Catacombe di San Sebastiano. The interest of 19th-century archaeologists and 20th- and 21st-century tourists has brought the catacombs back to life.

Numbers in the text and margin correspond to points of interest on the Catacombs and the Appian Way map.

A Good Walk

The initial stretch of the Via Appia Antica is not pedestrian-friendly—there is fast, heavy traffic and no sidewalk all the way from Porta San Sebastiano to the Catacombe di San Callisto. Also, the gardens and villas along this stretch are hidden behind walls, so there's really not much to see, except for the little church of **Domine Quo Vadis?** ①, a short way beyond Porta San Sebastiano.

To reach the catacombs and the prettier stretch of the Via Appia Antica, take bus 218 (which starts from San Giovanni in Laterano) at the stop near Porta San Sebastiano; the bus route follows Via Ardeatina, parallel to Via Appia Antica. You can get off at the stop nearer to the **Catacombe di San Callisto** ②, or at Via San Sebastiano, which you take to reach **Catacombe di San Sebastiano** ③. Alternately, to start farther down the road, take Metro line A to Colli Albani and bus 660 to the tomb of Cecilia Metella, or the J3 bus (separate ticket) from Termini.

Visit the catacomb of your choice; then walk south on Via Appia Antica. Opposite San Sebastiano are some Jewish catacombs, not open

126

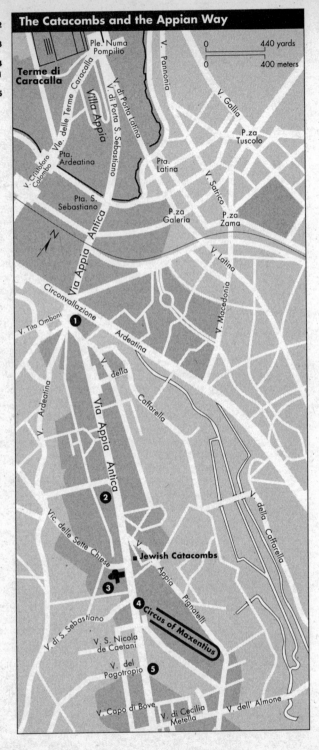

The Catacombs and the Appian Way

Ple. Numa
Pompilio

V. Pannonia

0   440 yards

0   400 meters

**Terme di
Caracalla**

V. Gallia

Villa Appia

V. di Porta Latina

V. di Porta S. Sebastiano

Vle. delle Terme Caracalla

P.za
Tuscolo

Pta.
Ardeatina

Pta.
Latina

V. Cristoforo Colombo

V. Satrico

Pta. S.
Sebastiano

P.za
Galeria

P.za
Zama

Via Appia Antica

V. Latina

N

Circonvallazione

V. Macedonia

❶

V. Tito Ombon

Ardeatina

V. della

V. Ardeatina

Via Appia Antica

Caffarella

❷

Vic. delle Sette Chiese

V. della Caffarella

V.
■ **Jewish Catacombs**

❸

Appia

V. di S. Sebastiano

❹ Circus of Maxentius

Pignatelli

V. S. Nicola
de Caetani

V. del
Pagotropio

❺

V. Capo di Bove

V. di Cecilia
Metella

V. dell' Almone

to the public. Also on the left are the ruins of the round Mausoleo di Romolo, built by Emperor Maxentius as a tomb for his son, Romulus, and the entrance to the **Circo di Massenzio** ④. Continue south to the **Tomba di Cecilia Metella** ⑤, which marks the beginning of the most interesting and evocative stretch of Via Appia, lined with vine-covered tombs and fragments of statuary. Cypresses and umbrella pines stand guard over the ruined sepulchers, and the occasional tracts of ancient paving stones are the same ones trod by Roman legions returning in triumph from southern conquests. In some stretches you can see the ruts worn in them by iron-clad cart wheels. Along the road are inconspicuous gateways to exclusive villas, residences of a lucky few.

Walk as far as you like along the road, but keep in mind that you have to retrace your steps to return to the bus stop. Among the more curious tombs here is a huge mass that seems balanced on a slender stem, and another tall mound on which a little house was built in a later age. You pass ruins of ancient villas, and to the left you can see the arches of an aqueduct.

TIMING

Weather is a determining factor, as the walk is almost entirely outdoors. There are no sidewalks along Via Appia Antica, so you will be walking mainly on beaten earth. Give a thought to carrying a picnic lunch or plan to dine at one of the pleasant restaurants near the catacombs. The walk takes about two hours, plus an hour for a visit to one of the catacombs, but allow another hour or so for the round-trip by bus, as service is not frequent.

Sights to See

★ ❷ **Catacombe di San Callisto** (Catacombs of St. Callistus). Burial place of many popes of the 3rd century, this is the oldest and among the most important and best-preserved underground cemeteries. One of the (English-speaking) friars who act as custodians of the catacomb will guide you through its crypts and galleries. ⊠ *Via Appia Antica 110,* ☎ *06/51301580.* ▨ *€4.15.* ⊙ *Thurs.–Tues. 8:30–noon and 2:30–5 (until 5:30 in summer).*

❸ **Catacombe di San Sebastiano** (Catacombs of St. Sebastian). The 4th-century church was named after the saint who was buried in the catacomb, which burrows underground on four different levels. This was the only early Christian cemetery to remain accessible during the Middle Ages, and it was from here that the term "catacomb" is derived—it's in a spot where the road dips into a hollow, known to the Romans as *catacumbas* (Greek for "near the hollow"). The Romans used the name to refer to the cemetery that had existed here since the 2nd century BC, and it came to be applied to all the underground cemeteries discovered in Rome in later centuries. ⊠ *Via Appia Antica 136,* ☎ *06/ 7887035.* ▨ *€4.15.* ⊙ *Mon.–Sat. 8:30–noon and 2:30–5 (until 5:30 in summer).*

❹ **Circo di Massenzio** (Circus of Maxentius). The ruins of the Circus of Maxentius, built in AD 309, give you an idea of what the Roman circuses looked like. You can see the towers at the entrance; the *spina,* the wall that divided it down the center; and the vaults that supported the tiers of seating for the spectators. The obelisk in Piazza Navona was found here. The adjacent **Mausoleo di Romolo** is a huge tomb built by the emperor for his son, Romulus, who died young. The tomb and circus were on the grounds of the emperor's villa, much of which is yet to be excavated. ⊠ *Via Appia Antica 153,* ☎ *06/7801324.* ▨ *€2.50.* ⊙ *Oct.–Mar., Tues.–Sun. 9–5; Apr.–Sept., Tues.–Sun. 9–7.*

① Domine Quo Vadis? (Lord, Where Goest Thou?). This church was built on the spot where tradition says Christ appeared to St. Peter as the Apostle was fleeing Rome and persuaded him to return and face martyrdom. A paving stone in the church bears an imprint said to have been made by the feet of Christ. ⊠ *Via Appia Antica at Via Ardeatina,* ☎ *06/5120441.* ⊙ *Daily 7–6:30.*

⑤ Tomba di Cecilia Metella (Tomb of Cecilia Metella). Originally this round tomb was a smaller version of the Mausoleum of Augustus. It was the burial place of a Roman noblewoman, wife of Crassus, one of Julius Caesar's generals. The original decoration includes a frieze of bulls' skulls near the top. The travertine stone walls were made higher and the crenellations added when the tomb was transformed into a fortress by the Caetani family in the 14th century. ⊠ *Via Appia Antica 162,* ☎ *06/7802465.* ▣ *Free.* ⊙ *Tues.–Sat. 9–1 hr before sunset, Sun. and Mon. 9–2.*

2   DINING

Since ancient times Romans have been known for great feasts and banquets, and though the days of the triclinium and the saturnalia are long past, dining out is still all the nightlife most Romans need. Don't look for star chefs here, or the latest trends— with a few notable exceptions, the city's food scene is a bit like its historical sites, well worn but still standing. Nonetheless, food-lovers have much to look forward to; in fact, a lingering meal alfresco is one of Rome's great pleasures.

Updated by
Jon Eldan and
Carla Lionello

ROMAN COOKING IS PREDOMINANTLY SIMPLE; dishes rarely have more than a few ingredients, and meat and fish are most often baked or grilled. Although many traditional recipes are based on innards, you won't find much of that on the menu in restaurants in the center of town, with the exception of *trippa alla romana* (tripe stewed in tomatoes with wild mint).

The typical Roman fresh pasta is fettuccine, a golden egg noodle that's at its classic best when laced with *ragù,* a thick, rich tomato and meat sauce. Spaghetti *alla carbonara* is tossed with a sauce of egg yolk, chunks of rendered *guanciale* (cured pork cheek), pecorino Romano cheese, and lots of freshly ground black pepper. Pasta *all'amatriciana* has a sauce of tomato, guanciale, pecorino, and chili or black pepper. Potato gnocchi, served with tomato sauce and a sprinkling of Parmesan or pecorino, are a Roman favorite for Thursday dinner. The best meat on the menu is often *abbacchio,* or milk-fed lamb. Legs are usually roasted with rosemary and potatoes, and the chops are grilled *alla scottadito* (to be eaten hot off the grill with your fingers). Most Mediterranean fish are light yet flavorful, among them *spigola* (sea bass), *triglia* (red mullet), and *rombo* (turbot or flounder).

Local cheeses are made from sheep's milk; the best known is the aged, sharp pecorino Romano. Fresh ricotta is a treat all on its own and finds its way into a number of dishes, including desserts. Typical wines of Rome are those of the Castelli Romani, the towns in the hills to the southeast: Frascati, Colli Albani, Marino, and Velletri. Though the water in Rome is good to drink, restaurants will usually have you choose between bottled *gassata* (sparkling) or *liscia* (not sparkling) water.

Many restaurants make a specialty of the *fritto misto* (mixed fry) with whatever vegetables are in season. Rome is famous for *carciofi* (artichokes; in season from November to April), traditionally prepared *alla romana* (stuffed with garlic and mint and braised), or *alla giudia* (fried whole). A special springtime treat is *vignarola,* a mixture of tender peas, fava beans, and artichokes, cooked with bits of guanciale.

One of the great joys of a meal in Italy is that most restaurants will not rush you out. Accordingly, service is often more relaxed than speedy, and the *conto* (bill) will not be brought until you ask for it. Though the *pane e coperto* (bread and cover charge) has been officially eliminated, many restaurants still charge extra for bread. Unless otherwise written on the menu, *servizio* (service) is included, so don't pay for service twice. Locals customarily reward particularly good service with a few euros per person. Almost all restaurants close one day a week (in most cases Sunday or Monday) and for at least two weeks in August.

In the late 1990s Romans discovered Sunday brunch, which has become an ongoing trend. It consists of a buffet offering in a restaurant or wine bar during the usual brunch hours. Besides salads, cheese, cold meats, and the like, you are likely to find *frittate* (Italian omelettes made with mixed vegetables), deep-fried vegetables (made to order), soups, cold pasta salads, and ethnic food from several countries. A varied selection of desserts might include American muffins and brownies.

Though no-smoking rooms are practically unheard of, these restaurants have no-smoking areas: Ai Tre Scalini, Alberto Ciarla, Albistrò, Al Bric, Antico Arco, Dal Bolognese, Dar Poeta (pizzeria), Enoteca Corsi, Ferrara, Il Convivio, La Pergola, L'Eau Vive, Le Sans Souci, Testa.

Prices

CATEGORY	COST*
$$$$	over €23
$$$	€18–€23
$$	€13–€18
$	under €13

Prices are for a second course (secondo piatto).

Aventine and Testaccio

$$$ ✕ **Checchino dal 1887.** Literally carved from a hillside composed of pot-sherds from Roman times, Checchino serves traditional Roman cuisine, carefully prepared and presented without fanfare or decoration, in a clean, sober environment. Though the slaughterhouses of Rome's Testaccio quarter—a short cab ride from the city center—are long gone, you can still try the various meats that make up the soul of Roman cooking: *trippa* (tripe), *testina* (head), *pajata* (intestine), *zampa* (trotter), and *coratella* (sweetbreads and heart of beef). There are also plenty of other dishes to choose from: house specialties include *coda alla vaccinara* (stewed oxtail), a popular Roman dish, and *abbacchio alla cacciatora* (braised milk-fed lamb) with seasonal vegetables. The restaurant also has one of the city's best wine lists. ⊠ *Via di Monte Testaccio 30,* ☎ *06/ 5746318. AE, DC, MC, V. Closed Sun., Mon., and Aug.*

$$ ✕ **Nel Regno di Re Ferdinando II.** For visitors to Italy who miss out on a trip to Naples, this place is the next best thing. Fresh ingredients and an emphasis on seafood are the hallmarks of Re Ferdinando. Start with linguine in a light squid sauce, or gnocchi *alla sorrentina* (with fresh tomatoes and mozzarella), and move on to stuffed *totano* (cuttlefish) or home-cooked meatballs. Neapolitan pastries are a good choice for dessert, and the wine list stays close to home, too, offering bottles from the Campania region. ⊠ *Via di Monte Testaccio 39,* ☎ *06/5783725. AE, DC, MC, V. Closed Sun. No lunch Mon.*

$ ✕ **Osteria ai Mercati.** Osteria ai Mercati may be a lot newer than other restaurants in the Testaccio area, but it feels like an old fit. Start with simple bruschetta with different toppings: fresh, sweet tomato, or smoked salmon and arugula. Potato-stuffed ravioli and *ciecamariti* (literally "blind the husbands," pasta in a spicy tomato sauce) are excellent, and second courses such as pork with porcini mushrooms and chestnuts are well executed. Homemade desserts and liqueur top off the meal. ⊠ *Piazza del Gazometro 1,* ☎ *06/5743091. AE, DC, MC, V. Closed 2 wks in mid-Aug. No lunch weekends.*

$ ✕ **Perilli.** A bastion of authentic Roman cooking and trattoria atmosphere since 1911 (the decor has changed very little), this is the place to go to try rigatoni *con pajata* (with veal intestines)—if you're into that sort of thing. Otherwise the amatriciana and carbonara sauces are classics. The house wine is a golden nectar from the Castelli Romani. ⊠ *Via Marmorata 39,* ☎ *06/5742415. AE, D, MC, V. Closed Wed. and Aug.*

Campo dei Fiori

$$ ✕ **Al Bric.** Roberto Marchetti, a fourth-generation Roman wine merchant, has created a bistro where wine reigns supreme, with a thick list (well over 1,000 labels) of carefully selected wines from regions in Italy and France. Fresh ingredients are one of the hallmarks of the Al Bric, and you can taste it in dishes such as artichoke charlotte with warm chèvre cheese or the inventive pappardelle with a pinot noir and duck sauce. A fantastic cheese cart and scrumptious desserts made in-house make Al Bric one of Rome's most interesting eateries. ⊠ *Via del Pel-*

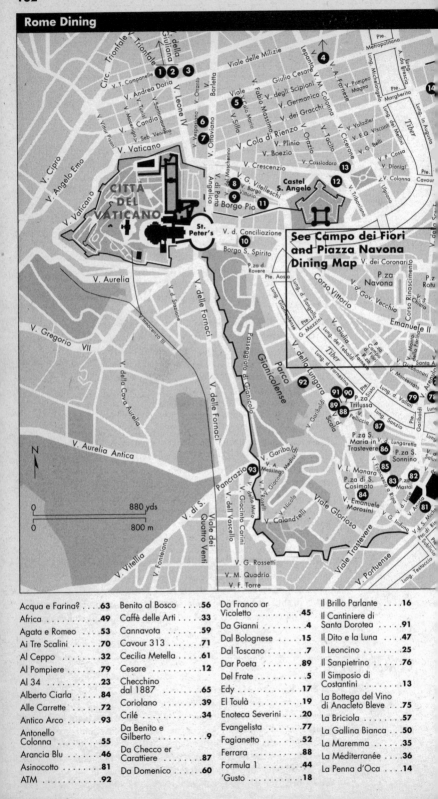

legrino 51, ☎ *06/6879533. AE, DC, MC, V. Closed Mon. and 2 wks in Aug. No lunch Tues.–Sat.*

$$ ✕ **Pierluigi.** Ever since Pierluigi opened in 1938, it's been a favorite with foreign residents of Rome and Italians in the entertainment field. On busy evenings tables are almost impossible to get, so make sure you reserve well in advance. Seafood dominates (if you're in the mood to splurge, try the lobster), but traditional Roman dishes are offered, too, including fried zucchini blossoms and simple spaghetti. Though the dining room, complete with stone arches, is perfectly pleasant, seats outside on the piazza are unbeatable in nice weather. ✉ *Piazza dei Ricci 144,* ☎ *06/6861302. AE, DC, MC, V. Closed Mon.*

$ ✕ **Albistrò.** Just a hop, skip, and a jump from Piazza Farnese, this small, surprisingly affordable restaurant turns out both classic Italian dishes and more varied, modern offerings. The small menu changes often, but you will always find interesting risottos, such as pumpkin with bits of almond cookies, and tasty second courses such as guinea fowl with chestnuts. One of the owners is from Switzerland, so be on the lookout for such regional specialties as *pavé,* a semolina pudding with fresh strawberries. ✉ *Via dei Banchi Vecchi 140/a,* ☎ *06/6865274. AE, DC, MC, V. Closed Wed. and 3 wks in July–Aug. No lunch Mon.–Sat., Sept.–June.*

$ ✕ **Café Malastrana.** Café Malastrana may be named after Prague's old town, but the food is all Italian, served in a sleek, modern space. Chef Antonio Giacomella provides a spirited variation on Roman classics: fried zucchini flowers with smoked salmon instead of anchovies, and pasta alla carbonara with the added kick of artichokes. The formula succeeds in other dishes as well, like *polpette di baccalà,* a creamy puree of salt cod rolled into balls, lightly breaded, and deep-fried. If your cholesterol level is still within designated limits, order the fried crepe for dessert, stuffed with pastry cream and topped with warm chocolate sauce, powdered sugar, and cinnamon. ✉ *Via Monserrato 32,* ☎ *06/6865617. MC, V. Closed Tues. and Aug. No lunch Sun.*

$ ✕ **Ditirambo.** Ditirambo's bistrolike atmosphere and delicious food attract glitterati such as Oscar winner Roberto Benigni, but Romans from all walks of life pack this restaurant every night. The kitchen offers dishes your grandmother might make, if she was a very good cook. Simple antipasti consist of vegetables and cured meats, and pastas range from cacio e pepe to gnocchi with Montasio cheese and radicchio. Grilled sea bass and veal chops with herbs baked in foil are favorite main courses. The homemade ricotta and sour cherry cake is a treat. ✉ *Piazza della Cancelleria 74/75,* ☎ *06/6871626. AE, DC, MC, V. Closed Aug. No lunch Mon.*

$ ✕ **Filetti di Baccalà.** The name says it all. For years, Filetti di Baccalà has been serving just that—battered, deep-fried fillets of salt cod—and not much else. The Roman specialty doesn't require much accompaniment. You'll find no-frills starters like *bruschette al pomodoro* (garlic-rubbed toast topped with fresh tomatoes and olive oil), and in winter months the cod is served alongside *puntarelle,* a crunchy Roman green topped with a delicious anchovy vinaigrette. It's a fun place, with a convivial waitstaff. ✉ *Largo dei Librari 88, near Campo dei Fiori,* ☎ *06/6864018. No credit cards. Closed Sun. and Aug. No lunch.*

$ ✕ **Grappolo d'Oro.** This central trattoria off Campo dei Fiori has been
★   a favorite for decades with locals and foreign residents. Although it was the subject of a *New Yorker* article on the "classic Roman trattoria," notoriety has not induced the graying, courteous owners to change their two half-paneled dining rooms or menu, which features pasta all'amatriciana and scaloppine any way you want them. Inquire about the day's special. ✉ *Piazza della Cancelleria 80,* ☎ *06/6864118. AE, DC, MC, V. Closed Sun. and Aug.*

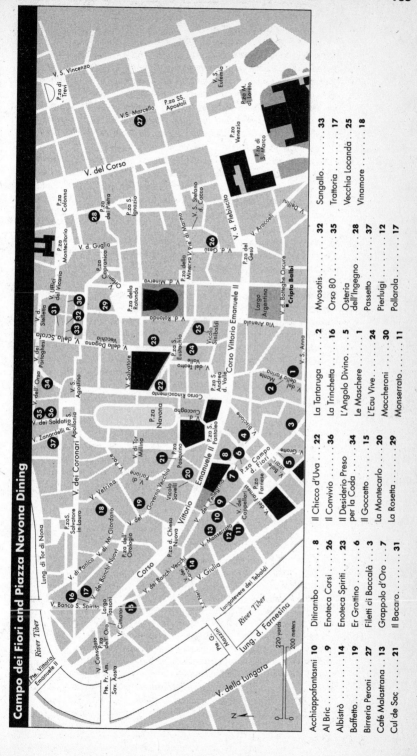

$ ✕ **Le Maschere.** For a taste of southern Italian (Calabrian) fare, try this informal cellar restaurant hidden away between Largo Argentina and Piazza Campo dei Fiori—in summer, look for the planters and the few outdoor tables. Dark rustic walls are hung with everything from paper garlands to old utensils; there are pottery wine jugs and rush-seat chairs. To start, order spicy Calabria salami or hit the expansive antipasto table, and then go on to pizza or pasta with broccoli or with tomato and eggplant sauce. Grilled meat and seafood make up the list of second courses. Try one of the up-and-coming Calabrian labels on the wine list. ✉ *Via Monte della Farina 29,* ☎ *06/6879444. DC, MC, V. Closed Mon. and 2 wks in Aug.*

$ ✕ **Monserrato.** Just off Piazza Farnese, this unassuming restaurant has maintained a high level of quality in an area chock-full of tourist traps. Monserrato's signature dishes are its fish specials: carpaccio *di pesce spada* (swordfish carpaccio, served with lemon and arugula), *insalatina di seppie* (cuttlefish salad), *bigoli con gamberi e asparagi* (homemade pasta with shrimp and asparagus), and grilled fish are all simply prepared, exalting the flavor of first-rate ingredients. Umbrella-covered tables on the small, adjacent piazza provide a lovely dining experience in nice weather. ✉ *Via di Monserrato 96,* ☎ *06/6873386. AE, MC, V. Closed Mon., 2 wks in Aug., and 1 wk at Christmas.*

$ ✕ **Pollarola.** This typical Roman trattoria, near Piazza Navona and Campo dei Fiori, has artificial flowers on the tables but—as a special feature—it also has an ancient, authentic Roman column embedded in the rear wall. Try a pasta specialty such as cannelloni with meat sauce, or *pollo in porchetta* (chicken with bacon and herbs). The house wines, white or red, are good. You can eat outdoors in nice weather. ✉ *Piazza della Pollarola 24 (Campo dei Fiori),* ☎ *06/68801654. AE, DC, MC, V. Closed Sun. and Aug.*

Colosseo

$$$ ✕ **San Teodoro.** With an enviable location on a quiet street behind the Roman Forum, the pleasant San Teodoro is a dependable choice for creative Italian cuisine, several Roman dishes, and delicate fish. The small but varied menu includes classic fried artichokes (among the best in the city), homemade ravioli *con cipolla di Tropea* (filled with red onion and tossed in balsamic vinegar), and fresh sole in a tomato, zucchini flower, and thyme broth. Service is courteous yet retains an air of familiarity, and the outdoor seating, abutting the theater of Marcellus and the Campidoglio, can't be beat. ✉ *Via dei Fienili 50,* ☎ *06/ 6780933. AE, DC, MC, V. Closed Sun.*

$$ ✕ **Ai Tre Scalini.** A high-quality restaurant near the Colosseum is a pleasant surprise. Sit outside in warm weather, but if it gets too hot, Ai Tre Scalini's naturally cool rooms on the lower level are fantastically refreshing. Sample chef Angelo Annarumi's playful salmon roulades with ricotta cheese and pink grapefruit, or the unusual radicchio and cheese-stuffed *zagnolotti* (small ravioli) in a delicious lobster sauce. A wide variety of second courses, from *orata in crosta di patate con vongole* (gilthead bream topped with crunchy potatoes and sprinkled with tasty baby clams) to simple beef with rosemary, are all served with flair. Excellent homemade almond ice cream comes with chocolate sauce. ✉ *Via SS. Quattro 30,* ☎ *06/7096309. AE, DC, MC, V. Closed Mon. and 10 days in Sept.*

Jewish Ghetto

$$$ ✕ **Piperno.** In the old Jewish Ghetto next to historic Palazzo Cenci, Piperno has been in business for more than a century. It is *the* place to go for Rome's extraordinary *carciofi alla giudia* (fried whole arti-

chokes). You eat in one of three small wood-paneled dining rooms or at one of a handful of tables outdoors. Try *filetti di baccalà* (fillet of cod), *pasta e ceci* (a thick soup of pasta tubes and chickpeas), and *fiori di zucca ripieni e fritti* (fried stuffed zucchini flowers). ⊠ *Monte dei Cenci 9,* ☎ *06/68806629. AE, DC, MC, V. Closed Mon. and Aug. No dinner Sun.*

$$ ✕ **Al Pompiere.** Something of a *hostaria*, or informal restaurant, in the heart of the old Jewish Ghetto, Al Pompiere has stayed the same over the years. Why should it change, when its Roman dishes such as fried zucchini flowers, battered salt cod, gnocchi, and tender beef strips with arugula are all consistently good? High ceilings, dark wood paneling, and a friendly atmosphere make you feel like you've stepped back in time. ⊠ *Via Santa Maria dei Calderari 38,* ☎ *06/6868377. AE, MC, V. Closed Sun. and Aug.*

$$ ✕ **Evangelista.** Evangelista is known throughout the city for its carciofi *al mattone,* roasted artichokes pressed flat between two hot bricks. Its fame is well deserved, but the artichokes are just the beginning. Try excellent pasta with fresh fava beans, pecorino cheese, and mint in spring, or roast pork loin with juniper berries in winter. Homemade desserts—don't miss the pastry with zabaglione cream and warm chocolate sauce—prompt service, and a comfortably elegant setting make Evangelista a winner. ⊠ *Via delle Zoccolette 11/a,* ☎ *06/6875810. MC, V. Closed Sun. and Aug. No lunch.*

$$ ✕ **Il Sanpietrino.** Named after the *sanpietrini*, or Roman cobblestones, that line the floor, this popular restaurant has a lovely, relaxing atmosphere. Beamed ceilings and tile walls remind diners of old-world Rome, yet the menu has a contemporary feel to it. Seafood dominates the bill, and dishes such as *panzerotti di pesce in salsa di mazzancolle* (homemade ravioli stuffed with fish, in a light prawn sauce) and *rombo in crosta di patate con salsa ai funghi porcini* (flounder baked in a potato crust, with porcini mushroom sauce) make the most of seasonal ingredients. Excellent desserts range from a pine-nut cake to a simple lemon sorbet with strawberry sauce. The short wine list is made up primarily of regional selections. ⊠ *Piazza Costaguti 15,* ☎ *06/68806471. AE, DC, MC, V. Closed Sun., 3 wks in Aug., and 1 wk in Jan. No lunch.*

$$ ✕ **Sora Lella.** What was once a simple trattoria ensconced on Tiberina Island (great view from the bathroom) is now a monument to the late founder herself, a beloved Roman personality. Inside are two small dining rooms lined with wood paneling and old wine bottles. Although prices are much higher than when Sora Lella presided over the cash desk, Lella's son has ensured that the cooking is still 100% Roman. Daily specials as well as menu standards are written on the chalkboard, but you'll usually find homey meatballs, *pasta e fagioli* (a thick soup of short pasta and beans), and *maialino all'antica roma* (suckling pig with prunes, pine nuts, and raisins). Leave room for the quintessential Roman ricotta cake. ⊠ *Via Ponte Quattro Capi 16,* ☎ *06/6861601. AE, DC, MC, V. Closed Sun. and Aug.*

Parioli

The Parioli neighborhood is a 10-minute cab ride from the city center, up Via Veneto and across Villa Borghese. It's a residential area known as an outpost of conspicuous wealth and political conservatism; you won't find tourist attractions here, but there are several good places to eat.

$$–$$$ ✕ **Al Ceppo.** This Sunday lunch favorite offers an ample selection of classic Italian dishes prepared with a creative flair. The menu changes daily but always includes a few specialties of the Marche region—where the owners come from—such as *olive ascolane* (large stuffed green olives, breaded and fried). Pasta is made fresh every day, and other hallmarks are *polpettine di melanzane al vapore* (steamed eggplant balls), the very Roman dish of pasta and broccoli in skate broth, and veal rolls stuffed with radicchio and Parmesan cheese. A wide selection of meats, fish, and vegetables grilled in the attractive fireplace in the front room rounds out the extensive menu. ⊠ *Via Panama 2,* ☎ *06/8419696. AE, DC, MC, V. Closed Mon. and 2 wks in Aug.*

$$ ✕ **La Méditerranée.** Chef Dominique Lesueur is French, but he combines influences from regions as different as Provence, Liguria, and Sicily, focusing most of all on seafood. Standouts include foie gras medallions with black truffle and steamed lobster; shellfish stew with saffron and garlic sauce; and grilled sea bream with fresh herbs over couscous. Desserts should not be missed. ⊠ *Via R. Fauro 2,* ☎ *06/80663694. AE, DC, MC, V. Closed Sun. and Aug.*

$$ ✕ **Ristorante & Wine Bar Testa.** With its stone arches, antique engravings lining the walls, and elegant atmosphere, Testa is one of the city's loveliest restaurants. The menu has been expanded and improved since its opening in the late 1990s, and the wine list offers some hard-to-find bottles. Dishes are updated classics such as pasta with clams and tuna roe, or roast pigeon with figs and honey. The "business lunch"—appetizer, main course, dessert, bottled water, and one glass of wine—is a steal at €18. ⊠ *Via Tirso 30,* ☎ *06/85300692. AE, DC, MC, V. Closed Sun. No lunch Aug.*

$ ✕ **Caffè delle Arti.** Rome's modern art museum, in the lovely green of the Villa Borghese park, also boasts a beautiful café that serves full meals. The food may not be the strongest Rome has to offer, but the restaurant's terrace alone is worth the tab. Best bets on the menu are salads and pastas, perfect lunch items. ⊠ *Via A. Gramsci 73,* ☎ *06/32651236. AE, D, MC, V. No dinner Mon.*

$ ✕ **Trattoria Fauro.** The Italian right wing made this spot its headquarters during the 2001 elections, proving that even Silvio Berlusconi appreciates a good bargain. Fish is especially strong—owner Franco Zambelli buys daily from the renowned fish market in the coastal town of Fiumicino. Menu items include roast octopus with fresh herbs, a fantastic house *crostino* (fatty bacon and shrimp on a slab of toasted bread), and sea bass with wild fennel—but the best thing to do is to toss the menu aside and place yourself in Franco's hands. Specialties from the northern city of Mantua are also on offer, courtesy of Franco's mother in the kitchen. ⊠ *Via R. Fauro 44,* ☎ *06/8083301. Reservations essential. AE, DC, MC, V. Closed Sun. and 2 wks in Aug.*

Piazza di Spagna

$$$$ ✕ **El Toulà.** Rome's prestigious and elegant El Toulà—one of the many spin-offs of its namesake in Treviso—has the warm, welcoming comforts of a 19th-century country house, with white walls, antique furniture in dark wood, heavy silver serving dishes, and spectacular fruit and flower arrangements. In the cozy bar off the entrance you can sip a *prosecco* (Venetian sparkling white wine), the aperitif best suited to the chef's Venetian specialties, such as *baccalà mantecato* (cod whipped with milk to a creamy consistency) or *fegato alla Veneziana* (sweet-and-sour liver with onions), which are always on offer, along with contemporary interpretations of Italian classics. ⊠ *Via della Lupa 29/b,* ☎ *06/6873750. Reservations essential. Jacket and tie. AE, DC, MC, V. Closed Sun. and Aug. No lunch Sat. or Mon.*

$$$$ ✕ **Roman Garden Lounge dell'Hotel Inghilterra.** Smack dab in the heart of the Piazza di Spagna shopping district, the Roman Garden Lounge of the Hotel Inghilterra provides an oasis of quiet charm. Mixed greens with tuna roe and steamed prawns with an artichoke flan make appetizing starters, and ravioli *con fave, cipolotti, e salsa d'agnello* (with fava beans, green onions, and lamb) and medallions of angler fish with eggplant are excellent choices for first and second courses. The menu changes with the season and focuses on fresh ingredients. Tables are close together; plan on eavesdropping neighbors. ⊠ *Via Bocca di Leone 14,* ☎ *06/699811. AE, D, MC, V.*

$$–$$$ ✕ **Dal Bolognese.** Long a haunt of the art crowd, this classic restaurant on Piazza del Popolo is a trendy choice for a leisurely lunch between sightseeing and shopping. An array of contemporary paintings decorates the dining room, but the real attraction is the lovely piazza—one of Rome's best for people-watching. As the name of the restaurant promises, the cooking here adheres to the hearty tradition of Bologna, with delicious homemade *tortellini in brodo* (filled pasta in broth), fresh pastas in creamy sauces, and steaming trays of boiled meats. Among the desserts, try the *dolce della mamma* (a concoction of gelato, zabaglione, and chocolate sauce) and the fruit-shape gelato. ⊠ *Piazza del Popolo 1,* ☎ *06/3611426. AE, D, MC, V. Closed weekends in July and Aug. No lunch Mon. or Tues.*

$$ ✕ **Al 34.** It can be hard to find a place to eat near Piazza di Spagna without spending outrageous sums, but Al 34 has been an affordable standby for many years. There are two seatings for dinner, at 7:30 and 9:30, and diners can choose from set menus featuring Roman specialties, seafood, and meat, or else order from the large à la carte menu. ⊠ *Via Mario de' Fiori,* ☎ *06/6795091. AE, DC, MC, V. Closed Mon. and Aug.*

$$ ✕ **'Gusto.** This is one of Rome's hot spots; even with room for more than 200 diners, it's still tough to get a reservation. Just off Via del Corso and not far from Piazza di Spagna, the two-story space has an airy, modernist feel. The kitchen seems to handle everything with a flair: a sophisticated menu fuses international influences with Italian traditions, resulting in such hybrids as wok-tossed spaghetti with vegetables and ginger, and eggplant and chickpea strudel with sesame–goat cheese sauce. The wine list has more than 800 labels, and the restaurant occasionally hosts live jazz and swing music. There's even a pizzeria that also serves salads and lighter fare at lunch, a wine bar, and a store selling cookbooks and kitchen gadgets. An efficient, professional staff keeps it all moving. ⊠ *Piazza Augusto Imperatore 9,* ☎ *06/ 3226273. Reservations essential. AE, MC, V. Closed Mon.*

$$ ✕ **La Penna d'Oca.** Owner Francesco Tola transformed an old osteria into one of the most interesting restaurants in the area near Piazza del Popolo. Harking back to his Sardinian seaside upbringing, he has created a menu primarily dedicated to fish. Marinated red mullet and rockfish are delicate starters, and homemade gnocchi with shrimp and radicchio in a butter and sage sauce are unusually light. Roast *sarago,* a hard-to-find Mediterranean fish, served with artichokes and potatoes, is a favorite, as is the succulent lobster. Be sure to place your dessert order for soufflé at the beginning of the meal. ⊠ *Via della Penna 53,* ☎ *06/ 3202898. AE, DC, MC, V. Closed Sun. and Aug. 10–31. No lunch Sat.*

$$ ✕ **Nino.** One of the most dependable restaurants in the historic center, Nino sticks to the classics, in food and decor (dark wood paneling and white tablecloths). To start, try its Tuscan cured meats or warm toasts spread with liver pâté. Move on to *pappardelle al lepre* (wide noodles with a rich hare sauce) or the grilled beef. Simple sweets, like *castagnaccio,* a chestnut dessert, are all worth the extra calories. Nino's location near Piazza di Spagna makes it an excellent choice for lunch after a morning of shopping. ⊠ *Via Borgognona 11,* ☎ *06/ 6786752. AE, DC, MC, V. Closed Sun. and Aug.*

$ ✕ **Edy.** This surprisingly affordable trattoria is right around the corner from the exclusive shops along the Via del Babuino. Fettuccine *ai carciofi* (with artichokes), spaghetti *al cartoccio con frutti di mare* (with mixed shellfish, brought to the table wrapped in foil), and lamb are all excellent choices. The house white, from the Castelli Romani, is a perfect, fruity accompaniment to the menu's offerings, especially in the heat of summer. Ask for a table outside in warm weather; otherwise, the tile interior with kitschy paintings of Roman scenes is more than adequate. ⊠ *Vicolo del Babuino 4,* ☎ *06/36001738. AE, DC, MC, V. Closed Sun. and 1 wk in mid-Aug.*

$ ✕ **Otello alla Concordia.** The clientele in this popular spot—it's off a shopping street near Piazza di Spagna—is about evenly divided between tourists and workers from shops and offices in the area. The former like to sit outdoors in the courtyard in any weather; the latter have their regular tables in one of the inside dining rooms. The menu offers classic Roman and Italian dishes, and service is friendly and efficient. Since every tourist in Rome knows about it, and since the regulars won't relinquish their niches, you may have to wait for a table; go early. ⊠ *Via della Croce 81,* ☎ *06/6791178. Reservations essential. AE, DC, MC, V. Closed Sun. and 3 wks in Jan.*

Piazza Navona

$$$$ ✕ **Il Convivio.** Chef Angelo Troiani's never-ending quest to find the freshest seasonal ingredients translates into original dishes like *cosce di quaglia in confit, vinaigrette all'aceto di lamponi, verza stufata* (confit of quail's legs with raspberry vinaigrette and braised cabbage); spaghetti with shrimp, artichokes, mint, and Roman sheep's-milk cheese; and *filetto di maiale arrostito, patate in porchetta, salsa di vin cotto* (roast pork served with bacon-wrapped potatoes in a wine sauce). The tasting menu, a good deal with five courses (but not including wine), changes every day. Massimo and Giuseppe manage the dining room and pour wine chosen from a vast cellar boasting more than 1,000 bottles. ⊠ *Vicolo dei Soldati 31,* ☎ *06/6869432. Reservations essential. AE, DC, MC, V. Closed Sun. and 1 wk in Aug. No lunch Mon.*

$$$$ ✕ **La Rosetta.** Chef-owner Massimo Riccioli took the nets and fishing
★ gear off the walls of his parents' trattoria to create what is widely known as *the* place to go in Rome to eat first-rate fish. The interior is simple elegance at its best, with warm wood paneling and fresh flowers. Start with the justifiably well-known selection of marinated seafood appetizers, each with a clear and distinct flavor. Pasta dishes are dressed with fish or seafood, alone or in combination with seasonal vegetables and fresh herbs. Even simpler dishes like the classic *zuppa di pesce* (fish soup) or perfectly grilled fish and crustaceans deserve star billing and command star prices. Desserts (made in-house) are worth saving room for and come with a glass of dessert wine. ⊠ *Via della Rosetta 9,* ☎ *06/6861002. Reservations essential. AE, DC, MC, V. Closed Sun. and Aug. No lunch Sat.–Wed.*

$$$ ✕ **Passetto.** Benefiting from a choice location near Piazza Navona, Passetto has been a favorite with Italians and tourists for many years: it's a place you can rely on for classic Italian food and friendly service, where the charm and grace of the waiters are reminiscent of a different era. If you can, eat on the terrace in the back—it's set on a quiet piazza; the mirrored dining room is more staid. Roman specialties, such as carbonara and abbacchio, are featured. ⊠ *Via Zanardelli 14,* ☎ *06/68803696. AE, DC, MC, V.*

$$-$$$ ✕ **Myosotis.** The Marsili family's decision to open a second, central
★ branch of their successful restaurant on the outskirts of town definitely paid off. Its popular location near the Pantheon, extensive menu, and great value make Myosotis a place you might want to return to again and again. The menu rides a delicate line between tradition and innovation, focusing more on the freshness and quality of the ingredients

than on elaborate presentation. Fresh pasta gets special attention: it's rolled out by hand to order for the *maltagliati alla delizia di mare* (pasta with seafood). There's a wide choice of fish (try the fish fry, a Roman staple), meat, and seasonal vegetables to choose from. The wine list is ample, the prices honest. ⊠ *Via della Vaccarella 3/5,* ☎ *06/6865554. AE, DC, MC, V. Closed Sun. and 2 wks in Aug.*

$$ ✕ **Il Bacaro.** This tiny candlelit spot near the Pantheon is perfect for a romantic evening. Marinated fish, pasta with sausage and broccoli, and excellent meats prepared in a variety of ways—such as *involtini di vitella con cipolotti e pinoli in salsa di olive nere* (tender veal rolled around scallions and pine nuts in a green olive sauce)—are some of the unpretentious but satisfying dishes on offer. The wine list is well above average and includes several varieties of after-dinner drinks, a rarity in Rome. ⊠ *Via degli Spagnoli 27,* ☎ *06/6864110. Reservations essential. DC, MC, V. Closed Sun. and 1 wk in Aug. No lunch Sat.*

$$ ✕ **Il Chicco d'Uva.** Standing right next to the Senate building, Il Chicco d'Uva has both a great location and stellar food. Appetizers include thinly sliced goose carpaccio with fresh peaches and steamed broccoli with fatty bacon and black truffle. Pastas vary from season to season and use both fish and meat, and second courses tend to favor carnivores, with such dishes as a delicate veal with zucchini flowers. Desserts are creative and satisfying; especially good are the *semifreddi,* soft ice cream in a variety of flavors with tasty toppings. ⊠ *Corso Rinascimento 70,* ☎ *06/6867983. AE, DC, MC, V. Closed Sun. and Aug. No lunch.*

$$ ✕ **Orso 80.** The good kind of tourist restaurant, this bright and bustling trattoria near Piazza Navona is well known for its fabulous antipasto table, heaped high with tasty vegetables, meat, and seafood. Try the homemade egg pasta or the *bucatini all'amatriciana* (pasta with tomatoes, sheep's milk cheese, and bacon); there's plenty of fish on the menu, too. For dessert, the ricotta cake, a genuine Roman specialty, is always good. ⊠ *Via dell'Orso 33,* ☎ *06/6864904. AE, DC, MC, V. Closed Mon. and Aug.*

$$ ✕ **Osteria dell'Ingegno.** With its stylish decor and happening feel, this upscale osteria almost seems out of place among the ruins of the old town. The short menu changes often, with simple dishes that emphasize fresh ingredients. Inventive salads big enough for lunch or a main course at dinner may be just the thing to order after several nights of three-course feasts. For those whose appetites remain hearty, ravioli *alle noci con fonduta di taleggio dolce e grana* (walnut ravioli in a silky sauce of taleggio and grana cheeses) and *anatra al forno con salsa agrodolce, uva e vin santo* (roast duck with a sweet and sour sauce, raisins, and sweet wine) are good choices. ⊠ *Piazza di Pietra 45, near the Pantheon,* ☎ *06/6780662. AE, DC, MC, V. Closed Sun. and 1 wk in Aug.*

$$ ✕ **Sangallo.** An intimate little restaurant not far from the Pantheon, Sangallo specializes in top-quality fish that is light, well cooked, and invitingly presented in dishes such as *tagliolini con pomodorini, mazzancolle, e scaglie di pecorino* (fresh pasta with cherry tomatoes, shrimp, and shavings of pecorino cheese) and *spigola in crosta di sale* (sea bass baked in a salt crust). The three tasting menus (fish, meat, and truffles) change monthly and are a better value than the à la carte offerings. ⊠ *Vicolo della Vaccarella 11/a,* ☎ *06/6865549. AE, DC, MC, V. Closed Sun. and first 3 wks in Aug. No lunch.*

$$ ✕ **Vecchia Locanda.** Sit outside in summer at this eatery on a tiny pedestrian street near Largo Argentina, and the world seems a better place. Vecchia Locanda has been in the restaurant business for more than 70 years and has managed to keep its antique charm intact. The menu offers classic Roman cuisine with a hint of creativity. Well-executed carbonara and amatriciana are great staples, but more inventive items such

as pasta with asparagus, clams, and shrimp, and beef strips with eggplant and cherry tomatoes are also good. Offerings change with the season, with heavier dishes of meat and game concentrated in the winter months. The wine list is impressive for such a small restaurant, and service is extremely courteous. ⊠ *Vicolo Sinibaldi 2,* ☎ *06/68802831. AE, DC, MC, V. Closed Sun. and Dec. 22–Jan. 20.*

$–$$ ✕ **L'Eau Vive.** This is definitely a unique Roman dining experience. For the last 29 years the restaurant, which serves (very good) classic French food, has been run by a society of French missionary nuns. Stick with French fare like foie gras and steak *au poivre* (pepper steak). The atmosphere throughout is serene and soothing, though rather plain (of course). Soft devotional music plays as the smiling sisters speedily bring plate after plate. They take a brief pause before dessert to sing "Ave Maria"—you are welcome to join in. The upstairs rooms, reserved for nonsmokers, have beautiful frescoes. Don't feel guilty if you order several courses; all proceeds go to charity. ⊠ *Via Monterone 85,* ☎ *06/68801095. AE, DC, MC, V. Closed Sun. and Aug.*

$ ✕ **Birreria Peroni.** This beer hall's long wooden tables, hard-backed booths, and simple northern Italian food (which resembles German fare) provide a nice respite from pasta and tomato sauce. Try the goulash or the many sausage specialties—with sauerkraut and potatoes, of course. The Peroni Gran Riserva beer, a domestic double malt, is terrific. ⊠ *Via di San Marcello 19,* ☎ *06/6795310. AE, DC, MC, V. Closed Sun. and Aug. No lunch Sat.*

$ ✕ **Il Desiderio Preso per la Coda.** Tucked behind Piazza Navona, this restaurant has a Tuscan slant and a laid-back feel. The walls are adorned with contemporary art, some of which was done by the wife of one of the owners. The small menu changes often and includes such dishes as *pappa al pomodoro* (a Tuscan bread and tomato soup), fig risotto, and *polpettone* (meat loaf), a great comfort food. ⊠ *Vicolo della Palomba 23,* ☎ *06/68307522. AE, DC, MC, V. Closed Mon. and Aug. No lunch.*

$ ✕ **Maccheroni.** This boisterous, convivial trattoria north of the Pantheon makes for a fun evening out. The modern decor and airy feel attract a young clientele, but the menu sticks to Roman basics like simple pasta with fresh tomatoes and basil or rigatoni *alla gricia* (with bacon, sheep's-milk cheese, and black pepper). Appetizers like prosciutto and buffalo mozzarella may not be exciting, but they're eminently satisfying. The homemade *panna cotta* (baked heavy cream) with chocolate or berry sauce is a perfect way to end the meal. ⊠ *Piazza delle Coppelle 44,* ☎ *06/68307895. AE, DC, MC, V. Closed Sun.*

$ ✕ **Trattoria.** No name, no menus—simply come in, sit down (go early to find a table), and wait for the mother-and-daughter team to start bringing out the food. Basic pastas with amatriciana, tomato sauce, or meat sauce; tripe; sausage; beef rolls simmered in tomato and onions; hearty cannellini beans; garlicky spinach—it's like eating at Grandma's. Don't ask questions in this most Roman of trattorias, just eat. ⊠ *Via dei Banchi Nuovi 8,* ☎ *no phone. No credit cards. Closed weekends and Aug.*

San Pietro

$$$ ✕ **Il Simposio di Costantini.** One of the classiest wine bars in town dou-
★ bles as one of Rome's better restaurants. Owner Arcangelo Dadini offers a sophisticated menu to match the elegance of the wrought-iron and velvet decor: spinach-stuffed pears drizzled with a sharp cheese sauce and chickpea soup with duck sausage and salt cod are typical of the bold, inspired entrées. Lighter fare includes a wide selection of marinated and smoked fish, top-quality salami and cured meats, pâtés, and

cheeses. Il Simposio benefits from having an enormous wine store attached; choose from 30 wines *degustazione* (available by the glass) or a multitude of Italian and foreign labels. ⊠ *Piazza Cavour 16,* ☎ *06/ 3211502. AE, DC, MC, V. Closed Sun. and Aug. No lunch Sat.*

$$–$$$ ✕ **Cesare.** An old standby in the residential area near the Vatican
★ known as Prati, Cesare is a willing slave to tradition. On offer are classic fish and meat dishes such as fresh marinated anchovies, homemade pasta with meat sauce, and thick Florentine steaks. Try the impressive array of cured meats, especially the *prosciutto di cervo* (salt-cured deer) or *lardo di Colonnata* (bacon). As with any other real Roman restaurant, gnocchi are served on Thursday and pasta with chickpeas on Friday. Cesare also has a fairly extensive wine list representing many regions. ⊠ *Via Crescenzio 13,* ☎ *06/6861227. AE, DC, MC, V. Closed Mon., Aug., and Easter wk. No lunch Sun.*

$$–$$$ ✕ **Da Benito e Gilberto.** Commonly known as "da Benito," this fish restaurant may look like all the other tourist-trap trattorias in the charming area near St. Peter's called Borgo Pio, but it's been a highly regarded staple among locals for years. Try their simple, classic seafood: heaping bowls of mussels and clams in a tomato broth, fettuccine with lobster, or their traditional fish fry, with shrimp, squid, and whatever else might be in season. Their refreshing dessert drink, a mixture of prosecco (dry sparkling white wine) and lemon sorbet, is perfect at any time of the year. ⊠ *Via del Falco 19,* ☎ *06/6867769. AE, D, MC, V. Closed Sun., Mon., and Aug.*

$$–$$$ ✕ **La Veranda dell'Hotel Columbus.** Deciding on whether to eat inside or outside at La Veranda is not easy, since both the courtyard—with trompe l'oeil designs, leafy trees, and nighttime torches—and the frescoed dining room with high-back wooden chairs are among Rome's most spectacular settings. The food matches the surroundings and ranges from classic Roman cuisine such as spaghetti alla carbonara to more updated Italian dishes such as fiori di zucca *con mazzancolle e salsa allo yogurt* (stuffed with prawns in a yogurt sauce) and roast beef in juniper-berry and bay-leaf sauce. In addition, chef Luca Urriera cooks up "historical" dishes, such as a 17th-century recipe for sea bream, baked in an almond crust. Call ahead, especially on Saturday, as the hotel often acts as a venue for weddings and the restaurant closes for such events. ⊠ *Borgo Santo Spirito 73,* ☎ *06/6872973. Reservations essential. AE, D, MC, V.*

$$ ✕ **Dal Toscano.** This family-run Tuscan trattoria near the Vatican has
★ an open, wood-fired grill and classic dishes such as *ribollita* (a thick bread-and-vegetable soup) and *pici* (fresh thick pasta, served with a wild hare sauce). The real attraction, though, is the grilled meat; when mad cow disease brought bistecca alla fiorentina off the menu, the result was an increased appreciation of the wonderful pork chops and lamb chops. Accompany them with a strong Chianti or a half liter of the Tuscan house wine. Desserts such as pastry cream tarts, apple strudel, and castagnaccio (a chestnut and pine-nut treat) in wintertime are all homemade. Service is friendly and speedy. There's outside dining in good weather. ⊠ *Via Germanico 58,* ☎ *06/39725717. AE, MC, V. Closed Mon., Aug., and Christmas–New Year's.*

$$ ✕ **Taverna Angelica.** The area surrounding St. Peter's Basilica isn't known
★ for culinary excellence, but Taverna Angelica is an exception. Its tiny size (just 20 seats) allows the chef to concentrate on each individual dish, and the results are impressive. The menu is creative without being excessive, and such dishes as chickpeas with a fondue of pecorino cheese, lentil soup with pigeon breast, and breast of duck in balsamic vinegar are exquisitely executed. The candlelit dining room, tasteful decor, and excellent service are icing on the cake. ⊠ *Piazza delle Vaschette 14/b,* ☎ *06/6874514. Reservations essential. AE, MC, V. Closed Sun. No lunch Mon.*

$ × **Osteria dell'Angelo.** At this boisterous and authentic eatery, the
★ mandatory prix-fixe menu at dinner is not a ploy to attract tourists,
it's just great food at a great price. If you go in a group, ask for fam-
ily-style portions and try a bit of everything they bring out. From
mixed antipasti of vegetables, beans, cured meats, and bruschetta to
spaghetti cacio e pepe and sautéed veal with mushrooms, it's all Roman
and it's all good. Dessert usually comes in the form of cookies to be
dunked in sweet wine. For dinner, reservations are a must. ⊠ *Via G.
Bettolo 24, near the St. Peter's Basilica Metro stop,* ☎ *06/3729470.
No credit cards. Closed Sun., Aug., and Christmas wk. No lunch
Wed., Thurs., and Sat.–Mon.*

$ × **Tre Pupazzi.** The "three puppets" after which the trattoria is named
were fragments of an ancient sarcophagus that once embellished the
building. Alas, they were removed during restoration work before the
millennium jubilee. On a byway near the Vatican, the tavern, founded
in 1625, wears its centuries lightly, upholding a tradition of good
food, courteous service, and reasonable prices. The menu offers classic Roman and Abruzzese trattoria fare, including fettuccine, homemade ravioli and abbacchio, plus pizzas at lunchtime (a rarity in Rome)
and well past midnight. ⊠ *Borgo Pio at Via dei Tre Pupazzi,* ☎ *06/
6868371. AE, MC, V. Closed Sun.*

Termini

$$$–$$$$ × **Agata e Romeo.** The husband-and-wife team of Agata Parisella and
Romeo Caraccio operate one of Rome's top-flight restaurants. Agata
runs the kitchen, turning out inspired cuisine that never loses sight of
its Roman roots, and Romeo acts as maître d' and expert sommelier.
Flan di pecorino con salsa di fichi secchi (sheep's-cheese flan with a
dried fig sauce), *vellutata di zucchini con fiore fritto* (a velvety zucchini
soup topped with a fried zucchini flower), and braised oxtail with cel-
ery puree are just a few of the delicious items on the small but balanced
menu. A tasting menu, complete with wine, is a smart bet if you want
to try a variety of specialties. Scrumptious desserts and an excellent
wine list place this among the city's finest eateries. ⊠ *Via C. Alberto
45,* ☎ *06/4466115. Reservations essential. AE, D, MC, V. Closed week-
ends, 2 wks in Jan., and 2 wks in Aug.*

$$–$$$ × **Monte Caruso.** Monte Caruso stands out from the pack of mediocre
places that surround the train station. Low arches and tiled floors cre-
ate a warm, elegant setting. The menu focuses on food from Lucania,
an area of Italy divided between the southern regions of Basilicata and
Calabria. Homemade pastas have strange-sounding dialect names, like
cautarogni (large cavatelli with Sicilian broccoli) and *cauzuni* (enor-
mous ricotta-stuffed ravioli), but the dishes are generally simple and
hearty. Don't miss the profiteroles for dessert, dressed at table with warm
chocolate sauce and whipped cream. ⊠ *Via Farini 12,* ☎ *06/483549.
AE, MC, V. Closed Sun. and Aug. No lunch Mon.*

$ × **Africa.** Africa is one of a handful of Ethiopian and Eritrean restau-
rants in Rome, testimony to the sizable local immigrant communities,
rather than a particular interest on the part of native Romans. Food
is eaten with the hands; scoop up meat and vegetables with the help
of soft, spongy bread. Try the classic *zighinì* (spicy beef), and if you're
tired of cappuccinos and *cornetti* (Italian croissants) in the morning,
Africa is open for traditional yogurt-based breakfasts. ⊠ *Via Gaeta
26,* ☎ *06/4941077. No credit cards. Closed Mon.*

$ × **Fagianetto.** Massive wooden beams on high are as solid as the rep-
utation of this family-run trattoria near Termini Station. It has a reg-
ular neighborhood clientele but also satisfies tourists' appetites with a
special menu for €13. But you may well be tempted by à la carte of-

ferings such as rigatoni *alla norcina* (with a sauce of crumbled sausage and cream) or osso buco *con funghi* (with mushrooms). Service is swift and courteous. ⊠ *Via Filippo Turati 21,* ☎ *06/4467306. AE, DC, MC, V. Closed Mon. and Aug.*

$ ✕ **Trattoria Monti.** Not far from Santa Maria Maggiore, the Camerucci family run one of the most dependable, moderately priced trattorias in the city. Try some of their specialties from the Marches region, such as homemade soups starring seasonal vegetables or *timballo di coniglio con patate* (rabbit casserole with potatoes). The house white wine is a very good Verdicchio also from the Marches. ⊠ *Via di San Vito 13,* ☎ *06/4466573. AE, D, MC, V. Closed Sun., Mon., Aug., and 1 wk each at Christmas and Easter.*

Trastevere

$$$ ✕ **Alberto Ciarla.** Look past the somewhat gaudy red and black decor
★ and you'll find Rome's most reliable fish restaurant. Owner Alberto Ciarla's attention to detail and dedication to finding the freshest of fish have won him the hearts of many diners over the years. In addition to the à la carte offerings, there are six tasting menus (including one focused on meat rather than fish). Raw fish is an excellent way to start, highlighting the flavors of swordfish, salmon, sea bass, and prawns. Continue with lovely pastas and fried, grilled, or roasted fish from the Mediterranean. Sumptuous desserts are worth splurging on, especially the *gelato affogato*, ice cream floating in coffee, topped with whipped cream. ⊠ *Piazza San Cosimato 40,* ☎ *06/5818668. AE, DC, MC, V. Closed Sun. and 2 wks in Jan. No lunch.*

$$$ ✕ **ATM.** With its minimalist decor, ATM almost has the feel of a New York sushi bar, which can be refreshing after too many wood-paneled trattorias. The menu is simple, with a good selection of sushi and sashimi. Eat at the bar or at one of the tables and enjoy the freshest of salmon, shrimp, swordfish, squid, sea bass, and whatever else owner Francesco Scarparo and his team of Japanese imports deem worthy of preparing that day. ⊠ *Via della Penitenza 7,* ☎ *06/68307053. AE, DC, MC, V. Closed Mon. and Aug. No lunch.*

$$$ ✕ **Trattoria da Umberto.** The wild boar's head adorning the wall makes it quite clear you are entering a game restaurant. "Franco the hunter" is the second name of this home-style eatery. Da Umberto represents a wonderful opportunity to be adventurous and try some of Franco's catches: boar, pigeon, guinea fowl, and hare are all delicious, whether in pastas, winter-warming stews, or on their own. ⊠ *Piazza San Giovanni della Malva 14/b,* ☎ *06/5816646. AE, DC, MC, V. Closed Wed. and 2 wks in Sept.*

$$–$$$ ✕ **Ostriche a Colazione.** Although "Oysters for Breakfast" is only open for dinner, its name illustrates the owner's obsession with seafood. The oysters are delicious, as one would expect, as are the many appetizing antipasti, like tartare of fresh cod or swordfish marinated in vinegar and thyme. Lobster, sea bass, grouper, and shrimp are all staples on the menu, with pasta or on their own. The service is efficient and the setting elegant. ⊠ *Via dei Vascellari 21,* ☎ *06/5898896. AE, DC, MC, V. Closed Sun. and Aug. No lunch.*

$$–$$$ ✕ **Paris.** On a small square just off Piazza Santa Maria in Trastevere, Paris (named after a former owner, not the city) has a reassuring, understated ambience, without the hokey flamboyance of so many other eating places in this neighborhood. It also has a menu offering the best of classic Roman cuisine: homemade fettuccine, delicate fritto misto, and, of course, baccalà. For dessert, try the fried ricotta balls, tastier than you might imagine. In fair weather opt for tables on the piazza.

⌧ *Piazza San Calisto 7/a,* ☎ *06/5815378. AE, DC, MC, V. Closed Mon. and 3 wks in Aug. No dinner Sun.*

$$–$$$ ✕ **Ripa 12.** This simple neighborhood fish restaurant has earned a faithful clientele. Marinated sea bass, spaghetti with lobster, and fresh fish of the day prepared according to the table's specifications are all simple but flavorful. In an area by now given over to set tourist menus, Ripa 12 is a gem. ⌧ *Via San Francesco a Ripa 12,* ☎ *06/5809093. AE, DC, MC, V. Closed Sun. and 10 days in mid-Aug.*

$$ ✕ **Antico Arco.** Run by three friends with a passion for wine and fine food, Antico Arco has won the hearts of Roman foodies with its culinary inventiveness. The wine list has a wide selection of Italian and French labels, plus a smattering from Australia and California. Particularly good are such starters as the parmigiano and onion soufflé with a tomato-basil sauce and such second courses as *carré d'agnello con composta di fichi* (rack of lamb with fig compote). Don't miss dessert, especially the chocolate cake with melted chocolate center: it's justly famous among chocoholics all over the city. ⌧ *Piazzale Aurelio 7,* ☎ *06/5815274. Reservations essential. AE, DC, MC, V. No lunch. Closed Sun. and Aug.*

$$ ✕ **Asinocotto.** Tucked away in a small street on the south side of Trastevere, Asinocotto is off the beaten track of tourist bars and restaurants. The menu includes delights like smoked tuna with fava beans and cinnamon and *minestra di fagioli cannellini con pasta alla castagna* (cannellini bean soup with chestnut pasta). The special of the day might be a Parmesan basket filled with spinach and quail, or sea bass with baby vegetables and ginger. For dessert try the chocolate torte with green tea granita or the delicious pears in vanilla. The wine list is carefully chosen, with sweet wines paired to match dessert dishes. Asinocotto also has an extensive selection of teas, a rarity in coffee-centric Italy. ⌧ *Via dei Vascellari 48,* ☎ *06/5898985. Reservations essential. AE, DC, MC, V. Closed Mon. and Jan. No lunch.*

$$ ✕ **Da Checco er Carettiere.** Maybe this is what all Italian restaurants once looked like: an aging doorman, garlic braids hanging from the ceiling, black-and-white photos in small frames lining the wood-paneled walls. All the Roman standards are here, more or less dependably prepared, plus plenty of local vegetables and a fair selection of fish. Family-run for three generations, Checco is a great place to soak up genuine Trastevere color and hospitality. ⌧ *Via Benedetta 10,* ☎ *06/5817018. AE, DC, MC, V. No dinner Sun.*

$$ ✕ **Ferrara.** It calls itself a wine bar, but Ferrara's menu makes it a bona fide restaurant with a wine list the length of a short novel. As you contemplate the labels from all over Italy, don't ignore the food at hand: an excellent mixed antipasto of marinated vegetables and cured meats; delicious homemade soups, especially *farro e funghi porcini* (farro grain and porcini mushrooms); and roast pork with prunes. Whether you're in the mood for a light snack or a four-course meal, Ferrara is sure to please. ⌧ *Via del Moro 1/a,* ☎ *06/5803769. AE, DC, MC, V.*

Via Appia Antica

$$ ✕ **Cecilia Metella.** From the entrance on Via Appia Antica, practically opposite the catacombs, you walk uphill to a low, sprawling construction designed for wedding feasts and banquets. There's a large terrace shaded by vines for outdoor dining. Although obviously geared to larger groups, Cecilia Metella also gives couples and small groups full attention, good service, and traditional Roman cuisine. The specialties are searing-hot *crespelle* (crepes), served in individual casseroles, and *pollo al Nerone* (chicken à la Nero; flambéed, of course). ⌧ *Via Appia Antica 125,* ☎ *06/5136743. AE, DC, MC, V. Closed Mon.*

$$ ✕ **L'Archeologia.** At this farmhouse just beyond the catacombs, you dine indoors beside the fireplace in cool weather or in the garden under age-old vines in the summer. The atmosphere is friendly and intimate, and specialties include homemade pastas, abbacchio scottadito, and seafood. ✉ *Via Appia Antica 139,* ☎ *06/7880494. AE, DC, MC, V.*

Via Veneto

$$$$ ✕ **La Terrazza dell'Eden.** The restaurant of the Eden hotel unfurls an unparalleled view of Rome's seven hills before your eyes, unfairly distracting you from some of the best food in the city. Modern yet simple Italian cuisine—high on flavor and herbs and low on butter and cream—is the rule. Always on the prowl for superior fresh ingredients, chef Enrico Derflingher has taken the search to a new level: how many other restaurants have their own fishing boat (in this case named after the hotel), which reserves the best of the day's catch for the chef? In addition to the ever-changing à la carte selections, there are always set *Romano* and macrobiotic menus. The restaurant is also open for breakfast (7–10). ✉ *Hotel Eden, Via Ludovisi 49,* ☎ *06/47812552. Reservations essential. Jacket and tie. AE, DC, MC, V.*

$$$$ ✕ **Le Sans Souci.** All the glitz and glamour of the dolce vita days of Rome in the 1950s live on in this overdecorated but superb subterranean sanctuary of gourmet delights. Impeccably dressed waiters slide over the carpeted floor, their gait reminiscent of finishing-school walking lessons, their smiles captivating but discreet. An elaborate coffered ceiling, mirrors, and painted ceramics from Perugia decorate the main room, in which carved wooden busts of Roman emperors look at one another over tables set in the French fashion. Couples share couches rather than sitting opposite one another (so much easier to see the show) while a guitarist plays sentimental songs. The menu presents both French and Italian dishes, among them truffled terrine de foie gras and various sweet and savory soufflés. ✉ *Via Sicilia 20,* ☎ *06/4821814. Reservations essential. Jacket and tie. AE, DC, MC, V. Closed Mon. and Aug. No lunch.*

$$$ ✕ **Papá Baccus.** Rome's best Tuscan restaurant has weathered the
★ mad-cow crisis, which robbed it of its signature dish, *bistecca alla fiorentina*, a thick, bone-in steak of prized Chianina beef. Owner Italo Cipriani has added delicious new dishes (many fish-based) to the menu, including *soppressata di polipo* (paper-thin slices of a fresh "salami" made from cooked octopus, dressed with herbs and olive oil) and *anello di alici* (fresh anchovies baked with artichokes and potato). Many ingredients are from Cipriani's native northern Tuscany, including delicate prosciutto and *cavolo nero* (Tuscan kale). The warm service, as well as a non-smoking room, help makes up for rather cold decor. ✉ *Via Toscana 36,* ☎ *06/42742808. AE, DC, MC, V. Reservation essential. Closed Sun., 2 wks in Aug., and 2 wks in Dec.–Jan. No lunch Sat.*

$$-$$$ ✕ **Tullio.** In the mood for a juicy steak? This Tuscan restaurant is still grilling beef—just not the bone-in *bistecca alla fiorentina*, which was dropped from the menu due to the mad-cow scare. Start off with thick bean or vegetable soup, or homemade *pappardelle al cinghiale* (wide egg noodles in a tomato and wild boar sauce). Meat dishes other than beef, such as lamb and veal, are also terrific. Splurge on a Chianti *riserva* to make the meal extra special. ✉ *Via San Nicola da Tolentino near Piazza Barberini,* ☎ *06/4745560. AE, DC, MC, V. Closed Sun. and Aug.*

$$ ✕ **Mariano.** At this restaurant near Via Veneto, Mariano's son-in-law and successor, Tonino, is an exponent of high quality and tradition. Since he leaves flights of culinary fancy to others, you can be sure of finding authentic Roman and central Italian cuisine here, including del-

icate egg pastas, game, and abbacchio in season. ⊠ *Via Piemonte 79,* ☎ *06/4745256. AE, DC, MC, V. Closed Sun. and Aug. No lunch Sat.*

Beyond the City Center

$$$$ ✕ **La Pergola.** High atop Monte Mario, the Cavalieri Hilton's rooftop
★   La Pergola restaurant offers a commanding view of the city below. Amply
          spaced tables and low lighting create an intimate atmosphere not
          matched by other restaurants in town. Celebrated wunderchef Heinz
          Beck is a skilled technician and brings Rome its finest example of
          Mediterranean *alta cucina* (haute cuisine); dishes such as risotto with
          quail and fresh herbs or shrimp over eggplant puree with chopped toma-
          toes and basil are balanced and light, and the presentation is striking.
          The wine list and the cheese cart offer ample and interesting choices
          from Italy and France. ⊠ *Cavalieri Hilton, Via Cadlolo 101,* ☎ *06/
          35092211. Reservations essential. Jacket and tie. AE, DC, MC, V. Closed
          Sun. and Mon. No lunch.*

$$$ ✕ **Il Dito e la Luna.** Good regional cooking can be hard to find in Rome;
          for updated Sicilian fare, head to Il Dito e la Luna. Pasta *con le sarde*
          (with fresh sardines, bread crumbs, pine nuts, and orange peel) is ex-
          cellent, as are other dishes made with eggplant, one of Sicily's staple
          vegetables. More creative dishes include rabbit with prunes and lamb
          chops with a sharp cheese sauce. Cannoli—standard in every Italian
          café in the States—are the real thing here: light, airy, and filled with
          delicious ricotta cheese. ⊠ *Via dei Sabelli 51,* ☎ *06/4940726. No credit
          cards. Closed Sun. and 2 wks in Aug. No lunch.*

$$–$$$ ✕ **Siciliainbocca.** Finally, Rome has a straight-up, no-nonsense Sicil-
          ian restaurant. Owners Roberto Di Stefano and Vincenzo Certo, both
          natives of the island, decided to open up Siciliainbocca after years of
          frustration at not finding a decent pasta *alla norma* (with eggplant,
          tomato sauce, and aged ricotta cheese) in the capital. Try specialties
          such as *caponata* (eggplant and peppers), risotto *ai profumi di Sicilia*
          (with lemon, orange, mozzarella, and zucchini), and delicious grilled
          swordfish, shrimp, and squid. Even in the dead of winter, Siciliainbocca's
          yellow walls and brightly colored ceramic plates will warm you up.
          There's outdoor seating in summer. ⊠ *Via E. Faà di Bruno 26,* ☎ *06/
          37358400. AE, DC, MC, V. Closed Sun.*

$$ ✕ **Coriolano.** The only tourists who find their way to this classic
          restaurant near Porta Pia are likely to be gourmets looking for quintessen-
          tial Italian cucina—and that means market-fresh ingredients, espe-
          cially seafood, light homemade pastas, and choice olive oil. The tables
          in the small antiques-filled dining room are set with immaculate white
          linen, sparkling crystal, and silver. Seafood dishes vary, but *tagliolini
          all'aragosta* (thin noodles with lobster sauce) is the house specialty; also
          order the seasonal porcini mushrooms (prepared with a secret recipe).
          The wine list is predominantly Italian but includes some French and
          California choices. ⊠ *Via Ancona 14,* ☎ *06/44249863. AE, DC, MC,
          V. Closed Aug.*

$–$$ ✕ **Da Domenico.** Da Domenico is one of those friendly neighborhood
          restaurants dishing up Roman cuisine to local regulars, which has man-
          aged to stay unchanged over the years. Near San Giovanni in Laterano,
          it provides a good lunch option after you visit the basilica and other
          churches in the area. Food is simple and hearty: fried vegetables, classic
          Roman pastas, and unadorned meats. ⊠ *Via Satrico 23–25,* ☎ *06/
          70494602. AE, D, MC, V. Closed Sun. and 3 wks in Aug. No lunch Mon.*

$ ✕ **Arancia Blu.** Many Italian restaurants don't quite understand the con-
          cept of being vegetarian; meat or fish often crops up in dishes even if
          not listed on menu descriptions. Arancia Blu, however, has grasped the

concept. Try potato and mint ravioli, or parsley pasta with peppers, olives, and capers. Eggplant parmigiana gets the inventive addition of a pastry crust. Excellent desserts and an extensive wine list make Arancia Blu a worthy choice even for meat eaters. ⊠ *Via dei Latini 65,* ☎ *06/4454105. No credit cards. Closed 10 days in mid-Aug. No lunch.*

$ ✕ **Cannavota.** On the square next to San Giovanni in Laterano, this place has a large and faithful following and has fed generations of neighborhood families over the years. Seafood dominates, but carnivores are satisfied also. Try one of the pastas with seafood sauce—fettuccine with scampi is a good choice—and then go on to grilled fish or meat. The cheerful atmosphere and rustic decor contribute to an authentically Roman experience. ⊠ *Piazza San Giovanni in Laterano 20,* ☎ *06/ 77205007. AE, DC, MC, V. Closed Wed. and 3 wks in Aug.*

$ ✕ **Da Franco ar Vicoletto.** In the heart of the city's student-filled San Lorenzo district, Da Franco ar Vicoletto is one of Rome's few remaining affordable fish restaurants. The prix-fixe menu is always more or less the same: an appetizer of sautéed mussels and/or clams; seafood lasagna; spaghetti with clams; pasta with beans and shellfish (a seemingly strange combination that succeeds heroically); and then grilled, roasted, and fried fish. It's the kind of place best visited in a group— the more people at your table, the more food that pours out of the kitchen. ⊠ *Via dei Falisci 1/b,* ☎ *06/4957675. No credit cards. Closed Mon. and 3 wks in Aug.*

$ ✕ **Da Gianni.** About a 20-minute walk from St. Peter's Basilica, this tiny trattoria is well worth the stroll. Also known as "Cacio e Pepe," Da Gianni turns out exclusively Roman food of good quality at a time when decent Roman trattorias are disappearing. While there are no antipasti on offer, heaping plates of tonnarelli cacio e pepe, tonnarelli alla carbonara, polpettone (meat loaf Italian-style), and fried anchovies are simple and satisfying main courses. Sit outside at folding wooden tables and check out the area's film and television crowd as they talk on their cell phones. ⊠ *Via G. Avezzana 11,* ☎ *06/3217268. No credit cards. Closed Sun. and Aug. No dinner Sat.*

$ ✕ **Pommidoro.** Mamma's in the kitchen and the rest of the family greets, serves, and keeps customers happy and well fed at this popular trattoria near Rome's main university, a short cab ride east of Stazione Termini. The menu—not so well translated—offers especially good grilled meats, game birds, and classic home-style *cucina* (cooking). You can dine outside in warm weather. ⊠ *Piazza dei Sanniti 44,* ☎ *06/4452692. No credit cards. Closed Wed. and Aug.*

$ ✕ **Tram Tram.** Across the streetcar tracks not far from Termini, Tram Tram offers simple cooking in a bustling trattoria ambience, snugly packed with hungry Romans. Fish is a good bet here; try homemade *orecchiette,* a pasta specialty with clams and broccoli from Puglia, where the cook grew up. They also do fantastic squid and shrimp in a tasty fish broth with potatoes on the side, and veggie lasagna good enough for any carnivore. For dessert, try the *crema di zabaglione* (custard made with eggs and marsala wine). ⊠ *Via dei Reti 44/46,* ☎ *06/490416. AE, D, MC, V. Closed Mon. and 1 wk in mid-Aug.*

$ ✕ **Uno e Bino.** Giampaolo Gravina's restaurant in an artsy corner of the San Lorenzo neighborhood is popular with Romans from all over town. He works the dining room, offering suggestions from an impressive list of the latest wines from well-known and smaller producers, and his sister Gloria is in the kitchen turning out inventive cuisine inspired by the family's Umbrian-Sicilian roots. Dishes such as octopus salad with asparagus and carrots, and spaghetti with swordfish, tomatoes, and capers are specialties. ⊠ *Via degli Equi 58,* ☎ *06/4460702. AE, D, MC, V. Closed Mon. and Aug. No lunch.*

Outside Rome

Some of Rome's best restaurants are found some distance from the city itself. All of those listed below can be reached by car in an hour or slightly more; they make for a pleasant drive in the country or a gourmet pit stop en route to other regions. Grottaferrata, part of the group of towns known as the Castelli Romani, can be reached by train, and the town is a lovely place for an afternoon of sightseeing and wine tasting. Trains also run to Ostia, the closest beach to Rome.

$$$$ ✕ **Antonello Colonna.** Antonello Colonna's emphasis on local products
★   is renowned throughout the region. Colonna himself selects all the restaurant's ingredients, and only the best of the best find their way onto his tables. After munching on the "chef's welcome," a small taste of things to come, try foie gras with apple compote, or pasta with garlic, meatballs, and Roman broccoli. Shoulder of goat with wild mint and pecorino cheese is wonderful, as is roast pigeon. Leave room for the cheese cart and dessert. ⊠ *Via Roma 89, Labico, 29 km (17½ mi) east of Rome off the A1 freeway (Valmontone exit),* ☎ *06/9510314. Reservations essential. AE, D, MC, V. Closed Mon. and Aug. No dinner Sun.*

$$$$ ✕ **Le Colline Ciociare.** "La Ciociaria" is an area southeast of Rome, immortalized by Sophia Loren in the film of the same name. Though sophisticated Romans may look down on the region, they certainly prize this restaurant, known throughout Lazio and beyond. Its tasting menu is a perfect way to try several dishes and can be modified according to your wishes. The restaurant's creative cuisine might include wild asparagus soup with warm ricotta, or quail and artichoke salad with herb-infused orzo. Veal and lamb from the surrounding hills are prepared with aplomb in a variety of ways. If you have room for dessert after such a feast, try the dense chocolate torte, a menu staple even in the height of summer. ⊠ *Via Prenestina 27, Acuto, 77 km (49½ mi) southeast of Rome,* ☎ *0775/56049. Reservations essential. AE, D, MC, V. Closed Mon. and 2 wks in Sept. No lunch Tues.*

$$ ✕ **Le Bizze de il Tino.** Ostia is known more for beach shacks and snack bars than elegant restaurants, but this is a noteworthy exception. As might be expected, fish is its raison d'être. Wine is included in il Tino's two tasting menus, and there are also wines by the glass for those interested in sampling different labels. Start with *millefoglie di alici freschi* (thin strips of pastry with fresh anchovies), which taste nothing like their tinned cousins, or crustacean tails stuffed with zucchini. Very good meat dishes are also available, but so close to the sea, fish is the real star. ⊠ *Via dei Lucilli 17/19, Ostia Lido, 28 km (17 mi) southeast of Rome (take the Ostiense Road),* ☎ *06/5622778. AE, D, MC, V. Closed Sun., Mon., first 2 wks in Jan., and 2 wks in mid-Aug. No lunch.*

$–$$ ✕ **Benito al Bosco.** Although the word *bosco,* or forest, suggests this place might favor game dishes, fish is the best choice here. Local specialties include cauliflower and cod soup, in addition to such Roman dishes as spaghetti all'amatriciana and fritto misto. Move on to red mullet stew and filet mignon prepared in a variety of ways. Benito makes his own olive oil and gathers both mushrooms and fresh produce from the surrounding hills. ⊠ *Contrada Morice 20, Velletri, 38 km (23 mi) southwest of Rome (take Via Appia),* ☎ *06/9641414. AE, D, MC, V.*

$ ✕ **La Briciola.** After a tour of the Castelli Romani, charming towns southeast of Rome, round out the day with a dinner at La Briciola. Adriana Montellanico has a certain way with her customers, making them feel at home immediately. Her well-known appetizer of fresh zucchini is outstanding, and soups such as wild fennel and bean or farro grain, chestnut, and chickpea, are delicious. Meat and game make for tasty main courses, and homemade desserts round off a lovely evening. Call ahead for one of the few tables outside in warm weather. ⊠ *Via G.*

D'Annunzio 12, Grottaferrata, 20 km (12 mi) southeast of Rome, ☎ *06/9459338. Reservations essential. No credit cards. Closed Mon. and 3 wks in Aug. No dinner Sun.*

Enoteche

It was not so long ago that wine in Rome (and other towns) was strictly local; you didn't have to walk far to find an osteria, where you could buy wine straight from the barrel or sit down to drink and nibble a bit, chat, or play cards. The tradition continues today, as many Roman wineshops are also open as *enoteche* (wine bars). The folding chairs and rickety tables have given way to designer interiors and chic ambience. Enormous barrels of Frascati have been replaced by shelves lined with hundreds of bottles from all over the country, representing the best in Italian wine making. Behind the bar you'll find a serious wine enthusiast—maybe even a sommelier—with several bottles open to be tasted by the glass. And the food has changed, too. There are usually carefully selected cheeses and cured meats, and a short menu of simple dishes and desserts, making a stop in an enoteca a great alternative to yet another three-course restaurant meal.

Campo dei Fiori

$$ ✕ **La Tartaruga.** This wine bar has less of a rustic atmosphere than most and feels like a small, elegant restaurant. The food matches the atmosphere, and offerings include risotto with asparagus, *vitello tonnato* (veal in a cold tuna sauce), and an excellent selection of cheeses and cold meats from all over Italy. ⊠ *Via del Monte della Farina 53,* ☎ *06/6869473. AE, D, MC, V. Closed Mon. and 1 wk in mid-Aug.*

$ ✕ **Il Goccetto.** Sergio Ceccarelli, one of Rome's most knowledgeable wine store owners, is more than willing to help perplexed customers. Choose from about 20 wines by the glass or from hundreds of bottles stocked on the wood shelves. Then curb your hunger with a wide selection of cheeses from all over Italy, marinated vegetables, and cured meats from the famed Falorni *salumificio* in Tuscany. Il Goccetto's location near Campo dei Fiori and its cool, quiet interior make it a welcome rest stop after sightseeing or a perfect place to sip an *aperitivo* before dinner at one of the neighborhood's many restaurants. ⊠ *Via dei Banchi Vecchi 14,* ☎ *06/6864268. AE, MC, V. Closed Sun. and last 3 wks in Aug.*

$ ✕ **L'Angolo Divino.** Stand at the bar and sip wine by the glass, or sit at wooden tables and folding chairs and choose from among the many bottles at L'Angolo Divino. Smoked fish, cured meats, cheeses, and salads make a nice lunch or light dinner. Ask about tasting evenings dedicated to single grapes or regions. ⊠ *Via dei Balestrari 12,* ☎ *06/ 6864413. MC, V. Closed Aug. No dinner Mon.*

Colosseo

$ ✕ **Cavour 313.** Wine bars are popping up all over the city, but Cavour 313 has been around much longer than most. Open for lunch and dinner, it serves an excellent variety of cured meats, cheeses, and salads. Choose from about 25 wines by the glass or uncork a bottle and stay a while. ⊠ *Via Cavour 313,* ☎ *06/6785496. AE, DC, MC, V. Closed Aug. No lunch weekends. No dinner Sun. June 15–Sept.*

Jewish Ghetto

$ ✕ **La Bottega del Vino di Anacleto Bleve.** This cozy wineshop in the Jewish Ghetto sets out tables and opens up for lunch. Owner Anacleto Bleve and his sons make the rounds, proposing the latest cheese they have procured from the farthest reaches of Italy. Instead of a menu, there's Mamma at the counter with a good selection of mixed salads, smoked fish, and sliced meats, as well as a few soups and *sformati* (thick flans). You point, and she serves it up. There are always wines to drink by the glass, or you can choose from the several hundred bottles on the shelves that surround you. ✉ *Via Santa Maria del Pianto 9/a,* ☎ *06/6865970. AE, D, MC, V. Closed Sun. and Mon. No dinner.*

Piazza di Spagna

$–$$ ✕ **Il Brillo Parlante.** Il Brillo Parlante's location near Piazza del Popolo makes it convenient for lunch or dinner after shopping in the area. Taste from 20 wines by the glass at the ground-floor bar, or eat downstairs in one of several wood-paneled and copper-piped rooms. The menu is extensive for a wine bar; choose from cured meats, *crostini* (toasted bread with various toppings such as pâté or prosciutto), pastas, grilled meats, and even pizzas. ✉ *Via della Fontanella 12,* ☎ *06/3243334. AE, D, MC, V. Closed Mon. and 1 wk in mid-Aug.*

$ ✕ **Enoteca Severini.** It's more of a hole in the wall than an actual wine bar, but if you want authenticity, come to Enoteca Severini. Each day, the eccentric owner opens up a few bottles on the counter for customers to sip. It's tiny, strange, yet charming and very, very Roman. ✉ *Via Bocca del Leone 44/a,* ☎ *06/6786031. MC, V. Closed Sat.*

$ ✕ **L'Enoteca Antica di Via della Croce.** This wine bar is always crowded, and for good reason. Its location near the Spanish Steps makes it a great stop for an *aperitivo* (pre-dinner drink) before hitting the area's restaurants. A small menu including cured meats, pastas, and salads also makes it a good lunch getaway after exercising your credit card in the neighborhood's boutiques. ✉ *Via della Croce 76/b,* ☎ *06/6790896. AE, D, MC, V. Closed 2 wks in Aug.*

Piazza Navona

$ ✕ **Cul de Sac.** This popular wine bar near Piazza Navona is among the city's oldest enoteche and offers a book-length selection of wines from Italy, France, the Americas, and elsewhere. Food is eclectic and ranges from Italian meats and cheeses to a fantastic onion soup that bears no resemblance to the famed French version, several vegetarian options, and delicious desserts. Outside tables get crowded fast, and Cul de Sac does not accept reservations, so get here early. ✉ *Piazza Pasquino 73,* ☎ *06/68801094. Reservations not accepted. MC, V. No lunch Mon.*

$ ✕ **Enoteca Corsi.** Very convenient to the historic center for lunch (no dinner) or an afternoon break, this little wine bar looks like it missed the revolution; prices and decor are *come una volta* (like once upon a time) when the shop sold—as the sign says—wine (red or white) and oil. The genuinely dated feel of the place has its charm: you can still get wine here by the liter, or choose from a good variety of fairly priced alternatives in bottles. There are also nicely prepared pastas and kind service. ✉ *Via del Gesù 88,* ☎ *06/6790821. AE, D, MC, V. Closed Sun. No dinner.*

$ ✕ **Enoteca Spiriti.** Located near the Pantheon, this modern wine bar makes a good stop for a light meal after seeing the sights in the historical center. At lunch there's always a pasta and soup selection, as well as fish and meat specials of the day. Dinner is lighter, focusing on cured meats and cheeses. ✉ *Via Sant'Eustachio 5,* ☎ *no phone. No credit cards. Closed Sun. and Aug. No lunch Sat.*

$ ✕ **La Trinchetta.** With a large dining menu and well chosen wine list, La Trinchetta has a faithful clientele. Choose from a vast array of unusual cured meats, terrines, rare cheeses, vegetable tarts, and simple desserts. A selection of 40 wines by the glass, and four pages of grappas, allows customers to experiment. ✉ *Via dei Banchi Nuovi 4,* ☎ *06/6830–0133. AE, MC, V. Closed last 2 wks in Aug. No lunch Sun.*

$ ✕ **Vinamore.** The name of this small wine bar tucked behind Piazza Navona means, aptly enough, "wine love." Wine shines most of all here, paired with simple dishes of cured meats, cheeses, and salads. Tasting classes are also available, and while the owners have yet to offer them in English, some things need no translation. ⊠ *Via Monte Giordano 63,* ☏ *06/68300159. AE, MC, V. Closed Aug. No lunch Mon.*

San Pietro

$-$$ ✕ **Del Frate.** This impressive wine bar, adjacent to one of Rome's noted wineshops, matches sleek and modern decor with a creative cuisine and three dozen wines available by the glass. In addition to cheeses, smoked meats, and composed salads, the house specialty is marinated meat and fish. For dessert, dip into the chocolate fondue. ⊠ *Via degli Scipioni 118,* ☏ *06/3236437. AE, MC, V. Closed 3 wks in Aug.*

Termini

$-$$ ✕ **Trimani Il Winebar.** In a town where most restaurants don't unlock the door before 8 PM, Trimani opens for snacks and cold plates at 6 PM, serves hot food starting at 7:30, and stays open until 11:30. There's always a choice of a soup and a few pasta plates, as well as second courses, *torte salate* (savory tarts), and plenty to choose from to drink. The atmosphere here is modern and casually reserved. Around the corner is the wineshop of the same name—one of the oldest in Rome. Call about wine tastings and short courses (in both Italian and English). ⊠ *Via Cernaia 37/b,* ☏ *06/4469630. AE, D, MC, V. Closed Sun. and 2 wks in Aug. No lunch Sat.*

Trastevere

$ ✕ **Il Cantiniere di Santa Dorotea.** With 35 wines by the glass, Santa Dorotea is a great place to meet for a drink after dinner, especially since it stays open until 2 AM. But its well-articulated menu, offering wine-bar fare like radicchio soup, *piadine* (a specialty from Romagna, flat bread stuffed with ham, cheese, and vegetables and then grilled), cured meats, salads, and cheeses, may persuade you to arrive earlier. ⊠ *Via di Santa Dorotea 9,* ☏ *06/5819025. AE, DC, MC, V. Closed Sun. and Aug.*

Pizzerias

It may have been invented somewhere else, but in Rome it's hard to walk a block without passing pizza in one form or another. Pizza from a bakery is usually made without cheese—pizza *bianca* (just olive oil and salt) or pizza *rossa* (with tomato sauce). Many small shops specialize in pizza *a taglio* (by the slice), priced by the *etto* (100 grams, about ¼ pound), according to the kind of topping. Both of these make a great snack any time of day. Here are few good by-the-slice choices: **Il Forno di Campo dei Fiori** (⊠ Campo dei Fiori, ☏ 06/68806662; closed Sun.) makes excellent pizza bianca and rossa all day. Just around the corner, **Pizza alla Pala** (⊠ Via del Pellegrino 11, ☏ 06/6865083; closed Sun.) has thicker-crusted pizza with multiple toppings; try it *ai porcini* (with mushrooms) or *piccante con pomodorini e prezzemolo* (with chilis, cherry tomatoes, and parsley). **Zi Fenizia** (⊠ Via Santa Maria del Pianto 65, ☏ 06/6896976; closed Sat. and Jewish holidays; no dinner Fri.) makes kosher pizza in the Jewish Ghetto. Behind Piazza Navona, an **unnamed bakery** (⊠ Via del Governo Vecchio 28, ☏ no phone; closed Sun.) makes wood-fired pizza bianca. Toppings are spread out along the bar; just point and choose to make a fantastic meal. **Panificio Renella** (⊠ Via del Moro 15-16, ☏ 06/5817265) is Trastevere's best bet for bakery pizza and is one of the few places open on Sunday; lines throughout the day are a testament to its pizza makers' bravura. Near the Vatican, **Pizzeria Vecchio Borgo** (⊠ Borgo Pio 27/a, ☏ 06/68806355; closed Sun. and Sat. afternoon in summer) churns out piping-hot pizzas; try the *boscaiola,* with sausage, mushrooms, and mozzarella, or *la bomba,* a truly explosive concoction with chili peppers.

Don't leave Rome without having sat down to a Roman pizza in a pizzeria. Most are open only for dinner, usually from 8 PM to midnight. Look for a place with a *forno a legna* (wood-burning oven), a must for a good thin-crust, plate-size Roman pizza. Standard models are the *margherita* (tomato, mozzarella, and basil), *napoletana* (tomato, mozzarella, and anchovy), and *capricciosa* (tomato, mozzarella, prosciutto, artichokes, olives, and a hard-boiled egg), but most pizzerias have a long list of additional options, including tasty *mozzarella di bufala* (buffalo-milk mozzarella). The wine at a pizzeria is worth skipping; Italians drink beer with pizza. There are sometimes other things to order on a pizzeria menu, but aside from bruschetta (grilled bread, usually topped with chopped fresh tomato, basil, garlic, and olive oil) and crostini (mozzarella toast), nonpizza items are often disappointing.

Aventine and Testaccio

$ ✕ **Acqua e Farina?** Not quite a pizzeria, trendy Acqua e Farina? sticks close to its name, which translates as "water and flour." The menu offers takeoffs on pizza, like *strufolini*, cylinders of pizza dough stuffed with mozzarella, anchovies, and zucchini flowers, or smoked provolone, mushrooms, and prosciutto. Try other shapes and fillings to create a fun meal. ⊠ *Piazza Θ. Giustiniani 2,* ☎ *06/5741382. Reservations not accepted. AE, MC, V. No lunch.*

$ ✕ **Remo.** Expect a wait at this perennial favorite in Testaccio fre-
★ quented by students and neighborhood locals. You won't find tablecloths or other nonessentials, just classic Roman pizza and boisterous conversation. ⊠ *Piazza Santa Maria Liberatrice 44,* ☎ *06/5746270. Reservations not accepted. No credit cards. Closed Sun., Aug., and Christmas wk. No lunch.*

Campo dei Fiori

$ ✕ **Acchiappafantasmi.** This popular restaurant near Campo dei Fiori offers a mind-boggling choice of pizzas. In addition to the traditional margherita and capricciosa, you'll find a spicy pizza with chili peppers and hot salami and one with fresh buffalo mozzarella and cherry tomatoes, perfect in summer. Appetizers are good, too; as well as the traditional fried goodies the menu includes a variety of items not standard to pizzerias, such as a spinach salad with bacon, mushrooms, and walnuts. ⊠ *Via dei Cappellari 66,* ☎ *06/6873462. Reservations not accepted. D, MC, V. Closed Tues. except in summer.*

$ ✕ **Er Grottino.** Among the many pizzerias and restaurants lining the Campo dei Fiori, Er Grottino is the best choice for crispy Roman pizza. No strange combinations here, just classics like mushroom, ham, or vegetable. The service is friendly, and it's open for lunch. ⊠ *Campo dei Fiori 32,* ☎ *06/68803618. Reservations not accepted. AE, DC, MC, V. Closed Tues. and Aug. 8–31.*

Colosseo

$ ✕ **Alle Carrette.** Tucked around the corner from the Forum on a tiny side street, Alle Carrette is easy to miss. Hunt it down for tasty Roman pizzas and the usual starters such as bruschetta and *supplì* (fried rice balls). It's one of the best pizzerias in the touristy area around the ruins. ⊠ *Vicolo delle Carrette 14,* ☎ *06/6792770. Reservations not accepted. MC, V.*

Parioli

$ ✕ **Crilé.** In the Parioli district north of Villa Borghese is a winning pizzeria famed for its pizza with radicchio and Gorgonzola. You can indulge meat cravings with its sausage, boiled prosciutto, and mushroom combo. They even have good beer; if Italy's Peroni fails to impress, sip on an English or German brew. ⊠ *Viale Maresciallo Pilsudski 46,* ☎ *06/8082690. Reservations not accepted. MC, V. Closed Sun. and 2 wks in Aug. No lunch.*

$ ✕ **La Maremma.** La Maremma has been one of the biggest draws in Parioli for years and its popularity has spawned a second outpost, closer to Via Veneto. Pizzas are available Roman-style with a thin crust, or Neapolitan-style, thicker and more filling. Outside tables can be had year-round, thanks to heaters that warm the terrace in winter. ✉ *Viale Parioli 93/c,* ☎ *06/8086002;* ✉ *Via Alessandria 119/d,* ☎ *06/8554002. Reservations not accepted. MC, V. Closed Mon. and Aug. No lunch.*

Piazza di Spagna

$ ✕ **Il Leoncino.** Lines out the door on weekends attest to the popularity of this fluorescent-lit pizzeria in the otherwise big-ticket neighborhood around Piazza di Spagna. It's one of the few pizzerias open for lunch as well as dinner. ✉ *Via del Leoncino 28, near Corso,* ☎ *06/6876306. Reservations not accepted. No credit cards. Closed Wed. and Aug. No lunch weekends.*

Piazza Navona

$ ✕ **Baffetto.** Down a cobblestone street not far from Piazza Navona, this is one of Rome's best-known pizzerias and a summer favorite for outside dining. The plainly decorated interior is mostly given over to the ovens, but there's another room with more paper-covered tables. Turnover is fast; this is not the place to linger. ✉ *Via del Governo Vecchio 114,* ☎ *06/6861617. Reservations not accepted. No credit cards. Closed Sun. and Aug. No lunch.*

$ ✕ **La Montecarlo.** Run by the niece of the owner of the pizzeria Baffetto, La Montecarlo has a similar menu and is almost as popular as its relative around the corner. It's open for both lunch and dinner. Crowds appreciate the inexpensive prices and fast service. ✉ *Vicolo Savelli 12,* ☎ *06/6861877. Reservations not accepted. No credit cards. Closed 2 wks in mid-Aug. and Mon. Nov.–Apr.*

San Pietro

$ ✕ **L'Isola della Pizza.** Right near the Vatican Metro stop, the "Island of Pizza" is also known for its copious antipasti. Simply ask for the house appetizers, and a waiter will swoop down with numerous plates of salad, seafood, bruschetta, prosciutto, crispy pizza bianca, and supplì. Though it's all too easy to fill up on these fun starters, the pizza is dependably good and meat-lovers can get a decent steak. ✉ *Via degli Scipioni 47,* ☎ *06/39733483. Reservations not accepted. AE, MC, V. Closed Sun., Aug., and Christmas wk. No lunch.*

Termini

$ ✕ **La Gallina Bianca.** This pizzeria's location right down the road from Termini station makes it a perfect place for a welcome-to-Rome meal. A bright, noisy locale, La Gallina Bianca attracts a young crowd and serves up classic thin-crust pizzas. Try the "full-moon" specialty, perfect for cheese-lovers, with ricotta, Parmesan, mozzarella, ham, and tomato. ✉ *Via A. Rosmini 5,* ☎ *06/4743777. Reservations not accepted. AE, MC, V. Closed Aug.*

Trastevere

$ ✕ **Dar Poeta.** Romans drive across town for great pizza from this neighborhood joint on a small street in Trastevere. Maybe it's the dough—the pizza is a bit cheaper than average, and made from a secret blend of flours that is reputed to be easier to digest than the competition. For dessert, there's an unusual calzone with Nutella chocolate-hazelnut spread and ricotta. ✉ *Vicolo del Bologna 45,* ☎ *06/5880516. Reservations not accepted. AE, DC, MC, V. No lunch.*

$ ✕ **Panattoni.** Nicknamed "the mortuary" for its marble tables, Panattoni is actually about as lively as you can get. Packed every night, this pizzeria offers crisp pizzas as well as a variety of tasty bean dishes. Panattoni stays open past midnight, convenient for dinner after catching a late movie at the English-language theater close by. ⊠ *Viale Trastevere 53–57,* ☎ *06/5800919. Reservations not accepted. No credit cards. Closed Wed. and 2 wks in mid-Aug. No lunch.*

$ ✕ **Popi-Popi.** This casual place attracts both tourists and locals, all of whom are drawn to the house specialty, pizza "Popi-Popi," with tomato, mozzarella, mushrooms, sausage, artichokes, and olives. If that doesn't satisfy, Popi-Popi also has moderately priced, good-quality steaks. ⊠ *Via delle Fratte di Trastevere 46,* ☎ *06/5895167. Reservations not accepted. AE, DC, MC, V. Closed Thurs. in Sept.–July.*

Beyond the City Center

$ ✕ **Formula 1.** Posters of Formula 1 cars and drivers past and present attest to the owner's love for auto racing. The atmosphere is casual and friendly and draws students from the nearby university as well as pizza-lovers from all over the city. Its location in the trendy San Lorenzo neighborhood makes it a convenient stop for dinner before checking out some of the area's bars. ⊠ *Via degli Equi 13,* ☎ *06/4453866. Reservations not accepted. No credit cards. Closed Sun. and Aug. No lunch.*

$ ✕ **La Soffitta.** You pay more, but hey, it's imported. Located northeast
★ of the city center, this is Rome's hottest spot for classic Neapolitan pizza (thick, though crusty on the bottom, rather than the crisp, paper-thin Roman kind) and the only pizzeria in town that has been certified by the Neapolitan Pizza Association to make the real thing. Desserts are brought in daily from Naples, of course. ⊠ *Via dei Villini 1/e,* ☎ *06/ 4404642. Reservations not accepted. AE, D, MC, V. Closed Sat. and Aug. No lunch Sun.*

Cafés

Rome doesn't have the grand cafés of Paris or Vienna, but there are hundreds of small places on pleasant side streets and piazzas to while away the odd half hour. The coffee is routinely of a high quality. Locals usually stop in for a quickie at the bar, which is also much less expensive than the same drink taken at table. Pricey **Antico Caffè Greco** (⊠ Via dei Condotti 86, ☎ 06/6791700) is a national landmark; its red-velvet chairs and marble tables have hosted the likes of Byron, Shelley, Keats, Goethe, and Casanova. **Caffè Sant'Eustachio** (⊠ P. Sant'-Eustachio 82, ☎ 06/6861309), traditionally frequented by Rome's literati, has outstanding coffee. (If you want your *caffè* without sugar here, ask for it *amaro*.) Don't miss the *gran caffè*, a secret concoction unlike anything else in the city. **Tazza d'Oro** (⊠ Via degli Orfani, near the Pantheon, ☎ 06/5835869) has many admirers who contend it serves the city's best cup of coffee. You can sit yourself down and watch the world go by at **Rosati** (⊠ Piazza del Popolo 5, ☎ 06/3225859). **Caffè della Pace** (⊠ Via della Pace 3, ☎ 06/6861216) is on a quiet street near Piazza Navona; it has long been the haunt of Rome's *belle monde*. Just around the corner from Caffè della Pace, **Bar del Fico** (⊠ Piazza del Fico 28, ☎ 06/6865205) is another spot to see and be seen. **Caffè Teichner** (⊠ Piazza San Lorenzo in Lucina 15–18, ☎ 06/6871683), just off the Corso, is a relatively pricey establishment on a lively piazza. **Bar Notegen** (⊠ Via del Babuino 159, ☎ 06/3200855) sits on one of Rome's most fashionable streets among the designer boutiques near the Spanish Steps. For a taste of Brussels, check out the Belgian chain **Le Pain Quotidien** (⊠ Via Tomacelli 24–25, ☎ 06/68807727); order the fresh bread, brought to the table with a selection of sweet spreads flavored with chocolate or chestnut. **Cafe Renault** (⊠ Via Nazionale 183, ☎ 06/47824966), on one of Rome's main shopping streets, is a big, popular café that serves a large selection of food. The exhibition hall **Palazzo delle Esposizioni** (⊠ Bar-only entrance on Via

Milano 7, ☎ 06/4828540) has an airy, modern café with a chic feel. Upstairs is a moderately priced cafeteria.

On Via Vittorio Veneto, Rome's hippest street in the 1950s and 1960s, you'll find the **Cafe de Paris** (⌗ Via Veneto 90, ☎ 06/4885284), which is also a *pasticceria* (pastry shop) and *gelateria* (gelato shop). Bring a book to **Bar Taruga** (⌗ Piazza Mattei 8, ☎ 06/6892299), in one of Rome's loveliest piazzas in the Jewish Ghetto, and curl up in one of the mismatched armchairs or sofas with a cappuccino or hot tea. **Bar Vezio** (⌗ Via de' Delfini 23, ☎ 06/6786036), in the Jewish Ghetto, is a tiny bar decorated with posters, slogans, banners, and photos from last century's socialist movements. In Piazza San Calisto, as you walk toward Viale di Trastevere, you'll discover the small and wonderfully down-at-the-heels **Bar San Calisto** (⌗ Piazza San Calisto 4, ☎ 06/5895678), immensely popular with the old local community and expat crowd, but still unfrequented by tourists. In Trastevere, conveniently located next to the English-language movie theater, is **Ombre Rosse** (⌗ Piazza Sant'Egidio 12, ☎ 06/5884155), a relaxed café that attracts a young clientele. It's good for a morning cappuccino, an afternoon tea, or an evening glass of wine. Trastevere's **Caffè della Scala** (⌗ Via della Scala 4, ☎ 06/5803610) is a mellow locale with old photos of jazz artists lining the walls. In upper-class Prati you'll find **Caffè Vanni** (⌗ Via Col di Lana 10, ☎ 06/32649001); the place attracts a media crowd, so bring your cell phone.

Gelaterias

Gelato is more a snack for Italians than a serious dessert. Italian ice cream is generally less creamy than its American counterpart. Flavors are simpler, the best tasting like the essence of pure fruit. Though you won't find the more Byzantine concoctions of the States (toffee pecan, double chocolate-chip brownie, and so on), you might just discover the best and the purest ice cream you've ever had. **Il Gelato di San Crispino** (⌗ Via della Panetteria 54, near Fontana di Trevi, ☎ 06/6793924; closed Tues.) makes perhaps the most celebrated gelato in all of Italy, without artificial colors or flavors. It's worth crossing town for—nobody else creates flavors this pure. For years **Giolitti** (⌗ Via degli Uffici del Vicario 40, ☎ 06/6991243) was considered the best gelateria in Rome, and it is still worth a stop if you are near the Pantheon. **Della Palma** (⌗ Via della Maddalena 20/23, ☎ 06/68806752) is close to the Pantheon on a street just north of the Piazza della Rotonda. It boasts 100 flavors of gelato, and for sheer gaudy display and range of choice it's a must. Immediately beside the Pantheon is **Cremeria Monteforte** (⌗ Via della Rotonda 22, ☎ 06/6867720), which has won several awards for its flavors. **Fiocco di Neve** (⌗ Via del Pantheon 51, ☎ no phone; closed Sun.) has excellent *granita di caffè* (coffee ice slush) as well as gelato. **Fonte della Salute** (⌗ Viale Trastevere, ☎ 06/5897471; closed 4 wks at Christmas) serves up about 50 flavors, as well as a wide variety of frozen yogurt.

Gelateria alla Scala (⌗ Via della Scala 51, ☎ 06/5813174; closed Dec.–Jan.) in Trastevere is a tiny place serving classic flavors of ice cream and a tart lemon ice. **Cremeria Ottaviani** (⌗ Via Leone IV 83/85, near the Vatican, ☎ 06/37514774; closed Wed.) is an old-fashioned gelateria with an excellent granita di caffè. You'll find a number of gelaterias in Via di Tor Millina, a street off the west side of Piazza Navona, where there are also a couple of good places for frozen yogurt and delicious *frullati*—shakes made with milk, crushed ice, and fruit of your choosing. On Prati's main shopping street, **Pellacchia** (⌗ Via Cola di Rienzo 3–5, ☎ 06/3210807; closed Mon.) is a classic *artigianale* (homemade) ice-cream parlor that has been going since the 1920s. **Al Settimo Gelo** (✉ Via Vodice 21/a, ☎ 06/3725567), in Prati, has been getting rave reviews for both classic flavors and newfangled inventions like cardamom and chestnut. West of Prati, on the hill of Monte Mario, **Lo Zodiaco** (✉ Viale del Parco Mellini 90, ☎ 06/35496640) is perhaps more remarkable for the city vista than for the ice cream. To the north of the city in the wealthy district of Parioli, **Caffè Parnaso** (✉ Piazza delle Muse 22, ☎ 06/8079741), as the name suggests, doubles as a café and pasticceria.

Pasticcerie

Romans are not known for having a sweet tooth, and there are few pastry shops in town that distinguish themselves with particularly good examples of the few regional desserts. One exception is the **Forno del Ghetto** (✉ Via del Portico d'Ottavia 2, ☎ 06/6878637; closed Fri. eve., Sat., and Jewish holidays). You might not expect a Jewish bakery in Rome, but this hole-in-the-wall—no sign, no tables, just a take-away counter—is an institution, preserving a tradition of Italian Jewish sweets that cannot be found anywhere else. The ricotta cake (with sour cherry jam or chocolate) is unforgettable. At **Dolceroma** (✉ Via del Portico d'Ottavia 20/b, ☎ 06/6892196; closed Mon. and 4 wks in July–Aug.), in the Jewish Ghetto, the apple strudel and Sacher torte may not be Italian, but Romans flock here just the same. A good bet for both Italian and foreign delights is **Dolci & Doni** (✉ Via delle Carrozze 85, ☎ 06/6782913), near Piazza di Spagna, where a wide range of goodies are served in a pleasant atmosphere. In the center, off Corso Vittorio, **La Deliziosa** (✉ Vicolo Savelli 50, ☎ 06/68803155; closed Mon.) serves fantastic ricotta cakes and a mean *bignè di San Giuseppe*, a cream-filled fried delight found around St. Joseph's Day in March. At **Bella Napoli** (✉ Corso Vittorio Emanuele 246, ☎ 06/6877048; closed Sat. and Aug.), the name gives away the house specialty: Neapolitan pastries like rum *babà* and *sfogliatelle*.

Across the Tiber in Trastevere, **Valzani** (✉ Via del Moro 37/b, ☎ 06/5803792; closed Mon.) is one of the few remaining old-style Roman pastry shops. Try the zabaglione cake, made with Marsala wine and egg yolks, or homemade chocolate Easter eggs. **Cecere** (✉ Via San Francesco a Ripa 151, ☎ 06/58332404; closed Thurs.) in Trastevere is famous for jam tarts. **Caffè Vanni** (✉ Via Col di Lana 10, ☎ 06/32649001) near Piazza Mazzini is a good place to enjoy proper Italian pasticcerie with coffee. At the corner of Piazza Barberini as you go toward Termini Station from the center of town, **Pepys Bar** (✉ Piazza Barberini 54, ☎ no phone) is a tiny but strangely charming stand-up emporium that sells a range of pastries and an impressive array of sandwiches. **Dagnino** (✉ entrance from Via V. Emanuele Orlando 75 or Via Torino 95, ☎ 06/4818660) is a well-known Sicilian pastry shop and bar in a covered gallery near Piazza Repubblica; specialties include Sicily's preeminent sweet, *cassata*, a ricotta cake with candied fruit.

3 LODGING

High-ceiling rooms in Renaissance *palazzi*,
sleek marble baths and plush carpets,
and the thrill of opening your window to
a view of the Pantheon's dome or a pretty
Baroque church facade are some of the
pleasures of Rome lodging. Even in budget
hotels, where the rooms may be smaller,
the furniture tackier, and the floors creakier,
you may enjoy the same views and a
sense of being in the heart of history. Rome
has a wide range of hotels, most of them
conveniently in the downtown area.

Updated by
Jude Barrand

PALATIAL SETTINGS, luxurious comfort, spacious rooms, and high standards of service can be taken for granted in Rome's top establishments, all in the very expensive price category. But in other categories, especially moderate and inexpensive, standards vary considerably. As a rule of thumb, in the moderate and inexpensive categories you have to expect to pay higher rates for less space and fewer comforts than you would for a hotel room in a comparable category in the United States. In renovated palazzi with a rigid structural scheme, space is at a premium; a few square feet of private bathroom space often has to be subtracted from the area of rooms that are not very big to start with.

International chains such as Hilton, Sheraton, Holiday Inn, and Marriott have luxury properties in Rome and maintain high standards of comfort. The Best Western group includes about eight moderately priced, independently owned and managed hotels in downtown Rome. Jolly hotels and Starhotels are Italy-based international chains with four-star hotels in Rome.

All Italian hotels are graded on a star scale, from five stars for the most deluxe hotels to one star for the most modest. This system is administered by local boards on the basis of a complicated evaluation of facilities and services, and it can be misleading. For tax purposes, hotels may prefer to have fewer stars than their amenities and services would warrant; as a result, their quality-price ratios may be excellent. The old-fashioned Roman pensione ceased to exist long ago as an official category, but many smaller inexpensive and moderate hotels preserve the homey atmosphere that makes visitors prefer them, especially for longer stays.

Five- and four-star hotels have all the amenities you would expect at top levels and rates, with full services, spacious lounges, bars, restaurants, and some fitness facilities. Three-star hotels may have minibars and in-room safes and double glazing to keep out street noise. Two- and three-star hotels will have private bathrooms and in-room direct-dial telephone and television, and most will have air-conditioning. In the less expensive places, you may have to pay extra for air-conditioning, and the shower may well be the drain-in-the-floor type that floods the bathroom. In one-star hotels you may have to share a bathroom and do without an elevator.

It can be hot in Rome from May through September. Always inquire about air-conditioning when booking a room for that time of year. Noise is also a concern. Romans are voluble—with or without cars and mopeds adding to the din. Rooms in all top hotels are soundproofed, but noise may be a problem in less expensive hotels anywhere in the city, especially in summer if there's no air-conditioning. Ask for an inside room if you're a light sleeper, but don't be surprised if it's on a dark courtyard.

The lodgings we list here are the cream of the crop in each price category. We always list the facilities that are available—but we don't specify whether they cost extra: when pricing accommodations, always ask what's included and what's not. Assume that hotels operate on the Continental Plan (CP, with a daily Continental breakfast) unless we specify that they use the European Plan (EP, with no meals included), the Modified American Plan (MAP, with daily breakfast and dinner), or the Full American Plan (FAP, with all meals included).

Most of the lodgings are in downtown Rome, where you can find hotels in all categories. There are obvious advantages to staying in a hotel within easy walking distance of the main sights, particularly because parts of downtown Rome are closed to traffic and are blessedly quieter than they once were. Stringent traffic and parking restrictions make a car a hindrance; if you have one, leave it in a garage and explore the city on foot. Staying in a central hotel means that you won't have to use crowded public transportation or take taxis all the time. The Termini Station area has the highest hotel density, but accommodations vary widely, from fine to seedy.

Always book in advance, even if only a few days ahead. Rome's religious importance makes it a year-round tourist destination, and there is never a period when Rome's hotels are predictably empty. However, July and August and late January to February are generally slack months. Inquire about special rates at all times. If you do arrive without reservations, try **HR** (Hotel Reservation service; ☎ 06/6991000), with desks at Leonardo da Vinci airport and Termini Station (an English-speaking operator is available daily 7 AM–10 PM). Municipal Information kiosks throughout the city can also help you find accommodations free of charge. **CTS** (⊠ Via Genova 16, ☎ 06/4620431), a student travel agency, can help find rooms. Don't rely on official-looking men who approach tourists at Termini Station: they tout for the less desirable hotels in the area.

You can book via e-mail or by telephoning and then following up with a letter or fax for confirmation. You will probably be asked to send a deposit; get a statement from the hotel about its refund policy before releasing your credit card number or mailing a money order. Always insist on receiving written confirmation from the hotel with details of the duration of your stay, room rate, extras if any, and location and type of room (single or double, twin beds or double; with or without bath or shower). When corresponding with hotels, remember that mail in Italy can be exasperatingly slow; telephone, fax, and e-mail are more effective.

Residence Hotels

If you want the independence offered by an apartment, consider staying in a residence hotel. Residence hotels have fully equipped kitchens and offer linens, laundry, and cleaning services. Most are available for monthly rentals; costs for an apartment for two range from about €1,300 for a week to €2,600 per month.

Palazzo al Velabro. (⊠ Via del Velabro 16, 00186, ☎ 06/6792758, FAX 06/6793790) is one of Rome's best-kept secrets. Right in the heart of the Boario Forum, adjacent to the Arch of Janus, it offers serene, understated luxury and great convenience. Guests are welcome to stay for as few as three nights in accommodations named after a Roman emperor, god, king, or poet.

Residence Aldrovandi (⊠ Via U. Aldrovandi 11, 00197, ☎ 06/3221430, FAX 06/3222181) is in the swish Parioli residential district north of Villa Borghese park, where you have to take a taxi or tram to reach downtown Rome. It is furnished with distinction and has concierge and maid service; guests can use the pool of the adjacent Hotel Aldrovandi.

Residence Ripetta (⊠ Via di Ripetta 231, 00186, ☎ 06/3231144, FAX 06/3203959), in the heart of the city, near Piazza del Popolo, is the most central of all of Rome's residence hotels. Its compact apartments are furnished in smart contemporary style, and it is well equipped for business travelers, with in-house meeting facilities.

Rates

Room rates in Rome are on a par with those of most other major European capitals. Rates are always inclusive of service, but it is customary

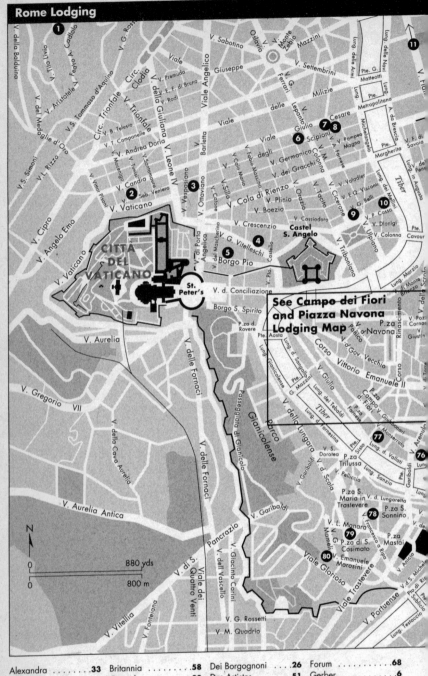

to tip porters, waiters, maids, and concierges. Taxes and breakfast are separate items in five-star hotels. In all other categories rates quoted for rooms generally include taxes, service, and breakfast, which may be continental or buffet. The standard Continental breakfast consists merely of coffee, cappuccino, or tea and a croissant or rolls, butter, and jam, though many hotels offer heartier buffet breakfasts, with cereals, yogurt, fresh fruit, and juice; sometimes bacon, eggs, and ham are served. In lower-priced hotels air-conditioning may add an extra charge of about €8–€10 per day. All hotels are supposed to have rate cards on the room doors or inside the closet. These specify exactly what you have to pay and detail any extras. Rates in any given hotel can vary according to the location and amenities of individual rooms.

Unless otherwise stated, the hotels reviewed here have elevators, TV (many with cable, including CNN) in the rooms, and telephones, and English is spoken. Few two-star hotels have minibars.

Highly recommended establishments are indicated by a star ★ (which bears no correlation to the Italian star rating system).

CATEGORY	COST*
$$$$	over €260
$$$	€180–€260
$$	€100–€180
$	under €100

*All prices are for two people in a standard double room, including tax and service.

Aventine and Testacio

$$$ 🏨 **Domus Aventina.** Marble, trompe l'oeil murals, classical artifacts, Piranesi prints, Baroque bouquets, and views of an ancient cloister— you will know you are in Rome in this friendly little hotel. The 17th-century facade is set amid the verdant, peaceful Aventine, steps away from some of the most important Roman monuments. All modern amenities are provided, and half the rooms have balconies. ⊠ *Via di Santa Prisca 11/b, 00153,* ☎ *06/5746135,* ℻ *06/57300044. 26 rooms. Free parking. AE, DC, MC, V.*

$$–$$$ 🏨 **Villa San Pio.** This hotel and the Hotel San Anselmo next door are
★ both under the same management, but Villa San Pio slightly outdoes its neighbor. It has Venetian rococo decor, spacious gardens, and vine-covered terraces; hand-painted decorations are everywhere. You'll find such comforts as air-conditioning throughout, an elevator, and hot tubs in many of the rooms. The location is ideal for peace and quiet within pleasant walking distance of the historic center. ⊠ *Via San Anselmo 19, 00153,* ☎ *06/5783214,* ℻ *06/5783604,* 🌐 *www.venere.it/roma/ villasanpio. 100 rooms. 2 bars, hot tub. AE, DC, MC, V.*

$$ 🏨 **Hotel San Anselmo.** Birdsongs emanating from the tree-lined avenues tell you the San Anselmo is as much a retreat as a hotel. It's located far from the bustle of the city center, perched on top of the Aventine Hill in the heart of ancient Rome. Rooms are clean and basic, but you'll be inclined to spend your time in the garden or at the terrace bar. ⊠ *Piazza San Anselmo 2, 00153,* ☎ *06/5745231,* ℻ *06/5783604,* 🌐 *www.aventinohotels.com. 45 rooms. Bar. AE, DC, MC, V.*

$$ 🏨 **Santa Prisca.** The Fascist-era architecture lends this place a rather institutional air (in fact, it's owned by an order of nuns), but it's comfortable and tastefully decorated. Rooms are spacious, and those on the third floor have French windows; some have small balconies. There's also an ample terrace. The extensive grounds offer plenty of parking. Satellite TV, air-conditioning, and colorful tiled bathrooms

with showers round out the amenities. ✉ *Largo M. Gelsomini 25, 00153,* ☎ *06/5741917,* ℻ *06/5746658. 50 rooms. Restaurant, bar, parking (fee). DC, MC. CP, EP, FAP, MAP.*

Campo dei Fiori

$$$ 🏨 **Cardinal.** Staying at this hotel is like stepping inside a Renaissance painting—it was built by Bramante, first architect of St. Peter's Basilica, and is set on magnificent Via Giulia, whose vistas have scarcely changed since the 15th century. Cardinals would feel right at home: the lobby is pale and cool, and the rooms upstairs are almost ascetic. Serene, severe, and subdued, many of the rooms have antique engravings and Olympian-high ceilings. ✉ *Via Giulia 62, 00186,* ☎ *06/68802719,* ℻ *06/6786376. 71 rooms. Bar. AE, DC, MC, V.*

$$$ 🏨 **Hotel Tiziano.** Outside, the Corso Vittorio Emanuele is teaming with shoppers, tourists, and denizens of the many neighborhood bars and restaurants. Inside, a cool, quiet marble lobby is a haven of calm. The guest rooms here are reasonably sized by Roman standards, and high ceilings, parquet floors, and classical furnishings give them an opulent feel. The English-speaking staff is polite and attentive. If you're interested in sampling the vibrant nightlife around Campo dei Fiori and Piazza Navona, Hotel Tiziano is an ideally located base. ✉ *Corso Vittorio Emanuele II, 110, 00186,* ☎ *06/6865019,* ℻ *06/6865019. 65 rooms. Restaurant, bar, parking (fee). AE, DC, MC, V.*

$$–$$$ 🏨 **Teatro di Pompeo.** Where else can you breakfast under the ancient
 ★ stone vaults of Pompey's Theater, historic site of Julius Caesar's assassination? At this intimate and refined little hotel in the heart of Old Rome you are part of that history; the restored beamed ceilings of the bedrooms date from the days of Michelangelo. The tastefully furnished rooms offer comfort as well as charm. Book well in advance. ✉ *Largo del Pallaro 8, 00186,* ☎ *06/68300170,* ℻ *06/68805531. 13 rooms. Bar. AE, DC, MC, V.*

$$ 🏨 **Albergo del Sole al Biscione.** Built on the ruins of the ancient The-
 ★ ater of Pompey, in the very heart of the timeless Campo dei Fiori area, this little gem has one of the quaintest multilevel terraces in old Rome; stunning views are guaranteed. The atmosphere is cozy—with open-beam ceilings and old-fashioned furnishings—and there are modern comforts, including an elevator. Rooms are set out in simple pension style, featuring early 20th-century wardrobes and veneer bed frames. ✉ *Via del Biscione 76, 00186,* ☎ *06/68806873,* ℻ *06/6893787,* 🌐 *www.venere.it/roma/sole. 58 rooms, 26 with bath. Parking (fee). No credit cards. EP.*

$$ 🏨 **Campo dei Fiori.** Frescoes, exposed brickwork, and elegant effects throughout this little hotel in Old Rome could well be the work of a set designer. There's an aura of fantasy and romanticism in the decoration, with the layout cleverly designed to make the most of limited space. A few rooms are so compact they're almost claustrophobic; others are larger, and all have some unusual decorative feature to remind you that you are in the heart of Rome. The hotel has no elevator, but the climb to the roof terrace rewards you with a marvelous view and a great area to relax. ✉ *Via del Biscione 6, 00186,* ☎ *06/68806865,* ℻ *06/6876003. 27 rooms, 14 with bath. MC, V. EP.*

$$ 🏨 **Hotel Rinascimento.** In an appealing old palazzo in the heart of the Campo dei Fiori district, this small hotel is ideal for exploring the back-street nooks and crannies of Rome. Its 19 rooms are done in a simple style that's neat and pleasant. The owners are charming and always helpful; their English is a bit hit-or-miss, so it helps to know a few key phrases in Italian (or have a phrase book handy). ✉ *Via del Pellegrino*

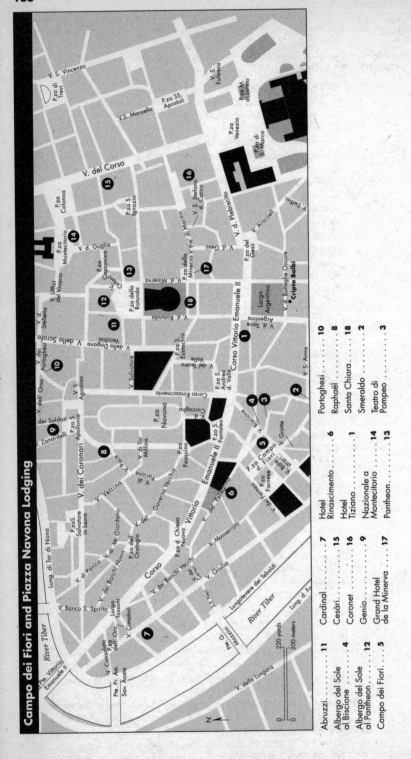

Campo dei Fiori and Piazza Navona Lodging

122, 00186, ☎ *06/6874813,* FAX *06/6833518. 19 rooms. Restaurant, bar, parking (fee). AE, DC, MC, V.*

$$ ⋆ 🏨 **Smeraldo.** The emerald-green marble entrance and other touches of marble throughout are only the beginning of what sets this bargain hotel (at the low end of this price category) apart from the rest. There are two terraces, air-conditioning, satellite TV in every room, and a bar. The rooms are fresh and immaculate, and some have private balconies. A handy location near Piazza Navona and Campo dei Fiori makes it ideal for taking in all the action. ✉ *Via dei Chiodaroli 9, 00186,* ☎ *06/6875929,* FAX *06/68805495. 39 rooms. Bar. AE, MC, V. EP.*

Colosseo

$$$$ ⋆ 🏨 **Forum.** This converted 18th-century convent offers spectacular views in the heart of ancient Rome. The Roof-Garden Restaurant overlooks the Fori Imperiali, with the Foro Romano, the Coliseum, and the Palatine Hill in the near distance. All amenities have been carefully provided and the walnut-paneled interiors are tastefully accented with period antiques. The bathrooms have been restyled using antique, decorated tiles. ✉ *Via Tor de'Conti 25–30, 00184,* ☎ *06/6792446,* FAX *06/6786479,* WEB *www.venere.it/roma/forum. 80 rooms. Restaurant, 2 bars, parking (fee). AE, DC, MC, V.*

$$$ 🏨 **Celio.** Magnificent murals, paintings, classical wallpaper, carpets, and choice pieces of furniture give this small hotel a plush yet intimate feel. Rooms are decorated with a keen eye for detail and harmony, and all have en suite bathrooms. Just behind the Colosseum, it's ideal for exploring ancient Rome's ruins. ✉ *Via dei Santi Quattro 35/c, 00184,* ☎ *06/70495333,* FAX *06/7096377. 20 rooms. Restaurant, bar. AE, DC, MC, V.*

$$$ ⋆ 🏨 **Duca d'Alba.** This elegant hotel has made a stylish contribution to the ongoing gentrification of the Suburra, the neighborhood near the Colosseum and the Roman Forum. The tasteful neoclassic decor is in character, with ancient Roman motifs, custom-designed furnishings, and marble bathrooms. All rooms are entirely soundproofed; a few have tiny terraces. The four-bed suite with kitchenette is an excellent money-saving option for a family or a group of friends. ✉ *Via Leonina 14, 00184,* ☎ *06/484471,* FAX *06/4884840,* WEB *www.hotelducadalba.com. 27 rooms, 1 suite. AE, DC, MC, V.*

$$$ 🏨 **Nerva.** History is truly on your doorstep at this charming hotel. The cobbled, narrow street is flanked by ruins of breathtaking splendor, and Colosseum enthusiasts need only wander a few paces to see the great Roman monument. The hotel itself is immaculate and rooms are soundproofed and air-conditioned. It has been decorated simply but tastefully and the staff is helpful and charming. ✉ *Via Tor de Conti 3, 00184,* ☎ *06/6781835,* FAX *06/6793764. 19 rooms. Restaurant, bar. AE, DC, MC, V.*

$$ 🏨 **Cavalieri.** This hotel opened its doors in 1999 to encouraging reviews. Its lobby, staffed by English-speaking receptionists, is stylishly understated, and rooms follow suit, with simple, contemporary decor. But the best thing about the place is the location, in a quiet alley just five minutes from the Colosseum, with enough archaeological wonders on its doorstep to keep the curious occupied for weeks. ✉ *Via Frangipane 34, 00184,* ☎ *06/6796246,* FAX *06/6797203,* WEB *www.cavalieri.it. 24 rooms. Bar, parking (fee). AE, DC, MC, V.*

$$ ⋆ 🏨 **Richmond.** Right at the beginning of Via Cavour, this charming little hotel is ideally situated for visits to the Forum, the Colosseum, and all the major sights of ancient Rome. There's an attractive rooftop terrace where you can have breakfast and take in the panoramic views. The decor is highlighted with tasteful, classical touches and the modern rooms feature hand-painted designs frescoes. The staff is helpful and multilingual. ⊠ *Largo Corrado Ricci 36, 00184,* ☎ *06/69941256,* FAX *06/69941254. 15 rooms. Bar, parking (fee). AE, DC, MC, V.*

Jewish Ghetto

$$ 🏨 **Arenula.** This hotel—with a luminous and cheerful all-white interior—has a good quality-price ratio. Rooms have pale-wood furnishings and gleaming bathrooms, as well as double-glazed windows and air-conditioning (in summer only; no help on warm spring or fall days). Two of the rooms accommodate four beds. The catch at the four-story Arenula is that the graceful oval staircase of white marble and wrought iron is the only way up—there is no elevator. The hotel stands on an age-worn byway off central Via Arenula, on the edge of the quaint Ghetto neighborhood and just across the Tiber from Trastevere. ⊠ *Via Santa Maria dei Calderari 47, off Via Arenula, 00186,* ☎ *06/6879454,* FAX *06/6896188. 50 rooms. DC, MC, V.*

Piazza di Spagna

$$$$ 🏨 **De La Ville Inter-Continental.** For the well-heeled, this is a fine option just a stone's throw from the top of the Spanish Steps. Guests often ask for the rooms their great-grandparents favored; regulars are treated like family here—one reason the place is usually booked solid. Other lures include a lobby replete with marble and gilt furnishings; tastefully subdued guest rooms; and a staff high on initiative. Don't miss the morning meal or Sunday brunch served in La Piazzetta restaurant: adorned with twinkling chandeliers, silky *bergères* (18th-century decorative chairs), and taffeta-draped French doors, it has to be the prettiest breakfast in Rome. ⊠ *Via Sistina 69, 00187,* ☎ *06/67331,* FAX *06/6784213,* WEB *www.interconti.com. 169 rooms, 23 suites. Restaurant, 2 bars, hair salon, parking (fee). AE, DC, MC, V.*

$$$$ 🏨 **Dei Borgognoni.** This quietly chic hotel is on a byway in the heart of the smart shopping district near Piazza San Silvestro. The centuries-old building has been remodeled to provide spacious lounges, a glassed-in garden, and stylishly furnished rooms that are cleverly arranged to create an illusion of space, though they are actually compact. Some rooms have balconies or terraces on an interior court. ⊠ *Via del Bufalo 126, 00187,* ☎ *06/69941505,* FAX *06/69941501,* WEB *www.hotelborgognoni.it. 50 rooms. Bar, business services, parking (fee). AE, DC, MC, V.*

$$$$ 🏨 **Grand Hotel Plaza.** The Plaza is one of the oldest and most presti-
★   gious of Rome's hotels. Built in 1860, it's awash with Edwardian and fin de siècle atmosphere. The main salon includes stained-glass skylights, elegant chandeliers, and frescoes on its coved ceiling. The rooms are equally regal, each one uniquely realized with rare antique furnishings and up-to-the-minute amenities. In the heart of Rome's most elegant district, it has several large rooftop terraces that offer stunning views all around. ⊠ *Via del Corso 126, 00186,* ☎ *06/69921111,* FAX *06/69941575,* WEB *www.hotelplazarome.com. 207 rooms, 10 suites. Restaurant, 2 bars. AE, DC, MC, V. EP.*

$$$$ 🏨 **Hassler.** At the top of the Spanish Steps, the Hassler has sweeping
★   views of Rome from its front rooms and rooftop restaurant; other rooms overlook the gardens of the Villa Medici. The hotel is run by the distinguished Wirth family of hoteliers, which assures a cordial atmosphere and imperial service from the well-trained staff whose discretion is appreciated by the showbiz celebrities who are regular guests. The public rooms have an extravagant 1950s elegance—especially the clubby winter bar; the summer garden bar; and the glass-roof lounge, with gold marble walls and a hand-painted tile floor. The comfortable guest rooms are decorated in a variety of classic styles, some with frescoed

walls. The penthouse suite, resplendent with antiques, has a huge terrace. ⊠ *Piazza Trinità dei Monti 6, 00187,* ☎ *06/699340,* FAX *06/678991,* WEB *www.hotelhasslerroma.com. 85 rooms, 15 suites. Restaurant, bar, hair salon. AE, DC, MC, V. EP.*

$$$$ 🏨 **Hotel de Russie.** This luxurious establishment, famed as a jet-set favorite, was once the preferred pied-à-terre of Picasso, Stravinsky, and Cocteau. After closing from 1997 to 2000 for renovations, it reopened with an entirely new design that still pays zealous attention to the hotel's historic past and maintains a true feel of elegance. In the romantic gardens (designed by neoclassic architect Valadier, who is also responsible for the facade) you can enjoy a cold drink or a meal at the Jardin de Russie restaurant, surrounded by an oasis of green in the heart of the Eternal City. ⊠ *Via del Babuino 9, 00187,* ☎ *06/328881,* FAX *06/ 32888888,* WEB *www.rfhotels.com. 130 rooms. Restaurant, bar, hair salon, spa, parking (fee). AE, DC, MC, V.*

$$$–$$$$ 🏨 **Hotel d'Inghilterra.** This old favorite sits on a quiet side street just
★ off Via Condotti. One hundred and fifty years ago the building belonged to the Torlonia princes, before it was transformed into a quietly opulent hotel. Most of the guest rooms are decorated with period furniture and elegant paintings, part of the hotel's private collection. Some of them are on the small side, however; rooms 133 and 433 are your best bet if you want extra space at no extra cost. ⊠ *Via Bocca di Leone 14, 00187,* ☎ *06/699811,* FAX *06/69922243,* WEB *www.charminghotels. it/inghilterra. 100 rooms. Restaurant, bar. AE, DC, MC, V. EP.*

$$$ 🏨 **Carriage.** The Carriage's location is what makes it special: it's just two blocks away from the Spanish Steps, in the heart of Rome. The stylish decor uses subdued Baroque accents and antique reproductions to give the hotel a touch of elegance. Though some of the rooms are pint-size, and a couple open onto an air shaft, several have little terraces, and all guests can use the roof garden. ⊠ *Via delle Carrozze 36, 00187,* ☎ *06/6990124,* FAX *06/6788279,* WEB *www.hotelcarriage.net. 27 rooms. Bar. AE, DC, MC, V.*

$$$ 🏨 **Condotti.** As its name suggests, this small hotel is only two blocks from Rome's premier shopping street, Via dei Condotti, and one block from the Spanish Steps. The emphasis here is on peace and comfort, created by elegant period furnishings and a relatively quiet location. All rooms are soundproofed and many enjoy views of the rooftops of Rome. Unfailing courtesy and hospitality are the keynotes among the multilingual staff. Room decor is a blend of modern and antique, with especially rich fabrics used for the curtains and bedspreads. Each room has its own temperature control. ⊠ *Via Mario de'Fiori 37, 00187,* ☎ *06/6794661,* FAX *06/6790457,* WEB *www.venere.it/roma/condotti. 16 rooms. AE, DC, MC, V.*

$$$ 🏨 **Homs.** Rome's most complete English-language bookshop, the Anglo-American, is directly across the street from this midsize hotel on a quiet street in the heart of the historic center. Two rooftop terraces, the larger one suitable for breakfast year-round, provide unforgettable views of the whole area. Rooms have all the amenities of much more expensive places, and while the furnishings are a bit plain overall, beautiful antiques accent strategic spots to create an air of graciousness. ⊠ *Via della Vite 71–72, 00187,* ☎ *06/6792976,* FAX *06/ 6780482. 48 rooms. Bar, parking (fee). AE, DC, MC, V.*

$$$ 🏨 **Hotel Valadier.** This sought-after hotel is in the vivacious heart of Rome, just off Piazza del Popolo. The bedrooms are decorated with flair and all have marble bathrooms. Best of all is the view from the rooftop terrace; the panorama of domes and cupolas is as good as any Rome has to offer. The food served at the roof-top restaurant, Valentino's, is first-rate, too. ⊠ *Via della Fontanella 15, 00187,* ☎ *06/3611998,*

FAX *06/3201558*, WEB *www.hotelvaladier.com. 50 rooms. 2 restaurants, piano bar. AE, DC, MC, V. EP.*

$$$ 🏠 **Locarno.** Art aficionados and people in the cinema have long ap-
★   preciated this hotel's preserved fin de siècle charm, intimate feel, and central location off Piazza del Popolo. Wallpaper and fabric prints are coordinated in the rooms, and some rooms have antiques. Everything is lovingly supervised by the owners, a mother-daughter duo. The buffet breakfast is ample, there's bar service on the panoramic roof garden, and complimentary bicycles are available if you feel like braving the traffic. ✉ *Via della Penna 22, 00186,* ☎ *06/3610841,* FAX *06/ 3215249,* WEB *www.hotellocarno.com. 46 rooms, 2 suites. Bar, lobby lounge, in-room data ports, parking (fee). AE, DC, MC, V.*

$$$ 🏠 **Trevi.** A romantic's dream, this delightful place is tucked away down one of Old Rome's quaintest alleys. The rooms are bright and clean. Some are small, but a few of the larger ones have antique furniture and wooden ceilings with massive beams. There's a roof-garden restaurant where you can eat marvelous pasta. ✉ *Vicolo del Babuccio 20, 00187,* ☎ *06/6789563,* FAX *06/69941407,* WEB *www. gruppotrevi.it/trevi/index.htm. 29 rooms. Restaurant, parking (fee). AE, DC, MC, V.*

$$$ 🏠 **Tritone.** This hotel is only a hundred yards from the Fontana di Trevi and within easy walking distance of virtually every important site in the historic center. Although the hotel is positioned on one of Rome's busiest thoroughfares, high-quality soundproofing ensures a good night's sleep. Rooms have modern decor with wall-to-wall carpeting, minibars, satellite TVs, and spacious bathrooms. A buffet breakfast can be taken in the roof garden, with panoramic views of the Eternal City. ✉ *Via del Tritone 210, 00187,* ☎ *06/69922575,* FAX *06/6782624,* WEB *www.tritonehotel.com. 43 rooms. Bar, minibars. AE, DC, MC, V.*

$$–$$$ 🏠 **Scalinata di Spagna.** An old-fashioned pensione that has hosted generations of romantics, this tiny hotel is booked solid for months—even years—ahead. Its location at the top of the Spanish Steps, inconspicuous little entrance, and view from the terrace where you breakfast make it seem like your own special, exclusive inn. ✉ *Piazza Trinità dei Monti 17, 00187,* ☎ *06/6793006,* FAX *06/69940598,* WEB *www. hotelscalinata.com. 16 rooms. Parking (fee). AE, MC, V.*

$$ 🏠 **Marcus.** The location, down the street from the Spanish Steps, is the premier feature of this small, homey hotel occupying a large apartment on one floor of an 18th-century cardinal's palazzo. Many rooms have antique fireplaces; all have modern bathrooms. The main living room has comfortable armchairs and a crystal chandelier. Double-glazed windows keep out most of the noise of central Rome. ✉ *Via del Clementino 94, 00186,* ☎ *06/68300320,* FAX *06/68300312,* WEB *www. venere.it/roma/marcus. 18 rooms. AE, MC, V.*

$$ 🏠 **San Carlo.** Marble accents are everywhere at this refurbished hotel, and the overall effect is refined and decidedly classical. It helps that it's on one of the historic center's quietest and most elegant streets. Rooms are bright and comfortable and some have their own terraces with rooftop views. A top-floor terrace is ideal for having breakfast or taking the sun throughout the day. ✉ *Via delle Carrozze 93, 00187,* ☎ *06/6784548,* FAX *06/69941197. 48 rooms. AE, MC, V.*

$ 🏠 **Margutta.** For location, good quality-price ratio, and friendly owner-managers, the Margutta is outstanding. The lobby and halls in this small hotel are unassuming, but rooms are a pleasant surprise, with a clean and airy look, attractive wrought-iron bedsteads, and modern baths. Three of the rooms have private terraces. Though it's in an old building, there is an elevator. The location is on a quiet side street between the Spanish Steps and Piazza del Popolo. ✉ *Via Laurina 34, 00187,* ☎ *06/3223674,* FAX *06/3200395. 21 rooms. AE, DC, MC, V.*

Piazza Navona

$$$$ ⊞ **Albergo del Sole al Pantheon.** This small hotel has stood opposite the Pantheon since the 15th century. Over the years, travelers have accepted the rather cramped quarters in exchange for the location on this historic square. The hotel has been tastefully decorated with a blend of modern and antique furnishings. Ceilings are high and floors are tiled in terra-cotta. Double-glazed windows shut out the din of the café scene below. ⊠ *Piazza della Rotonda 63, 00186,* ☎ *06/6780441,* FAX *06/69940689,* WEB *www.hotelsolealpantheon.com. 30 rooms. Bar. AE, DC, MC, V.*

$$$$ ⊞ **Grand Hotel de la Minerva.** The Minerva is the very stylish reincarnation of the hostelry that occupied this 17th-century palazzo for hundreds of years, hosting literati from Stendhal to Sartre and de Beauvoir. Entirely renovated in 1997, with a stunning stained-glass lobby skylight designed by architect Paolo Portoghesi, the Minerva has everything a guest could want in the way of comfort, as well as an absolutely central location. And from the lavish roof terrace, open for summer dining in fair weather, you can almost touch the dome of Hadrian's Pantheon. ⊠ *Piazza della Minerva 69, 00186,* ☎ *06/695201,* FAX *06/6794165. 118 rooms, 16 suites. Restaurant, piano bar, gym. AE, DC, MC, V. EP.*

$$$$ ⊞ **Nazionale a Montecitorio.** This is one of the most historic of Rome's hotels—at least with regard to postwar Italian politics. Given its prime location adjacent to the Parliament, this 16th-century palazzo has been the venue for any number of momentous meetings of Italy's top politicos. In keeping with its national importance, it offers every traditional service and modern comfort: homey yet regal rooms, a bar, a restaurant, meeting rooms, and first-class staff. The buffet breakfast is not only lavish but unforgettable, due to the eye-popping polychrome marble floors of the restaurant. The second-floor penthouse suite offers a private terrace and amazing views. ⊠ *Piazza Montecitorio 127, 00186,* ☎ *06/695001,* FAX *06/6786677,* WEB *www.nazionaleamontecitorio.it. 87 rooms, 1 suite. Restaurant, bar, 2 meeting rooms, parking (fee). AE, DC, MC, V.*

$$$$ ⊞ **Pantheon.** The Pantheon makes a wonderful place to stay right next door to the monument of the same name. The lobby and hallways offer a taste of Roman splendors from every epoch: art nouveau stained glass, ancient mosaics, medieval carved wood-beam ceilings, and a massive crystal chandelier. A print of one of Rome's obelisks on the door welcomes you to your room, where you'll find antique walnut furniture, fresh flowers, and more wood-beam ceilings. ⊠ *Via dei Pastini 131, 00186,* ☎ *06/6787746,* FAX *06/6787755,* WEB *www.hotelpantheon.com. 20 rooms, 1 suite. Bar. AE, DC, MC, V. EP.*

$$$$ ⊞ **Raphaël.** This may be Rome's most fascinating hotel. The location
★ is perfect—tucked away behind spectacular Piazza Navona—and the vine-covered facade creates an immediate feeling of cozy mystery. The extensive lobby features an array of sculptures, genuine antiques, and a collection of original Picasso ceramics. Each room is uniquely designed and decorated with its own treasures, and bathrooms are finished with travertine marble or hand-painted tiles. The bi-level Bramante Terrace, where guests can arrange to have meals, offers great city views. The Raphaël Restaurant is memorable, serving French and Mediterranean cuisine on Picasso-inspired dinnerware. Some suites have private terraces. ⊠ *Largo Febo 2, 00186,* ☎ *06/682831,* FAX *06/6878993,* WEB *www.raphaelhotel.com. 51 rooms, 7 suites, 10 apartments. Restaurant, bar, sauna, gym, parking (fee). AE, DC, MC, V. EP.*

$$$ ⊞ **Cesàri.** From the traffic-free street in front of this intimate and
★ quiet hotel in the center of Rome you can see the columns of an an-

cient temple that were incorporated into the side of the stock exchange. The hotel's exterior is as it was when Stendhal and German historian Gregorovius stayed here in the 1800s, but the interior has been thoroughly renovated and redecorated, with cream-color walls embellished with old prints of Rome and soft green drapes and bedspreads. A few rooms are furnished with antiques; all have smart two-tone blue marble bathrooms. ⊠ *Via di Pietra 89/a, 00186,* ☎ *06/6792386,* FAX *06/6790882,* WEB *www.venere.it/roma/cesari. 47 rooms. Parking (fee). AE, DC, MC, V.*

$$$ ⌂ **Santa Chiara.** Three historic buildings form this gracious hotel be-
★   hind the Pantheon. It has been in the same family for 200 years, and the personal attention shows in meticulously decorated and maintained lounges and rooms. Though not all the rooms are spacious, all have character and are quiet and well organized. Each has built-in oak headboards, a marble-top desk, and an elegant travertine bath. Double-glazed front windows overlook Piazza della Minerva. The excellent location and low rates in this category give it a good quality-price ratio. The hotel also has three apartments, for two to five people each, with full kitchens. The topmost has beamed ceilings, a fireplace, and a huge terrace with a view of the Pantheon's dome. ⊠ *Via Santa Chiara 21, 00186,* ☎ *06/6872979,* FAX *06/6873144,* WEB *www.albergosantachiara.com. 100 rooms, 4 suites, 3 apartments. Bar, parking (fee). AE, DC, MC, V.*

$$–$$$ ⌂ **Genio.** Rooms at the top of this medium-size hotel, located just at the ancient entrance to Piazza Navona, have terraces and citywide views. There's also a roof terrace for all, where you can have breakfast. Modeled after classic Roman taste, the lobby, public areas, and rooms make you feel right at home. Rooms are decorated in warm colors and have parquet floors and a harmonious mix of modern and antique reproduction furnishings. ⊠ *Via G. Zanardelli 28, 00186,* ☎ *06/6832191,* FAX *06/68307246. 60 rooms. Bar, parking (fee). AE, DC, MC, V.*

$$ ⌂ **Coronet.** You, too, can be a guest in the vast Palazzo Doria Pamphilj off Piazza Venezia. This small hotel occupies part of a floor in one wing of the palace; seven interior rooms overlook the aristocratic family's lovely private garden court. Antique-style stuccoes and moldings in the carpeted halls and beam ceilings in several rooms are in keeping with the historic surroundings. The good-size rooms have oldish baths, some very small. Several rooms can accommodate three or four beds. ⊠ *Piazza Grazioli 5, 00186,* ☎ *06/6792341,* FAX *06/69922705. 13 rooms, 10 with bath. AE, DC, MC, V.*

$$ ⌂ **Portoghesi.** In the heart of Old Rome, the Portoghesi is a small hotel
★   with big atmosphere and a truly European character. From a tiny lobby, an equally tiny elevator takes you to the quiet bedrooms, all decorated with floral prints and reproduction antique furniture. It has a charming roof garden with a view of the city's domes and rooftops. ⊠ *Via dei Portoghesi 1, 00186,* ☎ *06/6864231,* FAX *06/6876976,* WEB *www.hotelportoghesiroma.com. 22 rooms, 6 suites. MC, V.*

$ ⌂ **Abruzzi.** Rarely do magnificent views of world-famous ancient monuments come so cheap. From the windows of this old-fashioned little establishment, the Pantheon is literally in your face. Unfortunately the facilities also recall a Rome of yesteryear: sink in the room, bathroom down the hall, no TV, no air-conditioning, no credit cards, no fax, no frills. But the rooms are clean and the beds comfortable. To make your reservation, you have to send a signed traveler's check with the name of the hotel also on it. ⊠ *Piazza della Rotonda 69, 00186,* ☎ *06/6792021. 25 rooms without bath. No credit cards.*

San Pietro

$$$$ ⌂ **Giulio Cesare.** An aristocratic town house in the residential, but central, Prati district, the Giulio Cesare is a 10-minute walk across the Tiber

from Piazza del Popolo. It's beautifully run, with a friendly staff and a quietly luxurious air. The rooms are elegantly furnished, with chandeliers, thick rugs, floor-length drapes, and rich damasks in soft colors. Public rooms have Oriental carpets, old prints and paintings, marble fireplaces, and a grand piano. The buffet breakfast is a veritable banquet. ⊠ *Via degli Scipioni 287, 00192,* ☎ *06/3210751,* FAX *06/3215129,* WEB *www.venere.it/roma/giuliocesare. 90 rooms. Bar, parking (fee).* AE, DC, MC, V.

$$$$ 🏨 **Hotel Dei Mellini.** On the right bank of the Tiber between the Spanish Steps and St. Peter's Basilica, this place has class to match its setting. The understated but luxurious reception rooms are a weary sightseer's dream. Antique prints, fresh flowers, and carefully chosen furniture give warmth to the light-filled rooms. Marble en suite bathrooms complete the pampered feel. Free parking is available nearby. ⊠ *Via Muzio Clementi 81, 00193,* ☎ *06/324771,* FAX *06/32477801,* WEB *www.venere.it/roma/dei_mellini. 80 rooms. Restaurant, bar.* AE, DC, MC, V.

$$$–$$$$ 🏨 **Atlante Star.** The Atlante Star is famous for its spectacular 5,000-square-ft roof garden, with a unique 360-degree, panoramic view of Rome. The garden is home to the justly renowned Les Étoiles restaurant, the ideal place to breakfast. Rooms are filled with a variety of antique furnishings, walnut paneling, and wall silks; every multicolor marble bathroom has a full-size Jacuzzi. The friendly, multilingual staff will do their utmost to ensure that you have a perfect stay. A block away, at Via Crescenzio 78, is a less expensive annex, the Atlante Garden. ⊠ *Via Vitelleschi 34, 00193,* ☎ *06/6873233,* FAX *06/6872300,* WEB *www.atlanthotels.com. 65 rooms, 10 suites. Restaurant, bar, parking (fee).* AE, MC, V.

$$$ 🏨 **Farnese.** A totally renovated turn-of-the-20th-century mansion, the
★ Farnese is two Metro stops from the Spanish Steps and within walking distance of St. Peter's Basilica. Furnished with great attention to detail in belle epoque style, it has an intimate atmosphere, dazzling modern baths, charming trompe l'oeil fresco decorations, and a roof garden. The ample sitting rooms on the main floor and the high-ceiling bedrooms are soberly elegant, with lavish wainscoting and rich fabrics. Owner-run by the same family as the Giulio Cesare around the corner, it pampers guests with personalized attention. ⊠ *Via Alessandro Farnese 30, 00192,* ☎ *06/3212553,* FAX *06/3215129. 24 rooms. Bar, free parking.* AE, DC, MC, V. EP.

$$–$$$ 🏨 **Isa.** Just across the Tiber River from Piazza Navona and a 15-minute walk from St. Peter's Basilica, in the heart of a tree-lined shopping district, this medium-size hotel has been elegantly renovated. Many rooms are decorated with classical-style murals illuminated by lights recessed into the ceilings. Well-placed faux marble effects, sumptuous wall silks, and real marble bathrooms complete the luxurious setting. Most rooms have balconies. ⊠ *Via Cicerone 39, 00193,* ☎ *06/3212610,* FAX *06/3215882,* WEB *www.hotelisa.com. 40 rooms. Parking (fee).* AE, DC, MC, V.

$$–$$$ 🏨 **Sant'Anna.** An example of the gentrification of the old Borgo neighborhood in the shadow of St. Peter's Basilica, this fashionable small hotel has ample, air-conditioned bedrooms in art deco style. The frescoes in the breakfast room and fountain in the courtyard are typical Roman touches. The spacious attic rooms have tiny terraces. ⊠ *Borgo Pio 133, 00193,* ☎ *06/68801602,* FAX *06/68308717,* WEB *www.hotelsantanna.com. 20 rooms. Parking (fee).* AE, DC, MC, V.

$$ 🏨 **Alimandi.** On a side street only a block from the Musei Vaticani,
★ this family-operated hotel offers excellent value in a neighborhood with moderately priced shops and restaurants. A spiffy lobby and ample

Close-Up

CONVENTS AND CURFEWS

ROME HAS AT LEAST 150 convents and religious institutes that offer lodging, usually quite plain but clean and inexpensive. Beds are mainly singles, unmarried couples are usually not accepted, and there's often a strict curfew of 10 or 10:30 PM. To book by phone, you may need to speak Italian, or have someone standing by who does. Rates range from €30 to €50 for a single, from €45 to €60 for a double. Meals are usually available for a modest extra charge.

Casa di Santa Brigida. Book well in advance, for this is one of the best and best known of the convents that take paying guests. It has an enviable location off Piazza Farnese in the heart of Old Rome. The address is that of the church of Santa Brigida, but the guest-house entrance is around the corner at Via Monserrato 54. There are comfortable lounges and a roof terrace. Rooms have small private baths. The Brigidine sisters are known for their gentle manner; they wear a distinctive habit and veil with a caplike headband. ⊠ Piazza Farnese 96, 00186, ☎ 06/68892497. 24 rooms with bath. AE, DC, MC, V.

Fraterna Domus. Located on a byway near Piazza Navona, this guest house is run by nuns who do not wear religious habits. Rooms are spartan but have the essentials, including small private bathrooms. Meals are hearty and inexpensive, and the curfew is 11 PM. ⊠ Vicolo del Leonetto 16, 00186, ☎ 06/68802727. 20 rooms with bath.

San Giuseppe della Montagna. This convent is just outside the Vatican walls, near the entrance to the Vatican Museums. Some of the guest rooms have three beds and all have private bathrooms. Here there is no curfew; guests are given keys. ⊠ Viale Vaticano 87, 00165, ☎ 06/39723807. 15 rooms with bath.

— Barbara Walsh Angelillo

lounges, a tavern for night owls, terraces, and roof gardens are some of the perks here. Rooms are spacious, airy, and well furnished; many can accommodate extra beds. Handy public transportation gets you to downtown Rome in 10 minutes or so. ⊠ Via Tunisi 8, 00192, ☎ 06/39723948, FAX 06/39723943, WEB www.alimandi.org. 35 rooms. Parking (fee). AE, DC, MC, V. EP.

$$ 🏠 **Amalia.** Handy to St. Peter's Basilica, the Vatican, and the Cola di Rienzo shopping district, this small hotel is owned and operated by the Consoli family—Amalia and her brothers. On several floors of a 19th-century building, it has large, airy rooms with functional furnishings, TV sets, minibars, pictures of angels on the walls, and gleaming marble bathrooms (hair dryers included). The Ottaviano stop of Metro line A is a block away. ⊠ Via Germanico 66, 00192, ☎ 06/39723356, FAX 06/39723365, WEB www.hotelamalia.com. 30 rooms, 25 with bath or shower. Minibars, parking (fee). AE, MC, V.

$$ 🏠 **Gerber.** On a quiet side street not far from the Vatican and across the river from Piazza del Popolo, this intimate, unpretentious hotel offers genuinely friendly service. Immaculately maintained throughout, it features a garden and sun terrace for breakfast or a relaxed moment. Rooms have pleasant, neutral-tone modern furnishings. ⊠ Via degli Scipioni 241, 00192, ☎ 06/3219986, FAX 06/3217048, WEB www.hotelgerber. it. 27 rooms. Bar, parking (fee). AE, DC, MC, V.

Termini

$$$$ 🏨 **Empire Palace Hotel.** The restaurant, Aureliano, is the big draw at this long-established accommodation. Traditional dishes jostle for space on the menu with modern, zany concoctions such as lemon sorbet with balsamic vinegar. In the hotel, the spacious marble-floored lobby and sitting areas are decorated with works by contemporary artists. The guest rooms are luxurious, decorated in classical Roman style with antique furniture and fine paintings on the walls. There are meeting and banquet rooms and a gym area. The place also boasts a great location in the heart of Rome's shopping and business center. It's perfect for a stylish stay with great food and convenience thrown in. ⊠ *Via Aureliana 39, 00187,* ☎ *06/421281,* FAX *06/42128400,* WEB *www. venere.it/roma/empire. 110 rooms. Restaurant, bar, gym, business services. AE, DC, MC, V. EP.*

$$$$ 🏨 **Mascagni.** High-quality soundproofing has created an oasis of solitude on one of Rome's busiest and most central streets. The Mascagni has a cheerful staff and the particular charm of a small hotel. Decorated in early 1920s style, the rooms have handsome mahogany furnishings and coordinated fabrics. The intimate lounges and pleasant bar mirror the same decorating scheme, as does the breakfast room, where a lavish buffet is laid out in the morning. ⊠ *Via Vittorio Emanuele Orlando 90, 00185,* ☎ *06/48904040,* FAX *06/4817637,* WEB *www.hotelmascagni.com. 40 rooms. Bar, business services. AE, DC, MC, V.*

$$$$ 🏨 **Mediterraneo.** Run by the famous Bettoja hotelier family, this classy place is steps from the train station and within walking distance of some major sights. The foyer, with marble and rich wood paneling, has plush armchairs perfect for unwinding. Rooms are tastefully decorated, with modern amenities. Views of the city from the penthouse suites and roof garden are alone almost worth the high price. The restaurant next door in sister hotel Massimo d'Azeglio has superb regional Italian cuisine as well as Italian, French, and Californian wines from the family wine cellar. ⊠ *15 Via Cavour, 00184,* ☎ *06/4884051,* FAX *06/4744105,* WEB *www.bettojahotels.it. 258 rooms, 10 suites. Restaurant, bar, lobby lounge, in-room safes, minibars, room service, parking (fee). AE, DC, MC, V.*

$$$$ 🏨 **Mercenate Palace Hotel.** Named after ancient Rome's most important patron of the arts who lived at this location just over 2,000 years ago, this classy accommodation is situated on top of the Esquiline, one of the highest of Rome's famous seven hills. From the rooftop terrace there's a marvelous view of the bell tower of Santa Maria Maggiore. The rooms are in two adjacent buildings, which have been lovingly renovated to their original fin de siècle splendor. They are tastefully decorated, and the suites are furnished with 19th-century antiques. ⊠ *Via Carlo Alberto 3, 00185,* ☎ *06/44702024,* FAX *06/4461354,* WEB *www. venere.it/roma/mecenate. 59 rooms, 3 suites. Restaurant, parking (fee). AE, DC, MC, V.*

$$$$ 🏨 **Morgana.** The dashingly marbled lobby, the antique accents in fully
★ carpeted halls, the cordial atmosphere, and high-ceilinged, soundproofed rooms decorated with fine fabrics make this an elegantly conceived hotel, with luxurious touches throughout from the bathrooms to the bar. The service is superb, and the location is convenient to Termini Station. ⊠ *Via Filippo Turati 33, 00185,* ☎ *06/4467230,* FAX *06/4469142,* WEB *www.hotelmorgana.com. 100 rooms, 2 suites. Bar, in-room safes, airport shuttle, parking (fee). AE, DC, MC, V.*

$$$$ 🏨 **St. Regis Grand.** The Grand, a Roman landmark, reopened in 2000 after an 18-month refurbishment. A 100-year-old establishment of class and style, the hotel, only a few minutes from Via Veneto, caters to an elite international clientele. Off the richly decorated, split-level main salon—where afternoon tea is served every day—is an intimate bar, a chic rendezvous. Guest rooms are furnished in a combination of styles including Empire, Regency, and Louis XV. Every room has its own identity, with a hand-painted fresco above the headboard. The Grand also offers one of Italy's most beautiful dining rooms, called simply Le Restaurant. ✉ *Via Vittorio Emanuele Orlando 3, 00185,* ☎ *06/47091,* FAX *06/4747307,* WEB *www.stregis.com. 134 rooms, 36 suites. Restaurant, bar, free parking. AE, DC, MC, V.*

$$$ 🏨 **Art Deco.** The name says it all: the decor at this hotel is attuned to the elegant sensibilities of the 1920s, with whimsical accents in art deco paintings and antiques. Underlying the old style are reassuring modern amenities: a fail-safe electrical system, air-conditioning, and whirlpool baths. The hotel is in a residential neighborhood 10 minutes from Termini Station and handy to public transport. ✉ *Via Palestro 19, 00185,* ☎ *06/4457588,* FAX *06/4441483,* WEB *www.travel.it/roma/ artdeco. 49 rooms. Restaurant, bar, hot tub. AE, DC, MC, V.*

$$$ 🏨 **Britannia.** This fine small hotel, with frescoed halls and a buffet-
★   breakfast room, is a very special place, offering superior quality at reasonable rates. Its quiet but central location is one attraction; a caring management is another. Guests are coddled with English-language dailies and local weather reports delivered to their rooms each morning, with sybaritic marble bathrooms (some with hot tubs), and well-furnished rooms (two with roof terraces). ✉ *Via Napoli 64, 00184,* ☎ *06/4883153,* FAX *06/4882343,* WEB *www.venere.it/roma/britannia. 32 rooms, 1 suite. Free parking. AE, DC, MC, V.*

$$$ 🏨 **Marcella.** Known to connoisseurs as one of Rome's best midsize hotels, with the feel of a smaller, more intimate establishment, the Marcella is 10 minutes from Via Veneto and Termini Station. Here you can do your sightseeing from the roof terrace, taking in the view while you breakfast. Many rooms also have good views, and they are all furnished with flair, using tasteful color schemes, floral prints, and mirrored walls, echoing the elegant winter-garden decor of the lounges and bar. The spacious suites are ideal for families. ✉ *Via Flavia 106, 00187,* ☎ *06/42014591,* FAX *06/4815832,* WEB *www.hotelmarcella.com. 73 rooms, 2 suites. Bar. AE, DC, MC, V.*

$$–$$$ 🏨 **D'Este.** The fresh-looking decor in this distinguished 19th-century hotel evokes turn-of-the-20th-century comfort, with brass bedsteads and lamps as well as dark-wood period furniture. Rooms are quiet, light, and spacious; many can accommodate family groups. The attentive owner-manager likes to have fresh flowers in the halls and sees that everything works. He encourages inquiries about special rates, particularly during the slack summer months. It's within hailing distance of Santa Maria Maggiore and close to Termini Station (you can arrange to be picked up there, free of charge, by the hotel car). ✉ *Via Carlo Alberto 48/b, 00184,* ☎ *06/4465607,* FAX *06/4465601,* WEB *www.hotel-deste.com. 37 rooms. Bar. AE, DC, MC, V.*

$$–$$$ 🏨 **Doria.** A convenient location and reasonable rates are the advantages of this small hotel. Space is ingeniously exploited, from the minuscule elevator to the nicely furnished but smallish rooms. One of the hotel's most attractive features is the roof garden—again, not very large, but fine for enjoying an alfresco breakfast and an interesting view. The Doria has a clone, the Hotel Amalfi, across the street. Also owned by the courteous Nigro brothers, it has the same amenities and some larger rooms with three beds. ✉ *Via Merulana 4, 00185,* ☎ *06/ 4465888,* FAX *06/4465889. 20 rooms. Bar. AE, DC, MC, V.*

$$ 🏨 **Alpi.** The sweeping marble entrance here is cool and welcoming; it sets the tone for the rest of this good-value-for-the-price hotel. What you notice most is the feeling of space—high ceilings with elegant

chandeliers, white walls, and marble or parquet floors add to the understated grace. Some of the bedrooms have antique furniture, and all are well thought out and tastefully decorated. There are slightly formal lounges and a cozier bar downstairs, as well as a respectable restaurant. ⊠ *Via Castelfidardo 84/a, 00185,* ☎ *06/4441235,* FAX *06/ 4441257,* WEB *www.hotelalpi.com. 48 rooms. Restaurant, bar. AE, DC, MC, V.*

$$ ★ 🏨 **Des Artistes.** The three personable Riccioni brothers have transformed their hotel into one of the best in the Termini Station neighborhood in its price range, lavishing it with paintings, handsome furnishings in mahogany, attractive fabrics, marble baths, and amenities such as air-conditioning and minibars. There's a floor with 10 simpler rooms for travelers on a budget. This is a no-smoking hotel. ⊠ *Via Villafranca 20, 00185,* ☎ *06/4454365,* FAX *06/4462368,* WEB *www.hoteldesartistes.com. 40 rooms, 27 with bath. Bar, in-room data ports. AE, DC, MC, V.*

$$ 🏨 **Italia.** Off Via Nazionale, this family-run hotel offers luminous rooms with big windows, desks, parquet floors, bathrooms with marble-look tiles, and attractive art on the walls. Three rooms are triples. An eight-room annex across the street has high ceilings, double-glazed windows, and a slightly more upscale look. Rates are at the low end of this price category and include a generous buffet breakfast; ask for rate discounts in August and winter. ⊠ *Via Venezia 18, 00184,* ☎ *06/ 4828355,* FAX *06/4745550,* WEB *www.hotelitaliaroma.com. 23 rooms. AE, DC, MC, V.*

$$ 🏨 **Miami.** This low-key hotel, located in a dignified 19th-century building on Rome's important Via Nazionale, has tastefully decorated and soundproofed rooms, all en suite. It's well situated for sightseeing, shopping, and getting around in general: it's on main bus lines and near Termini Station and the Metro. Winter rates from November through February are a good bargain. The friendly family-style management is attentive and helpful. Rooms on the courtyard are quieter. ⊠ *Via Nazionale 230, 00184,* ☎ *06/4817180,* FAX *06/484562,* WEB *www. hotelmiami.com. 48 rooms, 3 suites. AE, DC, MC, V.*

$$ 🏨 **Montreal.** This compact hotel stands across the square from Santa Maria Maggiore, only three blocks from Termini Station, with bus and subway lines close by. On three floors of an older building, it offers fresh-looking, though smallish, rooms. The owner-managers are pleasant and helpful, and the neighborhood has plenty of reasonably priced places to eat. ⊠ *Via Carlo Alberto 4, 00185,* ☎ *06/4457797,* FAX *06/ 4465522. 22 rooms. AE, DC, MC, V.*

$$ 🏨 **Romae.** In the better part of the Termini Station neighborhood, the Romae has the advantages of a strategic location (within walking distance of many sights, and handy to bus and subway lines), a very friendly and helpful management, and good-size rooms that are clean and airy. The pictures of Rome in the small lobby and breakfast room, the luminous white walls and light-wood furniture in the rooms, and the bright little baths all have a fresh look. Amenities such as satellite TV, in-room safe, and hair dryer are unusual for a hotel of this price. (Rates are at the low end of the price category.) Families benefit from special rates and services. ⊠ *Via Palestro 49, 00185,* ☎ *06/4463554,* FAX *06/ 4463914,* WEB *www.hotelromae.com. 30 rooms. AE, DC, MC, V.*

$$ 🏨 **Siviglia.** You are transported back to a more opulent era in this freshly renovated 19th-century mansion in the quieter residential fringe of the Termini Station area. Like the several embassies in the neighborhood, it has bright flags flying at the entrance. Inside, Venetian glass chandeliers and reproduction antique furniture give the lounges considerable character; rooms are simpler, with a light, airy touch. ⊠ *Via Gaeta 12, 00185,* ☎ *06/4441198,* FAX *06/4441195. 40 rooms. Bar. AE, DC, MC, V.*

$$ 🏨 **Villa Della Rose.** The gorgeous courtyard full of roses and jasmine lures in the weary traveler as deftly as a Venus's-flytrap. The tranquillity of the outside is matched by the elegant and airy reception rooms; in the main room the eye is drawn irresistibly upward to a magnificent painted ceiling. The bedrooms are somewhat less impressive, but the hallmark taste of the hotel can be seen in every corner. ⊠ *Via Vincenza 5, 00185,* ☎ *06/4451788,* 𝔽𝔸𝕏 *06/4451639. 40 rooms. Bar. AE, DC, MC, V.*

$ 🏨 **Aphrodite.** This small hotel is right next door to Termini Station. It's clean and friendly, but basic. Some rooms are on the spartan side, but the overall feel is fresh and modern. White walls and curtains mean there's a peaceful, almost monastic quality to the place. You can't beat it for value. ⊠ *Via Marsala 90, 00185,* ☎ *06/491096,* 𝔽𝔸𝕏 *06/491579. 40 rooms. Bar. AE, DC, MC, V.*

Trastevere

$$ 🏨 **Cisterna.** On a quiet street in the very heart of medieval Trastevere, this basic but comfortable hotel is ideally located for getting to know Rome's most authentic neighborhood, a favorite of artists and bohemians for decades. Beamed ceilings add a rustic touch, and there's a marble terrace-garden with a classical fountain. All rooms have private bathrooms with shower, air-conditioning, and satellite TV. One room, number 40, has its own private terrace. ⊠ *Via della Cisterna 7–9, 00153,* ☎ *06/5881852,* 𝔽𝔸𝕏 *06/65810091. 18 rooms. DC, MC, V.*

$ 🏨 **Carmel.** Rome's only kosher hotel sits across the Tiber from the main synagogue. Although its room furnishings are spartan, the staff is very friendly and there's a charming vine-covered terrace. Most rooms have air-conditioning and double-glazed windows. There are two kitchens for use by Jewish guests, and prepared kosher meals can also be arranged. Breakfast is offered in the snack bar next door. ⊠ *Via Goffredo Mameli 11, 00153,* ☎ *06/5809921,* 𝔽𝔸𝕏 *06/5818853. 10 rooms. Parking (fee). MC, V.*

$ 🏨 **Trastevere.** This tiny hotel captures the unique charm of the village-within-a-city district that is Trastevere. The entrance hall features a mural of the famous Piazza di Santa Maria that's just a block away, and hand-painted art nouveau wall designs add a touch of graciousness throughout. Open medieval brickwork and a few antiques here and there complete the quaint mood. Most rooms face Piazza San Cosimato, where there's an old-fashioned market every morning except Sunday. ⊠ *Via Luciano Manara 24–25, 00153,* ☎ *06/5814713,* 𝔽𝔸𝕏 *06/5881016. 9 rooms. AE, DC, MC, V. EP, FAP, MAP.*

Via Veneto

$$$$ 🏨 **Barberini.** Here you can find about all you could ask for in a Rome hotel: charm, taste, and the good fortune to look out onto one of the best art galleries in town, Palazzo Barberini. The marble-floor lobby is light and welcoming, and upstairs each room is furnished with fixtures designed exclusively for the hotel. The breakfast buffet (not included in the price of the room) on the rooftop is in a league of its own: fresh, delicious, and copious. ⊠ *Via Rasella 3, 00187,* ☎ *06/4814993,* 𝔽𝔸𝕏 *06/4815211,* 𝕎𝔼𝔹 *www.hotelbarberini.com. 35 rooms, 4 suites. Restaurant, bar, parking (fee). AE, DC, MC, V. EP.*

$$$$ 🏨 **Bernini Bristol.** Since it opened its doors in 1870 this hotel has been a byword for luxury and elegance. The lounges—filled with antique furnishings and 18th-century tapestries—are a favored watering hole for Rome's well-heeled denizens. The rooms are decorated with a more low-key opulence. Like many accommodations in the area, the rooftop terrace has a great view across the bustling hub of the city. ⊠

Piazza Barberini 23, 00187, ☎ *06/4883051,* FAX *06/4824266,* WEB *www.sinahotels.com. 125 rooms, 1 suite. Restaurant, bar, gym. AE, DC, MC, V. EP.*

$$$$ ⊡ **Eden.** This superlative hotel combines dashing elegance and stun-
★ ning vistas of Rome with the warm charm of Italian hospitality. It has
an intimate air that's found favor with Hemingway, Ingrid Bergman,
Fellini, and many other luminaries. The precious antiques, sumptuous
Italian fabrics, linen sheets, and marble baths all have an understated
elegance, and the views from the rooftop bar and restaurant will take
your breath away. The La Terrazza dell'Eden restaurant has drawn well-
deserved raves. ⊠ *Via Ludovisi 49, 00187,* ☎ *06/478121,* FAX *06/
4821584,* WEB *www.hotel-eden.it. 112 rooms, 14 suites. Restaurant, bar,
gym, parking (fee). AE, DC, MC, V. EP.*

$$$$ ⊡ **Excelsior.** To Romans and many others, the white Victorian cupola
of the Excelsior is a symbol of Rome at its most cosmopolitan. The
hotel's porte cochere has long sheltered Europe's aristocrats and Hol-
lywood's royalty as they alighted from their Rollses and Ferraris. They
pass through polished doors that still open onto a world of luxury lav-
ished with mirrors, carved moldings, Oriental rugs, crystal chandeliers,
and huge, Baroque floral arrangements. The theme of gracious living
prevails throughout the hotel in splendidly appointed rooms and marble baths. ⊠ *Via Veneto 125, 00187,* ☎ *06/47081,* FAX *06/4826205,*
WEB *www.westin.com. 286 rooms, 35 suites. Restaurant, bar, gym,
parking (fee). AE, DC, MC, V. EP.*

$$$$ ⊡ **Imperiale.** The Imperiale hotel is housed inside a handsome stone
palazzo on the ever-popular Via Veneto. Polished parquet floors, airy
fabrics, and light-color walls set the tone of grace and style. The guest
rooms are decorated in a classical style that's in keeping with the
building itself. First-class cuisine can be had in the spacious dining room,
or you can enjoy a meal in the covered gazebo restaurant on Via
Veneto itself. ⊠ *Via Veneto 24, 00185,* ☎ *06/4826351,* FAX *06/4826343.
95 rooms. 2 restaurants, bar. AE, DC, MC, V.*

$$$$ ⊡ **Majestic.** In the 19th-century tradition of grand hotels, this establishment on Via Veneto offers sumptuous furnishings in turn-of-the-
20th-century style. The spacious rooms, swathed in fine fabrics, have
opulent white marble bathrooms and are equipped with up-to-date accessories well concealed so as not to spoil the atmosphere. Many suites
have whirlpool baths. There are authentic antiques in the public rooms.
The excellent restaurant looks like a Victorian conservatory, with a terrace overlooking Via Veneto. The intimate Ninfa grill-café on the
street level serves light meals and drinks. ⊠ *Via Veneto 50, 00187,* ☎
06/421441, FAX *06/4880984. 87 rooms, 8 suites. Restaurant, 2 bars,
parking (fee). AE, DC, MC, V. EP.*

$$$$ ⊡ **Marriott Grand Hotel Flora.** This handsome hotel, located at the top
of Via Veneto next to the Villa Borghese park, is something of a bea-
con on the Rome landscape, not least because it's painted deep pink.
Opinions may differ about the color choice, but there's little doubt that
Grand Hotel Flora's standard of excellence is among the highest in
the city. No expense has been spared in decorating the rooms and
suites. Each one is unique, and carefully chosen antiques grace them
all; the bathrooms are the last word in ablution chic. There's a lovely
roof-garden restaurant on the seventh floor and a large conference hall.
• ⊠ *Via Veneto 191, 00187,* ☎ *06/489929,* FAX *06/4820359,* WEB *www.
mariotthotels.com. 127 rooms, 24 suites. 2 Restaurants, bar, business
services, free parking. AE, DC, MC, V.*

$$$$ ⊡ **Regina Baglioni.** This former playground of kings and poets is
sumptuously decorated in art nouveau style and enjoys a commanding location on the famed Via Veneto, handy to Villa Borghese and the
dolce vita cafés of Roman high life. The rooms and suites are truly pala-

tial in their appointments, with Oriental carpets, luxury brocades, wall silks, and period antiques. Le Grazie restaurant is notable for its fine table settings of silver, porcelain, and crystal and for its equally fine cuisine. The seventh-floor suites enjoy superb views of the Eternal City. ✉ *Via Veneto 72, 00187,* ☎ *06/421111,* FAX *06/42012130,* WEB *www.baglionihotels.com. 123 rooms, 7 suites. Restaurant, bar, parking (fee). AE, DC, MC, V. EP.*

$$$ 🏨 **Alexandra.** This unassuming establishment with a slightly old-fashioned feel sits on what's arguably Rome's most evocative and glamorous street: Via Veneto. The reception rooms look as though they have remained untouched since King Vittorio Emanuele II's time. The bedrooms, however, are airy and spotlessly clean. All come with en suite bathrooms. Breakfast is served in a sunny conservatory. ✉ *Via Veneto 18, 00187,* ☎ *06/4881943,* FAX *06/4871804. 45 rooms. Restaurant, bar, parking (fee). AE, DC, MC, V.*

$$$ 🏨 **La Residenza.** It's primarily Americans who frequent this hotel in
★ a converted town house near Via Veneto, drawn by its first-class comfort and friendly atmosphere. The canopied entrance, spacious and well-furnished lounges, and bar and terrace are all what you would expect of a deluxe lodging. Rooms are done in aquamarine and beige, with bentwood furniture, large closets, and heated towel racks; a few have balconies. Rates include a generous American-style buffet breakfast. ✉ *Via Emilia 22, 00187,* ☎ *06/4880789,* FAX *06/485721. 29 rooms. Bar. AE, MC, V.*

$$$ 🏨 **Nuovo Hotel Quattro Fontane.** The opulence and glory of ancient Rome have inspired the decoration at this peaceful hotel. The reception hall's draped curtains, suits of armor, and banquet-hall ceilings leave you in a very evocative state of mind. The bedrooms are understated by comparison, and the dining room has a monastic simplicity about it that acts as a nice contrast. ✉ *Via 4 Fontane, 00184,* ☎ *06/ 4884480,* FAX *06/4814936. 36 rooms. Restaurant, bar, business services. AE, DC, MC, V.*

$$ 🏨 **Julia.** The Julia has been welcoming weary travelers since 1949. The small establishment is tucked away behind Piazza Barberini down a sinuous cobbled lane. Inside, the decor is surprisingly modern and straightforward. The rooms are functional, but although they lack character, they are spacious and clean. ✉ *Via Rasella 29, 00187,* ☎ *06/ 4881637,* FAX *06/4873413. 33 rooms. Bar. AE, DC, MC, V.*

$$ 🏨 **Sicilia.** This handy, medium-size hotel is just off the famous Via Veneto. The lobby furnishings are a bit suspect (the brown velour sofas aren't to everyone's taste) and the guest rooms have a 1970s feel, but overall the place is clean and spacious, and the staff is friendly and speaks English. What's lacking in style is made up for in location, with Villa Borgese a five-minute walk away and the delights of Via Veneto just around the corner. ✉ *Via Sicilia 24, 00187,* ☎ *06/4821913,* FAX *06/ 4821943,* WEB *www.hotelsicilia.it. 60 rooms. Restaurant, bar. AE, DC, MC, V.*

Beyond the City Center

$$$$ 🏨 **Cavalieri Hilton.** Though the Cavalieri is outside the imaginary confines of the city's center, distance has its advantages, one of them being the magnificent view from the hotel's hilltop site (ask for a room facing the city). This hotel is a stylish oasis of quiet and comfort, with good taste and a distinctive Italian flair. If you can tear yourself away from your balcony, the terraces, gardens, and swimming pool, you will find a courtesy shuttle bus leaving for the center of Rome every hour. Don't miss the deservedly acclaimed rooftop restaurant, La Pergola. ✉ *Via Cadlolo 101, 00136,* ☎ *06/35091,* FAX *06/35092241,* WEB *www.*

cavalieri-hilton.it. 349 rooms, 23 suites. 2 restaurants, 4 bars, 1 indoor and 1 outdoor pool, hair salon, spa, 2 tennis courts, gym. AE, DC, MC, V. EP.

$$$$ 🏨 **Duke Hotel.** This luxurious establishment is in the heart of the chic Parioli district. The Villa Glori and Villa Borghese parks flank it, giving it the feel of a country club in the center of the city. Beautiful furniture and the building's original features have been skillfully thrown into relief by plain, off-white walls and light-filled rooms. The Polo lounge has an intimate atmosphere. ⊠ *Via Archemede 69, 00197,* ☎ *06/367221,* FAX *06/36004104,* WEB *www.thedukehotel.com. 64 rooms, 14 suites. Bar, business services, free parking. AE, DC, MC, V.*

$$$$ 🏨 **Lord Byron.** This stylish hotel is a striking white art deco town house on the edge of Villa Borghese, the lush park in the center of Rome. It's a short taxi ride to the downtown area, a negligible inconvenience well compensated for by the quiet setting. Inside, modern and antique styles combine to create highly polished opulence. The downstairs bar—a magnificent piece of cabinetry—is a conversation piece, and the stylish Relais le Jardin restaurant earns consistently high marks. ⊠ *Via G. de Notaris 5, 00197,* ☎ *06/3220404,* FAX *06/3220405,* WEB *www.lordbyronhotel. com. 28 rooms, 9 suites. Restaurant, bar, parking (fee). AE, DC, MC, V. EP.*

$$$$ 🏨 **Parco dei Principi.** The 1960s-era facade of this large, seven-story hotel contrasts with the turn-of-the-20th-century Italian court decor, and the extensive botanical garden, right on the border of the exclusive Parioli district and the Villa Borghese park, adds a certain natural touch. The result is a brilliant combination of traditional elegance and contemporary pleasure: picture windows in every room with views over an ocean of green, surmounted by St. Peter's dome; a wonderful free-form swimming pool; a piano bar with stained-glass and carved walnut appointments; and chamber music in the garden. ⊠ *Via G. Frescobaldi 5, 00198,* ☎ *06/854421,* FAX *06/8845014. 160 rooms, 20 suites. 3 restaurants, bar, piano bar, pool, health club, business services, parking (fee). AE, DC, MC, V.*

$$$ 🏨 **Villa Glori.** This unassuming midsize hotel is a bit off the beaten path, but the neighborhood has lot of charm and it's only a 10-minute tram ride to the historic center. It's on a quiet cul-de-sac that, together with the next private street over, is called *piccola Londra* (little London) for its architectural style unique in all of Rome. The interior is pleasant: clean and homey, with furnishings in blond wood and beige leather. There's an American-style buffet breakfast. ⊠ *Viale del Vignola 28, 00196,* ☎ *06/3227658,* FAX *06/3219495. 57 rooms. Parking (fee). AE, DC, MC, V.*

$$–$$$ 🏨 **Hotel Villa Borghese.** There's a reason why this place is such great value: it's a little farther out of the city center than comparable hotels. Having said that, it overlooks Villa Borghese, the city's most famous park, and all the wonderful Borghese museums are just a short walk away. The reception rooms are decorated with flair and have a quiet sense of Continental sophistication. Antique furniture and paintings ranging from modern to classical are found throughout; the walls are predominantly white, giving the hotel a light, airy feel. Beware of the bedrooms that have a bathroom built into a "box" inside the room itself; make sure yours is truly en suite. ⊠ *Via Pinciana 31, 00198,* ☎ *06/85300919,* FAX *06/8414100. 32 rooms. Bar. AE, DC, MC, V.*

4 NIGHTLIFE AND THE ARTS

Rome is a magical city after dark. Its monuments are illuminated against the night sky, its cafés and piazzas crowded with people watching people, while behind inconspicuous doors, the rites of the evening are celebrated in music clubs, discos, and bars. When the late show at the cinema is over, the streets are suddenly as crowded as at midday. That's when the pizzerias do a booming business and traffic is more hectic than ever.

Updated by
John Eldan and
Carla Lionello

T**O MANY PEOPLE, ROME ITSELF IS ENTERTAINMENT** enough. The piazzas, fountains, and delicately colored *palazzi* make impressive backdrops for the living theater of the vivacious city, with a *fortissimo* of motor vehicles. Rome has learned to make the most of its spectacular cityscape, transforming its most beautiful places into settings for the performing arts, either outdoors in the summer or in splendid palaces and churches in the winter. When performances are held at locations such as Villa Celimontana, Piazza Trinità dei Monti, or the church of Sant'Ignazio, the venue often steals the show. Music is what Rome does best to entertain people until the wee hours, whether it be opera or jazz or disco. Theater, and especially the cinema, is a big draw for Italian-speakers, but late-night café-sitting in trendy spots is fun even if you don't speak the language.

THE ARTS

Though Romans used to take their culture rather distractedly, they now show a lively interest in the arts. They can't wait for the new concert hall designed by Renzo Piano to be finished (the location is near the Flaminio Stadium, north of Piazza del Popolo; promised for April 2002, the opening may be delayed due to the discovery of Roman ruins on the site). The city offers an array of cultural events throughout the year, at outdoor venues during the warmer months. For all outdoor events in the evening, take a jacket or sweater and something to cover bare legs: despite the daytime heat of a Roman summer, the nights can be cool. Events generally are poorly publicized; you can find out what's scheduled by keeping an eye on the posters announcing events and reading listings in newspapers and specialized publications.

The most comprehensive listings of what's going on in the city (movies, museum exhibitions, concerts, sporting and cultural events) are in the weekly *Romac'è* booklet, which comes out every Friday and has a short section in English at the back. Schedules of events are also published in the daily newspapers, in the *Trovaroma* Thursday supplement of *La Repubblica* newspaper, in the *Guest in Rome* booklet distributed free at hotel desks, and in flyers available at EPT offices and city tourist information kiosks. A biweekly English-language periodical, *Wanted in Rome,* available at many newsstands, has good coverage of events in the arts. Look for posters outside churches announcing free concerts and recitals of religious music. The RomaEuropa Festival, which begins in July but reaches its height in October, is a multivenue performing-arts program. If you visit Rome during the month of July or August, ask at the tourist office for a schedule of concerts and outdoor movies (some in English) that make up the *Estate Romana* festival.

Depending on the venue, concert tickets can cost anything from €7 to €25. Often, seating is open (identified in Italian as *posti non numerati*). Inquire about this when you buy the tickets; you may have to arrive early to get a good seat. Get opera and concert tickets in advance at the box office, or try just before the performance. **Roman Reference** (⊠ Via de' Capocci 94, ☎ 06/48903612) is basically a business that organizes short-term apartment rentals but is also happy to provide many types of personalized services for tourists, including ticket reservations for events in Rome and other parts of Italy. **Orbis** (⊠ Piazza Esquilino 37, ☎ 06/4827403) is a multipurpose ticket agency. **Genti e Paesi** (⊠ Via Adda 11, ☎ 06/85301755) will book tickets for concerts, theater, and museums.

Dance

The **Rome Opera Ballet** gives regular performances at the Teatro dell'Opera, often with leading international guest stars. Rome is regularly visited by ballet companies from all over the world; performances are at **Teatro dell'Opera** (⊠ Via Firenze 72, ☎ 06/4817003), Teatro Olimpico, or at one of the open-air venues in summer. **Teatro Olimpico** (⊠ Piazza Gentile da Fabriano 17, ☎ 06/3265991) is the venue for contemporary dance companies. In addition, throughout the year, small dance companies from Italy and abroad give performances in various places; check entertainment listings for information.

Film

For programs and show times, see the entertainment pages of daily newspapers, *Romac'è*, or Rome's English-language publications. Tickets are usually €6.20–€6.70; for matinees and shows all day Wednesday, the price drops to €4.15 or €5.15. Rome has dozens of movie houses, but the only one to show exclusively English-language films in English is the **Pasquino** (⊠ Piazza S. Egidio 10, just off Piazza Santa Maria in Trastevere, ☎ 06/58333310), with three screens. The **Quirinetta** (⊠ Via Minghetti 4, ☎ 06/6790012) shows international films in their original language, which is almost always English. The **Alcazar** (⊠ Via Merry del Val 14, ☎ 06/5880099) has movies in their original language with Italian subtitles on Monday only. The **Nuovo Sacher** (⊠ Largo Ascianghi 1, ☎ 06/5818116), owned by popular director Nanni Moretti, shows non-Italian movies in their original language on Monday and Tuesday. The **Nuovo Olimpia** (⊠ Via in Lucina 16/b, ☎ 06/6861068) is just off Via del Corso, and features classic films shown in their original language. The **Palazzo delle Esposizioni** (⊠ Via Nazionale 194, near Termini, ☎ 06/4745903) puts on film festivals where movies are usually shown in the original language. The €6.20 entrance fee gets you into the venue's exhibitions as well.

Fine Arts

Rome is not a city known for innovative exhibitions; the churches and permanent collections in its many museums are the star artistic attractions. Nonetheless, the **Palazzo delle Esposizioni** (⊠ Via Nazionale 194, near Termini, ☎ 06/4745903) often stages worthwhile shows. The **Acquario Romano** (⊠ Piazza M. Fanti 47, near Stazione Termini, ☎ 06/4468616) opens to the public for special shows and concerts. Academic institutions such as the **British School** (⊠ Piazzale W. Churchill 5, in the Villa Borghese, ☎ 06/3264939) often host special exhibitions and free lectures by visiting professors. The **American Academy** (⊠ Via A. Masina 5, on the Janiculum Hill, ☎ 06/5846) has shows and lectures by artists and scholars in residence. **Giulia** (⊠ Via Giulia 148, ☎ 06/6861443) is a small gallery that's worth a look. **Valentina Moncada** (⊠ Via Margutta 54, ☎ 06/3207956) is a small private gallery near Piazza di Spagna.

Music

Classical

Despite the long-standing criticism that Rome doesn't have a central concert hall (a new one is currently under construction), the city hosts a wide variety of classical music concerts at various small venues throughout the city. This can result in memorable performances in smaller halls and churches whose ambience makes up for the less-grand space. This is true particularly at Christmas and Easter, an especially busy concert season in Rome. A major concert series is organized year-round by the **Accademia di Santa Cecilia** (concert hall and box office: ✉ Via della Conciliazione 4, ☎ 06/68801044), featuring Rome's Orchestra dell'Accademia di Santa Cecilia and frequent guest soloists. The Accademia Filarmonica Romana concerts are performed at the **Teatro Olimpico** (✉ Piazza Gentile da Fabriano 17, ☎ 06/3265991). The internationally respected **Oratorio del Gonfalone** (✉ Via del Gonfalone 32, ☎ 06/6875952) series focuses on Baroque music. **Il Tempietto** (✉ Area Archaeolica del Palatino, Cortile di San Teodoro, Via di San Teodoro 7, ☎ 06/87131590) organizes music festivals and concerts throughout the year. Depending on the venue, tickets run from about €8 to €25.

In addition to the formal concert companies, many small concert groups perform in cultural centers and churches, often for free. The following events and venues are especially worth noting: From late June to early August, the courtyard of the Basilica di San Clemente hosts the **New Opera Festival** (☎ 06/5611519 or 347/0074348, WEB www.newoperafestivaldiroma.com), an Italo-American project to raise money for young musicians, with a varied program that often includes the likes of Mozart, Handel, Verdi, and Puccini. In the summer, the gardens of the **Museo Nazionale degli Strumenti Musicali** (✉ Piazza Santa Croce di Gerusalemme, ☎ 06/7014796) are the site of concerts. The **Orto Botanico** (✉ Largo Cristina di Svezia, ☎ no phone), off Via della Lungara in Trastevere, has a summer concert series. Look for posters outside churches announcing free concerts, particularly at the church of **Sant'-Ignazio** (✉ Piazza Sant'Ignazio, near the Pantheon, ☎ 06/6794560), which often hosts concerts in a spectacularly frescoed setting. Other churches that frequently host concerts are **Sant'Ivo alla Sapienza, San Francesco a Ripa,** and **San Paolo entro le Mura.**

Rock, Pop, and Jazz

Rock, pop, and jazz concerts are frequent, especially in summer, although even performances by big-name stars may not be well advertised. Most of the major acts perform outside the center, so it's worth asking about transportation *before* you buy your tickets. Tickets for larger musical performances are usually sold by **Orbis** (✉ Piazza Esquilino 37, ☎ 06/4827403). **Ricordi** music stores (✉ Via del Corso 506, ☎ 06/3612682; ✉ Viale Giulio Cesare 88, ☎ 06/3720216) sell concert tickets.

The **Estate Romana** (Roman Summer) program, organized by the local and regional governments, has been growing every year (corresponding with the increasing number of Romans who stay in town during July and August). The program now includes a diverse offering of well-publicized and well-organized cultural events, most set outdoors and all free or reasonably priced. Events spread from the center of town to the periphery and run from early June to early September. They include music of every sort, as well as outdoor cinema and theater. Most events are, of course, in Italian, but the following might well be interesting to English-speaking visitors:

Caracalla Festival (✉ Via delle Terme di Caracalla, ☎ 06/68801044, WEB www.santacecilia.it) is the summer season (July) of the Accademia Nazionale di Santa Cecilia. The venue is the much-loved Baths of Caracalla, but fear of damage to the site has led local authorities to limit the performances to small crowds (and left the summer opera series without a home). In addition to classical music from the Orchestra di Santa Cecilia, the program typically includes piano soloists and jazz and folk groups.

Fiesta! (✉ Via Appia Nuova 1245 [zona Capannelle], ☏ 06/71299855, WEB www.fiesta.it) is an enormous celebration of Latin American music and culture, which is very popular with Italians. The event features more than 4,000 hours of live Latin music and Italian pop every summer, along with exhibits related to Latin American culture, dozens of shops and stands selling food and goods from all over the world, and four outdoor dance floors. Events run in the evenings from mid-June through August, and the admission is €8.

Jazz & Image(✉ Villa Celimontana, Piazza della Navicella, ☏ 06/ 77591848 or 06/77591832) is the longest-running jazz festival in Europe. From mid-June to early September it brings a program of mostly classic jazz to the lawn of Villa Celimontana, on the hill adjacent to the Colosseum. Admission is typically €8.

Roma Incontra il Mondo (Rome Meets the World; ✉ Laghetto di Villa Ada, Via di Ponte Salario, WEB www.villaada.it) has grown in a few short years to become one of Europe's best world-music festivals. Live music most evenings from late June to early August starts at 8 PM, followed by dancing until 2 AM. Stands sell hand-made goods from around the world and Italian, Arab, and African food.

Romaestate al Foro Italico (✉ Viale delle Olimpiadi, ☏ 06/78074560) takes place from early June to late August, every night between 9 PM and 2 AM (last admission midnight). Since 1991 this spot has been one of Rome's main summer event venues, with 200 live concerts, a fitness area that includes a swimming pool and a roller park, food stands, and a playground. Admission is €5.50.

Opera

Rome's opera season runs from November or December to May, and performances are staged in the **Teatro dell'Opera** (✉ Via Firenze 72, ☏ 06/4817003). Tickets go on sale at the beginning of the season; the box office is open from 10 to 5. Prices range from about €16 to €80 for regular performances; they can cost much more for special events, such as an opening night or the appearance of an internationally acclaimed guest singer.

After the summer opera season was evicted from the ruins of the ancient **Terme di Caracalla,** the debate over a permanent open-air venue continues. The most likely choice is **Villa Pepoli,** a parklike area adjacent to the ruins of the Baths. The city's **Olympic Stadium** (✉ Stadio Olimpico, Foro Italico) is summer opera's temporary home. Call the Teatro dell'Opera (☏ 06/4817003) for tickets and information.

Theater

Rome's official theater is the **Teatro di Argentina** (✉ Largo Argentina, ☏ 06/68804601), but it only has plays in Italian. The **India** theater (✉ Lungotevere dei Papareschi, ☏ 06/68804601) is home to some productions in English. It is in a former soap factory in Testaccio. An interesting troupe is the "Off-Night Repertory Theatre," which mounts original, one-act plays in English once a week at the **Teatro dell'Arte** (✉ Via Urbana 107, ☏ 06/4885608).

NIGHTLIFE

After-hours entertainment in Rome consists mainly of late-night cafés, music clubs, and discos. Most spots except the big discos have a clubby atmosphere, with a regular clientele. The "in" places, especially the discos, change like the flavor of the month and may fade into oblivion after a brief season of popularity. Many simply change name and decor from one year to the next. Hubs of after-dark activity are Piazza Navona and the Pantheon area, Trastevere, and Testaccio. The Spanish Steps are strictly for tourists.

The best sources for an up-to-date list of late-night spots and of who's playing what at the music clubs are the weekly entertainment guides, *Romac'è* and *Trovaroma*.

Bars

There's a bar for every taste in Rome. One at a better hotel will offer elegant surroundings and soft music, with drinks mixed by an expert *barista* (bartender). Customers found at such a place are usually a mix of Italians and foreigners, and prices are fairly steep. Then there's a spate of informal, clubby cafés and wine bars catering to a fairly sophisticated crowd faithfully observing the Roman ritual of the evening aperitif between 6:30 and 9. The most radical change in the bar scene in Rome over the past few years has been the opening of a plethora of quaintly named English and Irish pubs, complete with Guinness, darts, and soccer on the TV. Italians love them even though they're seldom the real McCoy.

Cafés and Wine Bars

Antica Enoteca (⊠ Via della Croce 76/b, ☎ 06/6790896) is a wine bar occupying historic quarters on a corner near the Spanish Steps. In the daytime, check out the menu if you're in need of a light lunch.

Once a modest neighborhood coffee bar, **Bar del Fico** (⊠ Piazza del Fico 28, ☎ 06/6865205) is now a plastic-and-neon rendezvous for swingers who prefer the earthy to the intellectual; watch out for huge crowds on weekend and summer nights.

Celebrities and literati hang out at **Caffè della Pace** (⊠ Via della Pace 3, ☎ 06/6861216), a turn-of-the-20th-century-style café near Piazza Navona. The atmosphere ranges from relaxed to electric, depending on who's in town. It's a cult coffeehouse with an upscale pizzeria annex next door. But the prices are steep, and service can be infuriatingly distracted.

Cantiniere di Santa Dorotea (⊠ Via di Santa Dorotea 9, ☎ 06/5819025) in Trastevere has a friendly atmosphere and a good selection of wines and simple food. Try the port-soaked melon on a warm summer night.

Not far from the church of San Pietro in Vincoli, **Cavour 313** (⊠ Via Cavour 313, ☎ 06/6785496) has dark-wood booths and wine shelves bearing bottles from Chile and Australia as well as Italy.

Cul de Sac (⊠ Piazza Pasquino 73, ☎ 06/68801094), close to Piazza Navona, crams a counter and some wooden tables into a small space where you can sample good wines and a variety of food. It's a popular place, so come early.

The name **Il Piccolo** (⊠ Via del Governo Vecchio 74, ☎ 06/68801746) means "small," so don't expect much elbow room. Instead, you'll find sangria and rare *fragolino* wine, made with grapes that taste like strawberries.

Spiriti (⊠ Via Sant'Eustachio 5, ☎ no phone), near the Pantheon, is tiny, with limited seating inside and a few tables outdoors. Likewise, the wine list is limited, but good. Light lunches and suppers are served.

Taverna del Campo (⊠ Piazza Campo dei Fiori 16, ☎ 06/6874402) is a very friendly, popular place that draws a young crowd; it features big barrels of peanuts and free nibbles (olives, cheese) at the bar. There is also outdoor seating and a light food menu including delicious *crostini* (toasts).

With the resources of the huge Trimani wineshop behind it, the sophisticated two-level **Trimani Il Winebar** (⊠ Via Cernaia 37/b, ☎ 06/4469630) has an abundance of good wine and tasty food to go with it, taken either at the counter or at tables inside or out. It's closed on Sunday.

You never know who you'll find at **Vineria Reggio** (⊠ Piazza Campo de Fiori 15, ☎ 06/68803268). The crowd ranges from aging beatnik poets to smartly turned-out young executives, reflecting the heterogeneous character of this colorful market square.

Elegant Bars

Harry's Bar (⊠ Via Veneto 150, ☎ 06/474643), the namesake of similar, separately owned operations in Venice and Florence, is popular with American businessmen and journalists. The attached restaurant is pricey.

Though there's live music in the little room downstairs, the oval mahogany bar on street level is the main attraction at **Jazz Café** (⊠ Via Zanardelli 12, ☎ 06/6861990). It's a watering hole for well-dressed young Romans. It's closed on Monday.

Situated off the damask-hung lobby of a truly grand hotel, **Le Bar** (⊠ Grand Hotel, Via Vittorio Emanuele Orlando 3, ☎ 06/47901) is a perfect perch from which to watch the wealthy and powerful come and go.

Sotto Sopra (⊠ Via dei Chiavari 4–5, ☎ 06/68892857) is an "art bar" that mixes culture and good decor with food and drink, particularly cocktails. In the historic center, it's open from 8 PM onward.

Pubs

The wood-paneled walls and fireplace provide a cozy atmosphere at **Artù** (⊠ Largo F. Biondi 5, off Piazza S. Maria in Trastevere, ☎ 06/5880398), a popular hangout with an ample selection of beer, wine, and tasty food.

Birreria Marconi (⊠ Via di Santa Prassede 9/c, ☎ 06/486636), more a beer hall than a pub, occupies a corner overlooking Santa Maria Maggiore and has tables outdoors. Young Italians flock here for pizza and beer.

Birreria Santi Apostoli (⊠ Piazza Santi Apostoli 52, ☎ 06/6788285) is a pine-paneled beer hall near Piazza Venezia serving light meals and big steins of German beer.

Near Santa Maria Maggiore, **Fiddler's Elbow** (⊠ Via dell'Olmata 43, ☎ 06/4872110) is the oldest Irish pub in Rome, and its scruffy authenticity shows up the fancier usurpers that have opened all over town. Singing is encouraged.

Flann O'Brien (⊠ Via Napoli 32, ☎ 06/4880418), off Via Nazionale, serves the usual Irish beverages but can also make a decent cappuccino. Haunt of a young and multinational clientele, **La Bricola** (⊠ Via della Lungaretta 81, ☎ 06/5812260) is a beer hall in Trastevere serving Austrian brews as well as pastas, salads, and more than 100 kinds of sandwiches.

Sloppy Sam's (⊠ Campo dei Fiori 9–10, ☎ 06/68802637). This buzzing pub on one of the city's busiest piazzas attracts young Americans and Brits. The interior is in classic, dark tones and it gets full quickly in the evenings.

Victoria House (⊠ Via Gesù e Maria 18, ☎ 06/3201698). Off Via del Corso, a stone's throw from Piazza del Popolo, this was the first of the English pubs and is still considered the best. It has an authentic, run-down, slightly tea-color air, and a good range of beer.

Dance and Nightclubs

Most dance clubs open about 10:30 PM, but they really warm up only after midnight. They usually charge a cover of around €13 to €15, which sometimes also includes the first drink. Subsequent drinks cost about €5 to €8. Some clubs also open on Saturday and Sunday afternoon for the under-16s. Many relocate to the beach in the summer, so when it's warm it's best to call ahead to confirm details.

Alibi (⊠ Via Monte Testaccio 40, ☎ 06/5743448), the most famous gay disco in town, is a rambling locale with a terrace facing Mt. Testaccio that is open for dancing in the summer. Straights like it too, but the crowd is predominantly gay men. Events here are often organized by the **Circolo Mario Mieli** (☎ 06/5413985), a gay advocacy group. The glitzy haunt of movers and shakers from the worlds of politics, commerce, and showbiz, **Bella Blu** (⊠ Via Luciani 21, ☎ 06/3230490) is in the Parioli residential district. It's a supper club, with disco dancing and a piano bar.

Stark, postindustrial decor leaves plenty of room for young rockers to enjoy themselves at **Black Out** (⊠ Via Saturnia 18, ☎ 06/70496791), and there's a separate "off-music" room for chilling out. Under various names and guises, this disco has hosted generations of Roman youth. **Bush** (⊠ Via Galvani 46, ☎ 06/57288691) is a high-tech dance club, bringing big-screen monitors and booming techno music to the ancient neighborhood of Testaccio.

In trendy Testaccio, **Caffè Latino** (⊠ Via di Monte Testaccio 96, ☎ 06/57288556) attracts a thirtyish crowd with dancing, an occasional live music performance, and a separate music-video room and bar.

A tranquil, leafy street close to the Romanesque church of San Saba (near the Aventine Hill) is home to **Chic & Kitsch** (⊠ Via di San Saba 11, ☎ 06/5782022), one of Rome's oldest discos, with an over-the-top luxury decor and a wide variety of music from the house DJ.

Gilda (⊠ Via Mario dei Fiori 97, near Piazza di Spagna, ☎ 06/6784838) is the place to spot famous Italian actors and politicians. The sophisticated nightspot near the Spanish Steps has a piano bar as well as a restaurant and dance floors with live and disco music. Jackets are required.

Showbiz and sports personalities have no trouble getting past the doorman at **Jackie O'** (⊠ Via Boncompagni 11, ☎ 06/42885457), but common mortals are advised to call in advance; this glamorous place is often taken over for PR events. There's a restaurant, piano bar, and disco, all dressy. The piano bar is closed Sunday, the disco Monday.

Notorious (⊠ Via San Nicolo di Tolentino 22, near Via Veneto, ☎ 06/42010572) is a tiny one-room disco, dressed up with marble and portraits of ancient Romans on the walls. Locals come here to dance to commercial, house, and underground music.

In the Trieste district, **Piper** (⊠ Via Tagliamento 9, ☎ 06/8414459), one of Rome's first discos, is still hot, drawing a young clientele. It has dance music, live groups, pop videos, and gay nights once a week. Occasionally, there's ballroom dancing for an older crowd, and Sunday afternoon it's open for teenagers. It's closed Monday–Wednesday.

Qube (⊠ Via di Portonaccio 212, ☎ 06/4385445), open only on Friday and Saturday, is Rome's biggest underground disco, a veritable sea of young bodies dancing till they drop. The decor is minimal, but the lights are psychedelic and the decibels mind-blowing.

Music Clubs

Jazz, folk, pop, and Latin-music clubs are flourishing in Rome, particularly in the Trastevere and more workaday Testaccio neighborhoods. Jazz clubs are especially popular at the moment, with local talent sometimes joined by visiting musicians from other countries. For admission, many clubs require that you buy a membership card (usually about €5–€10, which may or may not include one drink).

Alexanderplatz (⊠ Via Ostia 9, ☎ 06/39742171), Rome's most important live jazz and blues club, consistently books the best of Italian and international performers. Near the Vatican, it has both a bar and a restaurant. Reservations are a good idea.

Big Mama (⊠ Vicolo San Francesco a Ripa 18, ☎ 06/5812551), a small club in Trastevere, is a Roman institution for live music, including jazz, blues, rhythm and blues, African, and rock. There's a bar, and snacks are available. It's closed Monday and from mid-June through September.

Latin rhythms are the specialty at **Caruso** (⊠ Via Monte Testaccio 36, ☎ 06/5745019) in Testaccio. Live music from the house band can be heard Monday through Saturday; on Sunday it's Arab music.

A few minutes by car from the center of town (beyond Porta Maggiore), **Circolo degli Artisti** (⊠ Via Casilina Vecchia 42, ☎ 06/70305684) is an informal live music venue, with exhibits and a dance space (a large outdoor dance floor in the summer). The clientele are mainly in their twenties.

Classico Village (⊠ Via Libetta, 3, ☎ 06/57288857), a multicultural space in a converted factory near the Ostiense train station, hosts an eclectic mix of theater and performance art, as well as live electronic and ethnic dance music. Call first to see what's on.

Edoardo II (⊠ Vicolo Margana 14, ☎ 06/69942419) is a music bar for gays, with kitschy medieval-castle decor that's vaguely in keeping with the location in Old Rome, near Piazza Venezia. It's open Tuesday through Saturday.

Near Castel Sant'Angelo, **Fonclea** (⊠ Via Crescenzio 82/a, ☎ 06/6896302) is a cellar with a publike atmosphere, a no-smoking policy, and live music every night of the week ranging from jazz to Latin American to rhythm and blues, depending on who's in town. The kitchen provides Italian and Mexican food.

Four XXXX Pub (⊠ Via Galvani 29, ☎ 06/5757296), a combination restaurant–beer hall–jazz club in the Testaccio neighborhood, has live jazz groups and a no-smoking section downstairs. The menu offers a mix of cuisines, including Latin American food.

In the heart of the after-hours scene near Piazza Navona, little **Il Locale** (⊠ Vicolo del Fico 3, ☎ 06/6879075) is jammed with a lively young crowd that likes to listen to what's new in rock from both sides of the Atlantic, live or recorded.

Jam Session Music (⊠ Via del Cardello 13/a, ☎ 06/4080956) alternates live performances of jazz and soul by internationally known musicians with disco and theme nights in a funky cellar formerly known as the St. Louis.

Near the Vatican, **Mississippi Jazz Club** (⊠ Borgo Angelico 18/a, ☎ 06/68806348) is a historic jazz club, with live performances by American and other international groups on Friday and Saturday.

A sophisticated crowd comes to **Spago** (⊠ Via di Monte Testaccio 35, ☎ 06/5744999) for cocktails and food until the wee hours. The club is carved into Monte Testaccio and decorated to look like an old Roman neighborhood. Canned music alternates with live, with a predilection for jazz.

5 OUTDOOR ACTIVITIES AND SPORTS

The Italians are sports crazy. To attend a
Lazio or Roma soccer game at the Foro
Italico is to witness the frenzy of the
Colosseum. The Romans don't just watch;
they also love to play. Every neighborhood
seems to have a multitude of tennis,
basketball, and volleyball courts. Bikers
and joggers fearlessly dodge the madness
of city traffic. For those with something more
relaxing in mind, white beaches are never
too far away.

Updated by
Norman
Roberson

IN ROME, soccer, tennis, and horseback riding are the sports that draw the biggest crowds and generate the most hype. The national-league soccer games at the Olympic Stadium, in the Foro Italico sports complex, from September to May and occasional international league games for the European championship are always an event; in May both the prestigious Italian Open tennis tournament and the Roman International Equestrian Competition attract a mixed audience of bona fide sports fans and celebrities gleaming for the ubiquitous TV cameras. Roman fans are enthusiastic about basketball and volleyball, too, and international matches in both sports are usually sold out. If you're more partial to sweating than cheering, you'll have plenty of opportunities for that as well. Running is the easiest sport for visitors to engage in, and perhaps the most fulfilling as well; if you plan your route appropriately, you can get in some wonderful sightseeing while you exercise.

BEACHES

Romans like to go to the beach in the summer months, and they seem none too bothered by the crowds they find there. Beaches, and public transportation to them, can become packed during July and August, especially on weekends. In the more developed areas nearer to Rome, beach-club concessions monopolize the sand; patches of free town beaches are usually seedier and more likely to be littered. The best clubs offer attractive cabanas, restaurants, and beach facilities for which you can pay by the day, week, or month. For cleaner water and more of a resort atmosphere, you have to go farther afield.

Ostia, officially called Lido di Ostia (*lido* means "beach"), is a busy urban center in its own right, a kind of satellite city 30 km (18 mi) southwest of Rome, and it's a major destination for Roman beach-goers. Ostia's own beach is badly eroded and its beach clubs rather seedy, but from here it's a quick trip to the more attractive Castelfusano and Castelporziano. Ostia is the place to come out of season for a walk on the *pontile* (pier), a dinner at the shore, and a gelato at **Sisto** (⊠ Piazza Anco Marzio 7, ☎ 06/5622982, closed Tues.). You can reach Ostia by COTRAL train from the Porta San Paolo station and the Magliana station on Metro B line.

Kursaal (⊠ Lungomare Catullo 36), reachable by Bus 06 from Ostia's Lido Station, is one of the better beach clubs and has a swimming pool, which is strongly recommended as an alternative to swimming in the sometimes murky waters of the sea around Rome.

The public beach at **Castelfusano,** about 33 km (20 mi) southwest of Rome and about 3 km (2 mi) southeast of Ostia, is well maintained in season. You can reach it by staying on the COTRAL Metro B train line from Rome past the Ostia stop, or by taking a bus south from Ostia along the shore boulevard.

Castelporziano, open only in summer, is a public beach area about 3 km (2 mi) southeast of Castelfusano. It's the closest thing to a wilderness beach in the vicinity of Rome: a few concessionaires have bathroom facilities and rent changing rooms, umbrellas, and beach chairs, but mostly it's just sand dunes and beach, and some walking is required to reach it from the road. None of this prevents it from becoming congested during peak periods. There's bus service to Castelporziano from the Cristoforo Colombo stop at the end of the COTRAL Metro B train line from Rome.

Fregene is a villa colony on the shore 37 km (23 mi) northwest of Rome. It can be reached from Rome by COTRAL bus from the Via Lepanto stop of Metro A train line. The sand is primarily the domain of beach clubs, where you pay for changing cabins, cabanas, umbrellas, and such, and for the fact that the sand is kept clean and combed. The beach club **La Nave** (⊠ Via Porto Rose, ☎ 06/66560703), as well as some of the others around Fregene, is also a lively nightspot.

PARTICIPANT SPORTS

Bicycling

Pedaling through Villa Borghese, along the Tiber, and through the center of the city when traffic is light can be an appealing way to see the sights. (In heavy traffic, exhaust fumes and dust can be unpleasant. Many local riders wear masks to help combat the problem.) Municipal bicycle paths have been laid out on mainly level ground. One of the longest paths starts at Viale Angelico, near the Vatican, and takes a northerly route to Foro Italico, where it turns away from the street to continue for a pleasant stretch along the Tiber. Another path goes through Villa Borghese, and a 7-km (4½-mi) path on the banks of the Tiber extends from Ponte Sublicio (connecting Porta Portese in Trastevere with Via Marmorata in Testaccio) to Ponte della Magliana, downstream.

There are bicycle rental concessions at the Piazza di Spagna and Piazza del Popolo Metro stops, Largo San Silvestro, Largo Argentina, Viale della Pineta in Villa Borghese, and Viale del Bambino on the Pincio, among others—all have good-quality bikes. At concessions and the agencies below, rental costs about €2.50 per hour, going up to about €3.60 for a mountain bike. Daily rates can be more convenient.

Collalti (⊠ Via del Pellegrino 82, ☎ 06/68801084), near Piazza Navona, can provide a regular one-speed bike, a mountain bike, a tandem, and even a pedal-powered rickshaw.

Happy Rent (⊠ Via Farini 3, ☎ 06/4818185), near Santa Maria Maggiore, has a good choice of bikes and gives you a free map of the city.

I Bike Rome (⊠ Underground parking lot, Section III, at Villa Borghese; entrance at Porta Pinciana, ☎ 06/3225240) is open daily; rates are competitive and include a helmet, chain, and padlock. The bikes are newish and in good condition.

Bowling and Boccie

Rome has its share of dedicated bowlers, most of them from the city's large expatriate population. For natives, bowling has never really supplanted the classic Italian equivalent of lawn bowling, boccie. The *bocciodromo* (boccie pitch) is often the scene of intense competition. Among the most central are those at Lungotevere Flaminio 39, at Via Austria in the Villaggio Olimpico development, and in Villa Ada park on Via Salaria.

For American-style bowling, head to **Bowling Roma** (⊠ Viale Regina Margherita 181, ☎ 06/8551184), where you'll find 16 lanes and a snack bar open 9 AM–2 AM (3 PM–2 AM July–August). Rates start at €1.80 per line on weekday mornings and go as high as €4.15 on the weekend. Shoe rental is included in the price.

Fitness Facilities

Big Gym (⊠ Foro Italico, Stadio dei Marmi, ☎ 06/3208666). From June through August the huge Olympic Stadium complex is open to the public for use in a wide range of fitness activities, including weightlifting, aerobics, and jogging. There are snack bars, dressing rooms, and extensive facilities, including basketball courts, a skating rink, and a climbing wall. The basic daily rate is €5, with additional charges for some activities.

Fitness Express (⊠ Via dei Coronari 46, ☎ 06/6864989), closed in August, is a compact gym in Old Rome with a program of personal training directed by American Linda Foster that offers classic and low-impact aerobics, stretching, and step. Day rates are available.

Navona Health Center (⊠ Via Banchi Nuovi 39, ☎ 06/6896104), closed Sunday May–October, is a workout center in a historic palazzo in Old Rome offering aerobics, body-building, a sauna, and a Turkish bath. The enrollment fee is waived for nonresidents; a workout and use of the sauna costs about €10.30.

Roman Sport Center (⊠ Via del Galoppatoio 33, ☎ 06/3201667; Parioli district, ⊠ Largo Somalia 60, ☎ 06/86212411) is the *in* place to work out. In vast underground premises adjacent to the Villa Borghese parking garage are two swimming pools, hydromassage, aerobic workout areas, gyms fully equipped for workouts and body-building, squash courts, Turkish baths, and saunas. The basic daily rate is about €25.

Sheraton Roma (⊠ Viale del Pattinaggio, ☎ 06/5453) has a heated outdoor pool, a tennis court, two squash courts, a sauna, and a fitness center, all open to nonguests.

Golf

Once considered a sport for the elite, golf has gained broader popularity in Italy. At the clubs listed here, all with 18-hole courses, nonmembers are allowed to play provided they present membership cards of their home golf or country clubs.

Circolo del Golf Roma (⊠ Via Acqua Santa 3, ☎ 06/7803407) is the oldest and most prestigious golf club in Rome. Off the Via Appia Antica, near the tomb of Cecilia Metella, it is the course closest to downtown and is part of Rome's most aristocratic country club.

Country Club Castelgandolfo (⊠ Via Santo Spirito 13, Castelgandolfo, ☎ 06/9312301) is in the Castelli Romani zone, 25 km (15 mi) southeast of Rome. The Robert Trent Jones–designed course has a 17th-century villa as a clubhouse.

Marco Simone (⊠ Guidonia Montecelio, ☎ 0774/366469), 7 km (4½ mi) east of the city, is one of Rome's newer courses. It is part of an upscale development adjacent to a medieval castle.

Olgiata Golf Club (⊠ Largo Olgiata 15, on Via Cassia, ☎ 06/30889141), 19 km (12 mi) north from the center of Rome, hosts tournament play and is a favorite with residents of the upscale northern suburbs.

Parco de' Medici (⊠ Viale Parco de' Medici 22, ☎ 06/6553477) is only 4½ km (3 mi) west of Rome, close to the clusters of gleaming high-rise office buildings in the Parco de' Medici and EUR business centers.

Horseback Riding

Riding is a long-standing tradition in the country around Rome, where trails cover ground once inhabited by the Etruscans. Cross-country riding can be arranged on weekends through local tourist offices and agritourism agencies.

Antiquitates (⊠ Civitella Cesi, 01010 Blera, ☎ 07/61415031, WEB www.plan-net.com/sangiovenale) organizes individual and group rides in the country around Rome. A full-day ride, at a cost of around €50 per person, includes a picnic lunch and a guide to take you through beautiful countryside peppered with Etruscan ruins and medieval castles.

Circolo Ippico Olgiata (✉ Largo Olgiata 15, ☎ 06/3788792), outside the city on the Via Cassia in the Olgiata suburb, has a riding ring and cross-country trails.

Running

The best bet for running in the central city is the **Villa Borghese**, which has an approximately ⅔-km (½-mi) circuit of the Pincio gardens, among the marble statuary. A longer run in the park might incorporate a loop around Piazza di Siena, a grass track measuring ¼ km (⅙ mi). Although most traffic is barred from Villa Borghese, buses, taxis, and official government and police cars speed through on the park's main roads. Be careful and stick to the side of the road. For a long run away from all traffic, try the quiet grounds of the renaissance **Villa Ada** on Via Salaria. **Villa Doria Pamphilj**, on the Janiculum, has pleasant grounds that are open to runners. If you really love history, take a run around the beaten-earth track of the old **Circus Maximus**, tracing the 1-km (½-mi) oval circuit that once hosted chariot races. A standard oval track open to runners is in the park along **Via delle Terme di Caracalla.**

Swimming

Aldovrandi Hotel (✉ Via Ulisse Aldovrandi 15, ☎ 06/3223993), in the tony Parioli residential district, allows nonguests to use the pool, set in a walled garden studded with tall pine trees.

Cavalieri Hilton (✉ Via Cadlolo 101, ☎ 06/35091) opens both its pools to nonguests. In fair weather you can lunch next to the outdoor pool, set in a lush oasis.

Piscina delle Rose (✉ Viale America, ☎ 06/54252185) is an Olympic-size pool open to the public from June to September.

Roman Sport Center (✉ Via del Galoppatoio 33, ☎ 06/3201667), in the heart of the city, has two Olympic-size swimming pools.

St. Peter's Holiday Inn (✉ Via Aurelia Antica 415, ☎ 06/6642) opens its 25-meter pool (as well as its two tennis courts) to nonguests.

Tennis

Increasingly popular with Italians, tennis is played in private clubs and on the many public courts that are rented by the hour. Your hotel concierge can direct you to the nearest courts and can book them for you. One of Rome's most prestigious private clubs is the **Tennis Club Parioli** (✉ Largo de Morpurgo 2, Via Salaria, ☎ 06/86200882), but in order to play there you have to be invited by a member.

SPECTATOR SPORTS

For schedules of sports events, look in the weekly *Romac'è* booklet at newsstands or inquire at Municipal Information kiosks.

Basketball

Good pro teams, many with players recruited from the United States, have boosted interest in basketball. The professional season is from October through March, and in Rome games are played at the **Palazzo dello Sport** (✉ Piazzale dello Sport, ☎ 06/5925107) in the EUR district.

Horseback Riding

The **Concorso Ippico Internazionale** (International Horse Show), held in May, draws a stylish crowd to the amphitheater of Piazza di Siena in Villa Borghese to witness the stiff competition. Every year the program includes a cavalry charge staged by the dashing mounted corps of the Carabinieri. For information contact the **Italian Federation of Equestrian Sports** (✉ Viale Tiziano 70, ☎ 06/3233806).

Horse Racing

There's horseback racing at the century-old **Capanelle** track (✉ Via Appia Nuova 1245, ☎ 06/716771), frequented by a chic crowd on big race days. Trotters run at the **Tor di Valle** track (✉ Via del Mare km 9.3, ☎ 06/5290270).

Marathon

The Colosseum is the starting point for the **Rome City Marathon** (☎ 06/30183016 or 06/5744246), run on the second Sunday in March, beginning at 9:30 AM. The route is the standard 42 km (26 mi) long and passes through some of Rome's most beautiful squares, including Piazza di Spagna and Piazza Navona. There's also a 7-km (4½-mi) route.

Soccer

Italy's favorite spectator sport stirs rabid enthusiasm among partisans. Games are usually held on Sunday afternoon throughout the September–May season, though some are played Saturday. Two professional soccer teams—Roma and Lazio—play their home games in Foro Italico's **Stadio Olimpico** (Olympic Stadium; ✉ Viale dei Gladiatori, ☎ 06/3336316). Tickets are on sale at the box office before the games; your hotel concierge may be able to help you get tickets in advance. The so-called curve, the end sectors behind the goal, where the cheering is loudest, has the least-expensive seats, costing about €15.50. Be aware, though, that these tickets are not usually sold to visitors.

Tennis

Rome's Tennis Stadium at **Foro Italico** is the scene of the Italian Open tournament in May. For information, call the **Italian Tennis Federation** (✉ Viale Tiziano 70, ☎ 06/36858510).

6   SHOPPING

Emo ergo sum, I shop therefore I am. For thousands of years the Romans have loved to haggle, barter, and spend in the city's shops and markets. Today Rome is a city of designer names such as Versace, Armani, Missoni: the streets are lined with the cream of high fashion, often available at a good price. Even if you're not buying, it's worth a stroll through the Piazza di Spagna or the Cola di Rienzo to take in the full-blown splendor of the window displays and the spectacle of Romans on the hunt for that perfect pair of shoes.

Updated by
·Jude Barrand

SHOPPING IN ROME is part of the fun, no matter what your budget. The Italian flair for transforming display windows into stunning artistic still lifes and whimsical theatrical tableaux makes window-shopping an aesthetic experience. If you're bent on buying, you're sure to find something that suits your fancy *and* your pocketbook. If you have something specific in mind, like Missoni or Benetton knitwear, Bruno Magli shoes, or Laura Biagiotti perfume, make a note of prices before you leave home, so you'll know whether you're getting a bargain by buying in Italy. The best deals here are still leather goods of all kinds—from gloves to bags to jackets—and silk goods and knitwear. Boutique fashions may be slightly less expensive in Rome than in the United States.

Some worthy old prints and minor antiques can be found in the city's interesting little shops, and full-fledged collectors can rely on the prestigious reputations of some of Italy's top antiques dealers. Genuine Italian handicrafts aren't so easy to find in these days of Asian imports, but some shops stock pottery and handwoven textiles made in Italy. Designer perfumes, from Versace to Armani to Moschino, may be a little cheaper here, but don't buy them in the designer boutiques; instead, look for them in the large *profumerie* (perfume and cosmetics stores), where you may be able to get a discount simply by asking for the *prezzo scontato* (discount price). Discounts are not generally given in other types of stores, though you can try to get one if you are making a large purchase.

Italian sizes are not uniform, so always try on clothing before buying, and measure gift items. Children's sizes are all over the place, and though they usually go by age, they are calibrated to Italian children. Average size-per-age standards vary from one country to another. Check washing instruction labels on all garments (often in English as well as Italian), as many are not washable at all, and those that are may not be preshrunk. Glove sizes are universal. In any case, remember that Italian stores generally will *not* refund your purchases and that they often cannot exchange goods because of limited stock.

Counterfeits

The Prada, Gucci, Fendi, and Vuitton bags sold by sidewalk vendors are fakes. An underground network organizes the illegal manufacture, distribution, and sale of these seemingly perfect counterfeits of stylish status symbols. Both manufacturers and vendors are always one jump ahead of the police. If an incredibly good buy in a name-brand product of any kind is proposed to you, examine the goods carefully. Reliable stores sell at the prices indicated by the manufacturers, so an enormous discount is suspect.

Credit Cards

Credit cards are widely accepted in Rome. Even some clothing vendors at outdoor markets honor them. Visa and MasterCard/CartaSì are the most common. Not all stores honor American Express or Diners Club cards, but you can expect them to be accepted in department stores.

Duty-Free Shopping

Value-added tax (IVA) is 20% on clothing and luxury goods, but it is already included in the amount on the price tag of consumer goods. If you are not a resident of the EU, you may be eligible, under certain conditions, for a refund of this tax on goods purchased here (☞ Taxes *in* Essential Information).

Mailing Purchases Home

Always take your purchases with you: having them shipped home from the shop may cause incomprehensible delays and unlimited grief. The mail is partly to blame; the cavalier attitude of some shop owners compounds the problem, especially if you have to correspond with them about delays. If circumstances are such that you can't take your goods with you, and if the shop seems reliable about shipping, get a detailed list of *what* is being shipped and a firm written statement of *when* and *how* your purchase will be sent. It might be wise to pay with a credit card.

Sales

Saldi (end-of-season sales) may mean real bargains in clothing and accessories. The main sale periods are in January (after January 6) and February, and mid-July to mid-September. Most stores adopt a no-exchange, no-return policy for sale goods. At other times of year, a *liquidazione* sign indicates a close-out sale, but take a good hard look at the goods; they may be bottom-of-the-barrel.

Shopping Districts

Cola di Rienzo

Between Piazza del Popolo and the Vatican, this broad avenue is lined with upscale shops that many Romans prefer to those around Piazza di Spagna because the wide sidewalks and big display windows make shopping easier. Clothing, housewares, gourmet foods, books, and, of course, shoes and bags, along with a Coin department store—Cola di Rienzo has it all, in a high-to-medium price range. Street-corner stands deal in bargain shoes and glassware. Near the Vatican at the west end of the avenue, off Piazza Risorgimento, a score of shops sell religious souvenirs, many of them on Via di Porta Angelica. Via Ottaviano, north of Piazza Risorgimento, has narrower sidewalks and lower-priced goods than Via Cola di Rienzo.

Old Rome: Pantheon and Via del Governo Vecchio

The narrow byways and gracious piazzas of Old Rome draw avant-garde shoppers. Via del Governo Vecchio is the place to browse in secondhand shops for the clothing of yesteryear and for hand-me-down Trifari jewelry. The secondhand shops on the streets are gradually being supplanted by minimalist boutiques known for trendy chic. True to its origins as a Roman circus, Piazza Navona has toy stores stocked with enormous stuffed animals. Around the Pantheon are reputable print and antiques stores. In May and October torches light the way on Via dei Coronari after dark, and shops are open late for the traditional antiques fair. Via Giulia and Via del Monserrato are also synonymous with art and antiques galleries. Romans shop Via dei Giubbonari for bargains in clothing, especially casual and funky young fashions and household linens.

Piazza Colonna and Piazza Barberini

The Rinascente department store, a large Rizzoli bookstore, and classic apparel shops for both sexes set a conservative tone for the lower edge of a hillside shopping district that takes in the more commercial areas of Via del Tritone and Via Barberini. The shopping atmosphere is more rarefied in the tony shops on Via Veneto. Shoes, bags, classic clothing, and leather apparel, at varying price levels, can be found throughout the area. One of Italy's most prestigious tailors and purveyors of classy men's ready-to-wear is Brioni, on Via Barberini. Via del Tritone has some medium-price and a few expensive shops offering a variety of goods. On Via Veneto are a scattering of high-price boutiques and shoe stores, as well as newsstands selling English-language newspapers, magazines, and paperback books.

Rome Shopping

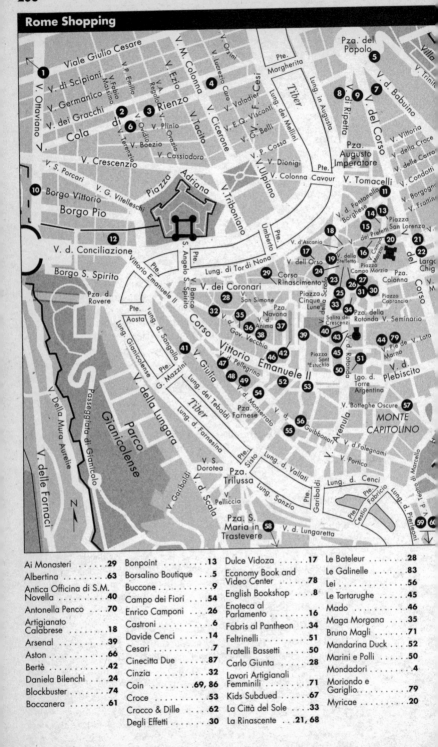

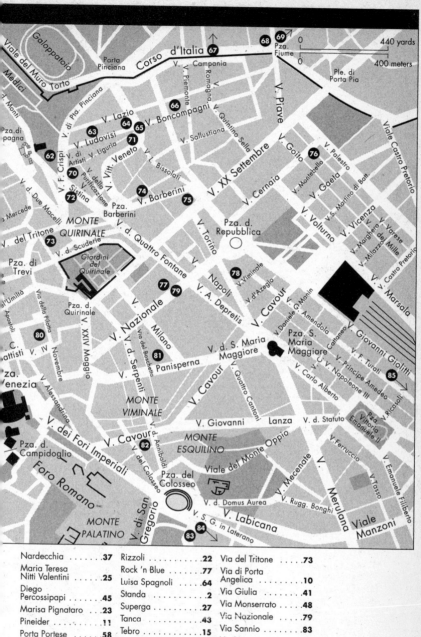

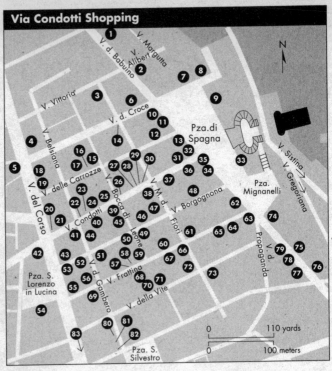

Via Condotti Shopping

Piazza di Spagna

The most elegant and expensive shops are concentrated in the area fanning out at the foot of the Spanish Steps. Via Condotti and Via Borgognona are lined with the boutiques of some of the leading names in high fashion: Armani, Versace, Prada, Mila Schön, and Gianfranco Ferré. Valentino has boutiques on Via Condotti and Via Bocca di Leone in addition to his palace-style headquarters and exhibition space on Piazza Mignanelli. From the bottom of the Spanish Steps and off to the right are Via Margutta, known for art galleries, and Via del Babuino, where the once-predominant antiques shops have had to make room for designer boutiques. Intersecting the top-price shopping streets are a number of others, such as Via del Corso, Via Frattina, and Via del Gambero, that are lined with specialty shops and boutiques of all kinds where goods are more competitively priced.

Via del Corso

Like a single-aisle shopping mall, this historic thoroughfare attracts droves of Romans and tourists who overflow the narrow sidewalks onto the street, dodging passing taxis and buses. Crowds are elbow-to-elbow in front of display windows chock-full of clothing and accessories. The stores adopt a what-you-see-is-what-you-get policy, putting most of their stock in the windows to help you make your selection even before you walk in the door. Young Rome comes here for jeans and inexpensive, trendy wear. Shoe shops have something for everyone. In the chic island of Piazza San Lorenzo in Lucina, smart and expensive specialty shops, such as the Profumeria Materozzoli, a 19th-century landmark, cater to the people from the patrician palaces in the area. Via Fontanella Borghese, between Via del Corso and the palace where Pauline Bonaparte Borghese lived, has a mix of boutiques and art and antiques galleries. Piazza della Fontanella Borghese, flanking the palace, is known for the permanent stalls selling prints and old books.

Via Nazionale

The merchandise is mainstream and prices are generally moderate along this wide thoroughfare near Stazione Termini. A host of shoe stores, handbag and luggage retailers, and off-the-rack clothing stores lines the avenue. There's a Upim department store, too. The museum shop in Palazzo delle Esposizioni, the big neoclassical exhibition building in white marble about halfway along the street, has some interesting small objects that make good gifts or souvenirs.

Blitz Tours

With most of the best shopping in Rome crammed into the Piazza di Spagna–Via Condotti–Via del Corso areas, you can dive into one shop after another for stylish treasures, hardly taking time to come up for air. The tours below are arranged by special interest and include addresses. For details about the stores, see the listings that follow.

Handbags and Luggage

Set off from Largo Goldini halfway down Via del Corso. From here head into the heart of the Via Condotti shopping district by turning east into Via delle Carrozze. On the left side of the street, between Via Belsiana and Via Bocca di Leone, you'll find **Amadei** (⊠ Via delle Carrozze 20) and its offbeat in-house styles. Continue up Via delle Carrozze to Piazza di Spagna to ogle the bags at **Furla** (⊠ Piazza di Spagna 22), and then head down Via Condotti. Those tourists you see with the Gucci shopping bags have beat you to the multilevel **Gucci** store (⊠ Via Condotti 8) on the left. Stop at **Redwall** (⊠ Via Condotti 56), on the right, for a look at the latest trends in designer bags. Ahead, on the same side of the street, see what **Ferragamo** (⊠ Via Condotti 66 and 73) is showing in the way of emphatic elegance. Turn left off Via Condotti onto Via Belsiana; that former church on the left is where **Gherardini** (⊠ Via Belsiana 48/b) displays a good selection of handbags and soft luggage. Continue straight ahead onto Via del Gambero and turn left onto Via della Vite to **Incontro Modo** (⊠ Via della Vite 44), for casual styles. By this time you may need an oversize tote to put all your purchases in. If you still don't want to say *"Basta!"* (Enough!) turn right onto Via del Moretto and then left onto Via della Mercedes. Head straight up the hill onto Via C. Le Case and then left onto Via F. Crispi. Cross over Via Sistina and on your right-hand side nestles **Antonella Penco** (⊠ Via F. Crispi 66), filled with inspired creations.

Leather Clothing

If you're looking for leather clothing with fashion sense, start off with **Renard** (⊠ Via Due Macelli 52); the shop has a large selection of some of the finest tailored leatherwear in Rome. On the same street, check out the styles at both of the **Skin** stores (⊠ Via Due Macelli 59/a; Via Due Macelli 87). For good buys in casual and classic styles in leather, head uphill from Via Due Macelli by way of Via Capo le Case to **Crocco & Dille** (⊠ Via Francesco Crispi 77), a tiny factory outlet. For a much larger selection of classic leather fashions for men and women, return down Via Francesco Crispi, following it all the way to Largo Tritone, where **Virdel** (⊠ Via del Tritone 75) has wraparound display windows on the corner. For lower prices, or if you want something made to order, take a taxi or the Metro to Via Cavour, where **Very Pel** (⊠ Via Cavour 174) has a workshop and lower price tags than the boutiques in the fancier Piazza di Spagna area.

Little Boutiques

For a strong fashion sense at prices much lower than Armani and friends, make the rounds of some boutiques where clothes are designed and made in-house. Start at **Mariella Burani** (⊠ Via Bocca di Leone 28), where the line between boutique fashion and designer ready-to-wear is a fine and very chic one. Then walk or take a taxi to **Dulce Vidoza** (⊠ Via dell'Orso 58) to consider the elegant pantsuits in stunning fabrics. Take another taxi to **Le Tartarughe** (⊠ Via Piè di Marmo 17, near Piazza Venezia), and try on knit separates and spare little dresses that adapt to any occasion. For a change of fashion pace, take a taxi or walk, skirting the rear of the Pantheon and the west end of Piazza Navona, to **Maga Morgana** (⊠ Via del Governo Vecchio 27), where the in-house styles have a distinctly retro look.

Department Stores

Rome has few department stores. The classiest are the two Rinascente stores and the three main Coin stores. They have welcome desks, multilingual guides, and tax-free refund desks. They are open all day and may be open on Sunday, too.

The first of several shopping malls in Rome and the handiest to reach is **Cinecittà Due** (⊠ Piazza di Cinecittà, Viale Palmiro Togliatti, ☎ 06/7220902); just take Metro line A to the Subaugusta stop. The mall has 100 shops, including a Coin department store branch, a big supermarket, snack bars, and cafés.

Coin (⊠ Via Cola di Rienzo 173, ☎ 06/36004298; ⊠ Piazzale Appio, ☎ 06/7080020; ⊠ Via Mantova 1/b, near Piazza Fiume, ☎ 06/8416279; ⊠ Cinecittà shopping mall, ☎ 06/7220931) is upscale, with merchandise arranged in well-spaced displays. The clothing ranges from classic and dressy to casual chic, with good separates and sportswear departments for men and women. The downstairs housewares department usually has a good stock of Italian ceramic ware. **La Rinascente** (✉ Piazza Colonna, ☎ 06/6797691; ✉ Piazza Fiume, ☎ 06/8841231) was Rome's first department store, and the early 1900s building in which it opened provides a fine showcase for five floors of clothing and accessories. Perfumes and cosmetics share the main floor with bags, costume jewelry, fun hats, and beautiful silk scarves. Upstairs are mainstream styles, both casual and dressy, for men and women. The Piazza Fiume location has more floor space and a wider range of goods than the older store on Piazza Colonna. The basement is devoted to housewares, and the top floors have furniture, toys, and children's departments. In between, accessories and apparel for men and women replicate what's available at the other store.

Budget

The low- to moderately priced Standa and Upim chains, with stores throughout Rome, have fair-to-middling quality goods. They are the places to go for a pair of slippers, bathing suit, underwear, and the like, to see you through until you get home. In addition, they carry toiletries and first-aid needs. Most Standa and Upim stores have invaluable while-you-wait shoe-repair counters.

Markets

Flea Markets

There's a flea market on Sunday morning at **Porta Portese** (✉ Via di Porta Portese, access from Via Ippolito Nievo, off Viale Trastevere); it offers mainly new or secondhand clothing, but there are still a few dealers in old furniture and sundry objects, much of it intriguing junk. Bargaining is the rule here, and it is imperative to take precautions against pickpockets. Though not strictly a flea market, the outdoor stalls at **Via Sannio** (✉ near the basilica San Giovanni in Laterano), open weekdays 10–1 and Saturday 10–6, offer bargains on used clothing and army surplus. You can also get great deals on shoes here. This is where you can buy good-quality name-brand shoes that have been used in the window displays of boutiques. A plethora of flea markets, some charging admission, have sprung up in such places as the **Borghetto Flaminio** (✉ Via Flaminia across from Ministry of the Navy). You can buy everything from clothes to jam to tattered old furniture here. In the garage on Via Ludovisi in the Via Veneto area you can find objects ranging from old silverware to watches and glasses. Most of the objects in this incongruous, underground market are period pieces and tend to be quite expensive. But there are always impromptu open-air markets in Rome. Look for schedules in the newspapers and in the *Romac'è* magazine and inquire at tourist information kiosks.

Food Markets

Rome's biggest and most colorful outdoor food markets are at **Campo dei Fiori** (near Piazza Navona), **Via Andrea Doria** (in the Trionfale neighborhood, north of the Vatican), and **Piazza Vittorio** (near Termini Station; this market is due to be moved from its traditional site skirting the piazza to another area close by). There are smaller outdoor markets in every neighborhood. All outdoor markets are open from Monday to Saturday from early morning to about 2; some markets (among them, Trionfale and Piazza dell'Unita, on Via Cola di Rienzo) are open all day.

Specialty Shops

Antiques and Prints

Antiques shopping in Rome can actually mean antiquities shopping; some shops showcase authentic ancient Roman works. Beyond those, the antiques scene is pretty much dominated by works and objects from the 17th century up to art deco. The stalls on Piazza Borghese are a happy hunting ground for old prints, postcards, and books at reasonable prices, and for the occasional rare edition or costly antique engraving. They are open all day, closed on Sunday, and do not accept credit cards.

Alinari (✉ Via Alibert 16/a, ☎ 06/6792923) is Italy's equivalent of the Bettman Archive. Generations of the Alinari family have photographed Italy since the 1800s, starting in Florence but gradually extending their activity throughout the peninsula. In their gallery-store off Via del Babuino you can find early photographs of Rome and views of Italy that make interesting mementos.

Daniela Bilenchi (✉ Via della Stelletta 17, ☎ 06/6875222) restores chinaware and porcelain, but she also sells antique lamps, showing a predilection for art nouveau and art deco styles.

Enrico Camponi (✉ Via della Stelletta 32, ☎ 06/6865249) offers a collection of old and antique glass vases, many of them by Venetian masters. Antique vases from Barovier, Venini, and Seguso may cost hundreds of dollars, but pretty little Murano glass ashtrays dating from the 1940s and '50s are inexpensive.

Le Bateleur (✉ Via S. Simone 71, ☎ 06/6877184), in a tiny 11th-century sacristy under a flight of stone steps, off Via dei Coronari, is what Grandma used to call a curiosity shop. It's packed with a jumble of objects in styles from the 17th to the 21st century.

Nardecchia (✉ Piazza Navona 25, ☎ 06/6869318) always has some of its large selection of beautiful prints of Rome in the big display window, vying for attention with the great Bernini fountain in the piazza. Romans consider Nardecchia one of the city's most reliable dealers.

Tanca (✉ Salita dei Crescenzi 12, near the Pantheon, ☎ 06/6875272) is a happy but cramped hunting ground for old prints. You can browse through piles and boxes to your heart's content in one of the three rather cluttered rooms; in another are showcases full of antique jewelry, old silver, and objets d'art.

Bookstores

Almost all of Rome's big bookstores have a few shelves of English-language books, and the newsstands on Via Veneto also sell paperbacks in English, but the broadest selections are available in the specialized English-language stores listed below.

Anglo-American (✉ Via della Vite 102, ☎ 06/6795222) carries books published in Britain and the States, including reference and scientific works. It also handles special orders. If you want to give an Italian friend a subscription to an English-language magazine, this is the place to arrange it.

Croce (✉ Corso Vittorio 156, ☎ 06/68802269) was a meeting place for literati and a showcase for their work for most of the 20th century, and it continues the tradition in the 21st. Its sharp look and large display windows attract the literary and the just plain curious.

Economy Book and Video Center (✉ Via Torino 136, ☎ 06/4746877) has a regular clientele of Americans and Brits living in Rome who know they can find the latest in hardcovers and paperbacks, calendars, greeting cards, and videos in English. The store is owned and run by Americans.

English Bookshop (✉ Via Ripetta 248, ☎ 06/3203301), specializing in English literature, translations of Italian literature, and a truly exhaustive stock of books in English about Italy—including guidebooks—packs as many volumes into fairly small premises. There is a wide selection of postcards, greeting cards, calendars, and children's books and videos.

Feltrinelli (⊠ Largo di Torre Argentina 6, ☎ 06/68803248) is the marketing branch of one of Italy's major publishing houses. The several stores in Rome are all well organized and well stocked with English-language paperbacks.

Mondadori (⊠ Piazza Cola di Rienzo 81, ☎ 06/3220188) is big and modern, with a luminous open plan. Sections are well marked; one is devoted entirely to English-language books. You'll also find an audio-video department, greeting cards, gadgets, and toys.

Rizzoli (⊠ Largo Chigi 15, ☎ 06/6796641) occupies two levels of the turn-of-the-20th-century Galleria at Piazza Colonna. It stocks many books in English; the wide selection of art books and cookbooks includes some English titles.

Ceramics

Artigianato Calabrese (⊠ Via d'Ascanio 5, ☎ 06/6877427) is a straightforward little store that sells a selection of typical Calabrian ceramics—heavy, no-nonsense pieces with the traditional bird motif. The store also carries handwoven and embroidered goods.

Carlo Giunta (⊠ Via Dei Coronari, 83-84, ☎ 06/6864192) is a brightly lit and alluring treasure trove that specializes in rare objects. Along with solid Italian artifacts, it has a good collection of bright Sicilian ceramics: jugs, plates, cachepots, and vases by some of the island's most respected potters.

Marini e Polli (⊠ Via del Pellegrino 85, ☎ 06/6869698) used to be a housewares store but has gradually become focused on ceramics in the colorful Vietri style and in unglazed terra-cotta. The ware is rustic and unrefined, and prices are moderate.

Myricae (⊠ Via Campo Marzio 11, ☎ 06/6892485) is bright with multicolor ceramics. Large vases and cachepots make handsome decorating accessories. Many are one-of-a-kind pieces by Tuscan artists, with hefty price tags.

Prestigio Interni (⊠ Via del Governo Vecchio 38, ☎ 06/68805134) has a mix of country-style Apulian ceramics and more artistic pieces, in addition to a scattering of antiques. The store is open only in the afternoon on weekdays and in the morning on Saturday.

Raku (⊠ Via dei Pastini, 20, ☎ 06/5803575) shows pottery in intriguing forms and colors with a distinctive, almost Asian look, though the pieces are made in Italy exclusively for this shop.

Clothing

CHILDREN'S CLOTHING

Shopping for the little ones can be a delight here, where even children's clothes have designer labels. But keep three things in mind. One, are the garments easy to care for? The prettiest things may not be washable, and cottons are not necessarily preshrunk. Two, are they practical? Features such as gripper-fastened leg openings and neck openings are not widely adopted in children's fashions here. Three, will they fit? Sizes are totally different from U.S. children's sizes, so take measurements before you leave home and bring along your tape measure, or get a good size-conversion chart.

Bonpoint (⊠ Piazza San Lorenzo in Lucina 25, ☎ 06/6871548) is a precious little emporium of French styles for children. They are expensive and exquisitely made, many embroidered and trimmed by hand. The Bonpoint look is picture-perfect.

Kids Subdued (⊠ Via R Giovannelli, 2, ☎ 06/8413046), despite the unusual English name, is an Italian store for children up to 12 years of age. It has irresistible linen smocks and knitwear for newborns and trendy clothes for fashionable preteens.

La Cicogna (✉ Via Frattina 138, ☎ 06/6791912; ✉ Via Cola di Rienzo 268, ☎ 06/6896557), a nationwide chain, has several stores in Rome. Each is like a small department store, with clothing, shoes, carriages, baby supplies, and so forth for children from infants to age 14. There's a maternity-wear department, too.

Quadrifoglio (✉ Via delle Colonnele 10, ☎ 06/6784917) is a shop for the well-dressed toddler in your life. Hand-embroidered smocks and high-quality fabric baby attire pack the clothes racks. Prices run the gamut from reasonable to expensive.

Rakel (✉ Vicolo del Bollo 6–7, ☎ 06/6864975) is a small, charming shop tucked down a side alley between Corso Vittorio Emanuele II and the Tiber. The clothes are all handmade from high-quality fabrics. Items in stock are for children up to the age of 7, and clothes are made to order for children up to 12.

HIGH-FASHION BOUTIQUES

Dolce & Gabbana (✉ Piazza di Spagna 82, ☎ 06/6792294) is where these unconventional designers show their slightly extravagant styles and offbeat chic to Romans.

Fendi (✉ Via Borgognona 39, ☎ 06/696661; ✉ Via Fontanella Borghese 57, ☎ 06/696661) is the fur-and-fashion emporium of this fashion dynasty; at its larger Via Fontanella store you can find bags and luggage and the Fendissime boutique, where price tags for fashion are relatively low.

Genny (✉ Piazza di Spagna 27, ☎ 06/6796074) sells classic but contemporary women's ready-to-wear fashions with a flair that is what Italian style is all about. Genny bags and shoes show the same dashing sense of style.

Giorgio Armani (✉ Via Condotti 77, ☎ 06/6991460) is a showcase for the designer's inimitable styles for men and women.

Krizia (✉ Piazza di Spagna 87, ☎ 06/6793772) sells her stunningly cut ready-to-wear line in an elegantly minimal setting.

Laura Biagiotti (✉ Via Borgognona 43, ☎ 06/6791205) has her understated dresses, suits, separates, and line of women's sizes in her spacious, central boutique.

Missoni (✉ Piazza di Spagna 78, ☎ 06/6792555) has samples of knitwear in the display windows facing the Spanish Steps. There is plenty more for men and women inside.

Prada (✉ Via Condotti 92, ☎ 06/6790897), demonstrating that a good bag is just a starting point for a complete fashion statement, has raised the Prada name to status symbol.

Sorelle Fontana (✉ Via di San Sebastianello 5, ☎ 06/6798652) is the doyenne of Rome's high-fashion houses, where the legendary sisters dressed Audrey Hepburn, Ava Gardner, and other celebs in the *La Dolce Vita* days. Now it shows ultraclassic clothes for the ultraelegant woman.

Valentino Donna (✉ Via Condotti 13, ☎ 06/6739420) shows the designer's superlative ready-to-wear collections for women in an elegant boutique.

Valentino Uomo (✉ Via Bocca di Leone 15, ☎ 06/6783656) is the ineffable Italian designer's men's boutique, where expensive elegance reigns supreme. Quality fabrics and faultless tailoring, together with a genius for style, are Valentino's signature.

Versace (✉ Via Bocca di Leone 27, ☎ 06/6780521) has helped transform a two-block area into Versaceville, with four other boutiques in addition to this one—three on Via Borgognona (Numbers 24 and 25) and one on Via Frattina.

KNITWEAR

Albertina (✉ Via Lazio 20, ☎ 06/4885876) elevates women's knitwear to the level of high fashion, imparting line and substance to creations for women that never go out of style. Coats, jackets, dresses, pants, and tops are made in exclusive wool, silk, or blended yarns.

De Clerq e De Clerq (✉ Via delle Carrozze 50, ☎ 06/6790988) caters to women of refined tastes and elevated budgets with exquisitely styled knitwear in cotton, silk, or wool.

Luisa Spagnoli (✉ Via Tritone 30, ☎ 06/69922769; ✉ Via Veneto 130, ☎ 06/42011281; ✉ Via Frattina 84/b, ☎ 06/6991706) is an internationally known name for women's knit fashions. The Spagnoli stores also carry a full range of ready-to-wear.

Marisa Pignataro (✉ Via della Scrofa 50, ☎ 06/6896476) has handmade knitwear for women in unusual yarns, mainly silk and wool. The selection includes shawls, dresses, and pants, many made with an ample, easy-to-wear line. The prices here are in keeping with the quality.

Mariselaine (✉ Via Condotti 70, ☎ 06/6795817) is a small, elegant women's boutique showing knitwear in fashion yarns and colors; every piece has something that takes it out of the ordinary. In addition, Mariselaine has classy, classic day and afternoon wear.

LEATHER CLOTHING

Leather clothing for men and women is a good buy in Italy, where skins imported from many countries are cut and tailored in styles ranging from casual to elegant.

Crocco & Dille (✉ Via Francesco Crispi 77, ☎ 06/6785735) is so tiny you may easily pass it by. But this minuscule factory outlet is worth your attention if you're looking for a casual leather jacket.

Fabris al Pantheon (✉ Via Degli Orfani, 87, ☎ 06/6795603) is a three-story shop just behind the Pantheon. It has a relatively small clothing line (most of the shop is given over to its bags and range of luggage) but don't let that mislead you—here you'll find the best-cut leather jackets in Rome. They are close-fitting, stylish, and made from very soft leather.

Renard (✉ Via Due Macelli 52, ☎ 06/6797004) is a leather boutique, displaying a selection of styles made exclusively in Italy. The store is large and airy, without the chock-full-of-goods look of sister stores.

Rock 'n Blue (✉ Via Nazionale 223, ☎ 06/4825510) is a jeans store that carries moderately priced young styles in leather, especially jackets to wear with jeans and the ever-popular aviator's jackets.

Skin (✉ Via Due Macelli 59/a, ☎ 06/6795856; ✉ Via Due Macelli 87, ☎ 06/6795856) is a double-barreled operation with sister stores across the street from one another. Both large, with big stocks, they have just about anything you could want in leather, and in any color, too. House styles are classic models of suits, skirts, jackets, and pantsuits. They also show high-fashion styles by Missoni and other designers.

Versari (✉ Via dei Due Macelli 115, ☎ 06/6790539) has a limited selection of styles. The store's specialty is jackets and coats, but it offers a token choice of skirts, pants, and such.

Very Pel (✉ Via Cavour 174, ☎ 06/4817640) is a small shop with a workroom on the premises. The mainly casual jackets, skirts, and pants in leather and suede are made on the spot, so if you don't see anything you like, you can have something made to order. Prices are lower than at the fancier leather boutiques.

Virdel (✉ Via del Tritone 75, ☎ 06/4885883) occupies an entire corner of the busy intersection with Via Francesco Crispi. Much of the merchandise, including bags and belts, is on display, making choosing easy. This is the place for classic styles in leather suits and jackets for men and women; there is little that would appeal to younger, trendier dressers.

MEN'S CLOTHING

Brioni (⊠ Via Barberini 79, ☎ 06/484517) has a well-deserved reputation as one of Italy's top tailors: the list of customers reads like a *Who's Who* of the international elite. Brioni also has a ready-to-wear line that has the same impeccable look as his custom-made styles.

Chenzo (⊠ Via Mario dei Fiori 111, ☎ 06/6786754) is two floors of everything from sportswear to classic suits with well-known labels, at moderate prices. The store is open daily.

Eddy Monetty (⊠ Via Condotti 63/a, ☎ 06/6794117) has the British look that Italians love, with Burberry a big seller. There are plenty of Italian labels to choose from, but nothing here comes cheap.

Enzo Ceci (⊠ Via della Vite 52, ☎ 06/6798882) caters to unconventional tastes, offering what Americans think Italian clothing should be: classic styles with a touch of extravagance, ties in flashy colors, wildly striped shirts, and three-piece suits in pale colors.

Ermenegildo Zegna (⊠ Via Borgognona 7/e, ☎ 06/6789143), of the unpronounceable name, is one of Italy's finest manufacturers of men's clothing. Zegna's classic ready-to-wear line is made of the firm's premier fabrics (the clothing line is a spin-off of the family's century-old textile industry). For outdoor wear, Zegna has developed innovative fabrics for rain jackets and car coats.

Grimas (⊠ Via del Gambero 11/a, ☎ 06/6784423) is a favorite with Romans who want to dress well without spending a lot. Both the wood-paneled store and the merchandise found within are classics.

Il Portone (⊠ Via della Carrozze 71, ☎ 06/6793355) embodies a tradition in custom shirt making. For decades, a man was a fashion nobody if he didn't have a few Portone shirts in his closet, identifiable by their cut and signature stripes. The store also carries nightshirts and underwear.

Osvaldo Testa (⊠ Via Frattina 42, ☎ 06/6790660) showcases Burberry to attract Anglophile Italians, but it also has some fine Italian labels, including Cerrutti. If your suitcase has been lost, this is the place to come for everything from boxers to suits to shoes.

MEN'S AND WOMEN'S CLOTHING

Battistoni (⊠ Via Condotti 61/a, ☎ 06/6976111) is a name that has been associated with smart, conservative style for generations. Classic Battistoni jackets, suits, shoes, and accessories are staples in the wardrobes of Rome's elegant set.

Belfe e Belfe (⊠ Via del Gambero 9, ☎ 06/6791725) stocks sportswear, including boat and golf shoes, as well as all-weather jackets, soft sweaters, and designer running suits.

Davide Cenci (⊠ Via Campo Marzio 1–7, ☎ 06/6990681) is a Roman classic for high-quality clothing and accessories for every occasion, from a sailboat party to a formal wedding. Trench coats, cashmeres, and beautifully tailored ready-to-wear are Cenci specialties.

Degli Effetti (⊠ Piazza Capranica 93, ☎ 06/6790202) has fashion on the cutting edge for men and women in separate stores on opposite sides of the piazza. This is the address of the women's store, which carries Miu Miu and Yoshi Yamamoto.

Red and Blue (⊠ Via Due Macelli 57, ☎ 06/6791933) has sporty casual wear for men and women, with a marked British accent. Burberry is featured in the large display windows, but the store also carries such fine Italian brands as Loro Piana.

Superga (⊠ Via della Maddalena 30/a, ☎ 06/6868737) sells the sneakers that every Italian wears, in classic white or a rainbow of colors, and it now has a line of sportswear for men and women.

TEENS' CLOTHING

Fiorucci (✉ Via Mario dei Fiori 54, ☎ 06/6792946) displays Fiorucci's signature angels on T-shirts and delights adolescents with kitschy gadgets and accessories.

Onyx (✉ Via Frattina 92, ☎ 06/6791509) is a teenagers' hangout, complete with high-volume music, where girls can find the up-to-the-minute separates that they love, including minimal tops and miniskirts, at moderate prices.

Replay (✉ Via della Rotonda 25, ☎ 06/6833073) has the look of an American country store but sells youthful casual styles made in Italy. Prices are moderate.

VINTAGE CLOTHING

Cinzia (✉ Via del Governo Vecchio 45, ☎ no phone) is known as a classic for vintage clothing, especially 1960s and '70s styles, including leather jackets and Mary Quant sunglasses.

Le Gallinelle (✉ Via del Boschetto 76, ☎ 06/4881017) makes over vintage clothing, using old fabrics in new garments or reconditioning vintage dresses to look like new. This tiny shop even has a men's corner, with mainly overcoats and trousers. Prices are very reasonable.

Mado (✉ Via del Governo Vecchio 89/a, ☎ 06/6875028) is like a trunk in Grandma's attic, full of vintage clothing and costume jewelry, with ostrich plumes tickling your nose.

WOMEN'S CLOTHING

Alexander (✉ Piazza di Spagna 49, ☎ 06/6791351) brings the street right into the shop with continuous cobblestone paving and street-smart fashions and shoes for women who like trendy, aggressive styles.

Arsenal (✉ Via del Governo Vecchio, 64, ☎ 06/6861380) is Italian design at its most inventive. This shop's sleek layout and low-key elegance stand out even in Rome.

Dulce Vidoza (✉ Via dell'Orso 58, ☎ 06/6893007) would be at home in New York's SoHo; it's minimal and elegant. It takes classic pantsuits out of the ordinary, using Nehru collars and unconventional fabrics and colors.

Elena Mirò (✉ Via Frattina 11, ☎ 06/6784367) is an attractive shop with a selection of stylish casual and dressy wear in women's sizes. Fabrics and colors reflect fashion trends.

Galassia (✉ Via Frattina 20, ☎ 06/6797896) has expensive, extreme, and extravagant women's styles by Gaultier, Westwood, and Yamamoto. This is the place for funky hats, feather boas, and flashy jewelry, at a price.

Lei (✉ Via dei Giubbonari 103, ☎ 06/6875432) has young styles from this side of the cutting edge—up-to-the-minute but not futuristic. Dolce & Gabbana and Romeo Gigli are represented by ready-to-wear that is sweet or sexy, or both.

Le Tartarughe (✉ Via Piè di Marmo 17, ☎ 06/6792240) makes a subtle fashion statement with a selection of versatile, easy-to-wear and easy-to-pack styles, many in knit fabrics, all designed in-house.

Maga Morgana (✉ Via del Governo Vecchio 27, ☎ 06/6879995) shows faux vintage styles in bare little 1930s flowered dresses or with a folk look, as well as knitwear, all designed and made exclusively for the shop.

Mariella Burani (✉ Via Bocca di Leone 28, ☎ 06/6790630) has classic chic with judiciously used high-fashion overtones. These clothes are ever-wearable and never boring.

Wazoo (✉ Via dei Giubbonari 28, ☎ 06/6869362) is one of Rome's trendiest boutiques for designer fashions for women, funky shoes, and very special dresses. Though small and divided into separate sections for shoes and clothing, the selection is wide and includes some of Vivienne Westwood's less outlandish styles.

Xandrine (⊠ Via della Croce 88, ☎ 06/6786201) has dressy retro styles, in a choice of classic or extravagant, at moderate prices.

Cosmetics/Beauty/Perfume

Antica Officina di Santa Maria Novella (⊠ Corso Rinascimento 47, ☎ 06/6872446), like a 16th-century pharmacy, is wood paneled and odorous of herbs, flowers, and a very special potpourri. The essences, soaps, creams, and lotions sold here are based on antique, natural formulas devised centuries ago by the monks of Santa Maria Novella in Florence.

Castelli (⊠ Via Frattina 54, ☎ 06/6790339; ⊠ Via Condotti 22, ☎ 06/6790998; ⊠ Via Oslavia 5, ☎ 06/3728312) is a perfumed paradise offering everything imaginable in the way of beauty aids, cosmetics, and hair accessories, plus a dazzling selection of high-quality costume jewelry. The shop on Via Frattina has a beauty salon (☎ 06/6780066), no kin to your neighborhood hairdresser in prices or atmosphere.

Materozzoli (⊠ Piazza San Lorenzo in Lucina 5, ☎ 06/68892686) is an antique herbalist's shop that has managed to preserve the old interior while modernizing its wares. There is a large selection of essences and naturally perfumed products, mainly English and French, and a good range of razors and brushes.

Fabrics

Italy is famous for silks and woolens. The country is one of the world's major textile manufacturers, so the choice is vast. You can find some real bargains when *scampoli* (remnants) are on sale.

Aston (⊠ Via Buoncompagni 27, ☎ 06/42871227) stocks couture-level fabrics for men and women. Though expensive, the goods cost much less here than at home.

Fratelli Bassetti (⊠ Corso Vittorio Emanuele II 73, ☎ 06/6892326) has a vast selection of world-famous Italian silks and fashion fabrics on several floors of a rambling palazzo.

Food, Wine, and Delicacies

Ai Monasteri (⊠ Corso del Rinascimento 72, ☎ 06/68802783) sells liqueurs, jams, and chocolate handmade by Cistercian monks from several Italian monasteries.

Buccone (⊠ Via di Ripetta 19, ☎ 06/3612154) is a landmark 1800s wineshop, with a wide selection of wines, sweets, and packaged candy. It serves light lunches, too.

Castroni (⊠ Via Cola di Rienzo 196, ☎ 06/6874383) has a broad and aromatic range of food products from all over the world. This is where members of foreign countries come to find specialties from home, but you'll see plenty of Italian-made goodies on the shelves, too.

Enoteca al Parlamento (⊠ Via dei Prefetti 15, ☎ 06/6873446) is one of the city's traditional wineshops, a haunt of journalists and politicos who stop in for wine by the glass. The Enoteca's prized bottle of Brunello di Montalcino, an early 1900s vintage, is defined as priceless.

Moriondo e Gariglio (⊠ Via Piè di Marmo 21, ☎ 06/6990856) is a tiny chocolate shop that has been catering to refined chocoholics' cravings for a century. Everything here is made in the store's own workshop.

Trimani (⊠ Via Goito 20, ☎ 06/4469661), one of Rome's best-stocked wine dealers, also has a broad selection of regional Italian delicacies.

Volpetti (⊠ Via Marmorata 47, ☎ 06/5742352) has the best cured meats in Rome, with a score of different salami. A vast selection of cheeses includes genuine buffalo-milk mozzarella. And the fresh pasta is heavenly.

Handbags and Luggage

A fine Italian handbag in leather or a stylish synthetic fabric is a worthwhile investment. Really good bags—the classic kind that you can carry for years—are not inexpensive. For styles that follow fashion, Redwall, Biasia, Evolution, the Bridge, and Zippo are names to look for.

Amadei (✉ Via delle Carrozze 20, ☎ 06/6783352) is a tiny shop with offbeat, trendy handbags for women. They're one of a kind, made by Amadei from leather or smart fabrics.

Antonella Penco (✉ Via F. Crispi 66, ☎ 06/42013393) has an eclectic and original range of in-house creations. Zany handbags are the specialty, but there are also beautiful baubles for the minimal chic brigade.

Furla (✉ Piazza di Spagna 22, ☎ 06/69200363) is the flagship store of a fleet with shops as far away as New York and Honolulu. They purvey chic bags and practical totes in bright colors, along with scarves and a selection of costume jewelry, all at moderate prices.

Gherardini (✉ Via Belsiana 48/b, ☎ 06/6795501) has taken over a deconsecrated church and transformed it into a showplace for the Gherardini label, associated with casual, easy-to-carry bags in leather and logo-stamped synthetic material. It has leather totes and bags in bright colors and a line of soft luggage.

Gucci (✉ Via Condotti 8, ☎ 06/6789340), for all the revamping by designer Tom Ford, still has groups of eager customers lined up at the door waiting for a chance to get at those perennial double-G logo bags and shoes.

Incontro Modo (✉ Via della Vite 44, ☎ 06/6788812) specializes in Italian-made handbags and luggage, as casual in style as the store's country-cabin decor. There are models for men and women, and the store carries a selection of Cerrutti and Zippo styles.

Mandarina Duck (✉ Corso Vittorio Emanuele II 16, ☎ 06/6789840) is the maker of soft bags and luggage in resistant synthetic fabrics, with the Mandarina Duck logo trim. Eminently practical in form and design (they can be folded up and slipped in a suitcase, and their capacity seems limitless), the bags are a boon to travelers.

Pier Caranti (✉ Piazza di Spagna 44, ☎ 06/6791621) displays a mountain of handbags in three big display windows. The store makes up in quantity and range of choice what it lacks in elegance. Though clearly tourist oriented, it has an Italian clientele, too.

Redwall (✉ Via Condotti 56, ☎ 06/6791973) is one of Italy's major handbag manufacturers and it produces under license for several leading designers, among them Armani and Moschino. The company has its own label, too. The spare decor of this small store leaves the spotlight to the bags, well made and hand finished.

Volterra (✉ Via Barberini 102, ☎ 06/4819315) has a good range of handbags from the best Italian manufacturers, and prices are competitive. The styles run the gamut from classy to casual.

Hats, Gloves, and Ties

Borsalino Boutique (✉ Piazza del Popolo 20, ☎ 06/32650838) has hats for men and women in signature styles, dressy, casual, and always classic, including Panama hats. The store also carries a line of shirts and ties.

Di Cori (✉ Piazza di Spagna 54a, ☎ 06/6784140) packs a lot of gloves into a tiny space, offering every type in every color imaginable. There is a limited selection of scarves and ties, too.

Merola (✉ Via del Corso 143, ☎ 06/6791961) has been selling expensive, top-quality gloves to Romans for decades. It also carries a line of scarves.

Roxy (✉ Via Frattina 115, ☎ 06/6796691; ✉ Via Barberini 112, ☎ 06/4883931) has the best selection of moderately priced ties to be found in Rome. The selection is bewilderingly large, and the stores are tiny and usually packed with customers.

Sermoneta (⊠ Piazza di Spagna 61, ☎ 06/6791960) has a huge stock of gloves in rainbow hues or classic blacks, whites, and browns. The quality is reliable.

Jewelry

Buccellati (⊠ Via Condotti 31, ☎ 06/6790329) is a tradition-rich Florentine jewelry house renowned for elaborately worked silver pieces and nostalgic jewelry recalling the days of grand décolletés and tiaras.

Bulgari (⊠ Via Condotti 10, ☎ 06/6793876) dazzles with enticing doses of opulence in small display windows. You ring at the door to be admitted to the treasure trove of distinctly contemporary jewels within.

Diego Percossipapi (⊠ Via Sant'Eustachio 16, ☎ 06/68801466) is a tiny shop with an upscale clientele. Often based on ancient Roman models, the jewels show masterful technique and a knowing choice of stones.

Maria Teresa Nitti Valentini (⊠ Via della Stelletta 4, ☎ 06/68308776) is known to connoisseurs for vintage jewelry (including some good costume jewelry), displayed along the narrow corridor that is the entrance to the minuscule shop.

Lingerie and Linens

Brighenti (⊠ Via Frattina 7, ☎ 06/6791484) looks like what it is—a traditional Roman shop of a gentler era, with art nouveau light fixtures and sculptured wooden shelves. The women's lingerie, in silk and satin, is lavish with lace in the most classic and feminine styles. The store also carries stylish bathing suits.

Cesari (⊠ Via Babuino 195, ☎ 06/3613451) is a Roman institution for frothy lingerie, quality household linens, and sumptuous decorator fabrics, and it has less-expensive gift items such as aprons, beach towels, and place mats.

Demoiselle (⊠ Via Frattina 93, ☎ 06/6793752) is a chic shop at the corner of Via Belsiana, with high-fashion lingerie, including La Perla's luscious Italian-made sleepwear and undergarments. The shop has a good selection of Missoni bathing suits in season.

Frette (⊠ Piazza di Spagna 10, ☎ 06/6790673) shows lingerie for fabulous trousseaux and has a large range of household linens in stylish prints and colors.

La Perla (⊠ Via Condotti 78, ☎ 06/69941934), small and minimally decorated, offers a selection of high-quality lingerie and underwear for women and for men. See their sexy pajamas.

Lavori Artigianali Femminili (⊠ Via Capo le Case 6, ☎ 06/6781100) offers embroidered household linens, exquisitely embroidered layettes and christening dresses, hand-knit suits for babies and small children, and women's blouses.

Marisa Padovan (⊠ Via della Carrozze 81, ☎ 06/6793946) is the place for exclusive, sometimes extravagant, lingerie in sumptuous styles, often trimmed with sequins and ostrich feathers.

Tebro (⊠ Via dei Prefetti 51, ☎ 06/6873441) is a large, classic Roman establishment with a long-standing reputation for quality and courtesy. This is where the well-heeled Roman shops for lingerie and household linens.

Venier e Colombo (⊠ Via Frattina 79, ☎ 06/6792979) has a breathtaking selection of lace-trimmed lingerie and linens and also sells lace by the yard.

Music and Videos

Most video stores have a section with English and American movies in the original language, sometimes with Italian subtitles. Though mainly a bookstore, the Economy Book and Video Center has a large selection of English-language videos.

Blockbuster (✉ Via Barberini 1, ☎ 06/4871666) has invaded Italy. This is just one of a dozen stores in Rome stocked with a megaselection of videos.

Economy Book and Video Center (✉ Via Torino 136, ☎ 06/4746877), though first and foremost a bookstore, also has a large selection of videos.

Messagerie Musicali (✉ Via del Corso 473, ☎ 06/684401) has central Rome's largest selections of tapes and CDs. It has a video department and sells sheet music and musical instruments, too.

Ricordi (✉ Via Cesare Battisti 120, ☎ 06/6798022) can provide any kind of music imaginable on tape or CD, from Italy's golden oldies to the latest on worldwide charts.

Rinascita (✉ Via Botteghe Oscure 2, ☎ 06/6797637) is in the building that houses the left-wing PDS (Partito Democratico della Sinistra, the former Communist Party). The floor below the big bookstore holds a music department with up-to-the-minute releases and a good choice of ethnic music.

Shoes

Rome's shoe stores seem to be as numerous as the mopeds buzzing around downtown. They range from custom-made-shoe boutiques to stores with huge displays of every model imaginable for men, women, and children. Most Italian shoes are made to a single, average width; if you need a narrower shoe you may have to try on many before you find the right fit. Valleverde and Melluso brands make wider, softer shoes for men and women.

Boccanera (✉ Via Luca della Robbia 36, ☎ 06/5750847), in the Testaccio neighborhood, is where the Romans go for great shoes, especially during sales, when the buys are terrific. The store hasn't changed much over the decades; it still has the relaxed elegance and courteous service once a tradition in Roman shops. Here you can find Prada, Tod's, Church, and other leading brands.

Bruno Magli (✉ Via del Gambero 1, ☎ 06/6793802) shows classy shoes in good-size corner display windows, but you will find many more styles inside, at high to moderate prices.

Campanile (✉ Via Condotti 58, ☎ 06/6783041) is the nonpareil name in classic Italian footwear for men and women. The shoes are costly but their quality is unbeatable.

Charles (✉ Via del Corso 109, ☎ 06/6792345) shows a host of styles in big display windows, offering practically all of the top-quality shoe labels, from Rossi to Rossetti. You choose your style in the window, then tell one of the bilingual clerks what you want. The store is clearly geared to tourists, but Romans come, too, for the wide selection and competitive prices.

Fausto Santini (✉ Via Frattina 120, ☎ 06/6784114) gives a hint of extravagance in minimally decorated, all-white show windows displaying surprising shoes that fashion mavens love. Santini's footwear for men and women is bright and trendy, sporting unusual forms, especially in heels. Coordinated bags and wallets add to the fun.

Ferragamo Donna (✉ Via Condotti 73, ☎ 06/6791565) has the ultimate in Italian fashion shoes for women, expensive and of excellent quality. Finding a bag or splashy Ferragamo scarf to match the shoes is no problem here.

Ferragamo Uomo (✉ Via Condotti 66, ☎ 06/6781130) shows classic styles in shoes for men, handcrafted in fine leather and in fabric for more sporty models.

Fratelli Rossetti (⊠ Via Borgognona 5/a, ☎ 06/6782676) combines classic quality and good looks in men's and women's shoes with the telling detail that puts them high in fashion.

Mada Shoes (⊠ Via della Croce 57, ☎ 06/6798660) has a selection of classic, conservative shoe styles for women with attractive details that make them distinctive.

Pollini (⊠ Via Frattina 23, ☎ 06/6798360) is a his-and-hers store, divided down the middle into narrow, separate shops. Pollini styles for both sexes are classic, with prices that are relatively high.

Sergio Rossi (⊠ Piazza di Spagna 97, ☎ 06/6783245) displays a discreet selection of classic men's and women's shoes in the windows of this store at the corner of Via della Croce. The styles are elegant and conservative.

Tod's (⊠ Via Borgognona 45, ☎ 06/6786828) has an English name, but the shoes are strictly Italian designed and made in Italy. This exclusive Tod's store has every model of the manufacturer's signature button-soled moccasin, as well as other styles.

Stationery

Pineider (⊠ Via della Fontanella Borghese 22, ☎ 06/6878369) is where Rome's aristocratic families have their wedding invitations engraved and their stationery personalized. For stationery and desk accessories, hand-tooled in the best Florentine leather, it has no equal.

Toys

Bertè (⊠ Piazza Navona 108, ☎ 06/6875011) is Rome's version of FAO Schwarz (though only one-twentieth the size). Romans always include a stop at Bertè's display windows in a stroll around Pizza Navona. The doll population is astounding—from crying, eating, and talking dolls to lace- and ribbon-bedecked old-fashioned beauties. The menagerie of stuffed animals ranges from tiny kittens to enormous elephants and polar bears that you would be hard put to find room for in your suitcase. There's also a line of toys and supplies for infants.

Galleria San Carlo (⊠ Via del Corso 114, ☎ 06/6790571) makes up in stock for what it lacks in decor. The store is basically composed of big display windows packed with toys; you show the clerks what you want and they will get it for you. There's an ample selection of Italian-made dolls and a whole forest of wooden Pinocchios.

La Città del Sole (⊠ Via della Scrofa 65, ☎ 06/6875404; ⊠ Piazza della Chiesa Nuova 22, Old Rome, ☎ 06/6872922) is the progressive parent's ideal store, chock-full of educational toys for all ages—even for adults (puzzles, tricks, and gadgets). Shelves and floor space are crammed with toys (in safe plastics and in wood) and with games, puzzles, and children's books, mainly in Italian. You won't find a Barbie here.

7 SIDE TRIPS FROM ROME

In the background of Renaissance portraits
of saints and princes you'll find dreamlike
landscapes dotted with medieval castles
and quaint villages. You have to look closely
to appreciate their beauty and wealth of
detail, but your attention is rewarded with
unexpected insight into a particular time and
place. Rome is the undisputed prince of the
Lazio region, dominating the foreground
and monopolizing attention, but, as in the
paintings, charming sights and unexpected
treasures are sprinkled throughout the
countryside around it.

By Barbara
Walsh
Angelillo

Updated by
Norman
Roberson

A BREATH OF COUNTRY AIR and a change of scenery can enhance your enjoyment of Rome and give you a new perspective on its disparate pleasures. For the greater part of 2,000 years, the grandeur and the glory of Rome have obscured the constellation of attractions in the region around it. Yet exploring Lazio (Latium, to the ancient Romans) is like applying a magnifying glass to an enormously complex painting replete with figures and action. By concentrating on one scene at a time, you get a much better understanding of the significance of the big picture.

One of the easiest excursions from the capital takes you west 25 km (15½ mi) to the sea, where tall pines stand among the well-preserved ruins of Ostia Antica, the main port of ancient Rome and an archaeological site that rivals Pompeii. A visit to Ostia Antica tells you more about the way the ancient Romans lived than the Roman Forum does. (And it brings home just how close Islamic troops came to overrunning Rome, as they would have if their fleet had not been defeated off Ostia in 849.)

The rolling landscape of Lazio along the coast northwest of Rome was once Etruscan territory, and at Cerveteri and Tarquinia it holds some intriguing reminders of a people who taught the ancient Romans a thing or two about religion, art, and a pleasurable way of life. The Etruscan sites here give you a very concrete impression of the people whose art and artifacts are displayed in the Museum of Villa Giulia in Rome. Deep in the countryside north of Rome, Viterbo has an intact medieval core and historic traces of its days as a papal stronghold. Close by, the gardens of Villa Lante at Bagnaia and Palazzo Farnese at Caprarola give an inkling of how Renaissance cardinals took a break from their duties at the papal court. And at Bomarzo a 16th-century prince created one of the first theme parks in Europe.

East of Rome lie some of the region's star sites, which could be combined along a route that loops through the hills where ancient Romans built their summer resorts. At Tivoli, Hadrian's Villa shows you the scale of individual imperial Roman egos, while Villa d'Este demonstrates that Renaissance egos were no smaller. Eastward at Palestrina lies a vast sanctuary from ancient times. At Subiaco, St. Benedict founded the hermitage that gave rise to Western monasticism. Southeast of Rome are three romantic sites little known outside Italy: a castle at Sermoneta that once belonged to Cesare Borgia, a fairy-tale garden at Ninfa, and the seaside citadel of Sperlonga. In addition to rewarding you with a refreshing break from city sightseeing, Lazio's attractions offer the key to a fuller Roman experience.

Numbers in the margin correspond to numbers on the Side Trips from Rome and Ostia Antica maps.

Pleasures and Pastimes

Dining

A day in the country for the Romans traditionally includes a midday meal at a favorite trattoria or restaurant, so there's no lack of good places to eat in the Lazio region. Prices are generally a little lower than in the capital. Each town has culinary specialties that are worth trying, as is the local wine. Many towns are known for local cheese and also for their bread—a crusty dark country loaf that makes the ultimate *bruschetta* (toasted bread doused with extra virgin olive oil, sprinkled with salt, an optional rubbing of garlic, and topped with vine-ripe tomatoes). Restaurants on the coast, of course, usually have seafood specialties.

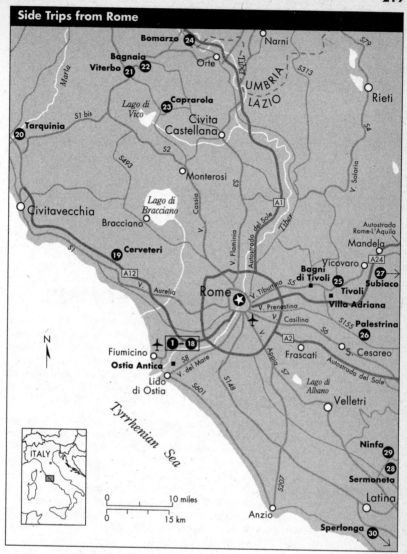

Bomarzo **24**
Narni
Bagnaia **22**
Viterbo **21**
Orte
UMBRIA
LAZIO
Caprarola **23**
Lago di Vico
Civita Castellana
Tarquinia **20**
Monterosi
Rieti
Civitavecchia
Lago di Bracciano
Bracciano
Cerveteri **19**
Mandela
Yicovaro
Bagni di Tivoli **25**
Tivoli
Villa Adriana
Subiaco **27**
Autostrada Rome-L'Aquila
A24
Rome
Palestrina **26**
S. Cesareo
1 **18**
Fiumicino
Ostia Antica
Frascati
Lido di Ostia
Lago di Albano
Velletri
ITALY
Tyrrhenian Sea
Ninfa **29**
Sermoneta **28**
Latina
10 miles
15 km
Anzio
Sperlonga **30**

N

Marta
S1 bis
S2
S493
V. Cassia
Tiber
S313
S79
S4
V. Salaria
A1
Autostrada del Sole
V. Flaminia
V. Tiburtina
S5
S155
A2
S6
V. Prenestina
V. Casilina
Appia
S7
Autostrada del Sole
V. Aurelia
A12
S1
S8
V. del Mare
S601
S148
S207
V.

CATEGORY	COST*
$$$$	over €18
$$$	€13–€18
$$	€8–€13
$	under €8

Prices are for a second course (secondo piatto).

Lodging

With relatively few exceptions (hotels in beach and hill resorts and spas such as Fiuggi), accommodations throughout the region cater more to commercial travelers than to tourists. For this reason the public rooms and guest rooms tend to be functional and anonymous, though adequate for an overnight.

CATEGORY	COST*
$$$$	over €155
$$$	€105–€155
$$	€55–€105
$	under €55

All prices are for two people in a standard double room, including tax and service.

OSTIA ANTICA: A PRETTIER POMPEII

Founded around the 4th century BC, Ostia served as Rome's port city for several centuries until the Tiber changed course, leaving the town high and dry. What has been excavated here is a remarkably intact Roman town in a pretty, parklike setting. Fair weather and good walking shoes are essential. On hot days, be here when the gates open or go late in the afternoon. A visit to the excavations takes two to three hours, including 20 minutes for the museum.

Ostia Antica was inhabited by a cosmopolitan population of rich businessmen, wily merchants, sailors, slaves, and their respective families. The great *horrea* (warehouses) were built in the 2nd century AD to handle huge shipments of grain from Africa; the *insulae* (forerunners of the modern apartment building) provided housing for the growing population. Under the combined assaults of the barbarians and the *Anopheles* mosquito, and after the Tiber changed course, the port was eventually abandoned. Tidal mud and windblown sand covered the city, which lay buried until the beginning of the 20th century. Now the **Scavi di Ostia Antica** (Ostia Antica excavations) have been extensively excavated and are well maintained. ✉ *Via dei Romagnoli,* ☎ *06/56358099,* WEB *www.itnw.roma.it/ostia/scavi.* 🎫 *€4.15 (includes admission to Museo Ostiense).* ☉ *Tues.–Sun. 9 AM–1 hr before sunset.*

Before exploring Ostia Antica's ruins, it's worthwhile to take a tour
❶ through the **Castello della Rovere** (Rovere Castle), located in the medieval *borgo* (town). This is the distinctive castle, easily spotted as you come off the footbridge from the train station, was built by Pope Julius II when he was the Cardinal Bishop of Ostia in 1483. Its triangular form is unusual for military architecture. Inside are (badly faded) frescoes by Michelangelo's pupil Baldassare Peruzzi.

❷ The **Porta Romana,** one of the city's three gates, is where you'll enter the Ostia Antica excavations. It opens onto the Decumanus Maximus, the main thoroughfare crossing the city from end to end. To your right, black-and-white mosaic pavements representing Neptune and Amphitrite
❸ decorate the **Terme di Nettuno** (Baths of Neptune). Directly behind the baths is the barracks of the fire department, which played an important role in a town with warehouses full of valuable goods and foodstuffs.

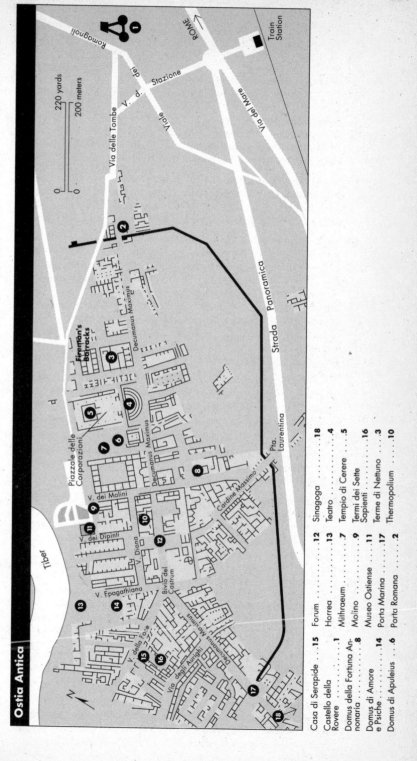

Ostia Antica

220 yards
200 meters

Tiber

ROME
Train Station

Romagnoli

Via delle Tombe
V. d. Pei
Stazione
Viale
Via del Mare
Strada Panoramica
Pta. Laurentina

Decumanus Maximus
Fireman's Barracks
Piazzale delle Corporazioni
V. dei Molini
V. dei Dipinti
Decumanus Maximus
Cardine Massimo
V. Diana
Bivio del Castrum
V. Epagathiana
V. della Foce
Decumanus Massimo
Via degli Aurighi

❹ On the north side of the Decumanus Maximus is the beautiful **Teatro** (theater), built by Agrippa and completely restored by Septimius Severus in the 2nd century AD. In the vast Piazzale delle Corporazioni,

❺ where trade organizations similar to guilds had their offices, is the **Tempio de Cerere** (Temple of Ceres), which is only appropriate for a town dealing in grain imports—Ceres, who gave her name to cereal, was the goddess of agriculture. You can visit the **Domus di Apuleius** (House

❻ of Apuleius), built in Pompeiian style, lower to the ground and with fewer windows than was characteristic of Ostia. Next door, the

❼ **Mithraeum** has balconies and a hall decorated with symbols of the cult of Mithras. This men-only religion, imported from Persia, was especially popular with legionnaires.

❽ On Via Semita dei Cippi, just off Via dei Molini, the **Domus della Fortuna Annonaria** (House of Fortuna Annonaria) is the richly decorated residence of a wealthy Ostian, which displays the skill of the mosaic artists of the period. One of the rooms opens onto a secluded garden.

❾ On Via dei Molini you can see a **molino** (mill), where grain for the warehouses next door was ground with stones that are still here. Along Via

❿ di Diana you come upon a **thermopolium** (bar) with a marble counter and a fresco depicting the fruit and foodstuffs that were sold here. At

⓫ the end of Via dei Dipinti is the **Museo Ostiense** (Ostia Museum), open Tuesday–Saturday 9–4:30 and Sunday 9–1:30, which displays sarcophagi (burial coffins), massive marble columns, and statuary too large to be shown anywhere else, including a beautiful statue of Mithras slaying the bull, which was taken from the underground Mithraeum. A snack bar, bookshop, and rest rooms are located behind the museum.

⓬ The **Forum**, on the south side of Decumanus Maximus, holds the monumental remains of the city's most important temple, dedicated to Jupiter, Juno, and Minerva; other ruins of baths; a basilica (which in Roman times served as a secular hall of justice); and smaller temples.

⓭ Via Epagathiana leads toward the Tiber, where there are large **horrea** (warehouses), erected during the 2nd century AD to receive the enormous amounts of grain imported into Rome during that period, the height of the Empire.

⓮ West of Via Epagathiana, the **Domus di Amore e Psiche** (House of Cupid and Psyche), a residence, was named for a statue found there (now on display in the museum); you can see what remains of a large pool in an enclosed garden decorated with marble and mosaic motifs. Even in ancient times a premium was placed on water views: the house faces the shore, which would have been only about ⅓ km (⅕ mi) away. The

⓯ **Casa de Serapide** (House of Serapis) on Via della Foce is a 2nd-century multilevel dwelling; another apartment building stands one street

⓰ over on Via degli Aurighi. Nearby, the **Termi dei Sette Sapienti** (Baths of the Seven Wise Men) are named for a group of bawdy frescoes found there.

⓱ The **Porta Marina** leads to what used to be the seashore. About 1,000

⓲ ft to the south are the ruins of the **sinagoga** (synagogue), one of the oldest in the Western world.

Dining

$$$$ ✕ **Cipriani.** Handily located in the little medieval borgo near the excavations, this elegant trattoria serves Roman specialties and seafood and has an exquisite wine list. ✉ *Via del Forno 11,* ☎ *06/56359560. AE, DC, MC, V. Closed Mon.*

Ostia Antica A to Z

To research prices, get advice from other travelers, and book travel arrangements, visit www.fodors.com.

CAR TRAVEL
Follow Via del Mare southwest, which leads directly from Rome to Ostia (a 30- to 40-minute trip).

TRAIN TRAVEL
Regular train service links the Ostia Antica station with Rome's Piramide Metro B Line station, near Porta San Paolo. Exit the Metro and go to the station called Ostia Lido adjacent to the Metro station. The ride takes about 35 minutes. Trains depart every half hour throughout the day. Call the FS toll-free number for train information (in Italian), or consult the FS Web site (which has an English version). A normal bus or Metro ticket covers the entire journey; just be sure you have not exceeded your 75-minute time limit on your ticket.

➤ TRAIN INFORMATION: **Ferrovie dello Stato** (FS; ☎ 848/888088, WEB www.fs-on-line.com).

CERVETERI AND TARQUINIA: ETRUSCAN LANDSCAPES

Northwest of Rome lie Etruscan sites on hills near the sea. The Etruscans were an apparently peaceable and pleasure-loving people who held sway over a vast territory north of Rome before the rise of the Roman Republic. They loved life and they were sure that they would enjoy the afterlife, too. The Etruscan necropolis, or "city of the dead," was a cemetery faithfully reproducing the homes and lifestyles of the living.

Beyond Rome's city limits, the countryside is green with pastures and endless fields of artichokes, a premium crop in these parts. You catch glimpses of the sea to the west, where the coast is dotted with suburban developments. Because the beaches in this area are popular with Romans, highways and public transportation can be uncomfortably crowded on weekends from spring to fall. Exploring the Etruscan sites requires some agility in climbing up and down uneven stairs, and you need shoes suitable for walking on rough dirt paths.

Cerveteri is the principal Etruscan site closest to Rome and features the Necropoli della Banditaccia, a sylvan setting among mossy stones and variously shaped monuments that are memorials to revered ancestors. Tarquinia is farther north but has even better tombs, as well as an excellent museum full of objects recovered from tombs throughout the region. On the way, you'll pass Civitavecchia, Rome's principal port. From the highway or train you can see the port installations, which include a fort designed by Michelangelo. The low mountains to the east are the Tolfa range, where the Etruscans mined metals for export to ancient Mediterranean markets.

Cerveteri

⑲ *42 km (26 mi) northwest of Rome.*

The nucleus of the town, in the shadow of a medieval castle, stands on a spur of tufa rock that was the site of the Etruscan city of Caere, a thriving commercial center in the 6th century BC. The necropolis is about 2 km (1 mi) from Cerveteri's main piazza, a trip you can make on foot or by taxi.

In the **Necropoli della Banditaccia** (Banditaccia Necropolis), the Etruscan residents of Caere left a heritage of great historical significance. In this monumental complex of tombs set in parklike grounds, they laid their relatives to rest, some in simple graves, others in burial chambers that are replicas of Etruscan dwellings. In the round tumulus tombs you can recognize the prototypes of Rome's tombs of Augustus and Hadrian (in the Mausoleo di Augusto and Castel Sant'Angelo) and the Tomb of Cecilia Metella on the Via Appia. Important tombs are open on a rotating basis, so you may not be able to enter all of them on a given day. Look for the **Tomba dei Capitelli**, with carved capitals; the **Tomba dei Rilievi**, its walls carved with reliefs of household objects; and the similar **Tombe degli Scudi e delle Sedie**. The **Tomba Moretti** has a little vestibule with columns. Some tombs have several chambers. ⊠ *Necropoli della Banditaccia.* 🎫 *€4.15.* ⏱ *May–Sept., Tues.–Sun. 9–7; Oct.–Apr., Tues.–Sun. 9–4.*

In Cerveteri's medieval castle, the **Museo Nazionale Cerite** is a small archaeological museum with some of the finds, mostly pottery, from the various Etruscan cemeteries that have been located in the area. (The more important objects found in the tombs are in Rome's Museo Etrusco di Villa Giulia and the Musei Vaticani.) ⊠ *Piazza della Necropoli,* ☎ *06/9940001,* 🌐 *www.etruschi.it/cittadine/cerveter.html.* 🎫 *Free.* ⏱ *Tues.–Sun. 9–7.*

Dining

$$ ✗ **Tuchulcha.** About ½ km (¼ mi) from the entrance to the Banditaccia necropolis, on the road leading to the site, this country trattoria offers simple and satisfying home-style food; two specialties are handmade fettuccine and locally grown artichokes served in various ways. You can dine outside in good weather. ⊠ *Via della Necropoli Etrusca,* ☎ *no phone. No credit cards. Closed Mon.*

Tarquinia

⑳ *About 90 km (55 mi) northwest of Rome; 50 km (30 mi) northwest of Cerveteri; 20 km (12 mi) north of Civitavecchia.*

Tarquinia sprawls on a hill overlooking the sea. Once a powerful Etruscan city, it was a major center in the Middle Ages, too. Though it lacks the harmony of better-preserved medieval towns, Tarquinia offers unexpected pleasures, among them views of narrow medieval streets opening onto quaint squares dominated by palaces and churches, and the sight of the majestic, solitary church of Santa Maria di Castello encircled by medieval walls and towers. To focus on Tarquinia's Etruscan heritage, visit the museum in Palazzo Vitelleschi, and then see the frescoed underground tombs in the fields east of the city. You can walk to the necropolis from town. From Piazza Matteotti, the town's main square, take Via Porta Tarquinia south past the church of San Francesco; go through the Porta Tarquinia, also known as Porta Clementina, and continue south on Via Ripagrotta. At the intersection with Via delle Croci, head east on the main road to reach the necropolis. There is infrequent bus service from Piazza Cavour to the necropolis, with only a couple of morning and afternoon departures.

The **Museo Nazionale Tarquiniense** (National Museum of Tarquinia) is housed in Palazzo Vitelleschi, a splendid 15th-century building that contains a wealth of Etruscan treasures. Even if pottery vases and endless ranks of stone sarcophagi leave you cold, what makes a visit here memorable are the horses. Two marvelous golden terra-cotta winged horses gleam warmly against the gray-stone wall on which they have been mounted in the main hall. They are from a frieze that once decorated an Etruscan temple, and they are strikingly vibrant proof of the degree of artistry attained by the Etruscans in the 4th century BC. The museum and its stately courtyard are crammed with sarcophagi from the tombs found beneath the meadows surrounding the town. The figures of the deceased recline casually on their stone couches, mouths curved in enigmatic smiles. Upstairs are vases and other Etruscan artifacts, together with some of the more precious frescoes from the tombs, removed to keep them from deteriorating. ✉ *Piazza Cavour.* 🎫 *€4.15, €6.20 including necropolis.* ⊙ *Tues.–Sun. 9–7.*

The entrance to the **Necropoli** (Necropolis), the Etruscan city of the dead, is about 1 km (½ mi) outside the town walls. Frequent, regularly scheduled guided tours (not mandatory) leave from the ticket office, visiting about 10 of the 100 most interesting tombs on a rotating basis. The tombs date from the 7th to the 2nd century BC, and they were painted with lively scenes of Etruscan life. The colors are amazingly fresh in some tombs, and the scenes show the vitality and highly civilized lifestyle of this ancient people. Of the thousands of tombs that exist throughout the territory of Etruria (there are 40,000 in the vicinity of Tarquinia alone), only a small percentage have been excavated scientifically. Many more have been found and plundered by "experts" called *tombaroli*, who dig illegally, usually at night. The tombs in the Tarquinia necropolis are bare; the only evidence of their original function is the stone platforms on which the sarcophagi rested. But the wall paintings are intriguing and in many cases quite beautiful. The visit takes about 90 minutes, and good explanations in English are posted outside each tomb. ✉ *Monterozzi, on the Strada Provinciale 1/b (Tarquinia–Viterbo),* ☎ *0766/856308; 06/9941098 for English-language tours.* 🎫 *€4.15, €6.20 including museum.* ⊙ *Tues.–Sun. 9 AM–1 hr before sunset.*

Dining and Lodging

$$$$ ✕🏠 **San Marco.** In a centuries-old former monastery across the square from the entrance to Tarquinia's archaeological museum, the restaurant caters to visitors who need sustenance after trudging through rooms of sarcophagi. The menu of classic Italian food is diversified with seasonal offerings, such as wild mushrooms. Tables are set outdoors in fair weather. The San Marco also has simple guest rooms ($$). ✉ *Piazza Cavour 18,* ☎ *0766/842234,* WEB *www.san marco.com. 16 rooms. Restaurant. AE, MC, V. Restaurant closed Tues.*

$$ ✕🏠 **Tarconte.** This modern hotel with wraparound windows is in a panoramic position just outside the center of town, about ½ km (¼ mi) south of the museum. It attracts business meetings and small conventions, but is also a haven for visitors who want to spend more than a day exploring Etruscan country. The hotel's Solengo Restaurant ($$$$) serves hearty pastas and *agnello scottadito* (grilled lamb chops), a local specialty. ✉ *Via della Tuscia 19,* ☎ *0766/856141. 53 rooms. Restaurant. AE, DC, MC, V.*

Cerveteri and Tarquinia A to Z

BUS TRAVEL
COTRAL buses leave for Cerveteri from the Lepanto stop of Metro A, with service every 40 minutes or so during the day. The ride takes about 70 minutes. Also from the Lepanto stop, COTRAL buses depart for Civitavecchia, where you have to change to another COTRAL bus to Tarquinia. The trip takes about two hours.
➤ BUS INFORMATION: **COTRAL** (✉ ☎ 800/431784).

CAR TRAVEL
For Cerveteri, take either the A12 Rome–Civitavecchia toll highway to the Cerveteri-Ladispoli exit, or take the Via Aurelia. The trip takes

about 40 minutes. To get to Tarquinia, take the A12 Rome–Civitavecchia highway all the way to the end, where you continue on the Via Aurelia to Tarquinia. The trip takes about one hour.

TRAIN TRAVEL

From Termini, Ostiense, and Trastevere stations in Rome, FS and Metropolitana suburban trains take you to the Cerveteri-Ladispoli station, where you can get a bus for Cerveteri. The train takes 30 minutes; the bus ride then takes 15 minutes. To get to Tarquinia, take an FS train (Rome–Genoa line) from Rome or from Cerveteri to the Tarquinia station, then a local bus from the station up to the hilltop town. The trip takes about 75 minutes.

➤ TRAIN INFORMATION: **Ferrovie dello Stato** (FS; ☎ 848/888088, WEB www.fs-on-line.com).

VISITOR INFORMATION

➤ TOURIST INFORMATION: **Tourist offices** (✉ Piazza del Castello, Cerveteri, ☎ 06/9941354; ✉ Piazza Cavour 1, Tarquinia, ☎ 0766/856384; WEB www.comune.tarquinia.vt.it).

VITERBO, BAGNAIA, CAPRAROLA, AND BOMARZO: WHERE POPES AND PRELATES TOOK THEIR EASE

The Viterbo region, north of the capital, is rich in history embodied in cameo scenes of dark medieval stone, dappled light on wooded paths, a prelate's palace worthy of Rome itself, and another prelate's pleasure garden, where splashing fountains were aquatic jokes played on unsuspecting guests. From Viterbo and Bagnaia to Caprarola and Villa Lante, this region has a concentration of first-rate attractions—with the surprising Renaissance theme park at Bomarzo thrown in for good measure. The city of Viterbo, which overshadowed Rome as a center of papal power for a time during the Middle Ages, lies in the heart of Tuscia, the modern name for the Etruscan domain of Etruria, a landscape of dramatic beauty punctuated by thickly forested hills and deep, rocky gorges. The farmland east of Viterbo conceals small quarries of the dark, volcanic *peperino* stone that shows up in the walls of so many buildings here, as well as in portals and monumental fireplaces. Lake Bolsena is an extinct volcano, and the sulfur springs still bubbling up in Viterbo's spas were used by the ancient Romans.

Bagnaia is the site of Villa Lante, where there are Italian gardens and a vast park; at Caprarola are the huge Renaissance palace and gardens designed for the Farnese family. Both were the work of the virtuoso architect Giacomo Barozzi (ca. 1535–ca. 1584), known as Vignola, who later worked with Michelangelo on St. Peter's. He rearranged the little town of Caprarola, too, to enhance the palazzo's setting.

The ideal way to explore this region is by car, making Bomarzo your first stop. By train, you can start at Viterbo and get to Bagnaia by local bus. If you're traveling by train and/or bus, you will have to check schedules carefully, and you may have to allow for an overnight if you want to see all four attractions.

Viterbo

㉑ *104 km (64 mi) north of Rome.*

Viterbo's moment of glory was in the 13th century, when it became the seat of the papal court. The medieval core of the city still nestles within 12th-century walls. Its old buildings, their windows bright with geraniums, are made of dark peperino, the local stone that colors the medieval part of Viterbo a dark gray, contrasted here and there with the golden tufa rock of walls and towers. Peperino is also used in the characteristic and typically medieval exterior staircases that you see throughout the old town. Viterbo's San Pellegrino district is a place to get the feel of the Middle Ages, seeing how daily life is carried on in a setting that has remained practically unchanged over the centuries. The Palazzo Papale and the cathedral enhance the effect. Since medieval times, the city has remained a renowned spa center for its natural hot springs just outside of town.

The Gothic **Palazzo Papale** (Papal Palace) was built in the 13th century as a residence for the popes who chose to sojourn here. At that time Rome was a notoriously unhealthy place, ridden with malaria and plague and rampaging factions of rival barons. In 1271 the palace was the scene of a novel type of rebellion. A conclave held here to elect a new pope had dragged on for months, apparently making no progress. The people of Viterbo were exasperated by the delay, especially as custom decreed that they had to provide for the cardinals' board and lodging for the duration of the conclave. So they tore the roof off the great hall where the cardinals were meeting, and put them on bread and water. Sure enough, a new pope—Gregory X—was elected in short order. The interior is not always open, but you can climb the stairs to what was once the loggia. ⊠ *Piazza San Lorenzo.*

The facade and interior of the cathedral, **Chiesa di San Lorenzo** (Church of St. Lawrence), date from the Middle Ages. On the ancient columns inside the church you can see the chips that an exploding bomb took out of the stone during World War II. ⊠ *Piazza San Lorenzo.*

The medieval district of **San Pellegrino** is one of the best preserved in Italy. It has charming vistas of arches, vaults, towers, exterior staircases, worn wooden doors on great iron hinges, and tiny hanging gardens. You pass many an antiques shop as you explore the little squares and byways. The **Fontana Grande** in the piazza of the same name is the largest and most extravagant of Viterbo's authentic Gothic fountains. ⊠ *Via San Pellegrino.*

Viterbo has been a spa town for centuries, and the **Terme dei Papi** continues the tradition. This excellent spa offers the usual rundown of health and beauty treatments with an Etruscan twist: try a facial with local volcanic mud, or a steam bath in an ancient cave, where scalding hot mineral water direct from the Bullicam spring splashes down a waterfall to a pool under your feet. The Terme dei Papi's main draw, however, is the *terme* (baths) themselves: a 100,000-square-ft **outdoor limestone pool** of Viterbo's famous hot water, which pours in at 59°C (138°F). Floats and deck chairs are for rent, but bring your own bathrobe or towel. ⊠ *Strada Bagni 12, Viterbo,* ☎ *0761/3501,* WEB *www.termedeipapi.it.* ⌚ *Weekdays €10.30; weekends €12.90.* ☉ *Pool daily 9–4:30, spa daily 9–5:30.*

Dining and Lodging

$$ ✕ **Enoteca La Torre.** Foodie paradise is found here, in a simple but elegant temple to good eating that's a real surprise so far off the beaten path. In addition to an ever-changing menu and a wine list cross-referenced with ratings from Italian wine guides, there are lists for cheeses, mineral waters, oils, and vinegars, the latter two from a stock kept in an old wooden chest in the front of the dining room. Chestnut fritters and rabbit stew are unusual delicacies, but rest assured that whatever you choose, it will be local, traditional, and of the highest quality. Next

door you can sample a reduced version of the restaurant menu at the casual La Cantina wine bar ($) or stop in for a wine-and-olive-oil tasting before dinner. ✉ *Via della Torre 5,* ☎ *0761/226467. AE, DC, MC, V. Closed Sun.*

$$$–$$$$ 🏨 **Hotel Niccolò V.** This peaceful, airy hotel attached to the spa at Terme
★   dei Papi would be a delight even without its views over the massive thermal pool that is its raison d'être. Marble baths and wooden floors give the quiet rooms an air of country-house elegance. Breakfast, a sumptuous buffet, is taken in an unusual wood-beamed gallery overlooking a small garden in back. Hotel guests are allowed free use of the pool and get a 15% discount on spa treatments. ✉ *Strada Bagni 12, 01100,* ☎ *0761/3501,* FAX *0761/352451,* WEB *www.terme.it. 20 rooms, 3 suites. Restaurant, bar, breakfast room, in-room safes, minibars, pool, meeting rooms. AE, DC, MC, V.*

Bagnaia

㉒   *5 km (3 mi) east of Viterbo.*

The village of Bagnaia, 5 km (3 mi) east of Viterbo, is the site of 16th-century cardinal Alessandro Montalto's summer retreat. Small twin residences are but an excuse for the hillside garden and park that surround them, designed by Vignola for a member of the papal court.

Villa Lante is a terraced extravaganza. On the lowest terrace a delightful Italian garden has a centerpiece fountain fed by water channeled down the hillside. On another, higher terrace a stream of water runs through a groove carved in a long stone table where the cardinal entertained his friends alfresco, chilling wine in the running water. And that is only one of the most evident and innocent of the whimsical water games that were devised for the cardinal. The symmetry of the formal gardens contrasts with the wild, untamed park adjacent to it, reflecting the paradoxes of nature and artifice that are the theme of this pleasure garden. ✉ *Via G. Barozzi 71.* ☎ *0761/288008.* 🎫 *€2.10.* ⊙ *Tues.– Sun. 9–1 hr before sunset.*

Caprarola

㉓   *19 km (12 mi) south of Viterbo.*

The wealthy and powerful Farnese family took over this sleepy village in the 1500s and endowed it with a palace that rivals the great residences of Rome.

The massive, magnificent, 400-year-old **Palazzo Farnese,** built on an unusual pentagonal plan, has an ingenious system of ramps and terraces designed by Vignola that leads right up to the main portal. This nicely allowed carriages and mounts to arrive directly in front of the door. Though the salons are unfurnished, the palace's grandeur is still manifest. An artificial grotto decorates one wall, the ceilings are covered with frescoes unabashedly glorifying the splendors of the Farnese family, and an entire room is frescoed with maps of the world as it was known to 16th-century cartographers. From the windows you can glimpse the Italian garden, which can be visited only by special permission. ✉ *Via Nicolai,* ☎ *0761/646052.* 🎫 *€2.10.* ⊙ *Tues.–Sun. 9– 1 hr before sunset.*

Bomarzo

㉔   *15 km (9 mi) east of Viterbo.*

☝ The eerie 16th-century **Parco dei Mostri** (Monster Park) is populated by weird and fantastic sculptures of mythical creatures and eccentric architecture. It was created by Prince Vicino Orsini for his wife, Giulia Farnese, who is said to have taken one look at the park and died of heart failure. No one really knows why the prince had the sculptures carved in outcroppings of stone in a dusky wood on his estate, but it probably has something to do with the artifices that were an artistic conceit of his time. Children love it, and there are photo ops galore. ⊠ *1½ km (1 mi) west of town.* 🎫 *€7.75.* ⊙ *Daily 8:30–1 hr before sunset.*

Viterbo, Bagnaia, Caprarola, and Bomarzo A to Z

BUS TRAVEL

COTRAL buses for Viterbo depart from the Saxa Rubra stop of the Ferrovie COTRAL train. The *diretta* (direct) bus takes about 75 minutes. Bagnaia can be reached from Viterbo by local city bus. For Caprarola, COTRAL buses leave from the Saxa Rubra station on the Roma Nord line.

➤ BUS INFORMATION: **COTRAL** (⊠ Piazzale Flaminio, ☎ 800/431784).

CAR TRAVEL

Head out of Rome on the A1 autostrada, exiting at Attigliano. Bomarzo is only 3 km (2 mi) from the autostrada. The trip takes one hour. It takes about 20 minutes to get to Viterbo from Bomarzo. Bagnaia, just east of Viterbo, can be visited before entering Viterbo. For Caprarola, head south on the Via Cimina; the ride takes 30 minutes.

TOURS

For Viterbo, authorized guides are available through the APT office (☞ Visitor Information, *below*).

TRAIN TRAVEL

The Rome–Viterbo train line should be operating by 2002 and will make travel between the two cities faster and easier. Trains will also stop at Bagnaia. For schedules and information, contact COTRAL.

➤ TRAIN INFORMATION: **COTRAL** (⊠ Piazzale Flaminio, ☎ 800/431784).

VISITOR INFORMATION

The Web site listed below has information on all the towns in the province of Viterbo.

➤ TOURIST INFORMATION: **APT Viterbo** (⊠ Piazza San Carluccio, ☎ 0761/304795, 🌐 www.provincia.vt.it/i_romea/index.htm).

TIVOLI, PALESTRINA, AND SUBIACO: FOUNTAINS, VILLAS, AND HERMITAGES

East of Rome are two of Lazio's star attractions—the Villa Adriana and the Villa d'Este in Tivoli—and, off the beaten path in the mountains beyond them, the lesser-known and wonderfully peaceful Palestrina and Subiaco. The road from Rome to Tivoli passes through some uninspiring industrial areas and burgeoning suburbs that used to be lush countryside. You'll know you're close to Tivoli when you see vast quarries of travertine marble and smell the sulfurous vapors of the little spa, Bagni di Tivoli. Both sites in Tivoli are outdoors and entail walking.

With a car, you can continue your loop through the mountains east of Rome, taking in two very different sights that are both focused on religion. The ancient pagan sanctuary at Palestrina is set on the slopes of Mt. Ginestro, from which it commands a sweeping view of the green plain and distant mountains. Subiaco, the cradle of Western monasticism, is tucked away in the mountains above Tivoli and Palestrina. Unless you start out very early and have lots of energy, plan an overnight stop along the way if you want to take in all three.

Tivoli

㉕ *36 km (22 mi) east of Rome.*

Villa Adriana (Hadrian's Villa), 6 km (4 mi) south of Tivoli, should be visited early, especially in summer, to take advantage of cool mornings. Hadrian's Villa was an emperor's theme park, an exclusive retreat where the marvels of the classical world were reproduced for a ruler's pleasure. Hadrian, who succeeded Trajan as emperor in AD 117, was a man of genius and intellectual curiosity. Fascinated by the accomplishments of the Hellenistic world, he decided to re-create it for his own enjoyment by building this villa over a vast tract of land below the ancient settlement of Tibur. From AD 118 to 130, architects, laborers, and artists worked on the villa, periodically spurred on by the emperor himself when he returned from another voyage full of ideas for even more daring constructions. After his death in AD 138, the fortunes of his villa declined. It was sacked by barbarians and Romans alike; many of his statues and decorations ended up in the Vatican Museums, but the expansive ruins are nonetheless compelling.

You should probably buy a map (€1.80) of the villa at the bookstore near the ticket office to help you make sense out of what can otherwise seem a maze of ruins. It's not the single elements but the peaceful and harmonious effect of the whole that makes Hadrian's Villa such a treat. Oleanders, pines, and cypresses growing among the ruins heighten the visual impact. A visit here should take about two hours, more if you like to savor antiquity slowly. After sunset on Friday a special one-hour tour under spotlights is available for €4.65. During the summer there's a sound-and-light show at night; check with your hotel concierge for the schedule. ⊠ *Bivio di Villa Adriana, off Via Tiburtina, 6 km (4 mi) southwest of Tivoli,* ☎ *06/39080739.* 🎫 *€4.15.* ⊙ *Daily 9 AM–90 mins before sunset.*

Villa d'Este, a late-Renaissance estate, is a playground of artistic whimsy, manifested in the 80-some fountains of all shapes and sizes that tumble down the vast, steep hillside garden. Cardinal Ippolito d'Este (1509–72), an active figure in the political intrigues of mid-16th-century Italy, set about proving his dominance over man and nature by commissioning this monument to architectural excess. His builders tore down part of a Franciscan monastery to clear the site, then diverted the Aniene River to water the garden and feed the fountains. History shows it was worth the effort—the Villa d'Este is still considered one of Italy's most beautiful spots. Tiny drinking fountains, massive reflecting pools, a fountain that once played music through organ pipes, and one that's a scale model of the great monuments of Rome show their years but are still a sight to see, and the green of the peaceful gardens is a pleasant break in summer. Allow an hour for this visit, and bear in mind that you'll be climbing a lot of stairs. In the summer the gardens and fountains are open at night. ⊠ *Piazza Trento 1,* ☎ *0774/312070.* 🎫 *€6.20.* ⊙ *Tues.–Sun. 9 AM–90 mins before sunset.*

Dining

$$$$ ✕ **Adriano.** At the entrance to Hadrian's Villa, this restaurant is a handy though pricey place to have lunch before heading up the hill to the Villa d'Este. The food is Italian with a gourmet touch, as in risotto *ai fiori di zucchine* (with zucchini flowers) or grilled porcini mushrooms in season. The atmosphere is relaxing. ✉ *Via di Villa Adriana 194,* ☎ *0774/ 382235. AE, DC, MC, V. No dinner Sun.*

$$ ✕ **Del Falcone.** A central location—on Tivoli's main street leading off Largo Garibaldi—means that this restaurant is popular and often crowded. In the ample and rustic dining rooms, you can try homemade fettuccine and cannelloni. Country-style grilled meats are excellent. ✉ *Via Trevio 34,* ☎ *0774/312358. AE, DC, MC, V.*

Palestrina

㉖ *27 km (17 mi) south of Tivoli on S636; 37 km (23 mi) east of Rome along Via Prenestina.*

Palestrina is surprisingly little known outside Italy, except to students of ancient history and music lovers. Its most famous native son, Giovanni Pierluigi da Palestrina, born here in 1525, was the renowned composer of 105 masses, as well as madrigals, magnificats, and motets. But the town was celebrated long before the composer's lifetime.

Ancient Praeneste (modern Palestrina) was founded much earlier than Rome. It was the site of the Temple of Fortuna Primigenia, which dates from the beginning of the 2nd century BC. This was one of the largest, richest, and most frequented temple complexes in all antiquity. People came from far and wide to consult its famous oracle. In modern times, however, no one had any idea of the extent of the complex until World War II bombings exposed ancient foundations that stretched far out into the plain below the town. It has since become clear that the temple area was larger than the town of Palestrina is today. Now you can make out the four superimposed terraces that formed the main part of the temple; they were built up on great arches and were linked by broad flights of stairs. The whole town sits on top of what was once the main part of the temple.

Large arches and terraces scale the hillside up to the **Palazzo Barberini,** built in the 17th century along the semicircular lines of the original temple. It's now a museum containing material found on the site, some dating from the 4th century BC. This splendid collection of Etruscan bronzes, pottery, and terra-cotta statuary as well as Roman artifacts takes second place to the chief attraction, a 1st-century BC mosaic representing the Nile in flood. This delightful work—a large-scale composition in which form, color, and innumerable details captivate the eye—is alone worth the trip to Palestrina. But there's more: a model of the temple as it was in ancient times, which will help you appreciate the immensity of the original construction. ✉ *Museo Nazionale Archeologico, Palazzo Barberini,* ☎ *06/9538100.* 🎫 *€2.05.* ⊘ *Daily 9–8; archaeological zone of the temple daily 9–1 hr before sunset.*

Dining and Lodging

$ ✕🏨 **Hotel Stella.** In the dining room ($$$) of this small, central hotel in Palestrina's public garden, you'll find simple decor, a cordial welcome, local dishes such as light and freshly made fettuccine served with a choice of sauces, and more unusual items such as *pasta e fagioli con frutti di mare* (pasta and bean soup with shellfish). The rooms are acceptable for an overnight. ✉ *Piazzale Liberazione, 3,* ☎ *06/9538172,* 🕸 *www.hotelstella.it. 28 rooms. AE, DC, MC, V.*

Subiaco

㉗ *54 km (33 mi) east of Rome.*

Tucked in among wooded mountains in the deep and narrow valley of the Aniene River, which empties into the Tiber in Rome, Subiaco is a modern town built over World War II rubble. It is chiefly important (aside from being the birthplace of Gina Lollobrigida, whose family name is common in these parts) as the site of the monastery where St. Benedict devised his rule of communal religious life in the 6th century, founding the order that was so important in transmitting learning through the ages. Even earlier, the place was a refuge of Nero, who built himself a villa here, said to have rivaled that of Hadrian at Tivoli, damming the river to create three lakes and a series of waterfalls. The road to the monastery passes the ruins of the emperor's villa.

Convento di Santa Scolastica (Convent of St. Scholastica), between the town of Subiaco and St. Benedict's hermitage on the mountainside, is the only one of the hermitages founded by St. Benedict to have survived the Lombard invasion of Italy in the 9th century. It has three cloisters; the oldest dates from the 13th century. The library, which is not open to visitors, contains some precious volumes; this was the site of the first print shop in Italy, set up in 1474. ⊠ *Road to Jenne and Vallepietra, 2½ km (1½ mi) east of Subiaco.* 🖼 *Free.* ☉ *Daily 9–12:30 and 4–7.*

The 6th-century **Monastero di San Benedetto** (Monastery of St. Benedict) is a landmark of Western monasticism. It was built over the grotto where the saint lived and meditated. Clinging to the cliff on nine great arches, it has resisted the assaults of humans for almost 800 years. Over the little wooden veranda at the entrance, a Latin inscription wishes PEACE TO THOSE WHO ENTER. Every inch of the upper church is covered with frescoes by Umbrian and Sienese artists of the 14th century. In front of the main altar, a stairway leads down to the lower church, carved out of the rock, with yet another stairway leading down to the grotto where Benedict lived as a hermit for three years. The frescoes here are even earlier than those above; look for the portrait of St. Francis of Assisi, painted from life in 1210, in the **Cappella di San Gregorio** (Chapel of St. Gregory), and for the oldest fresco in the monastery, in the **Grotta dei Pastori** (Shepherds' Grotto). ⊠ *Subiaco,* ☎ *0774/85039.* 🖼 *Free.* ☉ *Daily 9–12:30 and 3–6.*

Dining and Lodging

$$$ ✕ **Mariuccia.** This modern, barnlike restaurant close to the monasteries caters to wedding parties and other groups on weekends but is calm enough on weekdays. There's a large garden and a good view from the picture windows. House specialties are homemade fettuccine with porcini mushrooms and *scaloppe al tartufo* (truffled veal scallops). During the summer you can dine outdoors under bright umbrellas. ⊠ *Via Sublacense,* ☎ *0774/84851. MC, V. Closed Mon.*

$ ✕🖼 **Miramonte.** This small hotel and its restaurant, La Botte di Baccois ($$$), are on the road between Subiaco and the monasteries. The restaurant atmosphere is homey and cordial; specialties include homemade fettuccine with a tasty ragù sauce and grilled meats and sausages. Adequate for an overnight, the rooms are simply furnished. The restaurant is closed Tuesday. ⊠ *Viale Giovanni XXIII 4,* ☎ *0774/822843. 13 rooms, 1 suite. AE, DC, MC, V.*

Tivoli, Palestrina, and Subiaco A to Z

BUS TRAVEL

COTRAL buses serve the region. Buses leave Rome for Tivoli every 15 minutes from the terminal at the Ponte Mammolo stop on Metro B, but not all take the route that passes near Hadrian's Villa. Inquire which bus passes closest to the villa and tell the driver to let you off there. The ride takes about one hour. From Rome to Palestrina, take the COTRAL bus from the Anagnina stop on Metro A. Try to avoid buses that go on Via Casalina, as the trip takes much longer than on

Via Preneste. From Rome to Subiaco, take the COTRAL bus from the Rebibbia stop on Metro B; buses leave every 40 minutes; the circuitous trip takes one hour and 45 minutes. Bus service links Tivoli and Palestrina; check schedules locally.

➤ Bus Information: **COTRAL** (☎ 800/431784, toll-free).

CAR TRAVEL

For Tivoli, take Via Tiburtina or the Rome–L'Aquila autostrada (A24). To get to Palestrina directly from Rome, take either Via Prenestina or Via Casilina or take the Autostrada del Sole (A2) to the San Cesareo exit and follow signs for Palestrina; this trip takes about one hour. From Rome to Subiaco, take S155 east for about 40 km (25 mi) before turning left onto S411 for the remaining 25 km (15½ mi) to Subiaco; the trip takes about 70 minutes.

From Tivoli to Palestrina, follow signs for Via Prenestina and Palestrina. To get to Subiaco from either Tivoli or Palestrina, take the autostrada for L'Aquila (A24) to the Vicovaro-Mandela exit, then follow the local road to Subiaco.

TOURS

CIT has half-day excursions to Villa d'Este in Tivoli. American Express has tours to Hadrian's Villa. Appian Line has excursions to Hadrian's Villa. Carrani Tours has tours that include Hadrian's Villa.

➤ Fees and Schedules: **American Express** (☎ 06/67641). **Appian Line** (☎ 06/487861). **Carrani Tours** (☎ 06/4742501). **CIT** (☎ 06/478641).

TRAIN TRAVEL

FS trains connect Rome's Termini and Tiburtina stations with Tivoli in about 30 minutes; Villa d'Este is about a 20-minute uphill walk from the station at Tivoli. The FS train from Stazione Termini to Palestrina takes about 40 minutes; you can then board a bus from the train station to the center of town.

➤ Train Information: **Ferrovie dello Stato** (FS; ☎ 848/888088, WEB www.fs-on-line.com).

VISITOR INFORMATION

➤ Tourist Information: **Palestrina** (✉ Piazza Santa Maria degli Angeli, ☎ 06/9573176). **Subiaco** (✉ Via Cadorna 59, ☎ 0774/822013). **Tivoli** (✉ Largo Garibaldi, ☎ 0774/334522).

SERMONETA, NINFA, AND SPERLONGA: PICTURESQUE TOWNS AND ROMANTIC RUINS

A trio of romantic places south of Rome, set in a landscape defined by low mountains and a broad coastal plain, lure you into a past that seems centuries away from the city's bustle. Sermoneta is a castle town. Ninfa, nearby, is a noble family's fairy-tale garden that is open to the public only at certain times. Both are on the eastern fringe of the Pontine Plain, once a malaria-infested marshland that was ultimately reclaimed for agriculture by one of the most successful projects of Mussolini's regime. Several new towns were built here in the 1930s, among them Latina and Pontinia. Sperlonga is a medieval fishing village perched above the sea near one of emperor Tiberius's most fabulous villas. You really need a car to see them all in a day or so, and to get to Ninfa. But Sermoneta and Sperlonga are accessible by public transportation.

Sermoneta

28 *80 km (50 mi) southeast of Rome.*

In Sermoneta, the town and castle are one. Within concentric rings of walls, in medieval times, townspeople lived and farmers came to take shelter from marauders. The lords—in this case the Caetani family—held a last line of defense in the tall tower, where if necessary they could cut themselves off by pulling up the drawbridge.

The **Castello Caetani** (Caetani Castle) dates from the 1200s. In the 15th century, having won it by ruse from the Caetanis, Borgia Pope Alexander VI transformed it into a formidable fortress and handed it over to his son Cesare. The chiaroscuro of dark and light stone, the quiet of the narrow streets, and the bastions that hint at siege and battle take you back in time. ✉ *Via della Fortezza.* 🎟 *€2.60. Guided tours only.* ⏱ *Apr.–Oct., Fri.–Wed. 10–11, 3–4, and 5–6; Nov.–Mar., Fri.–Wed. 10–11:30, 2–3, and 4–5.*

Ninfa

29 *5 km (3 mi) north of Sermoneta.*

In the Middle Ages **Ninfa** was a thriving village, part of the Caetani family's vast landholdings around Sermoneta. It was abandoned when malaria-carrying mosquitoes infested the plain, and it fell into ruin. Now it is a place of rare beauty, a dream garden of romantic ruins and rushing waters, of exotic species and fragrant blooms. Ninfa is part of a World Wildlife Fund Oasis, managed in collaboration with the Caetani heirs. Preceding generations of the Caetani family, including English and American spouses and gardening buffs, created the garden over the course of the 20th century. ✉ *Via Ninfina, Doganella di Ninfa,* ☎ *0773/695407 (APT Latina-Provincial Tourist Office).* 🎟 *€6.20. Guided tours only.* ⏱ *Apr.–June, call for designated days; July–Sept., 1st weekend of month 9–noon and 2:30–6.*

Sperlonga

30 *127 km (79 mi) southeast of Rome.*

Sperlonga is a labyrinth of whitewashed alleys, arches, and little houses, like a casbah wrapped around a hilltop overlooking the sea, with broad, sandy beaches on either side. Long a favorite haunt of artists and artisans in flight from Rome's quick pace, the town has ancient origins. The medieval town gates, twisting alleys, and watchtower were vital to its defense when pirate ships came into sight. Now they simply make this former fishing town even more picturesque.

Under a cliff on the shore only 1 km (½ mi) south of Sperlonga are the ruins of a grandiose villa built for Roman emperor Tiberius and known as the **Grotta di Tiberio** (Grotto of Tiberius). The villa incorporated several natural grottoes, in one of which Tiberius dined with guests on an artificial island. The various courses were served on little boats that floated across the shallow seawater pool to the emperor's table. Showpieces of the villa were the colossal sculpture groups embellishing the grotto. The **Museo Nazionale** (National Museum) was built on the site especially to hold the fragments of these sculptures, discovered by chance by an amateur archaeologist. The huge statues had been smashed to pieces centuries earlier by Byzantine monks unsympathetic to pagan images. For decades the subject and appearance of the originals remained a mystery, and the museum was a work in progress as scholars there tried to put together the 7,000 pieces of this giant puzzle. Their achievement, the immense Scylla group, largest of the sculptures, is on view here. ⊠ *Via Flacca,* ☎ *0771/54028.* ☜ *€2.05.* ☉ *Mon.–Sat. 9–6, Sun. 9–8.*

Dining

$$–$$$ ✕ **Gli Archi.** Tucked into a landing of Old Sperlonga's myriad stairways, this attractive restaurant has brick-arch interiors and a courtyard for fair-weather dining. A touch of refinement puts it a cut above the establishments closer to the beach, and its owners take pride in serving high-quality ingredients with culinary simplicity. Seafood, including pasta with seafood sauces, predominates, but there are a few meat courses, too. ⊠ *Via Ottaviano 17,* ☎ *0771/54300. AE, DC, MC, V. Closed Wed. and Jan.*

$–$$ ✕ **La Bisaccia.** A favorite with locals, La Bisaccia is popular with seasonal residents, too. It is near the beach in the newer part of town, and you can walk to it in about 10–15 minutes from the center of Old Sperlonga. Book a table for lunch on weekends and in summer. Seafood comes just about any way you want it, from pasta with scampi to fried, baked, or grilled fish. And if you don't want fish, the menu has some basic meat dishes and a local specialty, creamy buffalo-milk mozzarella. ⊠ *Via Romita 19,* ☎ *0771/584576. AE, DC, MC, V. Closed Tues.*

Sermoneta, Ninfa, and Sperlonga A to Z

BUS TRAVEL

COTRAL buses for Sermoneta leave Rome from the EUR Fermi stop of Metro B. The ride takes about one hour. For Sperlonga, COTRAL buses leave from the same stop. The trip takes about 1½ hours.

➤ BUS INFORMATION: **COTRAL** (☎ 800/431784, toll-free).

CAR TRAVEL

The fastest route south is the Via Pontina, an expressway. An alternative is the Via Appia. For Sermoneta, turn east at Latina. The trip takes about 50 minutes. For out-of-the-way Ninfa, proceed as for Sermoneta, but before reaching Sermoneta, follow the signs for Doganella/Ninfa. An alternative is to follow the Via Appia to Cisterna and then look for signs for Doganella/Ninfa. The trip takes about one hour. For Sperlonga, take the Via Pontina to Latina, then the Via Appia to Terracina and Sperlonga. The trip takes about 1½ hours.

TRAIN TRAVEL

FS trains on the Rome–Formia–Naples line stop at Latina Scalo, where you can get a local bus to Sermoneta, though service is erratic. Traveling time is about one hour. For Sperlonga, on the same line, get off at the Itri station, from which buses leave for Sperlonga. The trip takes about 1½ hours.

➤ TRAIN INFORMATION: **Ferrovie dello Stato** (FS, ☎ 848/888088, WEB www.fs-on-line.com).

VISITOR INFORMATION

➤ TOURIST INFORMATION: **APT Latina** (⊠ Via Duca del Mare 19, Latina, ☎ 0773/695407, WEB www.aptlatinaturismo.it).

8 BASICS AND BACKGROUND

Smart Travel Tips A to Z

Map of Rome

Map of Italy

Portraits of Rome

Books and Videos

Chronology

Italian Vocabulary

ESSENTIAL INFORMATION

ADDRESSES

It's worth noting that the streets of Rome, even in the newer outskirts, are numbered erratically. Numbers can be even on one side of the street and odd on the other; sometimes numbers are in ascending consecutive order on one side of the street and descending order on the other.

AIR TRAVEL
TO AND FROM ROME

Price is just one factor to consider when booking a flight: frequency of service and even a carrier's safety record are often just as important. Major airlines offer the greatest number of departures. Smaller airlines—including regional and no-frills airlines—usually have a limited number of flights daily. On the other hand, so-called low-cost airlines usually are cheaper, and their fares impose fewer restrictions, such as advance-purchase requirements. In terms of safety, low-cost carriers as a group have a good history—about equal to that of major carriers.

BOOKING

When you book **look for nonstop flights** and **remember that "direct" flights stop at least once.** Try to avoid connecting flights, which require a change of plane. For more booking tips and to check prices and make on-line flight reservations, log on to www.fodors.com.

Two airlines may jointly operate a connecting flight, so ask if your airline operates every segment—you may find that your preferred carrier flies you only part of the way. International flights on a country's flag carrier are almost always nonstop; U.S. airlines often fly direct.

Ask your airline if it offers electronic ticketing, which eliminates all paperwork. There's no ticket to pick up or misplace. You go directly to the gate and give the agent your confirmation number. There's no worry about waiting on line at the airport while precious minutes tick by.

CARRIERS

When flying internationally, you must usually choose between a domestic carrier, the national flag carrier of the country you are visiting, and a foreign carrier from a third country. You may, for example, choose to fly Alitalia to Rome. National flag carriers have the greatest number of nonstops. Domestic carriers may have better connections to your hometown and serve a greater number of gateway cities. Third-party carriers may have a price advantage.

Charters usually have the lowest fares but are the least dependable. Departures are infrequent and seldom on time, and flights can be delayed for up to 48 hours or can be canceled for any reason up to 10 days before you're scheduled to leave. Itineraries and prices can change after you've booked your flight.

In the United States, the Department of Transportation's Aviation Consumer Protection Division has jurisdiction over charters and provides a certain degree of protection. The DOT requires that money paid to charter operators be held in escrow, so if you can't pay with a credit card, **always make your check payable to a charter carrier's escrow account.** The name of the bank should be in the charter contract. If you have any problems with a charter operator, contact the DOT (☞ Airline Complaints, *below*). If you buy a charter package that includes both air and land arrangements, remember that the escrow requirement applies only to the air component.

➤ MAJOR AIRLINES: **Alitalia** (☎ 800/ 223–5730). **Continental** (☎ 800/231–

0856). Delta (☎ 800/241–4141). Northwest (☎ 800/225–2525). US Airways (☎ 800/622–1015).

➤ FROM THE UNITED KINGDOM: Direct service from Heathrow is provided by **Alitalia** (☎ 08705/448–259 or 0870/5448–259) and **British Airways** (☎ 0845/773–3377). From Manchester there are at least three flights weekly to Rome.

➤ CHARTER CARRIERS: **Tower Air** (☎ 800/348–6937).

CHECK-IN & BOARDING

Assuming that not everyone with a ticket will show up, airlines routinely overbook planes. When everyone does, airlines ask for volunteers to give up their seats. In return, these volunteers usually get a certificate for a free flight and are rebooked on the next flight out. If there are not enough volunteers, the airline must choose who will be denied boarding. The first to get bumped are passengers who checked in late and those flying on discounted tickets, so **get to the gate and check in as early as possible,** especially during peak periods.

Always **bring a government-issued photo ID to the airport;** even when it's not required, a passport is best.

CUTTING COSTS

The least-expensive airfares to Rome are priced for round-trip travel and usually must be purchased in advance. It's smart to **call a number of airlines, and when you are quoted a good price, book it on the spot**—the same fare may not be available the next day. Airlines generally allow you to change your return date for a fee. If you don't use your ticket, you can apply the cost toward the purchase of a new ticket, again for a small charge. However, most low-fare tickets are nonrefundable. To get the lowest airfare, **check different routings.** Compare prices of flights to and from different airports if your destination or home city has more than one gateway. Also price off-peak flights, which may be significantly less expensive.

Travel agents, especially those who specialize in finding the lowest fares, can be especially helpful for booking a plane ticket. When you're quoted a price, **ask your agent if the price is likely to drop any lower.** Good agents know the seasonal fluctuations of airfares and can usually anticipate a sale or fare war. However, waiting can be risky: the fare could go *up* as seats become scarce, and you may wait so long that your preferred flight sells out. A wait-and-see strategy works best if your plans are flexible. If you must arrive and depart on certain dates, don't delay.

Consolidators are another good source. They buy tickets for scheduled international flights at reduced rates from the airlines, then sell them at prices that beat the best fare available directly from the airlines, usually without restrictions. Sometimes you can even get your money back if you need to return the ticket. Carefully read the fine print detailing penalties for changes and cancellations, and **confirm your consolidator reservation with the airline.**

➤ CONSOLIDATORS: **Cheap Tickets** (☎ 800/377–1000). **Discount Airline Ticket Service** (☎ 800/576–1600). **Unitravel** (☎ 800/325–2222). **Up & Away Travel** (☎ 212/889–2345). **World Travel Network** (☎ 800/409–6753).

ENJOYING THE FLIGHT

For more legroom, **request an emergency-aisle seat.** Don't sit in the row in front of the emergency aisle or in front of a bulkhead, where seats may not recline. If you have dietary concerns, **ask for special meals when booking.** These can be vegetarian, low-cholesterol, or kosher, for example. On long flights, try to maintain a normal routine, to help fight jet lag. At night, **get some sleep.** By day, **eat light meals, drink water** (not alcohol), and **move around the cabin** to stretch your legs. For additional jet-lag tips consult *Fodor's FYI: Travel Fit & Healthy* (available at bookstores everywhere).

Many carriers have prohibited smoking on all of their international flights; others allow smoking only on certain routes or certain departures, so **contact your carrier regarding its smoking policy.**

FLYING TIMES

Flying time to Rome is 7½–8½ hours from New York, 10–11 hours from Chicago, 12–13 hours from Los Angeles, and 2½ hours from London.

HOW TO COMPLAIN

If your baggage goes astray or your flight goes awry, complain right away. Most carriers require that you **file a claim immediately.**

➤ AIRLINE COMPLAINTS: U.S. Department of Transportation **Aviation Consumer Protection Division** (✉ C-75, Room 4107, Washington, DC 20590, ☎ 202/366–2220, WEB www.dot.gov/airconsumer). **Federal Aviation Administration Consumer Hotline** (☎ 800/322–7873).

RECONFIRMING

Although the trend on international flights is to drop reconfirmation requirements, many airlines still ask you to reconfirm each leg of your international itinerary. Failure to do so may result in your reservation's being canceled.

AIRPORTS & TRANSFERS

AIRPORTS

The principal airport for flights to Rome is **Leonardo da Vinci Airport,** commonly known by the name of its location, **Fiumicino.** It's 32 km (20 mi) southwest of the city, on the coast. It has been enlarged and equipped with computerized baggage handling and has a direct train link with downtown Rome. Rome's other airport is **Ciampino,** on Via Appia Nuova, 15 km (9 mi) south of downtown. Ciampino is a civil and military airport used by some international flights and most charter companies.

➤ AIRPORT INFORMATION: **Leonardo da Vinci Airport/Fiumicino** (☎ 06/65951). **Ciampino** (☎ 06/794941).

TRANSFERS BETWEEN FIUMICINO AND DOWNTOWN

When approaching by car, **follow the signs for Rome and the GRA** (the ring road that circles Rome). The direction you take on the GRA depends on where your hotel is located. If it is in the Via Veneto area, for instance, you would take the GRA in the direction of the Via Aurelia, turn off the GRA

onto the Via Aurelia, and follow it into Rome. **Get a map and directions** from the car-rental people at the airport.

A taxi ride from the airport to the center of Rome costs about €35, including supplements, and takes about 30–45 minutes depending on the traffic. Private limousines can be booked at booths in the Arrivals hall; they charge a little more than taxis but can carry more passengers. There is a taxi stand in front of the International Arrivals hall and a booth inside for taxi information. Use only licensed white or older yellow taxis. **Avoid gypsy drivers,** who may approach you in the arrivals hall; they charge exorbitant, unmetered rates.

Two trains link downtown Rome with Fiumicino: **inquire at the airport** (EPT tourist information counter in the International Arrivals hall or train information counter near the tracks) to determine which takes you closest to your destination in Rome. The 30-minute nonstop Airport-Termini express (marked FS and run by the state railway) goes directly to Track 22 at Termini Station, Rome's main train station, well served by taxis and hub of Metro and bus lines. Departures from the airport begin at 8 AM and run hourly, with the final departure at 8 PM. Hourly service from Termini Station to the airport begins at 7 AM and runs until 8 PM. Tickets cost €8.25. FM1, the other airport train, leaves from the same tracks and runs from the airport to Rome and beyond, serving commuters as well as air travelers. The main stops in Rome are at Trastevere (35 minutes), Ostiense (40 minutes), and Tiburtina (50 minutes); at each you can find taxis and bus and/or Metro connections to other parts of Rome. FM1 trains run from Fiumicino between 6:28 AM and 1:28 AM, with departures every 20 minutes, a little less frequently in off-hours; the schedule is similar going to the airport. Tickets cost €4.40. For either train, **buy your ticket at a vending machine** (you'll need to have euros on hand) **or at ticket counters** at the airport and at some stations (Termini Track 22, Trastevere, Tiburtina). At the airport, stamp the ticket at the gate. Remember when using the train at other stations to

stamp the ticket in the little yellow or red machine near the track before you board. During the night, **take COTRAL buses** from the airport to Tiburtina Station in Rome (45 minutes); they depart from in front of the International Arrivals hall at 1:15, 2:15, 3:30, and 5 AM. Buses leave Tiburtina Station for the airport at 2, 3, 4, and 5 AM. Tickets either way cost €3.60.

TRANSFERS BETWEEN CIAMPINO AND DOWNTOWN

By car, **go north on the Via Appia Nuova** into downtown Rome.

A taxi from Ciampino to the center of Rome can cost anywhere between €24 and €31, and the ride takes about 20 minutes. Make sure you choose a driver with an official-looking plate and avoid taking the first cab that approaches you.

A COTRAL bus connects the airport with the Anagnina Station of Metro line A, which takes you into the center of the city. Buses depart from in front of the airport terminal around 25 times a day between 6:50 AM and 11:40 PM. The fare is €1 and your ticket is also good for the Metro. Have change handy for the ticket machine, which is not always working. There is also a shop inside the terminal that can sell you a ticket, but it keeps erratic hours. If both purchasing options fail, board the bus and offer to pay the driver.

➤ TRANSFER CONTACTS: **COTRAL** (☎ 800/431784).**FS** (☎ 848/888088).

DUTY-FREE SHOPPING

As of July 1, 1999, duty-free sales were abolished between European Union countries, including Italy. But visitors traveling from a non-EU country to an EU country can still avail of the old duty-free privileges.

BIKE TRAVEL

This is a pleasant way to get around when traffic is light. But remember: Rome was built on seven hills and has since incorporated several more. Rental rates for standard bikes are about €2.50 for four hours to €15 or €20 for a full day.

There are rental concessions at the Metro stations at Piazza del Popolo and Piazza di Spagna, at Viale del Bambino on the Pincio, and at Viale della Pineta in Villa Borghese park.

➤ BIKE RENTALS: **Happy Rent** (⊠ Via Farini 3, ☎ 06/4818185). **I Bike Rome** (⊠ underground parking lot at Villa Borghese, Via del Galoppatoio 33, ☎ 06/3225240). **St. Peter Moto Rent** (⊠ Via di Porta Castello 43, ☎ 06/6875714 or 06/4885485; ⊠ Via Fosse di Castello 7, ☎ 06/6874909).

BIKES IN FLIGHT

Most airlines accommodate bikes as luggage, provided they are dismantled and boxed. Airlines sell bike boxes, which are often free at bike shops, for about $5 (it's at least $100 for bike bags). International travelers can sometimes substitute a bike for a piece of checked luggage at no charge; otherwise, the cost is about $100. Domestic and Canadian airlines charge $25–$50.

BUS & TRAM TRAVEL

Rome's integrated Metrebus transportation system includes buses and trams (ATAC), Metro (subway) and suburban trains and buses (COTRAL), and some other suburban trains (FS) run by the state railways. A ticket (BIT) valid for 75 minutes on any combination of buses and trams and one entrance to the Metro costs €0.75. Regular buses and trams run from 5:30 AM to midnight, plus there's an extensive network of night buses throughout the city. Time-stamp your ticket when boarding the first vehicle, stamping it again when boarding for the last time within 75 minutes. You **stamp the ticket** at Metro turnstiles and in the little machines near the stops for buses and trams. Tickets are sold at tobacconists, newsstands, some coffee bars, automatic ticket machines in Metro stations, some bus stops, and ATAC and COTRAL ticket booths (in some Metro stations and at a few main bus stops). You can buy them singly or in quantity; it's always a good idea to **have a few tickets handy** so you don't have to hunt for a vendor when you need one. A BIRG tourist ticket, valid for one day (only for the day it is stamped, not 24 hours) on all public transport, costs €3. A weekly ticket (*settimanale*, also known as CIS) costs €12.50 and can be purchased only at ATAC and

COTRAL booths—there's an ATAC kiosk at the bus terminus in front of Termini station.

If you're going farther afield, or planning to spend more than a week in Rome, think about getting a BIRG ticket from the railway station. A €7.75 ticket gives you unlimited travel all day on all state transport throughout the region of Lazio. This can take you as far as the Etruscan city of Tarquinia or medieval Viterbo. There are also weekly versions of the ticket.

Not as fast as the Metro, bus travel is more scenic. With reserved bus lanes and new tram lines, surface transportation has improved considerably in recent years, though it is still crowded during rush hours. Orange, gray-and-red, or blue-and-orange **ATAC** city buses and trams run from about 5:30 AM to midnight, with skeleton *notturno* (night) services on main lines through the night. Remember to board at the rear and to exit at the middle; you must **buy your ticket before boarding, and stamp it in a machine as soon as you enter.** If you find the bus too crowded to get to the ticket machine, manually cancel the ticket by writing on it the date and time you got on. The ticket is good for a transfer within the next 75 minutes.

There is no central bus terminal in Rome. Long-distance and suburban COTRAL bus routes terminate either near Tiburtina Station or at outlying Metro stops, such as Rebibbia and Ponte Mammolo (line B) and Anagnina (line A).

Also see Subway Travel, *below.*

➤ INFORMATION: **ATAC** urban buses (☎ 06/46951). **COTRAL & ATAC** (☎ 800/431784).

SMOKING

Smoking is not permitted on Rome buses, trams, or subway trains. There are smoking cars on aboveground trains.

BUS TRAVEL TO AND FROM ROME

An extensive network of bus lines that cover all of Lazio is operated by CO-TRAL (Consorzio Trasporti Lazio). There are several main bus stations from which departures and arrivals are made, depending upon where you want to go. Fares are reasonable, especially with the introduction of the day ticket called a BIRG (Biglietto Integrale Regionale Giornali), which allows you to travel on all of the lines (and some railroad lines) for a 24-hour period from the time of the ticket's first validation. The cost of a BIRG depends upon the distance to your destination. Because of the size and complexity of the system, it's a good idea to consult with your hotel concierge or telephone COTRAL central office when planning a trip.

➤ BUS INFORMATION: **COTRAL** (☎ 800/431784).

BUSINESS HOURS

BANKS & OFFICES

Banks are open weekdays 8:30–1:30 and 2:45–3:45 or 3–4. Exchange offices are open all day, usually 8:30–8.

Post offices are open Monday–Saturday 8–2; central and main district post offices stay open until 8 or 9 PM on weekdays for some operations. You can buy stamps at tobacconists.

GAS STATIONS

Only a few gas stations are open on Sunday, and most close for a couple of hours at lunchtime and at 7 PM for the night. Many, however, have self-service pumps that are operational 24 hours a day, and gas stations on autostrade are open 24 hours.

MUSEUMS & SIGHTS

Museum hours vary and may change with the seasons. Many important national museums are closed one day a week, often on Monday. The Roman Forum, other sites, and some museums may be open until late in the evening during the summer. **Always check locally.**

Most churches are open from early morning until noon or 12:30, when they close for two hours or more; they open again in the afternoon, generally around 4 PM, closing about 7 PM or later. Major cathedrals and basilicas, such as the Basilica di San Pietro, are open all day. Note that sightseeing in churches during religious rites is usually discouraged. Be sure to **have a fistful of coins handy** for the *luce* (light) machines that illuminate the works of art in the perpetual dusk of ecclesiastical interiors. A pair of binoculars will help you get a good look at painted ceilings and domes.

A tip for pilgrims and tourists keen to get a glimpse of the pope: avoid the weekly general audience on Wednesday morning in Piazza di San Pietro, and **go to his Sunday angelus instead.** This midday prayer service tends to be far less crowded (unless beatifications or canonizations are taking place) and is also mercifully shorter, which makes a difference when you're standing.

PHARMACIES

Most pharmacies are open Monday–Saturday 8:30–1 and 4–8; some are open all night. A schedule posted outside each pharmacy indicates the nearest pharmacy open during off-hours (afternoons, through the night, and Sunday).

SHOPS

Shop hours are flexible, and many shops in downtown Rome are open all day during the week and also on Sunday, as are some department stores and supermarkets. Alternating city neighborhoods also have general once-a-month Sunday opening days. Otherwise, most shops throughout the city are closed on Sunday. Shops that take a lengthy lunch break are open 9:30–1 and 3:30 or 4–7 or 7:30. All shops close for one half day during the week, Monday morning in winter and Saturday afternoon in summer.

Food shops are open 8–2 and 5–7:30, some until 8, and most are closed on Sunday. They also close for one half day during the week, usually Thursday afternoon from September to June and Saturday afternoon in July and August.

Traditionally the worst days to arrive in Rome, or do anything that hasn't been preplanned, are May 1 (Labor Day) and Christmas Day. Until very recently there was no transport whatsoever on Labor Day, and certainly no food shops open. Practices have changed a little in the last few years, but you may still expect to find many shops and businesses closed, and only a skeleton transport system working. New Year's Day is also problematic, as is Easter Sunday.

Barbers and hairdressers, with some exceptions, are closed Sunday and Monday.

CAMERAS & PHOTOGRAPHY

The *Kodak Guide to Shooting Great Travel Pictures* (available at bookstores everywhere) is loaded with tips.

➤ PHOTO HELP: **Kodak Information Center** (☎ 800/242–2424).

EQUIPMENT PRECAUTIONS

Don't pack film and equipment in checked luggage, where it is much more susceptible to damage. X-ray machines used to view checked luggage are becoming much more powerful and therefore are much more likely to ruin your film. Always **keep film and tape out of the sun.** Carry an extra supply of batteries, and **be prepared to turn on your camera or camcorder** to prove to security personnel that the device is real. Always **ask for hand inspection of film,** which becomes clouded after repeated exposure to airport X-ray machines, and **keep videotapes away from metal detectors.**

FILM & DEVELOPING

All types of film for common use is readily available throughout the city. A roll of 35 mm film costs €2.60 to €3.60, depending on the speed. One-hour photo developers are common in the city center and around the Vatican; they charge around €6.20 for a 24-exposure roll of 35 mm print film.

VIDEOS

The European norm for videotape is PAL, and unless you have a special machine you will not be able to play videos bought in Italy back in the States. So **bring your own videotapes from home.**

CAR RENTAL

Rates in Rome begin at around $70 a day and $210 a week for an economy car with air-conditioning, a manual transmission, and unlimited mileage. This includes the 20% tax on car rentals. Note that Italian legislation now permits certain rental wholesalers, such as Auto Europe, to drop the VAT.

➤ MAJOR AGENCIES: **Alamo** (☎ 800/522–9696; 020/8759–6200 in the U.K.,

WEB www.alamo.com). **Avis** (☎ 800/ 331–1084; 800/879–2847 in Canada; 02/9353–9000 in Australia; 09/525– 1982 in New Zealand; 0870/606– 0100 in the U.K.; WEB www.avis.com). **Budget** (☎ 800/527–0700; 0870/ 156–5656 in the U.K.; WEB www. budget.com). **Dollar** (☎ 800/800– 6000; 0124/622–0111 in the U.K., where it's affiliated with Sixt; 02/ 9223–1444 in Australia; WEB www. dollar.com). **Hertz** (☎ 800/654–3001; 800/263–0600 in Canada; 020/8897– 2072 in the U.K.; 02/9669–2444 in Australia; 09/256–8690 in New Zealand; WEB www.hertz.com) **National Car Rental** (☎ 800/227–7368; 020/ 8680–4800 in the U.K.; WEB www. nationalcar.com).

CUTTING COSTS

To get the best deal, **book through a travel agent, who will shop around.**

Also **ask your travel agent about a company's customer-service record.** How has the company responded to late plane arrivals and vehicle mishaps? Are there often lines at the rental counter? If you're traveling during a holiday period, does a confirmed reservation guarantee you a car?

Do **look into wholesalers,** companies that do not own fleets but rent in bulk from those that do and often offer better rates than traditional car-rental operations. Payment must be made before you leave home.

➤ WHOLESALERS: **Auto Europe** (☎ 207/ 842–2000 or 800/223–5555, FAX 207/ 842–2222, WEB www.autoeurope.com). **DER Travel Services** (✉ 9501 W. Devon Ave., Rosemont, IL 60018, ☎ 800/782–2424, FAX 800/282–7474 for information, 800/860–9944 for brochures, WEB www.dertravel.com). **Europe by Car** (☎ 212/581–3040 or 800/223–1516, FAX 212/246–1458, WEB www.europebycar.com). **Kemwel Holiday Autos** (☎ 800/678–0678, FAX 914/825–3160, WEB www. kemwel.com).

INSURANCE

When driving a rented car you are generally responsible for any damage to or loss of the vehicle. Before you rent, see what coverage your personal auto-insurance policy and credit cards provide.

Before you buy collision coverage, check your existing policies—you may already be covered. However, collision policies that car-rental companies sell for European rentals usually do not include stolen-vehicle coverage. Note that in Italy, all car-rental companies make you buy theft-protection policies.

REQUIREMENTS & RESTRICTIONS

In Italy your own driver's license is acceptable. An International Driver's Permit is a good idea; it's available from the American or Canadian Automobile Association and, in the United Kingdom, from the Automobile Association or Royal Automobile Club. These international permits are universally recognized, and having one in your wallet may save you a problem with the local authorities.

SURCHARGES

Before you pick up a car in one city and leave it in another, **ask about drop-off charges or one-way service fees,** which can be substantial. Note, too, that some rental agencies charge extra if you return the car before the time specified in your contract. To avoid a hefty refueling fee, **fill the tank just before you turn in the car,** but be aware that gas stations near the rental outlet may overcharge.

CAR TRAVEL

EMERGENCY SERVICES

Major rental agencies often provide roadside assistance, so **check your rental agreement** if a problem arises. Also, ACI (Auto Club of Italy) Emergency Service offers 24-hour road service. **Dial 116 from any phone,** 24 hours a day, to reach the nearest ACI service station.

➤ BREAKDOWNS: **ACI Emergency Service** (✉ Servizio Soccorso Stradale, Via Solferino 32, 00185 Rome, ☎ 116; 06/44595 or 06/441060).

GASOLINE

Only a few gas stations are open on Sunday, and most close for a couple of hours at lunchtime and at 7 PM for the night. Many, however, have self-service pumps (accepting currency, not credit cards) that are operational

24 hours a day. Gas stations on autostrade are open 24 hours. Gas can cost up to €1.30 per liter.

PARKING

Parking space is at a premium. Parking in an area signposted ZONA DISCO is allowed for limited periods (from 30 minutes to two hours or more—the limit is posted); if you don't have the cardboard disk to show what time you parked, you can use a piece of paper. The *parcometro*, the Italian version of metered parking, has been introduced in Rome. It's advisable to **leave your car only in guarded parking areas.** Unofficial parking attendants can help you find a space but offer no guarantees. Your car may be towed away if illegally parked.

ROAD CONDITIONS

Italians drive fast and are impatient with those who don't, a tendency that can make driving on the congested streets of Rome a hair-raising experience. Traffic is heaviest in morning and late-afternoon commuter hours, and on weekends. Watch out for mopeds.

RULES OF THE ROAD

Driving is on the right, as in the United States. Regulations are largely as in Britain and the United States, except that the police have the power to levy on-the-spot fines. The use of horns is forbidden in most areas; a large sign, ZONA DI SILENZIO, indicates where. Speed limits are 130 kph (80 mph) on autostrade and 110 kph (70 mph) on state and provincial roads, unless otherwise marked. Fines for driving after drinking are heavy, with the additional possibility of six months' imprisonment.

CHILDREN IN ROME

Although Italians love children and are generally very tolerant and patient with them, they provide few amenities for them. Discounts do exist. Always ask about a *sconto bambino* (child's discount) before purchasing tickets. Children under a certain height ride free on municipal buses and trams. Children under 18 who are EU citizens are admitted free to state-run museums and galleries, and there are similar privileges in many municipal or private museums. Discounts on concert tickets may be available for young people with student ID.

Be sure to plan ahead and **involve your youngsters** as you outline your trip. When packing, include things to keep them busy en route. On sightseeing days try to schedule activities of special interest to your children.

Fodor's Around Rome with Kids (available in bookstores everywhere) can help you plan your days together.

If you are renting a car, don't forget to **arrange for a car seat** when you reserve. For general advice about traveling with children, consult *Fodor's FYI: Travel with Your Baby*, available in bookstores everywhere.

➤ VACATION PACKAGES WITH CHILDREN: **Grandtravel** (✉ 6900 Wisconsin Ave., Suite 706, Chevy Chase, MD 20815, ☎ 301/986–0790 or 800/247–7651) for people traveling with grandchildren ages 7–17. **Rascals in Paradise** (✉ 650 5th St., Suite 505, San Francisco, California 94107, ☎ 800/U–RASCAL or 415/978–9800, ⨳ 415/442–0289). **Young Family Travelers** (✉ 235 Wanaque Ave., Suite 201, Pompton Lakes, NJ 07442, ☎ 888/968–6432, ⨳ 973/616–4654).

FLYING

If your children are two or older, **ask about children's airfares.** As a general rule, infants under two not occupying a seat fly at greatly reduced fares or even for free. When booking, **confirm carry-on allowances** if you're traveling with infants. In general, for babies charged 10% of the adult fare you are allowed one carry-on bag and a collapsible stroller; if the flight is full, the stroller may have to be checked or you may be limited to less.

Experts agree that it's a good idea to use safety seats aloft for children weighing less than 40 pounds. Airlines set their own policies: U.S. carriers usually require that the child be ticketed, even if he or she is young enough to ride free, since the seats must be strapped into regular seats. Do **check your airline's policy about using safety seats during takeoff and landing.** And since safety seats are not allowed everywhere in the plane, get your seat assignments early.

When reserving, **request children's meals or a freestanding bassinet** if you need them. But note that bulkhead seats, where you must sit to use the bassinet, may lack an overhead bin or storage space on the floor.

FOOD

In restaurants and trattorias you may find a high chair or a cushion for the child to sit on, but rarely do they offer a children's menu. **Order a *mezza porzione*** (half portion) of any dish, or **ask the waiter for a *porzione da bambino*** (child's portion).

LODGING

Most hotels in Rome allow children under a certain age to stay in their parents' room at no extra charge, but others charge for them as extra adults; be sure to **find out the cutoff age for children's discounts.**

SIGHTS & ATTRACTIONS

Places that are especially appealing to children are indicated by a rubber-duckie icon (🐤) in the margin throughout this book.

COMPUTERS ON THE ROAD

Getting on-line in Rome isn't difficult: public Internet stations and Internet cafés, some open 24 hours a day, are becoming more and more common. Prices differ from place to place, so **spend some time to find the best deal.** This isn't always readily apparent: a place might have higher rates, but because it belongs to a chain you won't be charged an initial flat fee again when you go to a different location of the same chain. Some hotels have in-room modem lines, but, as with phones, using the hotel's line is relatively expensive. Always check modem rates before plugging in. You may need an adapter for your computer for the European-style plugs. As always, if you are traveling with a laptop, carry a spare battery and an adapter. Never plug in your computer into any socket before asking about surge protection. IBM sells a pea-size modem tester that plugs into a telephone jack to check if the line is safe to use.

➤ INTERNET CAFÉS: **Bibli Bookshop** (✉ Via dei Fienarole 27/8, ☎ 06/5884097 or 06/5814534). **Internet Café** (✉ Via Marruccini 12, ☎ 06/4454953).

Internet Centre (✉ Via delle Fosse di Castello 8, ☎ 06/6861464). **The Netgate** (✉ Via in Arcione 103, near Fontana di Trevi, ☎ 06/69922320; ✉ Borgo Santo Spirito 17, near the Vatican, ☎ 06/6893445).

CONCIERGES

Concierges, found in many hotels, can help you with theater tickets and dinner reservations: a good one with connections may be able to get you seats for a hot show or prime-time dinner reservations at the restaurant of the moment. You can also turn to your hotel's concierge for help with travel arrangements, sightseeing plans, services ranging from aromatherapy to zipper repair, and emergencies. Always, **always tip** a concierge who has been of assistance (☞ Tipping, *below*).

CONSUMER PROTECTION

Whenever shopping or buying travel services in Rome, **pay with a major credit card**, if possible, so you can cancel payment or get reimbursed if there's a problem. If you're doing business with a particular company for the first time, **contact your local Better Business Bureau and the attorney general's offices** in your state and (for U.S. businesses) the company's home state as well. Have any complaints been filed? Finally, if you're buying a package or tour, always **consider travel insurance** that includes default coverage (☞ Insurance, *below*).

➤ BBBs: **Council of Better Business Bureaus** (✉ 4200 Wilson Blvd., Suite 800, Arlington, VA 22203, ☎ 703/276–0100, FAX 703/525–8277, WEB www.bbb.org).

CUSTOMS & DUTIES

When shopping, **keep receipts** for all purchases. Upon reentering the country, **be ready to show customs officials what you've bought.** If you feel a duty is incorrect or object to the way your clearance was handled, note the inspector's badge number and ask to see a supervisor. If the problem isn't resolved, write to the appropriate authorities, beginning with the port director at your point of entry.

IN AUSTRALIA

Australian residents who are 18 or older may bring home $A400 worth of souvenirs and gifts (including jewelry), 250 cigarettes or 250 grams of tobacco, and 1,125 ml of alcohol (including wine, beer, and spirits). Residents under 18 may bring back $A200 worth of goods. Prohibited items include meat products. Seeds, plants, and fruits need to be declared upon arrival.

➤ INFORMATION: **Australian Customs Service** (Regional Director, ✉ Box 8, Sydney, NSW 2001, Australia, ☎ 02/9213–2000, FAX 02/9213–4000, WEB www.customs.gov.au).

IN CANADA

Canadian residents who have been out of Canada for at least seven days may bring home C$750 worth of goods duty-free. If you've been away fewer than seven days but more than 48 hours, the duty-free allowance drops to C$200; if your trip lasts 24–48 hours, the allowance is C$50. You may not pool allowances with family members. Goods claimed under the C$750 exemption may follow you by mail; those claimed under the lesser exemptions must accompany you. Alcohol and tobacco products may be included in the seven-day and 48-hour exemptions but not in the 24-hour exemption. If you meet the age requirements of the province or territory through which you reenter Canada, you may bring in, duty-free, 1.14 liters (40 imperial ounces) of wine or liquor or 24 12-ounce cans or bottles of beer or ale. If you are 19 or older you may bring in, duty-free, 200 cigarettes and 50 cigars. Check ahead of time with the Canada Customs Revenue Agency or the Department of Agriculture for policies regarding meat products, seeds, plants, and fruits.

You may send an unlimited number of gifts worth up to C$60 each duty-free to Canada. Label the package UNSOLICITED GIFT—VALUE UNDER $60. Alcohol and tobacco are excluded.

➤ INFORMATION: **Canada Customs Revenue Agency** (✉ 2265 St. Laurent Blvd. S, Ottawa, Ontario K1G 4K3, Canada, ☎ 204/983–3500 or 506/636–5064; 800/461–9999 in Canada, WEB www.ccra-adrc.gc.ca).

IN ITALY

Of goods obtained anywhere outside the EU or goods purchased in a duty-free shop within an EU country, the allowances are as follows: (1) 200 cigarettes or 100 cigarillos or 50 cigars or 250 grams of tobacco; (2) 2 liters of still table wine or 1 liter of spirits over 22% volume or 2 liters of spirits under 22% volume or 2 liters of fortified and sparkling wines; and (3) 50 ml of perfume and 250 ml of toilet water.

Of goods obtained (duty and tax paid) within another EU country, the allowances are as follows: (1) 800 cigarettes or 400 cigarillos or 400 cigars or 1 kilogram of tobacco; (2) 90 liters of still table wine plus (3) 10 liters of spirits over 22% volume plus 20 liters of spirits under 22% volume plus 60 liters of sparkling wines plus 110 liters of beer.

➤ INFORMATION: **Italian Customs, Fumicino Airport** (Circoscrizione Dogonale Roma 2, ☎ 06/65011555). **Italian Customs, Rome** (Circoscrizione Dogonale Roma 1, ✉ Via Scalo San Lorenzo, 8, ☎ 06/448871).

IN NEW ZEALAND

Homeward-bound residents 17 or older may bring back $700 worth of souvenirs and gifts. Your duty-free allowance also includes 4.5 liters of wine or beer; one 1,125-ml bottle of spirits; and either 200 cigarettes, 250 grams of tobacco, 50 cigars, or a combination of the three up to 250 grams. Prohibited items include meat products, seeds, plants, and fruits.

➤ INFORMATION: **New Zealand Customs** (Custom House, ✉ 50 Anzac Ave., Box 29, Auckland, New Zealand, ☎ 09/300–5399, FAX 09/359–6730, WEB www.customs.govt.nz).

IN THE U.K.

If you are a U.K. resident and your journey was wholly within the European Union (EU), you won't have to pass through customs when you return to the United Kingdom. If you plan to bring back large quantities of alcohol or tobacco, check EU limits beforehand.

➤ INFORMATION: **HM Customs and Excise** (✉ St. Christopher House, Southwark, London SE1 0TE, U.K.,

☎ 020/7928–3344, WEB www.hmce.
gov.uk).

IN THE U.S.

U.S. residents who have been out of
the country for at least 48 hours (and
who have not used the $400 allow-
ance or any part of it in the past 30
days) may bring home $400 worth
of foreign goods duty-free.

U.S. residents 21 and older may bring
back 1 liter of alcohol duty-free. In
addition, regardless of your age, you
are allowed 200 cigarettes and 100
non-Cuban cigars. Antiques, which
the U.S. Customs Service defines as
objects more than 100 years old,
enter duty-free, as do original works
of art done entirely by hand, including paintings, drawings, and
sculptures.

You may also mail or ship packages
home duty-free: up to $200 worth of
goods for personal use, with a limit
of one parcel per addressee per day
(except alcohol or tobacco products
or perfume worth more than $5);
label the package PERSONAL USE and
attach a list of its contents and their
retail value. Do not label the package
UNSOLICITED GIFT or your duty-free
exemption will drop to $100. Mailed
items do not affect your duty-free
allowance on your return.

➤ INFORMATION: **U.S. Customs Service**
(✉ 1300 Pennsylvania Ave. NW, Room
6.3D, Washington, DC 20229, WEB www.
customs.gov; inquiries ☎ 202/
354–1000; complaints c/o ✉ 1300
Pennsylvania Ave. NW, Room 5.4D,
Washington, DC 20229; registration
of equipment c/o Office of Passenger
Programs, ☎ 202/927–0530).

DINING

The restaurants we list are the cream
of the crop in each price category.
Properties indicated by an ✕☷ are
lodging establishments whose restaurant warrants a special trip.

MEALTIMES

Unless otherwise noted, the restaurants listed in this guide are open
daily for lunch and dinner.

PAYING

In most Roman restaurants, the *conto*
(bill) will not be brought until you

ask for it. Though the *pane e coperto*
(bread and cover charge) has been officially eliminated, many restaurants
still charge extra for bread. Unless
otherwise written on the menu, *servizio* (service) is included, so **don't
pay for service twice.** Locals customarily reward particularly good service
with a few euros per person.

RESERVATIONS & DRESS

Reservations are always a good idea:
we mention them only when they're
essential or not accepted. Book as far
ahead as you can, and reconfirm as
soon as you arrive. We mention dress
only when men are required to wear
a jacket or a jacket and tie.

DISABILITIES & ACCESSIBILITY

ACCESS IN ROME

Italy has only recently begun to provide facilities such as ramps, telephones, and rest rooms for people
with disabilities; such things are still
the exception, not the rule. Travelers'
wheelchairs must be transported free
of charge, according to Italian law, but
the logistics of getting a wheelchair on
and off trains and buses can make this
requirement irrelevant. High, narrow
steps for boarding trains create problems. Seats are reserved for people
with disabilities on public transportation, but few buses have lifts for
wheelchairs. Rome's newer gray-and-
red city buses are equipped for easy
boarding and securing of wheelchairs.
In many monuments and museums,
even in some hotels and restaurants,
architectural barriers make it difficult,
if not impossible, for people with
disabilities to gain access. In Rome,
however, the Basilica di San Pietro, the
Cappella Sistina, and the Musei Vaticani are all accessible by wheelchair.
The terminals of the Fiumicino Airport–Rome Ostiense rail connection
have elevators for wheelchairs.

Throughout Rome parking spaces
near major monuments and public
buildings are reserved for cars transporting people with disabilities. The
narrow streets of the city's center,
parked cars hugging the buildings, the
lack of sidewalks, and uneven cobblestone pavement add up to hard going.

Bringing a Seeing Eye dog into Italy
requires an import license, a current

certificate detailing the dog's inoculations, and a letter from your veterinarian certifying the dog's health. Contact the nearest Italian consulate for particulars.

The Italian Government Tourist Board (ENIT) can provide a list of accessible hotels and the addresses of Italian associations for travelers with disabilities.

➤ LOCAL RESOURCES: **Italian Government Tourist Board** (ENIT; ✉ 630 5th Ave., New York, NY 10111, ☎ 212/245–4822, FAX 212/586–9249; see *Visitor Information*, below, *for a list of other ENIT locations*).

RESERVATIONS

When discussing accessibility with an operator or reservations agent, **ask hard questions.** Are there any stairs, inside *or* out? Are there grab bars next to the toilet *and* in the shower/tub? How wide is the doorway to the room? To the bathroom? For the most extensive facilities meeting the latest legal specifications, **opt for newer accommodations.**

➤ COMPLAINTS: **Aviation Consumer Protection Division** (☞ Air Travel to & from Rome, *above*) for airline-related problems. **Civil Rights Office** (✉ U.S. Department of Transportation, Departmental Office of Civil Rights, S-30, 400 7th St. SW, Room 10215, Washington, DC 20590, ☎ 202/366–4648, FAX 202/366–9371, WEB www.dot.gov/ost/docr/index.htm) for problems with surface transportation. **Disability Rights Section** (✉ U.S. Department of Justice, Civil Rights Division, Box 66738, Washington, DC 20035-6738, ☎ 202/514–0301 or 800/514–0301; 202/514–0383 TTY; 800/514–0383 TTY, FAX 202/307–1198, WEB www.usdoj.gov/crt/ada/adahom1.htm) for general complaints.

TRAVEL AGENCIES

In the United States, the Americans with Disabilities Act requires that travel firms serve the needs of all travelers. Some agencies specialize in working with people with disabilities.

➤ TRAVELERS WITH MOBILITY PROBLEMS: **Access Adventures** (✉ 206 Chestnut Ridge Rd., Scottsville, NY 14624, ☎ 716/889–9096,

dltravel@prodigy.net), run by a former physical-rehabilitation counselor. **CareVacations** (✉ No. 5, 5110–50 Ave., Leduc, Alberta T9E 6V4, Canada, ☎ 780/986–6404 or 877/478–7827, FAX 780/986–8332, WEB www.carevacations.com), for group tours and cruise vacations. **Flying Wheels Travel** (✉ 143 W. Bridge St., Box 382, Owatonna, MN 55060, ☎ 507/451–5005 or 800/535–6790, FAX 507/451–1685, WEB www.flyingwheelstravel.com).

DISCOUNTS & DEALS

Be a smart shopper and **compare all your options** before making decisions. A plane ticket bought with a promotional coupon from travel clubs, coupon books, and direct-mail offers or on the Internet may not be cheaper than the least expensive fare from a discount ticket agency. And always keep in mind that what you get is just as important as what you save.

DISCOUNT RESERVATIONS

To save money, **look into discount reservations services** with toll-free numbers, which use their buying power to get a better price on hotels, airline tickets, even car rentals. When booking a room, always **call the hotel's local toll-free number** (if one is available) rather than the central reservations number—you'll often get a better price. Always ask about special packages or corporate rates.

When shopping for the best deal on hotels and car rentals, **look for guaranteed exchange rates,** which protect you against a falling dollar. With your rate locked in, you won't pay more, even if the price goes up in the local currency.

➤ AIRLINE TICKETS: ☎ 800/AIR–4LESS.

➤ HOTEL ROOMS: **Hotel Reservations Network** (☎ 800/964–6835, WEB www.hoteldiscount.com). **Players Express Vacations** (☎ 800/458–6161, WEB www.playersexpress.com). **Steigenberger Reservation Service** (☎ 800/223–5652, WEB www.srs-worldhotels.com). **Travel Interlink** (☎ 800/888–5898, WEB www.travelinterlink.com). **Turbotrip.com** (☎ 800/473–7829, WEB www.turbotrip.com).

PACKAGE DEALS

Don't confuse packages and guided tours. When you buy a package, you travel on your own, just as though you had planned the trip yourself. Fly-drive packages, which combine airfare and car rental, are often a good deal. In cities, ask the local visitors' bureau about hotel packages that include tickets to major museum exhibits or other special events. If you **buy a rail-drive pass,** you may save on train tickets and car rentals. All Eurail- and Europass holders get a discount on Eurostar fares through the Channel Tunnel.

ELECTRICITY

To use electric-powered equipment purchased in the United States or Canada, **bring a converter and adapter.** The electrical current in Italy is 220 volts, 50 cycles alternating current (AC); wall outlets take Continental-type plugs, with two round prongs.

If your appliances are dual-voltage, you'll need only an adapter. Don't use 110-volt outlets marked FOR SHAVERS ONLY for high-wattage appliances such as blow-dryers. Most laptops operate equally well on 110 and 220 volts and so require only an adapter.

EMBASSIES & CONSULATES

➤ AUSTRALIA: **Australian Embassy** (✉ Via Alessandra 215, Rome, ☎ 06/852721).

➤ CANADA: **Canadian Embassy** (✉ Via G.B. de Rossi 27, Rome, ☎ 06/445981).

➤ NEW ZEALAND: **New Zealand Embassy** (✉ Via Zara 28, Rome, ☎ 06/4417171).

➤ UNITED KINGDOM: **U.K. Embassy** (✉ Via XX Settembre 80/a, ☎ 06/4825441).

➤ UNITED STATES: **U.S. Embassy** (✉ Via Veneto 121, ☎ 06/46741).

EMERGENCIES

No matter where you are in Italy, **dial 113 for all emergencies,** or find somebody (your concierge, a passerby) who will call for you, as not all 113 operators speak English; the Italian word to use to draw people's attention in an emergency is *Aiuto!* (Help!, pronounced "ah-*you*-toh").

Pronto soccorso means "first aid" and when said to an operator will get you an *ambulanza* (ambulance). If you just need a doctor, you should ask for "*un medico*"; most hotels will be able to refer you to a local doctor. Don't forget to ask the doctor for *una ricevuta* (an invoice) to show to your insurance company in order to get a reimbursement. Other useful Italian words to use in an emergency are "*Al fuoco!*" (Fire!, pronounced "ahl fuh-*woe*-co") and "*Al ladro!*" (Follow the thief!, pronounced "ahl *lah*-droh").

Italy has a national police force (*carabinieri*) as well as local police (*polizia*). Both are armed and have the power to arrest and investigate crimes. **Always report the loss of your passport to either the carabinieri or the police,** as well as to your embassy. Local traffic officers are known as *vigili* (though their official name is *polizia municipale*)—they are responsible for, among other things, giving out parking tickets and clamping cars, so before you even consider parking the Italian way, make sure you are at least able to spot their white (in summer) or black uniforms (many are women). Should you find yourself involved in a minor car accident, you should contact the vigili. A country-wide toll-free number is used to call the carabinieri in case of emergency.

Most pharmacies are open Monday–Saturday 8:30–1 and 4–8; some are open all night. A schedule posted outside each pharmacy indicates the nearest pharmacy open during off-hours (afternoons, through the night, and Sunday). **Dial 1100 for an automated list of three open pharmacies** closest to the telephone from which you call. Farmacia Internazionale Barberini, on Piazza Barberini, is open 24 hours and has English-speaking staff. The hospitals listed below have English-speaking doctors. Rome American Hospital is about 30 minutes by cab from the center of town.

➤ CONTACTS: Emergencies (☎ 113). Carabinieri (☎ 112).

➤ HOSPITALS: **Rome American Hospital** (✉ Via Emilio Longoni 69, Tor Sapienza, ☎ 06/22551, WEB www.rah.it). **Salvator Mundi International Hospital** (✉ Viale delle Mura Gianicolensi 66,

Monte Verdi Vecchio, ☎ 06/588961, WEB www.smih.pcn.net).

➤ PHARMACIES: For American and British products, or their equivalents, and English-speaking staff: **Farmacia Cola di Rienzo** (✉ Via Cola di Rienzo 213, ☎ 06/3243130). **Farmacia Internazionale Barberini** (✉ Piazza Barberini 49, ☎ 06/4825456). **Farmacia Internazionale Capranica** (✉ Piazza Capranica 96, near the Pantheon, ☎ 06/6794680).

ENGLISH-LANGUAGE MEDIA

BOOKS

English-language books in Rome are expensive; most are imported from England, so prices in Rome reflect the strong pound and shipping costs. The Anglo-American Bookstore and the Economy Book and Video Center have the widest selection of genres. Trastevere's Corner Bookstore carries lots of offbeat new fiction and has a vast history section. For used books at lower prices, try the Open Door.

➤ CONTACTS: **Anglo-American Bookstore** (✉ Via della Vite 102, ☎ 06/6795222, WEB www.aab.it). **Corner Bookstore** (✉ Via del Moro 48, Trastevere, ☎ 06/5836942). **Economy Book and Video Center** (✉ Via Torino 136, ☎ 06/4746877, WEB www.booksitaly.com). **Lion Bookshop** (✉ Via dei Greci 33/36, ☎ 06/32654007). **Open Door** (✉ Via della Lungaretta 25, Trastevere, ☎ 06/5896478).

NEWSPAPERS & MAGAZINES

The ubiquitous *International Herald Tribune* is published in Italy with the four-page *Italy Daily* insert, an English-language summary of main Italian news stories and local cultural events. Major English and American newsmagazines and a few daily papers are available at some newsstands, including those on Via Veneto, Via del Corso (at Via del Tritone), and Campo dei Fiori.

GAY & LESBIAN TRAVEL

Local gays and lesbians generally maintain low visibility in Rome; favorite clubs and bars are usually mixed rather than exclusively homosexual.

➤ GAY AWARENESS ORGANIZATIONS: **Arcigay Arcilesbica Pegaso** (✉ Via Acciaresi 7, ☎ 06/41730752). **Circolo Mario Mieli** (✉ Via Ostiense 202, ☎ 06/5413985).

➤ GAY- & LESBIAN-FRIENDLY TRAVEL AGENCIES: **Different Roads Travel** (✉ 8383 Wilshire Blvd., Suite 902, Beverly Hills, CA 90211, ☎ 323/651–5557 or 800/429–8747, FAX 323/651–3678, lgernert@tzell.com). **Kennedy Travel** (✉ 314 Jericho Turnpike, Floral Park, NY 11001, ☎ 516/352–4888 or 800/237–7433, FAX 516/354–8849, WEB www.kennedytravel.com). **Now Voyager** (✉ 4406 18th St., San Francisco, CA 94114, ☎ 415/626–1169 or 800/255–6951, FAX 415/626–8626, WEB www.nowvoyager.com). **Skylink Travel and Tour** (✉ 1006 Mendocino Ave., Santa Rosa, CA 95401, ☎ 707/546–9888 or 800/225–5759, FAX 707/546–9891, WEB www.skylinktravel.com), serving lesbian travelers.

GUIDEBOOKS

Plan well and you won't be sorry. Guidebooks are excellent tools—and you can take them with you. You may want to check out color-photo-illustrated *Fodor's Exploring Rome,* thorough on culture and history; pocket-size *Citypack Rome,* which includes a supersize foldout map; or *Fodor's Holy Rome,* a photo-filled guide to the Christian sights. All are available at on-line retailers and bookstores everywhere.

HEALTH

FOOD & DRINK

The Centers for Disease Control and Prevention (CDC) in Atlanta caution that most of southern Europe is in the "intermediate" range for risk of contacting traveler's diarrhea. Part of this risk may be attributed to an increased consumption of olive oil and wine, which can have a laxative effect on stomachs used to a different diet. The CDC also advises all international travelers to swim only in chlorinated swimming pools, unless they are absolutely certain the local beaches and freshwater lakes are not contaminated.

Tap water is drinkable across Rome itself, and the city is renowned for the high quality of its water that comes from plentiful underground springs. Throughout the city, in almost every square and side street, you will find drinking fountains, often labeled *acqua marcia,* with a little bronze or brass drinking spout pierced by a hole. The only water you should not drink is the water that gushes into ornamental fountains, which often has cleansing chemicals in it, and any fountain that has the words *non potabile,* meaning undrinkable, written over it.

Beginning in 2001, mad cow disease has had a significant impact on Italian dining habits. Although as of that summer there were no cases of the disease in humans in Italy, and only two Italian cows were found infected, many Italians stopped eating beef altogether. The beloved *bistecca alla fiorentina,* the thick T-bone steak cut from Tuscan beef, was banned by the European Union; restaurants famous for this specialty switched to grilled pork. Other traditional dishes at least temporarily unavailable included *osso buco* (braised veal shank), oxtail, and offal specialties prepared throughout the country. *Vitello* (veal), *vitellone* (young beef), and *manzo* (beef) are considered safe to eat by both the Italian government and the European Union (these are cuts that don't come in touch with spinal marrow). Yet consumers tend to trust veal only. As a result, some restaurants experimented with "alternative meats" such as *struzzo* (ostrich) and *canguro* (kangaroo). *Cavallo* (horse meat, which is sweet and lean), *buffalo* (buffalo, like beef but less tender), and *coniglio* (rabbit) can be found at many butchers. The price of lamb and pork rose 20%, while the price of fish remained stable.

HOLIDAYS

New Year's Day; January 6 (Epiphany); Easter Sunday and Monday; April 25 (Liberation Day); May 1 (Labor Day or May Day); June 29 (Sts. Peter and Paul, Rome's patron saints); August 15 (Assumption of Mary, also known as Ferragosto); November 1 (All Saints' Day); December 8 (Immaculate Conception); Christmas Day and Boxing Day.

INSURANCE

The most useful travel-insurance plan is a comprehensive policy that includes coverage for trip cancellation and interruption, default, trip delay, and medical expenses (with a waiver for preexisting conditions).

Without insurance you will lose all or most of your money if you cancel your trip, regardless of the reason. Default insurance covers you if your tour operator, airline, or cruise line goes out of business. Trip-delay covers expenses that arise because of bad weather or mechanical delays. Study the fine print when comparing policies.

When you're traveling internationally, a key component of travel insurance is coverage for medical bills incurred if you get sick on the road. Such expenses are not generally covered by Medicare or private policies. U.K. residents can buy a travel-insurance policy valid for most vacations taken during the year in which it's purchased (but check preexisting-condition coverage). British and Australian citizens need extra medical coverage when traveling overseas.

Always **buy travel policies directly from the insurance company**; if you buy them from a cruise line, airline, or tour operator that goes out of business you probably will not be covered for the agency or operator's default, a major risk. Before making any purchase, **review your existing health and home-owner's policies** to find what they cover away from home.

➤ TRAVEL INSURERS: In the United States: **Access America** (⊠ 6600 W. Broad St., Richmond, VA 23230, ☎ 800/284–8300, 𝔽𝔸𝕏 804/673–1491, 𝕎𝔼𝔹 www.etravelprotection.com). **Travel Guard International** (⊠ 1145 Clark St., Stevens Point, WI 54481, ☎ 715/345–0505 or 800/826–1300, 𝔽𝔸𝕏 800/955–8785, 𝕎𝔼𝔹 www.travelguard.com).

➤ INSURANCE INFORMATION: In Australia: **Insurance Council of Australia** (⊠ Level 3, 56 Pitt St., Sydney NSW 2000, ☎ 02/9253–5100, 𝔽𝔸𝕏 02/9253–5111, 𝕎𝔼𝔹 www.ica.com.au). In Canada: **RBC Travel Insurance** (⊠ 6880 Financial Dr., Mississauga, Ontario L5N 7Y5, ☎ 905/791–8700; 800/668–4342 in Canada, 𝔽𝔸𝕏 905/

816–2498, WEB www.royalbank.com).
In New Zealand: **Insurance Council of New Zealand** (⊠ Level 7, 111–115 Customhouse Quay, Box 474; Wellington, ☎ 04/472–5230, FAX 04/473–3011, WEB www.icnz.org.nz). In the United Kingdom: **Association of British Insurers** (⊠ 51–55 Gresham St., London EC2V 7H, U.K., ☎ 020/7600–3333, FAX 020/7696–8999, WEB www.abi.org.uk).

LANGUAGE

In Rome, language is usually not a problem. You can always find someone who speaks at least a little English, albeit with a heavy accent; remember that the Italian language is pronounced exactly as it is written—many Italians try to speak English as it is written, with bewildering results. You may run into a language barrier in the countryside, but a phrase book and close attention to the Italians' astonishing use of pantomime and expressive gestures will go a long way.

Try to **master a few phrases for daily use,** and familiarize yourself with the terms you'll need to decipher signs and museum labels. To get the most out of museums, you'll need English-language guidebooks to exhibits; look for them in bookstores and on newsstand, as those sold at the museums are not necessarily the best.

LANGUAGES FOR TRAVELERS

A phrase book and language-tape set can help get you started. *Fodor's Italian for Travelers* (available at bookstores everywhere) is excellent.

LANGUAGE-STUDY PROGRAMS

Private language schools and U.S.- and U.K.-affiliated educational institutions offer a host of Italian language study programs in Rome.

➤ LANGUAGE SCHOOLS: **American University of Rome** (⊠ Via Pietro Rosselli 4, ☎ 06/58330919). **Arco di Druso** (⊠ Via Tunisi 4, ☎ 06/39750984). **Berlitz** (⊠ Via Torre Argentina 21, ☎ 06/68806951). **Centro Linguistico Italiano Dante Alighieri** (⊠ Piazza Bologna 1, ☎ 06/44231400). **Ciao Italia** (⊠ Via delle Frasche 5, ☎ 06/4814084). **Dilit International House** (⊠ Via Marghera 22, ☎ 06/4462602).

LODGING

The lodgings we list are the cream of the crop in each price category. We always list the facilities that are available—but we don't specify whether they cost extra: when pricing accommodations, always ask what's included and what costs extra. Properties marked ✕⊡ are lodging establishments whose restaurants warrant a special trip.

APARTMENT & VILLA RENTALS

For stays of a week or more, especially for families or groups of friends, an apartment or villa rental may be more convenient than a hotel. Always insist on photos, a map with indication of location, and a detailed description of the property. Homes International offers short- and long-term accommodations in Rome. Property International handles monthly and weekly rentals in Rome and Tuscany. The English-language biweekly *Wanted in Rome* lists rentals available privately.

➤ LOCAL AGENTS: **Homes International** (⊠ Via Bissolati 20, 00187, ☎ 06/4881800, FAX 06/4881808, homesint@tin.it). **Property International** (⊠ Viale Aventino 79, 00153, ☎ 06/5743170, FAX 06/5743182, Property.rm@flashnet.it).

➤ RENTAL LISTINGS: *Wanted in Rome* (WEB www.wantedinrome.it).

➤ ITALY-ONLY AGENCIES: **Cuendet USA** (⊠ 165 Chestnut St., Allendale, NJ 07041, ☎ 201/327–2333; ⊠ Suzanne T. Pidduck, c/o Rentals in Italy, 1742 Calle Corva, Camarillo, CA 93010, ☎ 800/726–6702). **Vacanze in Italia** (⊠ 22 Railroad St., Great Barrington, MA 01230, ☎ 413/528–6610 or 800/533–5405).

➤ INTERNATIONAL AGENTS: **At Home Abroad** (⊠ 405 E. 56th St., Suite 6H, New York, NY 10022, ☎ 212/421–9165, FAX 212/752–1591, WEB www.athomeabroadinc.com). **Drawbridge to Europe** (⊠ 98 Granite St., Ashland, OR 97520, ☎ 541/482–7778 or 888/268–1148, FAX 541/482–7779, WEB www.drawbridgetoeurope.com). **Hideaways International** (⊠ 767 Islington St., Portsmouth, NH 03801, ☎ 603/430–4433 or 800/843–4433,

FAX 603/430–4444, WEB www.hideaways.com; membership $129). **Hometours International** (✉ Box 11503, Knoxville, TN 37939, ☎ 865/690–8484 or 800/367–4668, WEB thor.he.net/~hometour/). **Interhome** (✉ 1990 N.E. 163rd St., Suite 110, N. Miami Beach, FL 33162, ☎ 305/940–2299 or 800/882–6864, FAX 305/940–2911, WEB www.interhome.com). **Vacation Home Rentals Worldwide** (✉ 235 Kensington Ave., Norwood, NJ 07648, ☎ 201/767–9393 or 800/633–3284, FAX 201/767–5510, WEB www.vhrww.com). **Villanet** (✉ 11556 1st Ave. NW, Seattle, WA 98177, ☎ 206/417–3444 or 800/964–1891, FAX 206/417–1832, WEB www.rentavilla.com). **Villas International** (✉ 950 Northgate Dr., Suite 206, San Rafael, CA 94903, ☎ 415/499–9490 or 800/221–2260, FAX 415/499–9491, WEB www.villasintl.com).

➤ IN THE UNITED KINGDOM: **CV Travel** (✉ 43 Cadogan St., London SW3 2PR, ☎ 020/7581–0851). **Magic of Italy** (✉ 227 Shepherds Bush Rd., London W6 7AS, ☎ 020/8748–7575).

HOME EXCHANGES

If you would like to exchange your home for someone else's, **join a home-exchange organization**, which will send you its updated listings of available exchanges for a year and will include your own listing in at least one of them. It's up to you to make specific arrangements.

➤ EXCHANGE CLUBS: **Intervac U.S.** (✉ Box 590504, San Francisco, CA 94159, ☎ 800/756–4663, FAX 415/435–7440, WEB www.intervacus.com; $93 yearly fee includes one catalog and on-line access).

HOSTELS

No matter what your age, you can **save on lodging costs by staying at hostels.** In some 4,500 locations in more than 70 countries around the world, Hostelling International (HI), the umbrella group for a number of national youth-hostel associations, offers single-sex, dorm-style beds and, at many hostels, rooms for couples and family accommodations. Membership in any HI national hostel association, open to travelers of all

ages, allows you to stay in HI-affiliated hostels at member rates; one-year membership is about $25 for adults (C$26.75 in Canada, £9.30 in the United Kingdom, $30 in Australia, and $30 in New Zealand); hostels run about $10–$25 per night. Members have priority if the hostel is full; they're also eligible for discounts around the world, even on rail and bus travel in some countries.

➤ ORGANIZATIONS: **Hostelling International—American Youth Hostels** (✉ 733 15th St. NW, Suite 840, Washington, DC 20005, ☎ 202/783–6161, FAX 202/783–6171, WEB www.hiayh.org). **Hostelling International—Canada** (✉ 400–205 Catherine St., Ottawa, Ontario K2P 1C3, ☎ 613/237–7884; 800/663–5777 in Canada, FAX 613/237–7868, WEB www.hostellingintl.ca). **Youth Hostel Association Australia** (✉ 10 Mallett St., Camperdown, NSW 2050, ☎ 02/9565–1699, FAX 02/9565–1325, WEB www.yha.com.au). **Youth Hostel Association of England and Wales** (✉ Trevelyan House, 8 St. Stephen's Hill, St. Albans, Hertfordshire AL1 2DY, U.K., ☎ 0870/8708808, FAX 01727/844126, WEB www.yha.org.uk). **Youth Hostels Association of New Zealand** (✉ Level 3, 193 Cashel St., Box 436, Christchurch, ☎ 03/379–9970, FAX 03/365–4476, WEB www.yha.org.nz).

➤ IN ROME: The **IYHF Ostello della Gioventù Foro Italico** (✉ Viale Olimpiadi 61, Foro Italico sports complex, near Tiber north of downtown Rome, ☎ 06/3236279, FAX 06/3242613) can be reached from Termini station by taking Metro line A to Ottaviano/S. Pietro station (Via Barletta exit), then bus 32.

HOTELS

For information about hotels in Rome, see Chapter 3, Lodging.

➤ TOLL-FREE NUMBERS: **Atahotels** (✉ Via Lampedusa 11/a, 20141 Milan, ☎ 02/895–261; 1678/23013 toll-free in Italy, FAX 02/846–5568; some bookable through E&M Associates, ☎ 212/599–8280 or 800/223–9832).**Best Western** (☎ 800/528–1234, WEB www.bestwestern.com). **Choice** (☎ 800/221–2222, WEB www.choicehotels.com). **Comfort** (☎ 800/

228–5150, WEB www.comfortinn.com).
Forte (☎ 800/225–5843, WEB www.
forte-hotels.com). **Hilton** (☎ 800/
445–8667, WEB www.hilton.com). **Holiday Inn** (☎ 800/465–4329, WEB www.
basshotels.com). **Inter-Continental**
☎ 800/327–0200, WEB www.interconti.
com). **Italhotels** (☎ 1678/01004 toll-
free in Italy). **ITT-Sheraton/The Luxury Collection** (⊠ 745 5th Ave., New
York, NY 10151, ☎ 800/221–2340,
1678/835–035 toll-free in Italy, FAX 212/
421–5929). **Jolly** (⊠ 22 E. 38th St.,
New York, NY 10016, ☎ 800/247–
1277 in New York State; 800/221–
2626 elsewhere in the U.S.; 800/237–
0319 in Canada; 167/07703 toll-free
in Italy). **Le Meridien** (☎ 800/543–
4300, WEB www.lemeridien-hotels.
com). **Marriott** (☎ 800/228–9290,
WEB www.marriott.com). **Quality Inn**
(☎ 800/228–5151, WEB www.qualityinn.
com). **Sheraton** (☎ 800/325–3535,
WEB www.starwoodhotels.com). **Space
Hotels** (☎ 1678/13013 toll-free in
Italy; 416/927–1133 or 800/843–3311
to book through Supranational). **Starhotels** (⊠ Via Belfiore 27, 50144 Florence, ☎ 055/36921; 1678/60200
toll-free in Italy; 800/448–8355;
FAX 055/36924). **Westin Hotels &
Resorts** (☎ 800/228–3000, WEB www.
westin.com).

MAIL & SHIPPING

Outgoing mail will reach its destination faster if mailed from the Vatican,
with Vatican stamps. You can buy
them in the post offices on either side
of Piazza di San Pietro, one next to
the information office and the other
under the colonnade opposite. During
peak tourist seasons a Vatican Post
Office mobile unit is set up in Piazza
di San Pietro.

➤ POST OFFICES: **Main Rome post
office** (⊠ Piazza San Silvestro 19,
☎ 06/6798495).

OVERNIGHT SERVICES

While DHL and UPS offices are
far out of the city center, FedEx has
walk-in service on Via Barberini; all
three companies will pick up packages from anywhere in Rome.

➤ MAJOR SERVICES: **DHL** (800/
345345). **Federal Express** (⊠ Via
Barberini 115, ☎ 800/123800). **UPS**
(☎ 800/877877).

POSTAL RATES

Airmail letters (lightweight stationery)
to the United States and Canada cost
€0.67 for the first 19 grams and an
additional €0.26 for every additional
unit of 20 grams. Airmail postcards
cost €0.62 if the message is limited to
a few words and a signature; otherwise, you pay the letter rate. Airmail
letters and postcards to the United
Kingdom cost €0.47. You can buy
stamps at tobacconists.

RECEIVING MAIL

Mail service is generally slow (sometimes excruciatingly so); allow up to
10 days for mail from Britain, 15
days from North America. Corre-
spondence can be addressed to you
care of the Italian post office. Letters
should be addressed to your name,
"c/o Ufficio Postale Centrale," followed by "Fermo Posta" on the next
line, and the name of the city (preceded by its postal code—Rome's
central post office's is 00187) on the
next. You can collect it at Rome's
central post office at Piazza San Silvestro by showing your passport or
photo-bearing ID and paying a small
fee. American Express also has a
general-delivery service. There's no
charge for cardholders, holders of
American Express traveler's checks,
or anyone who booked a vacation
with American Express.

MONEY MATTERS

Rome's prices are comparable to
those in other major capitals, such as
Paris and London. The days when
Italy's high-quality attractions came
with a comparatively low Mediterranean price tag are long gone. With
the cost of labor and social benefits
rising and an economy weighed down
by the public debt, Italy is therefore
not a bargain, but there is an effort to
hold the line on hotel and restaurant
prices, which had become inordi-
nately high by U.S. standards. Depending on season and occupancy,
you may be able to obtain unadver-
tised lower rates in hotels; always
inquire. If you want the luxury of
$$$$ and $$$ hotels, be prepared to
pay top rates.

Unless you dine in the swankiest
places you'll still find Rome one of
the cheapest European capitals in

which to eat. Clothes and leather goods are also generally less expensive than in northern Europe. Public transport is relatively cheap.

Admission to the Musei Vaticani is €9.30. The cheapest seat at Rome's Opera House runs €15.50; a movie ticket is €6.20. A daily English-language newspaper is €1.65.

A Rome 2-km (1-mi) taxi ride costs €5.25. An inexpensive hotel room for two, including breakfast, is about €100; an inexpensive dinner is €20. A simple pasta item on the menu is about €6.75, and a ½-liter carafe of house wine €3. A McDonald's Big Mac is €2.50, with prices doubled if you sit down. A pint of beer in a pub is around €4.25.

Prices throughout this guide are given for adults. Reduced fees are sometimes available for children, students, and senior citizens.

For information on taxes, *see* Taxes, *below*.

ATMS

ATMs are fairly common in Rome and are the easiest way to get euros. Be sure you **have a four-digit PIN**; longer numbers won't work in Italian ATMs.

CREDIT CARDS

Should you use a credit card or a debit card when traveling? Both have benefits. A credit card allows you to delay payment and gives you certain rights as a consumer (☞ Consumer Protection, *above*). A debit card, also known as a check card, deducts funds directly from your checking account and helps you stay within your budget. When you want to rent a car, though, you may still need an old-fashioned credit card. Although you can always *pay* for your car with a debit card, some agencies will not allow you to *reserve* a car with a debit card.

Otherwise, the two types of cards are virtually the same. Both will get you cash advances at ATMs worldwide if your card is properly programmed with your personal identification number (PIN). (For use in Rome, your PIN must be four digits long.) Both offer excellent, wholesale ex-

change rates, and both protect you against unauthorized use if the card is lost or stolen. Your liability is limited to $50, as long as you report the card missing.

Throughout this guide, the following abbreviations are used: **AE**, American Express; **DC**, Diners Club; **MC**, MasterCard; and **V**, Visa.

➤ REPORTING LOST CARDS: **American Express** (☎ 336/668–5110 international collect). **Diners Club** (☎ 702/797–5532 collect). **MasterCard** (☎ 800/870–866 toll-free in Italy). **Visa** (☎ 800/821–001).

CURRENCY

The unit of currency in Italy as of January 1, 2002, is the euro of the European Monetary Union. Under the euro system, there are eight coins: 1 and 2 euros, plus 1, 2, 5, 10, 20, and 50 centimes, or cents, of the euro. All coins have one side that has the value of the euro on it and the other side with each country's own unique national symbol. There are seven notes: 5, 10, 20, 50, 100, 200, and 500 euros. Notes are the same for all countries.

CURRENCY EXCHANGE

For the most favorable rates, **change money through banks.** Although ATM transaction fees may be higher abroad than at home, ATM rates are excellent because they are based on wholesale rates offered only by major banks. You won't do as well at exchange booths in airports or rail and bus stations, in hotels, in restaurants, or in stores. To avoid lines at airport exchange booths, **get a bit of local currency before you leave home.**

At press time, the exchange rate was about 1.13 euros to the U.S. dollar; 0.75 euros to the Canadian dollar; 1.61 euros to the pound sterling; 0.58 euros to the Australian dollar; and 0.47 euros to the New Zealand dollar.

➤ EXCHANGE SERVICES: **International Currency Express** (☎ 888/278–6628 for orders, WEB www.foreignmoney. com). **Thomas Cook Currency Services** (☎ 800/287–7362 for telephone orders and retail locations, WEB www.us.thomascook.com).

TRAVELER'S CHECKS

Do you need traveler's checks? It depends on where you're headed. If you're going to rural areas and small towns, go with cash; traveler's checks are best used in cities. Lost or stolen checks can usually be replaced within 24 hours. To ensure a speedy refund, buy your own traveler's checks—don't let someone else pay for them: irregularities like this can cause delays. The person who bought the checks should make the call to request a refund.

PACKING

In your carry-on luggage, **pack an extra pair of eyeglasses or contact lenses and enough of any medication** you take to last the entire trip. You may also ask your doctor to write a spare prescription using the drug's generic name, since brand names may vary from country to country. In luggage to be checked, **never pack prescription drugs or valuables.** To avoid customs delays, carry medications in their original packaging. And don't forget to carry with you the addresses of offices that handle refunds of lost traveler's checks. Check *Fodor's How to Pack* (available in bookstores everywhere) for more tips.

CHECKING LUGGAGE

How many carry-on bags you can bring with you is up to the airline. Most allow two, but not always, so make sure that everything you carry aboard will fit under your seat or in the overhead bin, and get to the gate early. Note that if you have a seat at the back of the plane, you'll probably board first, while the overhead bins are still empty.

Note that when flying internationally, baggage allowances may be determined not by piece but by weight—generally 88 pounds (40 kilograms) in first class, 66 pounds (30 kilograms) in business class, and 44 pounds (20 kilograms) in economy.

Airline liability for baggage is limited to $1,250 per person on flights within the United States. On international flights it amounts to $9.07 per pound or $20 per kilogram for checked baggage (roughly $640 per 70-pound bag) and $400 per passenger for un-checked baggage. You can buy additional coverage at check-in for about $10 per $1,000 of coverage, but it excludes a rather extensive list of items, shown on your airline ticket.

Before departure, **itemize your bags' contents** and their worth, and label the bags with your name, address, and phone number. (If you use your home address, cover it so potential thieves can't see it readily.) Inside each bag, **pack a copy of your itinerary.** At check-in, **make sure that each bag is correctly tagged** with the destination airport's three-letter code. If your bags arrive damaged or fail to arrive at all, file a written report with the airline before leaving the airport.

PACKING LIST

Rome generally has mild winters and hot, sticky summers. Take a medium-weight coat for winter; a lightweight all-weather coat for spring and fall; and a lightweight jacket or sweater for summer evenings, which may be cool. Brief summer thunderstorms are common, so take a folding umbrella. As interiors can be cold and sometimes damp in the cooler months, take woolens or flannels. Plan your wardrobe in layers, no matter what the season. Casual clothes are the general rule, especially during the summer. In all seasons, Italians dress exceptionally well; to them, casual means easy but elegant, even in jeans. Though men aren't required to wear jackets or ties anywhere, except in the grander hotel dining rooms and some deluxe restaurants, they are expected to look reasonably sharp. Formal wear is the exception rather than the rule at the opera, though people in expensive seats usually do get dressed up. Wear sturdy walking shoes or sandals, preferably with thick soles, to get around in comfort on Rome's many cobblestone streets and the gravel paths that surround some of the historic buildings. In general, avoid wearing shorts, halter tops, and thong sandals.

If you're coming during the summer months be careful to avoid bringing too many clothes. You'll probably wear only half of what you bring, and anything more than light cotton clothes is unbearable in the humid heat.

Dress codes are strict for visits to the Basilica di San Pietro and the Musei Vaticani: for both men and women, shorts, tank tops, and halter tops are taboo. Shoulders must be covered. Women should carry a scarf or shawl to cover bare arms if the custodians insist. Those who do not comply with the dress code are refused admittance. Although there are no specific dress rules for the huge outdoor papal audiences, you will be turned away if you're in shorts or a revealing outfit. The Vatican Information Office in Piazza di San Pietro will tell you the dress requirements for smaller audiences. Dress codes for churches are similar, though less strictly applied.

To protect yourself against purse snatchers and pickpockets, carry a money pouch or belt. Don't keep your passport and large sums of money in your handbag or hip pocket. Any kind of bag, shoulder bag, or camera case is a target. If you must carry one, choose one with long straps that you can sling across your body, bandolier style. Avoid carrying a bag if you can, or carry one that is obviously just a tote for your guide book and sundries.

PASSPORTS & VISAS

When traveling internationally, **carry your passport** even if you don't need one (it's always the best form of ID) and **make two photocopies of the data page** (one for someone at home and another for you, carried separately from your passport). If you lose your passport, promptly call the nearest embassy or consulate and the local police.

ENTERING ITALY

All U.S., Canadian, U.K., Australian, and New Zealand citizens, even infants, need only a valid passport to enter Italy for stays of up to 90 days.

PASSPORT OFFICES

The best time to apply for a passport or to renew is in fall and winter. Before any trip, check your passport's expiration date, and, if necessary, renew it as soon as possible.

➤ AUSTRALIAN CITIZENS: **Australian Passport Office** (☎ 131–232, WEB www.passports.gov.au).

➤ CANADIAN CITIZENS: **Passport Office** (☎ 819/994–3500, 800/567–6868 in Canada, WEB www.dfait-maeci.gc.ca/passport).

➤ NEW ZEALAND CITIZENS: **New Zealand Passport Office** (☎ 04/494–0700, WEB www.passports.govt.nz).

➤ U.K. CITIZENS: **London Passport Office** (☎ 0870/521–0410, WEB www.ukpa.gov.uk) for fees and documentation requirements and to request an emergency passport.

➤ U.S. CITIZENS: **National Passport Information Center** (☎ 900/225–5674; calls are 35¢ per minute for automated service, $1.05 per minute for operator service; WEB www.travel.state.gov/npicinfo.html).

REST ROOMS

Public rest rooms are rather rare in Rome. While there are public toilets in Piazza di San Pietro, Piazza di Spagna, at the Roman Forum, and in a few other strategic locations (all with a charge of €0.25), the locals seem to make do primarily with well-timed pit stops and rely on the local bar. Private businesses can refuse to make their toilets available to the passing public, but most bars will allow you to use the rest room if you ask politely. Alternatively, it is not uncommon to pay for a little something—a few cents for a mineral water or espresso—in order to get access to the facilities. Standards of cleanliness and comfort vary greatly. Restaurants, hotel halls, department stores like La Rinascente and Coin, and McDonald's restaurants tend to have the cleanest rest rooms. Pubs and bars rank among the worst. In general, it is in your interest to carry tissues with you. There are bathrooms in all airports and train stations (in major train stations you'll also find well-kept pay toilets for €0.25–€0.50) and in most museums. There are also bathrooms at highway rest stops and gas stations: a small tip to the cleaning person is always appreciated. There are no bathrooms in churches, post offices, public beaches, or subway stations.

SAFETY

The best way to protect yourself against purse snatchers and pickpockets is to **wear a money belt** (☞ Packing, *above*). Wear a bag or camera slung across your body bandolier-style, and don't rest your bag or camera on a table or chair at a sidewalk café or restaurant. In Rome, **beware of pickpockets** on buses, especially Line 64 (Termini–St. Peter's train station); the new line 40 Express, which takes a slightly different route and takes you closer to the basilica; and subways—and when making your way through the corridors of crowded trains. Pickpockets may be active wherever tourists gather, including the Roman Forum, Piazza Navona, and Piazza di San Pietro. Purse snatchers work in teams on a single motor scooter or motorcycle: one drives and the other grabs.

"Gypsy" children and young women (often with babes in arms) are present around sights popular with tourists, especially the Colosseum, and are adept pickpockets. One modus operandi is to approach a tourist and proffer a piece of cardboard with writing on it. While the unsuspecting victim attempts to read the message *on* it the children's hands are busy *under* it, trying to make off with wallets and valuables. If you see such a group (usually recognizable by their unkempt appearance), do not even allow them near you—they are quick and know more tricks than you do. The phrases *"Vai via!"* (Go away!) and *"Chiamo la polizia"* (I'll call the police) usually keep them at bay. Yelling anything at them at the top of your voice can be a deterrent.

WOMEN IN ROME

Foreign women can expect to attract extra attention from Italian men, but this is usually harmless flirtation and rarely will become a safety issue. Use common sense.

SCOOTERS

As bikes are to Beijing, so scooters are to Rome; that means they are everywhere. Riders are required to wear helmets, and traffic police are tough in enforcing this law. Producing your country's driver's license should be enough to convince most rental firms that they're not dealing with a complete beginner; but if you're unsure of exactly how to ride a scooter think twice, and at least ask the assistant for a detailed demonstration.

➤ RENTAL AGENCIES: **Scoot-a-Long** (✉ Via Cavour 302, ☎ 06/6780206). **St. Peter Moto Rent** (✉ Via di Porta Castello 43, ☎ 06/6875714).

SENIOR-CITIZEN TRAVEL

Senior-citizen discounts are not widely offered in Italy unless they are part of a tour package (☞ *below*). EU citizens over 60 are entitled to free admission to state museums as well as to many other museums—always ask at the ticket office. Older travelers may be eligible for special fares on Alitalia and other airlines. When renting a car, **ask about promotional car-rental discounts**, which can be cheaper than senior-citizen rates.

Senior travelers should be aware that few public buildings, including museums, restaurants, and shops, in Rome are air-conditioned. Public toilets are few and far between, other than those in restaurants and hotels, and in department stores. Toilets in coffee bars may be locked to keep out undesirables; if so, ask for the key at the cashier. There are public toilets in Piazza di San Pietro, Piazza di Spagna, at the Roman Forum, and in a few other strategic locations. Wheelchairs are available for free for use at the Vatican Museums.

➤ EDUCATIONAL PROGRAMS: **Elderhostel** (✉ 11 Ave. de Lafayette, Boston, MA 02111-1746, ☎ 877/426–8056, FAX 877/426–2166, WEB www.elderhostel.org). **Interhostel** (✉ University of New Hampshire, 6 Garrison Ave., Durham, NH 03824, ☎ 603/862–1147 or 800/733–9753, FAX 603/862–1113, WEB www.learn.unh.edu).

SHOPPING

The notice PREZZI FISSI (fixed prices) means just that: in shops displaying this sign it's a waste of time to bargain unless you're buying a sizable quantity of goods or a particularly costly object. Always bargain, however, at outdoor markets (except food markets) and when buying from street vendors. For a comprehensive introduction to the joys of shopping, Italian-style, *see* Chapter 6.

SIGHTSEEING TOURS

ORIENTATION TOURS

American Express, Appian Line, Carrani, CIT, and other operators offer three-hour tours in air-conditioned 60-passenger buses with English-speaking guides. There are four itineraries: "Ancient Rome" (including the Roman Forum and Colosseum); "Classic Rome" (including the Basilica di San Pietro, Fontana di Trevi, and the Janiculum Hill); "Christian Rome" (including some major churches and the catacombs); and "The Vatican Museums and Sistine Chapel." Most cost between €21 and €26, but the Musei Vaticani tour costs about €31. American Express tours depart from Piazza di Spagna and CIT from Piazza della Repubblica, both with some hotel pickups; Carrani and Appian Line pick you up at centrally located hotels.

American Express and other operators can provide a luxury car for up to three people, a limousine for up to seven, a minibus for up to nine, all with English-speaking driver, but guide service is extra. Almost all operators offer "Rome by Night" tours, with or without dinner and entertainment. You can book tours through travel agents.

Though operators and names change, a sightseeing bus following a continuous circle route through the center of town is usually operating. It makes scheduled stops at important sites, where you can get on and off at will. Check with the Rome tourist information kiosks or inquire at your hotel for the name of the current operator and schedules.

The least expensive organized sightseeing tour of Rome is that run by ATAC, the municipal bus company. Bus 110 tours leave from Piazza dei Cinquecento, in front of Termini Station, last about three hours, and cost about €7.75. The driver provides a commentary, and you're given an illustrated guide with which to identify the sights. Buy tickets at the ATAC information booth in front of Termini Station. There is at least one tour daily, departing at 2:30 PM (3:30 in summer).

Even less expensive are the sightseeing "tours" of Rome that can be had from certain buses and trams that pass major sights. With a single €0.75 ticket you can get in 75 minutes of sightseeing (or an entire day, with a €3.10 *giornaliero* ticket). Time your ride to avoid rush hours. The little electric Bus 116 scoots through the heart of Old Rome, with stops near the Pantheon, the Spanish Steps, and Piazza del Popolo, among others. The route of Bus 117 takes in San Giovanni in Laterano, the Colosseum, and the Spanish Steps.

Since the pedestrianization of many parts of the city, and restrictions on buses by the municipality, many companies no longer provide bus tours as such but tours in taxis, which are a little more intimate but can negotiate the traffic better.

➤ BUS LINE: **ATAC** (☎ 167/431784).

➤ TOUR OPERATORS: **American Express** (☎ 06/67641). **Appian Line** (☎ 06/487861). **Carrani** (☎ 06/4880510). **CIT** (☎ 06/4746555 or 06/42014239).

SPECIAL-INTEREST TOURS

You can make your own arrangements (at no cost) to attend a public papal audience at the Vatican or at the pope's summer residence at Castel Gandolfo. You can also book through a travel agency for a package that includes coach transportation to the Vatican for the audience and some sightseeing along the way, returning you to your hotel, for about €21. The excursion outside Rome to Castel Gandolfo on summer Sundays for the pope's blessing costs about €25. Agencies that arrange these tours include Appian Line, Carrani, and CIT.

Tourvisa Italia organizes boat trips on the Tiber, leaving from Ripa Grande, at Ponte Sublicio. Depending on the season, they may include excursions to Ostia Antica, with a guided visit of the excavations and return by bus. A scheduled river bus service operates from spring to fall, depending on the conditions of the river.

To experience a Roman kitchen, contact Fodor's updater Carla Lionello, who offers private, half-day cooking workshops. You create a four-course meal while discussing the techniques and traditions involved.

▶ TOUR OPERATORS: **Appian Line** (☎ 06/487861). **Carla Lionello** (☎ 06/69920435, WEB www.cookinginrome. com). **Carrani** (☎ 06/4880510). **CIT** (☎ 06/42014239). **Tourvis Italia** (☎ 06/4463481).

WALKING TOURS

Scala Reale organizes day and evening walking tours, theme walks, and excursions for very small groups, together with personalized consulting on what to see and do. Genti e Paesi is an Italian cultural association that offers walking tours and museum visits in English. Book at least one day in advance. If you have a reasonable knowledge of Italian, you can take advantage of the free guided visits and walking tours organized by Rome's cultural associations and the city council for museums and monuments. These usually take place on weekends. Programs are announced in the daily papers and in *Roma c'è*.

▶ TOUR OPERATORS: **Enjoy Rome** (✉ Via Varese 39, ☎ 06/4451843). **Genti e Paesi** (✉ Via Adda 111, ☎ 06/85301755). **Scala Reale** (✉ Via Varese 52, ☎ 06/4451477, FAX 617/2490186 in the U.S., ☎ FAX 06/44700898 in Italy).

EXCURSIONS

Most operators offer half-day excursions to Tivoli to see the fountains and gardens of Villa D'Este. Appian Line's morning tour to Tivoli also includes a visit to Hadrian's Villa, with its impressive ancient ruins. Most operators also have full-day excursions to Assisi, to Pompeii and/or Capri, and to Florence.

▶ TOUR OPERATOR: **Appian Line** (☎ 06/487861).

PERSONAL GUIDES

You can arrange for a personal guide through American Express, CIT, or the main EPT (Ente Per Turismo) Tourist Information Office.

▶ TOUR OPERATORS: **American Express** (☎ 06/67641). **CIT** (☎ 06/42014239).

EPT Tourist Information Office (☎ 06/488991 or 06/48899253).

SMOKING

To the dismay of many clean-air-loving travelers, Italians are unrepentant smokers. Although the number of smokers is dropping slowly each year, Italians are known for disregarding the many no-smoking laws that do exist, which are seldom seriously enforced. If you ask someone to smoke elsewhere or not to smoke in no-smoking areas, don't expect him or her to respond or respect your request. By Italian law, restaurants and bars should be equipped with ventilation systems, but many restaurants seem not to comply adequately. Your best bet for finding as smoke-free an environment as possible is to stick to large establishments and, weather permitting, to eat outside. All FS trains have no-smoking cars: always specify your preference when you make reservations.

STUDENTS IN ROME

LOCAL RESOURCES

The **Centro Turistico Studentesco** (CTS) is a student and youth travel agency with offices in major Italian cities; CTS helps its clients find low-cost accommodations and bargain fares for travel in Italy and elsewhere and also serves as a meeting place for young people of all nations. CTS is also the Rome representative for EuroTrain International.

▶ AGENCY: **Centro Turistico Studentesco** (✉ Via Andrea di Vesalio 6, northeast of Termini Station, ☎ 06/441111; ✉ Via Genova 16, ☎ 06/4620431 or 06/4679271).

TRAVEL AGENCIES

To save money, **look into deals available through student-oriented travel agencies.** To qualify you'll need a bona fide student ID card. Members of international student groups are also eligible.

▶ IDs & SERVICES: **Council Travel** (CIEE; ✉ 205 E. 42nd St., 15th floor, New York, NY 10017, ☎ 212/822–2700 or 888/268–6245, FAX 212/822–2699, WEB www.councilexchanges.org) for mail orders only, in the United

States. **Travel Cuts** (✉ 187 College St., Toronto, Ontario M5T 1P7, Canada, ☎ 416/979–2406 or 800/667–2887 in Canada, FAX 416/979–8167, WEB www.travelcuts.com).

➤ STUDENT TOURS: **AESU Travel** (✉ 2 Hamill Rd., Suite 248, Baltimore, MD 21210-1807, ☎ 410/323–4416 or 800/638–7640, FAX 410/323–4498). **Contiki Holidays** (✉ 300 Plaza Alicante, Suite 900, Garden Grove, CA 92840, ☎ 714/740–0808 or 800/266–8454, FAX 714/740–2034).

SUBWAY TRAVEL

The Metro is the easiest and fastest way to get around Rome. There are stops near most of the main tourist attractions. The Metro has two lines—A and B—which intersect at Termini Station. Line A runs from the eastern part of the city, with stops, among others, at San Giovanni in Laterano, Piazza Barberini, Piazza di Spagna, Piazzale Flaminio (Piazza del Popolo), and Ottaviano/San Pietro, near the Basilica di San Pietro and the Musei Vaticani. Line B has stops near the Colosseum, the Circus Maximus, the Pyramid (Ostiense Station and trains for Ostia Antica), and the Basilica di San Paolo Fuori le Mura. The Metro opens at 5:30 AM, and the last trains leave the last station at either end at 11:30 PM (on Saturday night the last train leaves at 12:30 AM). A ticket (BIT) valid for 75 minutes on any combination of buses and trams and one entrance to the Metro costs €0.75.

TAXES

HOTELS

The service charge and IVA, or value-added tax, are included in the rate except in five-star deluxe hotels, where the IVA (15% on luxury hotels) may be a separate item added to the bill at departure.

RESTAURANTS

Many, but not all, Rome restaurants have eliminated extra charges for service and for *pane e coperto* (a cover charge that includes bread, whether you eat it or not). If it is an extra, the service charge may be 12%–15%. Only part, if any, of this amount goes to the waiter, so an additional tip is appreciated (☞ Tipping, *below*).

If a waiter scribbles out an nonitemized bill (which likely as not comes to less than you expected) it means that the establishment is probably not abiding by the letter of the law and not paying its full share of taxes. You may think this a boon, but remember that you, as the customer, are legally liable, too. **Always ask for an itemized bill** and a *scontrino*, or receipt. Officially you have to keep this receipt with you for 600 ft from the restaurant or store and be able to produce it if asked by the tax police. Sounds absurd? It's something of a desperate measure for the country with the highest taxes in Europe and the highest levels of tax evasion/avoidance, and there have been cases of unwitting customers falling foul of the law.

VALUE-ADDED TAX

Value-added tax (IVA) is 20% on luxury goods. On most consumer goods, it is already included in the amount shown on the price tag; on services, such as car rentals, it is an extra item.

To get an IVA refund, when you are leaving Italy take the goods and the invoice to the customs office at the airport or other point of departure and have the invoice stamped. (If you return to the United States or Canada directly from Italy, go through the procedure at Italian customs; if your return is, say, via Britain, take the Italian goods and invoice to British customs.) Under Italy's IVA-refund system, a non-EU resident can obtain a refund of tax paid after spending a total of €155 in one store (before tax—and note that price tags and prices quoted, unless otherwise stated, include IVA). Shop with your passport and ask the store for an invoice itemizing the article(s), price(s), and the amount of tax. Once back home—and within 90 days of the date of purchase—mail the stamped invoice to the store, which will forward the IVA rebate to you.

Global Refund is a VAT refund service that makes getting your money back hassle-free. The service is available Europe-wide at 130,000 affiliated stores. In participating stores, **ask for**

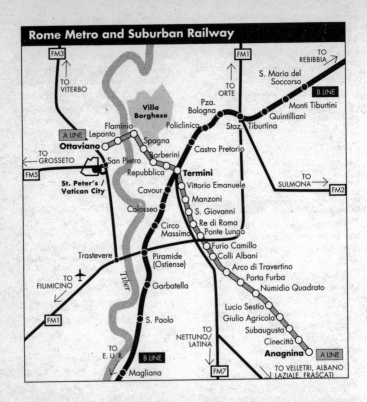

Rome Metro and Suburban Railway

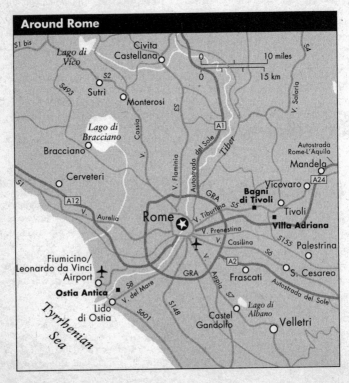

Around Rome

the **Global Refund refund form** (called a Shopping Cheque). Have it stamped like any customs form by customs officials when you leave the European Union (be ready to show customs officials what you've bought). Then take the form to one of the more than 700 Global Refund counters—conveniently located at every major airport and border crossing—and your money will be refunded on the spot in the form of cash, check, or a refund to your credit-card account (minus a small percentage for processing).

➤ VAT REFUNDS: **Global Refund** (✉ 99 Main St., Suite 307, Nyack, NY 10960, ☎ 800/566–9828, FAX 845/ 348–1549, WEB www.globalrefund. com).

TAXIS

Taxis in Rome do not cruise, but if free they will stop if you flag them down. They wait at stands but can also be called by phone, in which case you're charged a supplement. The various taxi services are considered interchangeable and are referred to by their phone numbers rather than names. The one exception is Radio Taxi, which is distinctive in that it accepts American Express and Diners Club. (Specify when calling that payment will be made by credit card.)

The meter starts at €2.30; there are supplements for night service (€2.60 extra from 10 PM to 7 AM) and on Sunday and holidays, as well as for each piece of baggage. Unfortunately, these charges do not appear on the meter, causing countless misunderstandings. If you take a taxi at night and/or on a Sunday, or if you have baggage or have had the cab called by phone, the fare will legitimately be more than the figure shown on the meter. Use only licensed, metered white or yellow cabs, identified by a numbered shield on the side, an illuminated taxi sign on the roof, and a plaque next to the license plate reading SERVIZIO PUBBLICO. Avoid unmarked, unauthorized, unmetered gypsy cabs (numerous at Rome airports and train stations), whose drivers actively solicit your trade and may demand astronomical fares.

➤ CALLING A CAB: Dial ☎ 06/3875, 06/3570, 06/4994, 06/5551, or 06/ 8433. **Radio Taxi** (☎ 06/3875).

TELEPHONES

AREA & COUNTRY CODES

The country code for Italy is 39. The area code for Rome is 06. When dialing an Italian number from abroad, do not drop the initial 0 from the local area code.

The country code is 1 for the United States, 61 for Australia, 1 for Canada, 64 for New Zealand, and 44 for the United Kingdom.

DIRECTORY & OPERATOR ASSISTANCE

For general information in English, dial 176. To place international telephone calls via operator-assisted service (or for information), dial 170 or long-distance access numbers (☞ *below*).

INTERNATIONAL CALLS

Hotels tend to overcharge, sometimes exorbitantly, for long-distance and international calls. Use your AT&T, MCI, or Sprint card. Or buy an international phone card, which you can use from designated pay phones. Or make your calls from Telefoni offices, designated TELECOM, where operators will assign you a booth, sell you an international telephone card, and help you place your call. You can make collect calls from any phone by dialing ☎ 1721011, which will get you an English-speaking operator. (When calling from pay telephones, insert a €0.10 coin, which will be returned upon the completion of your call.) You automatically reach an operator in the country of destination. Rates to the United States are lowest round the clock on Sunday and 10 PM–8 AM, Italian time, on weekdays.

LOCAL CALLS

Phone numbers in Rome, and throughout Italy, don't have a set number of digits. All calls in Rome are preceded by the city code 06, with the exception of three-digit emergency numbers (113 is for general emergencies). Emergency numbers can be called for free from pay phones.

LONG-DISTANCE CALLS

Throughout Italy, long-distance calls are dialed in the same manner as local calls: the city code plus the number. Rates vary depending on the time of day, with the lowest late at night and early in the morning.

LONG-DISTANCE SERVICES

AT&T, MCI, and Sprint access codes make calling long distance relatively convenient, but you may find the local access number blocked in many hotel rooms. First ask the hotel operator to connect you. If the hotel operator balks, ask for an international operator, or dial the international operator yourself. One way to improve your odds of getting connected to your long-distance carrier is to travel with more than one company's calling card. (A hotel may block Sprint, for example, but not MCI.) If all else fails, call from a pay phone.

➤ ACCESS CODES: **AT&T Direct** (☎ 1721011). **MCI WorldPhone** (☎ 1721022). **Sprint International Access** (☎ 1721877).

PUBLIC PHONES

At press time, speculation was that upon the changeover from lire to euros, public phones would no longer accept coins but instead would be operational only with a *scheda telefonica* (prepaid calling card). You buy the card (values vary—€2.50, €5, and so on) at Telefoni offices, post offices, newsstands (called *edicole*), and tobacconists. Tear off the corner of the card and insert it in the slot. When you dial, its value appears in the window. After you hang up, the card is returned so you can use it until its value runs out. The *scheda telefonica internazionale* (values vary from €6.20 to €51.65) is an international calling card that can be used at designated public phones to call many foreign countries, including Canada and the United States.

TIME

Rome is 1 hour ahead of London, 6 ahead of New York, 7 ahead of Chicago, and 9 ahead of Los Angeles. Rome is 9 hours behind Sydney and 11 behind Aukland.

TIPPING

Many Rome restaurants have done away with the service charge of about 12%–15% that used to appear as a separate item on your check—now service is almost always included in the menu prices. It's customary to leave an additional 5%–10% tip for the waiter, depending on the quality of service. Tip checkroom attendants €0.25–€0.50 per person, rest-room attendants €0.25; in both cases tip more in expensive hotels and restaurants. Tip €0.05–€0.10 for whatever you drink standing up at a coffee bar, €0.25 or more for table service in a café. At a hotel bar tip €1 and up for a round or two of cocktails, more in the grander hotels.

Tip taxi drivers 5%–10% of the meter amount. Railway and airport porters charge a fixed rate per bag. Tip an additional €0.50, more if the porter is very helpful. Not all theater ushers expect a tip; if they do, tip €0.25 per person, more for very expensive seats. Give a barber €1–€1.50 and a hairdresser's assistant €1.50–€4 for a shampoo or cut, depending on the type of establishment and the final bill; 5%–10% is a fair guideline.

On sightseeing tours, tip guides about €1 per person for a half-day group tour, more if they are very good. In museums and other places of interest where admission is free, a contribution is expected; give anything from €0.25 to €1 for one or two persons, more if the guardian has been especially helpful. Service station attendants are tipped only for special services.

In hotels, give the *portiere* (concierge) about 15% of his bill for services, or €2.50–€5 if he has been generally helpful. For two people in a double room, leave the chambermaid about €1 per day, or about €3–€6 a week, in a moderately priced hotel; tip a minimum of €0.50 for valet or room service. Increase these amounts by one half in an expensive hotel, and double them in a very expensive hotel. In very expensive hotels, tip doormen €0.50 for calling a cab and €1 for carrying bags to the check-in desk, bellhops €1.50–€2.50 for carrying your bags to the room, and €1.50–€2.50 for room service.

TOURS & PACKAGES

Because everything is prearranged on a prepackaged tour or independent vacation, you spend less time planning—and often get it all at a good price.

BOOKING WITH AN AGENT

Travel agents are excellent resources. But it's a good idea to collect brochures from several agencies, as some agents' suggestions may be influenced by relationships with tour and package firms that reward them for volume sales. If you have a special interest, **find an agent with expertise in that area**; the American Society of Travel Agents (ASTA; ☞ Travel Agencies, *below*) has a database of specialists worldwide.

Make sure your travel agent knows the accommodations and other services of the place being recommended. Ask about the hotel's location, room size, beds, and whether it has a pool, room service, or programs for children, if you care about these. Has your agent been there in person or sent others whom you can contact?

Do some homework on your own, too: local tourism boards can provide information about lesser-known and small-niche operators, some of which may sell only direct.

BUYER BEWARE

Each year consumers are stranded or lose their money when tour operators—even large ones with excellent reputations—go out of business. So **check out the operator.** Ask several travel agents about its reputation, and try to **book with a company that has a consumer-protection program.** (Look for information in the company's brochure.) In the United States, members of the National Tour Association and the United States Tour Operators Association are required to set aside funds to cover your payments and travel arrangements in the event that the company defaults. It's also a good idea to choose a company that participates in the American Society of Travel Agents' Tour Operator Pro-

gram (TOP); ASTA will act as mediator in any disputes between you and your tour operator.

Remember that the more your package or tour includes the better you can predict the ultimate cost of your vacation. Make sure you know exactly what is covered, and **beware of hidden costs.** Are taxes, tips, and transfers included? Entertainment and excursions? These can add up.

➤ TOUR-OPERATOR RECOMMENDATIONS: **American Society of Travel Agents** (☞ Travel Agencies, *below*). **National Tour Association** (NTA; ✉ 546 E. Main St., Lexington, KY 40508, ☎ 859/226–4444 or 800/682–8886, WEB www.ntaonline.com). **United States Tour Operators Association** (USTOA; ✉ 342 Madison Ave., Suite 1522, New York, NY 10173, ☎ 212/599–6599 or 800/468–7862, FAX 212/599–6744, WEB www.ustoa.com).

TRAIN TRAVEL
TO AND FROM ROME

State-owned FS trains are part of the Metrebus system (☞ Bus & Tram Travel, *above*) and also serve some destinations on side trips outside Rome. The main FS stations in Rome are Termini, Tiburtina, Ostiense, and Trastevere. Suburban trains use all of these stations. The Ferrovie COTRAL line departs from a terminal in Piazzale Flaminio, connecting Rome with Viterbo.

CLASSES

FS trains have first and second classes. On local trains the higher, first-class fare gets you a clean doily on the headrest of your seat, a little more legroom, and a little less crowding. On long-distance trains (to Florence and Venice, for instance), first-class travel is worth the difference, and it is essential to **make seat reservations** in either class, which can be done through FS or most travel agencies.

CUTTING COSTS

To save money, **look into rail passes.** But be aware that if you don't plan to cover many miles you may come out ahead by buying individual tickets.

FARES & SCHEDULES

For destinations within 100 km (62 mi) of Rome, you can buy a *kilometrico* ticket. Like bus tickets, they can be purchased at some newsstands and in ticketing machines, as well as at FS ticket windows. Buy them in advance so you won't waste time in line at station ticket booths. Like all train tickets, they must be date-stamped in the little yellow or red machines near the track before you board. Within a range of 100 km (62 mi) they are valid for six hours from the time they are stamped, and you can get on and off at will at stops in between for the duration of the ticket's validity.

➤ TRAIN INFORMATION: FS (☎ 848-888088, WEB www.fs-on-line.com).

TRANSPORTATION

AROUND ROME

Although most of Rome's sights are in a relatively circumscribed area, the city is too large to be seen solely on foot. Take the Metro (subway), a bus, or a taxi to the area you plan to visit, and expect to do a lot of walking once you're there. Wear a pair of comfortable, sturdy shoes to cushion the impact of the *sampietrini* (cobblestones). Heed our advice on security. Get away from the noise and polluted air of heavily trafficked streets by taking parallel streets whenever possible. You can get free city and transportation-route maps at municipal information booths; the transportation maps are probably more up-to-date than those you can buy at newsstands.

TRAVEL AGENCIES

A good travel agent puts your needs first. Look for an agency that has been in business at least five years, emphasizes customer service, and has someone on staff who specializes in your destination. In addition, **make sure the agency belongs to a professional trade organization.** The American Society of Travel Agents (ASTA)—the largest and most influential in the field with more than 26,000 members in some 170 countries—maintains and enforces a strict code of ethics and will step in to help mediate any agent-client disputes if necessary.

ASTA (whose motto is "Without a travel agent, you're on your own") also maintains a Web site that includes a directory of agents. (If a travel agency is also acting as your tour operator, *see* Buyer Beware *in* Tours & Packages, *above*.)

➤ LOCAL AGENT REFERRALS: **American Society of Travel Agents** (ASTA; ✉ 1101 King St., Suite 200, Alexandria, VA 22314 ☎ 800/965–2782 24-hr hot line, FAX 703/739–7642, WEB www.astanet.com). **Association of British Travel Agents** (✉ 68–71 Newman St., London W1T 3AH, ☎ 020/7637–2444, FAX 020/7637–0713, WEB www.abtanet.com). **Association of Canadian Travel Agents** (✉ 130 Albert St., Suite 1705, Ottawa, Ontario K1P 5G4, ☎ 613/237–3657, FAX 613/237–7052, WEB www.acta.net). **Australian Federation of Travel Agents** (✉ Level 3, 309 Pitt St., Sydney NSW 2000, ☎ 02/9264–3299, FAX 02/9264–1085, WEB www.afta.com.au). **Travel Agents' Association of New Zealand** (✉ Level 5, Paxus House, 79 Boulcott St., Box 1888, Wellington 10033, ☎ 04/499–0104, FAX 04/499–0827, WEB www.taanz.org.nz).

VISITOR INFORMATION

TOURIST INFORMATION

In Rome, there is an EPT (Ente Per Turismo) Tourist Information Office in the city center, and there are EPT booths at Termini Station and Leonardo da Vinci Airport. EPT provides information about cultural events, museums, churches, and other landmarks in the city. Its free map of the city is very good. Information regarding travel outside of Rome can be found at the office of the ENIT (Italian Government Tourist Board).

➤ AT HOME: **Italian Government Tourist Board** (ENIT; ✉ 630 5th Ave., New York, NY 10111, ☎ 212/245–4822, FAX 212/586–9249; ✉ 401 N. Michigan Ave., Chicago, IL 60611, ☎ 312/644–0990, FAX 312/644–3019; ✉ 12400 Wilshire Blvd., Suite 550, Los Angeles, CA 90025, ☎ 310/820–0098, FAX 310/820–6357; ✉ 1 Pl. Ville Marie, Suite 1914, Montréal, Québec H3B 3M9, ☎ 514/866–7667, FAX 514/392–1429; ✉ 1 Princes St., London

W1R 8AY, ☎ 020/7408–1254, FAX 020/7493–6695).

➤ IN ROME: **ENIT** (Italian Government Tourist Board; ⌗ Via Marghera 2–6, ☎ 06/48899253). **EPT Tourist Information Office** (⌗ Via Parigi 5–11, ☎ 06/488991), open Monday–Saturday 9–7.

➤ U.S. GOVERNMENT ADVISORIES: **U.S. Department of State** (⌗ Overseas Citizens Services Office, Room 4811 N.S., 2201 C St. NW, Washington, DC 20520, ☎ 202/647–5225 for interactive hot line, WEB travel.state.gov); enclose a self-addressed, stamped, business-size envelope.

WEB SITES

Do check out the World Wide Web when planning your trip. You'll find everything from weather forecasts to virtual tours of famous cities. Be sure to **visit Fodors.com** (www.fodors.com), a complete travel-planning site. You can research prices and book plane tickets, hotel rooms, rental cars, vacation packages, and more. In addition, you can post your pressing questions in the Travel Talk section. Other planning tools include a currency converter and weather reports, and there are loads of links to travel resources.

For more information specifically on Italy, visit: www.initaly.com and www.wel.it. Other sites that might be of interest are www.romeguide.it, www.romaonline.it, and www.italyhotel.com.

The Web site www.nerone.cc is a quirky personal view of the city, and www.museionline.it has invaluable links to almost all the city's many museums and galleries together with news of the latest exhibitions, opening hours, and prices.

The Web site www.rome2000.net is a resource for pilgrims coming to the Vatican, and the state railways' excellent and user-friendly site at www.fs-on-line.com will help you plan any rail trips in the country.

WHEN TO GO

The main tourist season in Rome starts shortly before Easter (when the greatest number of visitors flock to the city) and runs through October. Spring and fall are the best seasons in Rome, as far as the weather goes, though tourist attractions are still crowded. It's neither too hot nor too cold, there's usually plenty of sun, and the famous Roman sunsets are at their best. In July and August, come if you like, but learn to do as the Romans do—get up and out early, seek shady refuge from early afternoon heat, take a nap if you can, resume activities in the late afternoon, and stay up late to enjoy the evening breeze. During August many shops and restaurants close, and on the August 15 holiday Rome is a ghost town. Roman winters are relatively mild, with some persistent rainy spells. During the winter months, especially January–March, you have a better chance of getting into the major tourist attractions without having to wait in line.

CLIMATE

Recent summers in Rome have been some of the driest and hottest on record.

➤ FORECASTS: **Weather Channel Connection** (☎ 900/932–8437), 95¢ per minute from a Touch-Tone phone.

ROME

The following are average daily maximum and minimum temperatures for Rome.

Jan.	52F	11C	May	74F	23C	Sept.	79F	26C
	40	5		56	13		62	17
Feb.	55F	13C	June	82F	28C	Oct.	71F	22C
	42	6		63	17		55	13
Mar.	59F	15C	July	87F	30C	Nov.	61F	16C
	45	7		67	20		49	10
Apr.	66F	19C	Aug.	86F	30C	Dec.	55F	13C
	50	10		67	20		44	6

FESTIVALS AND SEASONAL EVENTS

Contact the Italian Government Tourist Board (☞ Visitor Information, *above*) for exact dates and further information on all the festivals held in Rome.

➤ JAN. 5–6: On the eve of **Epiphany,** Piazza Navona's toy fair explodes in joyful conclusion, with much noise and rowdiness to encourage Befana, an old woman who brings toys to good children and pieces of coal (represented by similar-looking candy) to the naughty.

➤ FEB.: **Carnival** celebrations reach a peak of masquerading fun on the Sunday and Tuesday before Lent begins. On the evening of Martedí Grasso (Mardi Gras) many restaurants hold special carnival parties—you'll need to make reservations well in advance.

➤ MAR.–APR.: **Easter** is the big event of the season, preceded by the solemn rites of Holy Week, in which the pope takes an active part. Concerts of sacred music abound in churches all around town. The Good Friday procession, led by the pope near the Colosseum, is both moving and spectacular. The Monday after Easter, known as Pasquetta, is a holiday and traditionally a day for an outing into the country. This is one of the busiest weeks of the year in Rome; make reservations well in advance. In March watch for the **Museums Week,** a week of cultural heritage when museums and archaeological sites are free.

➤ LATE APR.: The Piazza di Spagna bursts into bloom, with the Spanish Steps covered by azaleas. Nearby, Via Margutta holds an **outdoor art show.**

➤ LATE APR.–EARLY MAY: The **International Horse Show** (Federazione Italiana Sport Equestri, ✉ Viale Tiziano 74, ☎ 06/36858528) brings sleepy Piazza di Siena, an amphitheater in Villa Borghese, to life with stirring competition and a chic crowd of spectators.

➤ EARLY MAY: The **Community Rose Garden Show** (Roseto Comunale, ✉ Via della Murcia, ☎ 06/5746810) opens at Valle Murcia on the slopes of the Aventine Hill overlooking the Circus Maximus and continues into June.

➤ MID-MAY: An **antiques fair** is held in the beautiful old Via dei Coronari in Old Rome, when shops stay open late and the street is lit by torches. Don't expect to find many bargains among the seductive antiques shops. The fair is repeated in October.

➤ LATE MAY: The **Italian International Tennis Tournament** (Federazione Italiana Tennis, ✉ Viale Tiziano 74, ☎ 06/36858510) is held at the Foro Italico.

➤ MID-JUNE–MID-JULY: The **Pontine Music Festival** is held in the Caetani castle in Sermoneta and in the abbeys of Fossanova and Valvisciolo, all within reach of Rome. It's a week of contemporary music, there's a concert every evening, and master classes and seminars for musicians.

➤ MID-JUNE–OCT.: The French Academy at Villa Medici holds a festival of performing arts called **RomaEuropa.** It's Rome's biggest arts festival, with an international array of acts. June is really the curtain raiser, with the bulk of the main events in September and October. The **Estate Romana** program, sponsored by several of the national academies in the city, involves a large number of outdoor concerts, plays, and movies throughout the city. Check with the local tourist office to find out what is going on. Movie buffs can choose from half a dozen film festivals in the summertime in Rome—the most interesting being the **Massenzio** in the Parco dell'Appia Antica, and the **L'Isola del Cinema** on the Gianicolo Hill near Trastevere. Consult local magazine listings for details.

Rome has a **Jazz Festival** from the end of June to the end of August, designed to rival the more famous Umbria Jazz Festival. There are concerts most evenings in the delightful Villa Celimontana on the Celian Hill.

In June and July there are concerts of classical, jazz, and ethnic music every Wednesday evening in the gardens of Villa Mazzanti on the hill of **Monte Mario** northwest of the Vatican.

Opera lovers can enjoy fine performances in the magnificent setting of the Roman **Villa Adriana** in Tivoli, just outside of Rome. The short season runs from the end of June to the beginning of July. A few symphonic concerts and some ballet are also included.

➤ JUNE 23: On the eve of the **Feast of St. John the Baptist,** June 24, the neighborhood of San Giovanni bursts with festive activities, mainly gastronomic.

➤ JUNE 29: The **Feast of St. Peter,** patron saint of Rome, is marked by solemn celebrations in St. Peter's Basilica, when the interior of the church is ablaze with light, and by showy fireworks over the Aventine Hill.

➤ MID-JULY: The **Festa di Noantri** in Trastevere combines religious processions with concerts of traditional Roman music and a sidewalk fair. There's a season of **ancient Greek drama** held at the beautiful Roman amphitheater at Ostia Antica, 23 km (15 mi) west of Rome. It's organized by the Teatro di Roma. The **Festival of Spoleto,** held in a beautiful Umbrian hill town 1½ hours from Rome, is also well worth a trip.

➤ AUG. 5: The **Feast of the Madonna of the Snow** is marked in the Basilica of Santa Maria Maggiore by a high mass, during which rose petals are thrown to represent the miraculous August snowfall that indicated where the church should be built.

➤ AUG. 15: **Ferragosto** marks the height of the summer vacation period. Most shops, restaurants, and museums are closed; public transport is at a minimum; and the city is the quietest it will ever be. There are special celebrations in the church of Santa Maria in Trastevere.

➤ LATE SEPT.–EARLY OCT.: In September and October the attractive medieval town of Viterbo holds a **Festival of Baroque Music.** A **Handicrafts Fair** in Rome brings torchlight, street stalls, and animation to Via dell'Orso.

➤ EARLY OCT.: In the Alban Hills southeast of Rome, the **Grape Harvest Festival** in Marino features parades and fountains spouting wine.

➤ OCT.: Look for the fall version of the semiannual **antiques fair** on Via dei Coronari in Old Rome.

➤ DEC. 8: This is the day of the **Feast of the Immaculate Conception,** when Rome's fire department replaces the garland atop the statue of the Virgin Mary in Piazza di Spagna and the pope comes over from the Vatican to pay his respects.

➤ MID-DEC.: Rome's **opera** season begins.

➤ LATE DEC.: **Presepi** (Christmas crèches) go on display in many churches; some of them are antique and quite elaborate. They often remain into the new year.

➤ DEC. 24 AND 25: **Christmas** is very much a family holiday in Rome. There are no public celebrations other than solemn religious rites, beginning on Christmas Eve; these are especially beautiful in the city's older churches and in St. Peter's Basilica, where the pope officiates both at midnight mass and at the late-morning mass on Christmas Day before imparting his blessing to the faithful in the square. Rome has more churches per square foot than any other city in the world. A Christmas service in one of the city's ancient places of worship is not to be missed.

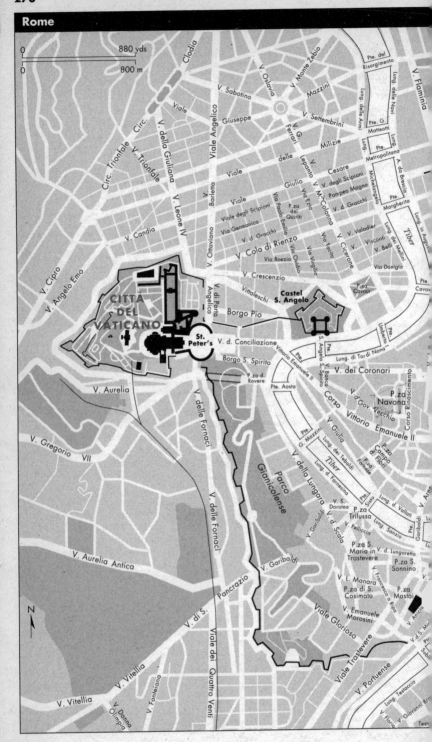

Italy

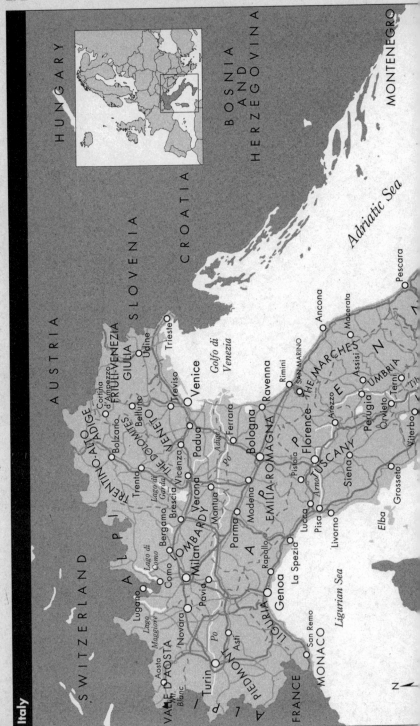

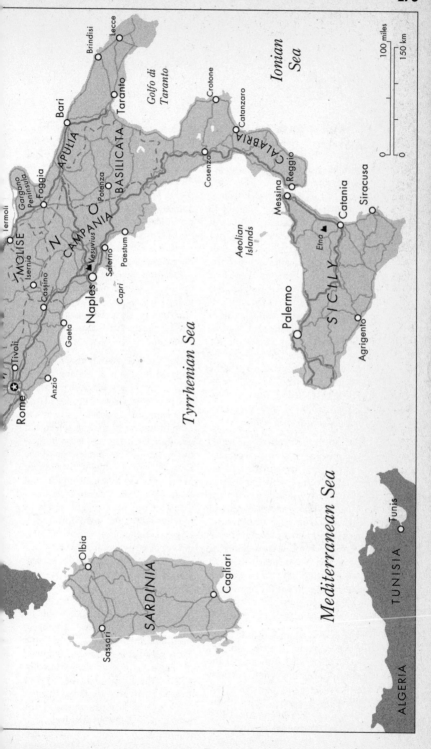

CREATIVE ROME: GLIMPSES OF GLORY

FOR THE LOVER OF ART, Rome remains the richest city in the world, its accumulated treasures inexhaustible despite centuries of plundering and decay. The epic time span of its art and architecture is immediately apparent when you arrive at the train station: while still under the daring modern sweep of the station's curving forecourt roof (finished in 1950) you can see to the right imposing fragments of the first city walls (of the 4th century BC, but traditionally ascribed to the 6th-century BC King Servius Tullius), and a walk across the piazza leads to Michelangelo's brilliant adaptation for Christian use in the 1560s of the last of the great imperial Roman baths (finished by Diocletian in AD 306). In fact, the idlest stroll in town still offers a succession of subtle or dramatic pleasures for the eye.

Conservation and export regulations give some protection to the city against property developers and rapacious collectors, and the biggest threat to the city's marble monuments since the barbarians and the Barberini now comes from the automobile, whose exhaust fumes cause rain to fall as corrosive sulfuric acid on triumphal arches and ancient columns. Even the Colosseum may have to be given a protective covering until scientists or politicians come up with a solution—or the world's oil runs out.

Given Rome's reputation as an artistic center and source of inspiration, it is surprising, but significant, that it has almost never had a native school of art; most of the distinguished works to be seen are imports, copies, or the work of outsiders in the service of kings, consuls, emperors, or popes. The story of the earliest Roman art is that of domination by the neighboring Etruscans (and, through them, by the colonizing Greeks). The first great temple—that of Jupiter, Juno, and Minerva on the Campidoglio (Capitol)—was built for the last of the ancient kings, Tarquin the Proud, by "workmen summoned from every part of Etruria," among them the first named artist to work in Rome, sculptor Vulca from Veii. Only the blocks of the temple's base survive—a large portion came to light in 1998 under the pavement of Palazzo Caffarelli, on the Campidoglio—but its lively, colored terra-cotta ornament can be judged from the grinning faces on antefixes preserved in museums, especially in the Etruscan Museum in Villa Giulia.

From the Etruscans, the Romans adopted the habit of making graven images of their gods and probably also of casting statues in bronze. (There are reports of bronzes made at the time of the first Etruscan kings, but among the earliest and most numerous to survive are renderings of the Capitoline Wolf—vigilantly offering her teats to the infants Romulus and Remus—and these are of later date.) Etruscan, too, is the practice that was to prevail throughout antiquity of setting up commemorative portrait statues in public—of kings and of women but, principally, of military heroes. The victorious Republican Spurius Carvilius used the enemy armor he captured in 293 BC to have a giant figure of Jupiter made; and, from the filings left over after the chasing, a statue of himself was cast—one of the many precursors to the splendid marble Augustus now in the Vatican. In 158 BC the Forum had become so crowded with portrait statues that the consuls removed those that had not been authorized. Portraits were also commonly made for family reasons. Wax masks of the dead (which could be worn by the living so that a man's ancestors could be present at his funeral) and images, along with triumphal spoils, might be displayed on the lintels of the family house. Portraits were frequent also on the later marble coffins, or sarcophagi, in which even freed slaves might be buried. Although neither sarcophagi nor portraits were invented by the Romans, their eventual mastery (and occasional monotony) of portraiture is legendary; the early bronze bust of "Brutus" on the Campidoglio is a noble example.

Even the ornament on everyday objects produced in early Rome is Etruscan in style; witness the mirrors and the cylindrical copper toiletry box, known as the Cista Ficoroni, in Villa Giulia, its elegantly incised figures showing how strongly the Etruscans had been influenced by the Greeks.

Elegance was in general a marked feature of early Roman taste. But the expulsion of the Etruscans and the kings, and the expansion in the last centuries BC of the republican state that was to dominate Italy and eventually the whole Mediterranean, brought with them a massive influx into the capital city of foreign booty; not just captured weapons but captured gods and works of art, carried in the triumphal processions of returning generals along with (presumably newly commissioned) paintings of their exploits and set up later as public ornaments. "Prior to this," says Pliny, "Rome knew nothing of these exquisite and refined things . . . rather it was full of barbaric weapons and bloody spoils; and though it was garlanded with memorials and trophies of triumphs there was no sight which was joyful to refined spectators." As the old-fashioned Cato is reported to have said, "Now I hear far too many people praising and marveling at the ornaments of Corinth and Athens, and laughing at our terra-cotta antefixes of the Roman gods."

Rome was thus exposed to a much more direct contact with Greek art, and the new conquests brought Greek artists and materials as well as finished works. Temples retained some traditional Etruscan features in plan but began to look more Greek, such as those in Largo Argentina or the 2nd-century BC Temple of Fortuna Virilis by the Tiber, built of rough local tufa and travertine. The nearby circular Temple of Vesta (originally the Temple of Hercules, as an inscription discovered in the 20th century has shown), which dates from the 3rd century, is made of the more "luxurious" material of marble. Not all old-style macho Romans welcomed this, and when Lucius Crassus used foreign marble for his house on the Palatine he was dubbed the "Palatine Venus." The great orator Cicero was not unusual in collecting examples of Greek art for his villa (a practice he called "my voluptuous pleasure"). Similarly, public art galleries were set up. Masterpieces of Greek sculpture were indeed in such demand that war booty did not suffice and many works were mechanically copied by the "pointing" process (invented by the Greeks and now used for the first time on a large scale)—so many in fact that a great proportion of the surviving antique statues in Rome's museums, even the Belvedere Apollo in the Vatican, are Roman copies or adaptations of Greek originals.

Art in Republican Rome was not entirely the consequence of plunder or imported labor. There were some exceptional native artists, principally in the more socially acceptable field of painting, in which a noble, Fabius Pictor, worked as early as the 4th century BC and later emperors such as Nero and Hadrian are reported to have excelled. Mural painting is also a genre in which one can speak of a distinctively Roman contribution. Compared with Pompeii, however, sadly little ancient painting or interior decoration survives in Rome, particularly from the early period. A noteworthy find, made in 1998, is a large bird's-eye view of a city that may be Rome itself, painted in Nero's time on a wall of the emperor's fabulous Domus Aurea (Golden House). There are some very fine examples of 1st-century BC painting and stucco—the charming landscape garden of Livia's villa and the "picture gallery" decor of the Farnesina House—in the Museo

Nazionale Romano in Palazzo Massimo alle Terme and on the Palatine.

The transition from a republican to an imperial form of government in the late 1st century BC was achieved gradually, by stealth as well as force. Subtly, but extensively, Julius Caesar and Augustus used public art as propaganda to buttress their positions. Famously, this involved big building projects and the claim that Augustus "found Rome brick and left it marble." Marble had of course been introduced earlier, but the forum Augustus built contains a greater variety of foreign colored marbles imported from the subject provinces of the Mediterranean than had been used before. Similarly, he was responsible for the introduction to Rome of the first Egyptian obelisks, which came to play such a distinctive role in the urban fabric. (The one at Montecitorio was originally used as a giant sundial.)

The triple-bayed triumphal arch built for him in the Forum (whose fragments helped to build St. Peter's) also prefigures a characteristically Roman form, but Augustus's patronage was not overwhelmingly self-promoting. He was responsible for, but did not give his name to, the Theater of Marcellus and other buildings. He built a temple in honor of the deified Julius Caesar, but he would not allow temples to be dedicated to himself unless they were also dedicated to Rome. The most attractive and best-preserved monument from his day is the Ara Pacis (Altar of Augustan Peace), reconstructed near his mausoleum in the 20th century. Its sophisticated carving is interesting as a revival of classical Greek style, though the use of historical imagery, with its portrait scenes, allegories, and episodes from the early history of the city, is characteristically Roman.

Augustus's successors did not need to be so circumspect. While Tiberius followed in his footsteps and left little personal mark on the city, and Claudius busied himself more with practical matters such as the aqueducts (most imposingly represented by the Porta Maggiore), Caligula and

Nero were notorious megalomaniacs—Nero wanted to rename the city Neropolis. Many of Nero's public buildings—the Circus and the first great public baths—and the city planning undertaken after the great fire of AD 64 benefited the city as a whole, but the most extensive project of his reign was the enormous Domus Aurea he built for himself, an engineering marvel set in parklike surroundings. When it was finished he said he was "at last beginning to live like a human being." The revolving ivory ceilings of the dining rooms are gone, but its dark ruins are still brightened by the paintings of the fastidious Famulus, who always wore a toga as he painted.

The succeeding Flavian emperors erased the traces of Nero's work. Nero's Colossus (a 115-ft gilt statue of him) was converted into an image of the sun, and an amphitheater was built by Vespasian nearby on the site of the Domus Aurea's ornamental lake. This was the Colosseum, most famous of all Rome's buildings and scene of the grisly spectacles with which all classes of the Roman welfare state, including the slaves, were kept amused. It is also a distinguished piece of engineering, embodying another of the comparatively few architectural forms invented by the Romans—the amphitheater. Not that the Flavians were against self-advertisement. They continued to use the triumphal arch as a billboard to boast of their victories and assert their divinity (a notable survivor is the Arch of Titus, where the emperor is carried to heaven by an eagle), and the style of their sculpture was more robust and confidently ornamental than ever before.

Under the Spaniard Trajan (AD 98–117) the empire reached its widest extent. He was the last to add to the series of Imperial Fora. (The adjacent market is still fairly intact.) The largest forum to date, his was financed by the booty from his campaigns against the Dacians in what is modern-day Romania. Trajan's exploits are immortalized in the continuous sculpted narrative spiraling round the innovative 120-ft column that still dominates the area.

Trajan's ward Hadrian (117–138)— the first bearded emperor, a keen hunter, singer, and devotee of the arts, and nicknamed "the little Greek"— was perhaps less concerned with his own fame, but no less active in embellishing the city. To him we owe the rebuilding of the Pantheon, a masterpiece of mathematical proportion and the only surviving building in which we can appreciate the spectacular impression created by the Romans' increasing use of cladding in colored marble from the imperial provinces. (Most of the marble from the other ancient buildings, like the great baths, has long since been stripped off and now adorns the churches and palaces of Christian Rome.) Hadrian was an enthusiastic builder and frequenter of public baths, which, besides offering exercise and hygiene for the body, pleased the eye with their marble and mosaic decorations and their collections of sculpture (the Farnese Hercules, now in Naples, was found in the Baths of Caracalla), as well as nourishing the mind with the literature kept in their libraries.

Having made plans for the most elaborate mausoleum in the city (which was later converted into the fortress of Castel Sant'Angelo), Hadrian in fact spent his last years almost exclusively at his sumptuous villa at Tivoli a few miles outside the city. This complex is notable both for the variety and beauty of its experimental architecture, with its references to famous sites in the Hellenistic world that Hadrian knew so well, and for the classical Greek Revival sculpture that has been found here. Notable among these are the Erechtheum caryatids beside the Canopus canal and the figure of Hadrian's beautiful Syrian friend Antinoös, now in the Capitoline Museum (one of the many statues of him, sometimes in the guise of a god, that Hadrian caused to be set up throughout the empire).

The Greek tradition dominated most Roman art until the time of Hadrian, but with his successors other ideals emerged, the change being particularly evident in the differing styles of the two sculpted panels of the base of the column of Anoninus Pius (circa 161), now in the Vatican, in the Arch of Septimius Severus (203), and, later, in the magnificent, if highly eclectic, Arch of Constantine (circa 315). On this latter arch, reliefs and statues from earlier monuments of Trajan, Hadrian, and Marcus Aurelius are juxtaposed, perhaps deliberately, with Constantinian reliefs, which are striking in their formality, severity, frontality, and, it must be said, crudity. The first two of these characteristics are often connected with the increasing absolutism of the Imperial Court.

The age of Constantine was a great turning point in the history of Rome and its art. The city was no longer the center of the empire (Diocletian had spent most of his time in Italy in Milan) and was not safe from external attack (as Aurelian had judged in 270, when he began building the massive walls that still ring the city). Constantine himself is famous for having founded the "New Rome" of Constantinople (previously named Byzantium and now known as Istanbul) in 330, but he did make a notable impact on the old city. Primarily this involved the discreet promotion, with imperial backing, of his adopted religion, Christianity, and the building of impressive churches for Christian worship and the privilege of burial. But this did not mean immediately abandoning all the old values, and indeed one of his principal achievements as emperor was the completion of what is now the dominant structure in the Forum, the Basilica, which had been begun by, and retains the name of, his rival, Maxentius. In its apse was placed for veneration a gigantic seated figure of the emperor, whose scale can be judged from the fragments of head, hand, and foot in the courtyard of Palazzo dei Conservatori on the Campidoglio.

For his Christian churches Constantine adopted a form that had long served a variety of functions in Roman secular life and was to remain a standard church design for hundreds of years: the colonnaded basilica, with a flat roof and semicircular apse (a barnlike structure with two rows of pillars down its length and one rounded end). The principal ones, San Giovanni in Laterano and old St. Peter's, were on a massive scale, but it is worth noting that Constantine's churches were rather plain externally and placed on the outskirts of the city on imperial property. They were not assertively imposed on Rome's civic and religious heart.

San Giovanni in Laterano and St. Peter's have since been remodeled or rebuilt, but a Constantinian interior, though smaller in scale and circular in plan, may be seen at Santa Costanza, the mausoleum built for the emperor's daughter, who was buried in an awe-inspiring imperial porphyry sarcophagus, now in the Vatican. Here the artistic continuity between pagan and Christian Rome is neatly exemplified. The column capitals are not all of the same type and, like so much of the building material used for subsequent churches, were clearly taken from earlier buildings, while the grape-crushing putti in the mosaics (and on the sarcophagus) had long been popular as a Bacchic motif and were now adopted by Christians as an allusion to the Eucharist.

No paintings survive in the early Christian basilicas, but paintings can be seen in the many catacombs, such as those of Sant'Agnese, near Santa Costanza. (The catacombs had been used for Christian burials not from fear of persecution or as hiding places but because land for burial was expensive.) In these paintings, too, we see a similar transfer of pagan forms to Christian uses.

After Constantine, no emperor returned to reside permanently in Rome, and the next century saw a struggle by the early Church to assert itself in the face of old, established pagan power. Churches were built closer to the center, such as the original San Marco, near the Campidoglio, and the impressively Roman authority of Christian imagery can be seen in the apse mosaics of Santa Pudenziana (circa 400), where the Apostles wear togas.

By 408 imperial edicts had forbidden the use of pagan temples (or any other place) for pagan worship (though it was not until 609 that the Pantheon became the first pagan temple to be used as a Christian church). The sack of Rome in 410 by the Visigoths (the first major military disaster for the city in 1,000 years) was traumatic but did not prevent the emergence of the Church as the unrivaled heir to the grand cultural dominance exercised previously by the now-absent emperor. This is visibly expressed in the large 5th-century churches of Santa Maria Maggiore—where the well-preserved mosaics on the triumphal arch show the Virgin Mary as an empress with a jeweled crown—and Santa Sabina, restored in the 1930s as the most graceful and perfect example of an early Christian basilica, its 20 Corinthian columns taken from classical buildings.

But the centuries of decline had already begun. The city was sacked again—by the Vandals in 455—and taken over by the Goths. When Gregory the Great became pope in 590, Rome had been for years a mere outpost of Byzantium, its population shrunk and its urban fabric reduced to a skeleton by decades of war and natural disasters. The Byzantine commander, when cornered in Hadrian's mausoleum, had repelled besieging Goths by having its statues smashed and the pieces catapulted at them. The erection of new churches had not entirely stopped: in the 520s the city prefect's audience hall in the Forum was converted into the church of Santi Cosma e Damiano and given mosaics in the more formal and abstract Byzantine style—and the administration of the city increasingly fell into the hands of the Church. But the future was bleak.

In the eight turbulent centuries that followed, the city's prosperity—and art—depended on the patchy success with which the pope could maintain his claim to temporal and spiritual power in the "Western" world, keeping the marauding Lombards, Saracens, and Normans at bay and the population of Rome in order. A major revival was signaled in 800, when the German Emperor Charlemagne, who saw himself as a new Constantine, acknowledged the supreme authority of the pope in the West by receiving his crown from Leo III in St. Peter's. Impressive new basilicas such as San Prassede were built and, not surprisingly, given Charlemagne's revivalist ideology, their form and mosaic decoration owed more to the art of Constantine's early church in Rome than to contemporary Byzantium.

But the revival was short-lived, not to be matched until the early 12th century, which saw a crop of new churches. In basic form they are almost monotonously traditional basilicas, innocent of developments taking place elsewhere in Europe, but they have attractive extras: tall brick bell towers (Santa Maria in Trastevere); cool colonnaded cloisters (Santi Quattro Coronati) and porticoes (San Lorenzo fuori le Mura); and lavish ancient marble fittings and pavements of the kind the Cosmati family were to specialize in, as well as mosaics (San Clemente). At San Clemente in particular, the charming still-life details and lush acanthus scrolls of the mosaics show a renewed interest in the pagan ingredients of early Christian art. But these ingredients had long been absorbed into Christian culture, and the examples of purely pagan art that survived had, to judge from pilgrim guidebooks, acquired superstitious, magical connotations—like the ancient marble mask installed in the portico of Santa Maria in Cosmedin, reputed to bite the hands of liars.

Further revivals occurred in the 13th century, not so much in architecture—despite Rome's one concession to the Gothic, the now-transformed Santa Maria sopra Minerva—as in painting and mosaic. In the 1290s, and especially in Cavallini's mosaics of the Life of the Virgin in Santa Maria in Trastevere, methods changed so that pictures of people, buildings, and whole stories became more lifelike than before, changes that later helped Giotto revolutionize pictorial narrative. Giotto himself worked in Rome, painting the triptych for the high altar of the old St. Peter's, now in the Musei Vaticani. But development in Rome suddenly ground to a halt, as the popes moved to Avignon (1309), and for 100 years the city became a back-

water. Petrarch lamented the state of "widowed Rome," cows wandered in the Forum, and the only artistic event of note was the building of the massive stairs up to Aracoeli, part of the populist Cola di Rienzo's fantasy of reviving the ancient Roman Republic on the Campidoglio.

The schism caused by the move of the popes to Avignon ended with the emergence of Martin V, a Roman, as undisputed pope (1417–31). He began the long process of restoration and renewal that, over the next three centuries, eventually resulted in spectacular and successful attempts to rival and surpass the achievements of the ancients.

To begin with, this involved the restoration of civil order and much repair work, but Martin V and his successors lived at a time of artistic resurgence in the rest of Italy, particularly in Florence, and they were able to import distinguished talent from outside. The great Florentine painter Masaccio came to Rome in the 1420s; his colleague Masolino's attractive frescoes survive at San Clemente as the first example of the new, more naturalistic style in painting with its mathematical perspective, while other Florentines—Donatello and Filarete—produced idiosyncratic but impressive sculpture for St. Peter's. All these artists were stimulated by what they could see of ancient Rome, and their patrons by what they could read of its literature. In particular, Nicholas V (1447–55) was a classical scholar and, convinced that the only way of impressing the authority of the Church on the feeble perceptions of the illiterate was by means of "outstanding sights . . . great buildings . . . and divine monuments," he produced an ambitious plan of building and decoration for Rome in general and the Vatican in particular, doubtless with the help of his friend and fellow scholar, the artist Alberti.

His successor, Pius II (1458–64), remarked that if the projects "had been completed, they would have yielded to none of the ancient emperors in magnificence," but little progress was in fact made. A rare exception was the decoration of the chapel of Nicholas V in the 1440s by Fra Angelico, with, for him, extraordinarily monumental frescoes. More substantial results were achieved by the Franciscan Sixtus IV (1471–84), who built a new bridge across the Tiber—only two had survived from antiquity, at the island and at Castel Sant'Angelo—and a large up-to-date hospital (Santo Spirito) near the Vatican, both designed to accommodate the pilgrims who flocked to Rome in Jubilee years. Churches, such as Santa Maria del Popolo, and palaces for cardinals, such as the enormous Cancelleria, were begun in new styles that paid increasing if still limited attention to ancient example. Property development was encouraged by new legislation. Although he was something of a philistine in his artistic taste, Sixtus did choose to import such outsiders as Botticelli and Perugino to decorate his large new chapel in the Vatican and tried to organize painters in Rome by setting up a guild. Although he was not especially interested in classical culture, and, like all the popes of his period, continued to use the ancient ruins as quarries, he performed an important service by setting up on the Campidoglio the first modern public museum of antique sculpture.

Such at this point was the enthusiasm, and excavation, for antique sculpture that his nephew Julius II (1503–13) was quickly able to stock the sculpture garden that he in turn set up in the Vatican Belvedere with the choicest pieces, such as the Laocoön group, dug up in 1506. And it is partly due to the presence in Rome of these rediscovered and revalued treasures that the artists he employed, notably Raphael and Michelangelo, were inspired to evolve their grand styles of painting and sculpture, which we may think of as specifically Roman, even though their art owed so much to Florence.

They must also have been responding to the imperial vision of their employer, the aggressive warrior-pope, who, in his determined efforts to continue his uncle's policy for the city, ordered the demolition of Constantine's St. Peter's, to be replaced by an au-

dacious structure planned by his architect Bramante, nicknamed the "Wrecker," which would, in scale and design, have "placed the dome of the Pantheon on the vaults of the Temple of Peace." For Julius, although he identified with previous popes in the dramatic propaganda decoration that Raphael painted in the Stanza of Heliodorus in the Vatican, also compared himself with Trajan in murals painted in his castle at Ostia. On his return from an expedition in 1507 a copy of the Arch of Constantine, depicting a history of his own exploits, was erected at the Vatican. Michelangelo's decoration of the Sistine Chapel ceiling, with its grand ensemble of sculptural figures, medallions, and reliefs, is clearly an imaginative exercise in this imperial genre, and his original design for the pope's tomb (which is in San Pietro in Vincoli) "surpassed every ancient and imperial tomb ever made . . . in its beauty and magnificence, wealth of ornament and richness" (Vasari).

The luxury-loving Medici pope, Leo X (1513–21), who followed, asked Raphael to decorate the largest room in the papal apartments with scenes from the life of Constantine, but he also borrowed jokes from Augustus and is reported to have said, "Since God has given us the papacy, let us enjoy it." There is plenty to enjoy in the long private loggia that Raphael and his pupils decorated next door, where tiny scenes from the Bible are overwhelmed by hundreds of painted and stucco images, mimicking ancient cameos and the kind of ancient fantasy painting to be seen in what had become the grottoes of Nero's Domus Aurea when it was rediscovered in the 1480s. Hence was born the name "grotesque" for the style of painting that was to become enormously popular in Roman and, with the spread of engravings, European interior decorations in subsequent years. It was also used in Raphael's saucy decoration of the nearby (but not visitable) bathroom of Cardinal Bibbiena and on a grand scale in the imposing unfinished villa that Raphael designed for Leo's cousin, Villa Madama. This is hard to visit, too, but other attractive villas of the day exist—the Farnesina, also decorated by Raphael, and the later Villa Giulia.

Villa Madama was a conscious re-creation of the ancient Roman villa as described by Pliny, and contemporary palaces tried to re-create the ancient-Roman house with its atrium and courtyards, as described by the Roman architect Vitruvius. Palazzo Farnese, finished by Michelangelo, is a stunning example, while Peruzzi's Palazzo Massimo is on a smaller scale but no less impressive. The courtyards of Palazzo Massimo alle Colonne and Palazzo Mattei also show how contemporaries displayed their prize antique sculptures—by setting them in the wall as decorations. Many less wealthy Romans imitated this fashion by having monochrome sculpturelike frescoes on their facades. A lonely survivor is Palazzo Ricci in Via di Monserrato.

But in 1527 the fun had to stop when German soldiers sacked the city, giving a glimpse of Purgatory and causing an exodus of artists (with further diffusion of their ideas) and, it is often believed, a change of heart in the city's art. Certainly Michelangelo's Last Judgment in the Sistine Chapel is a tremendous warning to the wicked, but artists such as Salviati and Perino del Vaga continued to paint in the most exuberant and deliciously witty styles, for example at Castel Sant'Angelo.

The Church did attempt to reform itself from inside, however, and among the churches built for the new religious orders after the Council of Trent (1545–63) were the Gesù for the Jesuits, originally rather severe inside, and the Chiesa Nuova for the Oratorians, one of the many churches to be influenced by the design of the Gesù, with a broad nave for preaching to large congregations. Here, St. Philip Neri, the founder of the Oratorians, was frequently found in a state of ecstasy in front of the painting of the Visitation by Barocci, his (and many others') favorite artist.

Spiritual excitement and intensity, theatrically presented, were to become dominant themes in the next century's art—most obviously in Bernini's chapel in Santa Maria della Vittoria, where members of the Cornaro family look out from their boxes at an ethereal vision of the ecstasy of St. Teresa, bathed in light, the whole executed in the most splendid ancient and modern marbles and other materials. Not all artists, though, looked so resolutely to heaven, and the most brilliant and influential painter in the period after Barocci was the passionate criminal Caravaggio, whose dramatically illuminated and controversial work ranged from luscious homosexual pornography for clerics to profound but distinctly earthy religious subjects—notice the obtrusively dirty feet of the adoring peasant in his St. Agostino altarpiece. Other distinguished painters of the day were more traditional—indeed, Annibale Carracci and his relatives pioneered a revival and extension of the styles of Raphael and Michelangelo, notably the opulent Galleria in Palazzo Farnese (circa 1600). Their work can be compared to (and contrasted with) that of Caravaggio in Santa Maria del Popolo.

Humble details such as Caravaggio's dirty feet may have moved the lower orders, but art was still effectively commanded by popes and cardinals: if Julius II's artistic propaganda had been grandiose, it was almost eclipsed by the whopping stories put out for the 17th-century Church. In painting this means, among others, the extraordinary achievements of Pietro da Cortona, who extended the powerful language of Michelangelo's decorations with a Venetian fluency and sense of color in his exaltation of the Barberini family on the ceiling of their palace's salone. But the most spectacularly theatrical effects were created in public architecture, both on a large scale in Bernini's piazza for St. Peter's, for example, where hundreds of huge travertine columns provide encircling porticoes, and on a smaller scale in innumerable projects such as Pietro da Cortona's brilliant scenographic setting for Santa Maria della Pace. Perhaps the most gifted and inventive of these architects was Borromini, a difficult (and in the end suicidal) person who did not get the biggest commissions. But his San Carlo and Sant'Ivo show how he could convert a restricted site into a tight ensemble of exhilarating power.

While this architecture was designed to impress, attempts were also afoot to make the city more comfortable. Bernini's porticoes not only broadcast the fame of Alexander VII but protected pilgrims from rain and sun. From the 16th century on, popes had striven to create straighter, wider streets, making it easier to visit the principal basilicas and speeding the progress of carriages. They also restored some of the ancient Roman aqueducts. The latter provided increasingly necessary water for the populace and supplied the impressive sculpted fountains that, from Bernini's Fontana dei Quattro Fiumi in Piazza Navona to Salvi's Fontana di Trevi, continue to delight and refresh the populace.

The Fontana di Trevi, the Spanish Steps, and Galilei's facade for San Giovanni in Laterano were among the last great spectacles of the late 17th and early 18th centuries. The artistic importance of 18th-century Rome lay not so much in what was done for the city as in what the city did for its many visitors. These were now the foreign artists studying the history paintings of Raphael and the religious works of Michelangelo in Rome's academies and the grand tourists, rather than the pilgrims of old. Piranesi's prints, fighting a magnificent rear-guard action for the grandeur of Rome against the growing popularity of a different—more purely Greek—view of antiquity, provided souvenirs for them; Batoni elegantly painted their portraits; and most of Canova's cool poetic sculptures were produced for export. The most distinguished building commissioned by the Vatican in this period was a museum—the Museo Pio-Clementino.

The power of the popes, and the city's art, continued to decline in importance in the 19th century as Rome emerged as the secular capital of the modern Italian state. Large but creaking and empty edifices were erected to its ideals—the monument to King Vittorio Emanuele and the Palace of Justice. The city was besieged by suburbs, and the river embanked to cope with flooding and traffic, but it survived remarkably well even the ambitions of Mussolini. His attempts to re-create something of the glory of the Roman Empire produced monotonous boulevards through the Forum and at St. Peter's, spoiling the effect of Bernini's piazza. But his grandiosity also gave birth to the striking architecture of the suburb of EUR.

Nor, in modern times, has Rome been an international center of the musical and theatrical arts, though ancient theaters and triumphal arches testify to the early Roman love of spectacle—even emperors performed and sang. Nero, who made his operatic debut with a group of sycophants in Naples, put his stage clothes on and sang (not fiddled) to a select audience while Rome burned. Opera-lovers can recapture something of this experience at open-air performances of Verdi's *Aida*, traditionally staged each summer with great gusto.

At the summer-long, outdoor, multi-screen movie festival one can see what gives Rome its claim to modern preeminence in the arts—the cinema. Successive generations of filmmakers working in the city and at Cinecittà (Italy's largest production studio) since World War II—Rossellini, Pasolini, and Fellini—have created an enduring art, perceptively chronicling and imaginatively exploring the inside and the outside of modern life and particularly, and most endearingly, of Roman society.

— Roger Jones

FEASTING
AT ROME'S TABLES

THERE IS NO SUCH THING as Italian cuisine. The Italian food that almost everybody loves to eat is really regional cooking. Lasagna and tortellini come from Bologna, veal cutlet and creamy risotto from Milan, *pasta e fagioli* (pasta and bean soup) and tiramisu from Venice, pizza and spaghetti with tomato sauce from Naples. Rome, too, has its very own culinary specialties, drawn from a tradition that goes back to the days when ancient Romans bought their groceries in the brand-new market that Emperor Hadrian had built. Yet Roman cooking seems to have had few ambassadors abroad.

Even in Rome, genuine Roman cooking is not easy to find. Restaurants and trattorias serve the cooking of other regions and other countries, catering to an increasingly heterogeneous population. The "Romans of Rome," a distinction that can be claimed only by those who have seven generations of Rome-born ancestors, are outnumbered by the "new" Romans— Italians from other regions and foreign residents, including legal and illegal immigrants from Asia, Africa, and Eastern Europe. Creeping mediocrity among Rome's eating places is making it increasingly difficult to get a really good taste of authentic Roman cooking.

The merit of Roman cooking is based on local ingredients, many of which are at their best only at certain times of year—milk-fed lamb, glorious globe artichokes from the sandy coastal plains, fresh vegetables from the farms of the Campagna Romana, as the countryside around Rome has been called since the time of the Caesars. Now, thanks to technology and imports from faraway continents, most ingredients are available year-round. But die-hard Roman cooks

know there's no substitute for the real thing—food that nature has made ready for eating, not for traveling.

Simple, hearty, and redolent of herbs, genuine Roman cooking comprises the economical dishes of the carters, shopkeepers, and artisans of Old Rome along with the refined and elaborate specialties concocted in the kitchens of popes, emperors, and kings. In the 1st century Juvenal wrote of dining on "a kid from the Agro Tiburtino, tenderest of the flock, who had not yet tasted grass and had more milk than blood in its veins." Martial, writing in the same era, sings the praises of the "lettuce, leeks, mint and dandelion greens, joys of the garden" brought to him by a farmer's wife. True to Roman tradition, he includes in his menu a baby lamb, "saved from the wolf's cruel jaws" only to meet a similar fate on Martial's table.

Celery, the indispensable ingredient of today's oxtail stew and bean soup, was covered with honey in ancient Rome and served as a dessert. Fish has also been a Roman choice through the centuries. In Trajan's time, slaves selected their master's favorite fish live from large tanks in the market, choosing between fresh- and saltwater varieties. At the entrance to the church of Sant'Angelo, at Portico d'Ottavia in the Ghetto, site of the old fish market, a curious plaque with a Latin inscription warns that the head of any fish surpassing the length of the plaque is to be cut off "up to the first fin" and given to the Conservators of the Capitol under pain of a fine of 10 gold florins. The heads were used to make a superb soup and were considered a great delicacy.

Eating habits have changed rapidly in Rome over the past few decades. Breakfasts are still sketchy: people usually start their day with a cappuccino and *cornetto* (brioche) at a neighborhood bar. Then, when mid-morning hunger pangs strike, they go to the nearest bakery for a square of crisp pizza *all'olio*, also known as pizza *bianca* (baked pizza dough, salt, and olive oil) hot from the oven. Romans love to eat it slathered with fresh ricotta cheese or dotted with sliced fresh figs. Pizza recurs throughout the day as a quick snack or fast meal; you can find it in bakeries and from morning to evening in the ubiquitous pizza *rustica* places where you can buy squares of crusty pizza with all kinds of toppings to take out or eat standing up. Pizzerias keep restaurant hours and serve classic round pizzas that are made to order and served at your table. Pizzerias also offer *bruschetta* (toasted garlic bread, often topped with sliced tomatoes) and *crostini* (rounds of toasted bread topped with grilled mozzarella and prosciutto or anchovies).

On their coffee breaks Romans have an espresso. Like all Italians they consider the cappuccino, half coffee and half frothy milk, strictly a morning drink, like *caffè latte* (much more milk than coffee)—they would never order it after a meal. If they want their coffee diluted, they'll ask for *caffè lungo*, made with a little more water, or *caffè macchiato* (espresso with a splash of steamed milk added at the counter). Many bars serve what they call *caffè americano*, a cup of American-style coffee. Caffè Hag is the best-known brand of decaffeinated coffee. *Caffè freddo* has little in common with iced coffee; it's more like coffee syrup and is served cold, not iced. *Granità di caffè* is frozen coffee slush that is sweetened and usually served with whipped cream. *Thè freddo* is presweetened tea served cold but not iced. It may be served *alla pesca* (with peach flavoring) or *al limone* (with lemon flavoring). Ice is something the Italians use little of, other than in a granità. Except in top hotels and restaurants, if you ask for ice in Rome you're likely to get only a few small pieces served on the side. It's for your own good, the Italians would say; iced drinks are harmful, as they upset the all-important di-

gestion and can cause collapse. It's not easy to get a really cold beer, either. But you can try: ask for whatever you want *molto freddo* (very cold), and emphasize the molto!

In theory, the main midday meal consists of several courses. However, problems of time and distance have forced Rome's working population to accept the idea of a light lunch, especially since offices and even stores have done away with the three-hour lunch break. As a result more and more places have sprung up in the city where you can find one-course meals, salads and such, with table or cafeteria-style service. Some restaurants also offer lunch menus.

A classic full Roman meal starts with an antipasto (hors d'oeuvre). In its simplest form, antipasto usually consists of a few slices of salami and prosciutto with olives and pickled vegetables and a butter curl (butter isn't served with bread anywhere in Italy, except in the most tourist-conscious places). A summertime delicacy is *melone* (chilled melon) or *fichi* (fresh figs) with prosciutto. *Antipasto di mare* is a seafood salad, usually already dressed with a citronette or vinaigrette sauce. Some restaurants are famed for their antipasto tables. This poses the question of how to order. As a rule of thumb, consider the antipasto the equivalent of one course. Throughout Italy pasta or soup is considered a first course; that's why these dishes are called *primi* (first). A normal meal would include a *primo* and a *secondo* (a main meat or seafood course). A basic restaurant or trattoria meal thus consists of two courses, with antipasto, vegetables and/or salad, and dessert as individually priced options. To have only the antipasto is to snub the kitchen and to cut into the proprietor's cost-profit ratio. If you want to do as the Romans do, have one other course before or after the antipasto, perhaps a pasta or a second course or even a vegetable (a *carciofo*, or artichoke, nicely substitutes for a first or main course).

Though you'll find all sorts of primi on the menu, from the tortellini of the Emilia Romagna region to the risotto of northern Italy, remember that the truly Roman pasta is fettuccine: light golden ribbons of egg pasta cooked al dente and served with a savory meat sauce (*al ragù*) or *alla papalina,* in a delicate sauce of butter, ham, and mushrooms (sometimes with peas, too). Fettuccine may also be served with seasonal vegetables such as artichokes and porcini mushrooms.

You'll hear several versions of the origin of spaghetti *alla carbonara,* served piping hot with raw egg, chunks of *guanciale* (unsmoked bacon), and lots of freshly ground black pepper. The one holding that the flecks of pepper evoke the image of a carbonara (one of the sturdy women who sold coal on the streets of Old Rome) is as good as any. Another Roman favorite is pasta *all'amatriciana,* served with a sauce of tomato, unsmoked bacon, and a bit of hot chili pepper, with a generous dusting of pecorino (sheep's-milk cheese). Pasta *alla gricia,* dressed with hot oil, unsmoked bacon, and plenty of black pepper, also is typically Roman, though it's not found on many menus. For an utterly simple and delicious summer dish, try pasta *alla checca,* steaming hot pasta that is tossed with fresh, uncooked chopped tomatoes, garlic, olive oil, and basil. "*Giovedì gnocchi!*" (Thursday gnocchi), is a weekly tradition in Roman restaurants and trattorias. Gnocchi are tiny dumplings of semolina or potatoes, served as a first course with tomato sauce and lots of cheese.

The truly Roman soup is *stracciatella,* steaming chicken broth with a beaten egg stirred into it together with Parmigiano cheese and a dash of nutmeg. The egg cooks as it's carried to the table.

Among the main courses, *abbacchio,* the baby lamb mentioned by Martial, is a classic choice. Spring is the best time for this dish. It is either roasted or served *al scottadito*—that is, grilled in the form of tiny chops that may burn your fingers (scotta dito) as you pick them up, a practice quite acceptable here.

On the menu, in addition to the usual *bistecca* (steak; with the exception of Tuscan meat, beef tends to be tough) and *cotoletta* (cutlet), you'll probably find *saltimbocca alla romana* (tender veal cutlets with sage and prosciutto) and *straccetti* (paper-thin slices of beef sautéed in oil). *Involtini* are little meat rolls, and *polpette* are meatballs. *Pollo alla diavola,* grilled chicken with a touch of lemon, is a simple main course. Many varieties of seafood are offered, from scampi (large shrimp) to *dentice* or *orata* (types of bream) and *rombo* (turbot). Though seafood dishes are generally more expensive, they are in great demand, so many Rome restaurants make seafood a specialty. "He's a baccalà" the Romans say, meaning that a person is stupid, perhaps unjustly maligning the *baccalà,* or codfish, which they otherwise esteem, especially in the form of crunchy hot fillets fried in batter.

The Roman way with innards is a story in itself. Centuries ago the men who cleaned and tanned the hides of the animals butchered in Rome were given the animals' innards to take home as a bonus. Ingenious housewives used these humble ingredients to create numerous dishes that have become staples of authentic Roman cooking. The most famous is *coda alla vaccinara,* oxtail simmered for hours in a tomato and celery stew. *Trippa* (tripe) is another favorite and a tradition on Saturday. *Coratella* (sautéed lamb's innards) and *pagliata* (baby lamb's intestines, usually served with rigatoni pasta) are still specialties of the restaurants and trattorias of Testaccio, where the slaughterhouses used to be. *Fritto misto alla romana* consists of batter-fried tidbits of artichokes or zucchini, ricotta, apples, brains, and sweetbreads. Roman trattorias may also serve *fagioli con le cotiche,* beans with pork rind.

Green vegetables are good in Rome. You'll see them on open-air market stalls in the morning and in the gastronomic still lifes that greet you in restaurants. Order *piselli e prosciutto* (peas and ham) in the spring, green salads, *cipolline in agrodolce* (baby onions in a sweet-sour sauce), and by all means try *puntarelle,* a truly Roman specialty, a variety of tender chickory curled in ice water and served with a garlicky anchovy dressing. It's usually available only in winter and spring.

The queen of Roman vegetables is the carciofo *romanesco* (globe artichoke), grown mainly in the iron-rich fields of the coastal plain north of Rome. It is particularly delicate when prepared *alla giudia,* the Jewish way, just as it originated in the kitchens of the Ghetto. Tender young artichokes are deep-fried and opened out to take the form of a flower, with each petal crisp and light enough to melt in your mouth. Carciofo *alla romana* is sautéed whole with garlic and parsley or mint.

As in most of Italy, Romans like to finish off their meal with fresh fruit or *macedonia* (fruit cup). Tiramisu is popular, as is *panna cotta,* milk custard that may be served with berries. Gelato (ice cream) is usually available and may be served *affogato* (literally, "drowned," with whisky). *Torta di ricotta* is the Roman version of cheesecake, made with ricotta. The local cheeses are mild caciotta and sharp, hard pecorino. You may be offered a liqueur by your host, and it will probably be *limoncello,* the popular lemon liqueur.

The ideal accompaniment to Roman food is the wine produced in the nearby hill towns known as the Cas-

telli Romani and in the wineries around Lake Bolsena, a bit farther afield. Among the Castelli Romani wines, Frascati is a dry, fruity white; when it's good it's very, very good, but too often the stuff served in carafes as Frascati is a poor substitute for the real thing. When in doubt, ask for a bottled wine. Colli Albani is quite similar to Frascati. Lanuvio is dry, golden-yellow, and rather robust. Marino may be either dry (*secco*) or slightly sweet (*abboccato*); it is either white or red. Velletri also produces a dry white and a red that ranges in color from pale to ruby red. The dry white Est Est Est of Montefiascone, on Lake Bolsena, turns up on Roman tables, as do some unpretentious but good whites from Capena and Cerveteri and whites and reds from Vignanello, near Viterbo.

Not many Romans indulge in the full banquet anymore, except on special occasions, mainly family get-togethers. But Romans do consider eating an essential component of traditional conviviality. With fast-food chains encroaching and the pace of life quickening, they defend their sociable and relaxed lifestyle by seizing every opportunity to gather in noisy family groups to enjoy good food and wine and congenial company.

— Barbara Walsh Angelillo

WHAT TO READ AND WATCH BEFORE YOU GO

Books

The Italians, by Luigi Barzini, is a comprehensive, lively analysis of the Italian national character published in 1964 (Atheneum). More recent musings on Italian life include *Italian Days*, by Barbara Grizzuti Harrison (Ticknor & Fields), and *That Fine Italian Hand*, by Paul Hoffman (Henry Holt), for many years *New York Times* bureau chief in Rome. *The New Italians*, by Charles Richards (Penguin), is also a well-researched overview of modern Italy's society and psyche by a British journalist. In *Rome: The Biography of a City* (Penguin), Christopher Hibbert provides a well-written and informative view of the city's eminent past and complex present. *When in Rome* (Robson Books) is an anthology of whimsical passages about Rome written by such famous authors as Dickens. Eleanor Clark's *Rome and a Villa* is a passionate evocation of the city as it was in the mid-20th century.

Classics of the travel essay genre include Elizabeth Bowen's *A Time in Rome* (Penguin) and James Lee Milne's *Roman Mornings* (New Amsterdam). Historic musings about Italy are offered in Henry James's perceptive *Italian Hours* (offered in many editions, including *Traveling in Italy with Henry James: Essays*, William Morrow) and in Edith Wharton's *Italian Backgrounds and Italian Villas and their Gardens* (Ecco Press). Stendhal, Goethe, and Dickens all wrote lengthily about Rome, and you'll find some intriguing passages in the collection *Italy in Mind* (Vintage), edited by Alice Leccese Powers. For lovers of detective fiction, Michael Dibdin's *A Long Finish* (Faber) is an enjoyable case for his irascible Rome detective Aurelio Zen.

For historical background, Edward Gibbon's *Decline and Fall of the Roman Empire* is available in three volumes (Modern Library). Consult Giorgio Vasari's *Lives of the Artists* and the *Autobiography of Benvenuto Cellini* (both available in Penguin Classics) for eyewitness accounts of the 16th century. An enlightening study of the complexities of Italy's contemporary history is offered by Paul Ginsborg's *A History of Contemporary Italy: Society and Politics 1943–1988* (Penguin).

A comprehensive introduction to Italian art is Frederick Hartt's *History of Italian Renaissance Art* (Abrams); Peter and Linda Murray's *The Art of the Renaissance* (Thames and Hudson) is a useful handbook. For aficionados of Rome's artistic treasures, Georgina Masson's *Companion Guide to Rome* (University of Rochester Press) is available in an updated edition.

For lively historical fiction, pick up *I Claudius* and *Claudius the God* by Robert Graves, available in a single edition (Penguin). Irving Stone's *The Agony and the Ecstasy* (NAL) relates a fictionalized version of the life of Michelangelo. Rome's inhabitants are portrayed during and after World War II in *History: A Novel*, by Elsa Morante (Vintage Aventura). Some of modern Italy's best literature has been set in Rome: try Carlo Emilio Gadda's *Quer Pasticciaccio Brutto de Via Merulana*, Pier Paolo Pasolini's *Ragazzi di Vita*, Gabriele D'Annunzio's *Il Piacere*, and Alberto Moravia's *Donna di Roma*, all of which can be found in English translation.

Videos

Set in a Rome that was recovering from World War II, Roberto Rossellini's *Rome, Open City* (1946) and Vittorio De Sica's *Shoeshine* (1946) and *The Bicycle Thief* (1948) are classics of the postwar cinema's neorealism. The delightful *Roman Holiday* (1953) won Audrey Hepburn an Oscar. Federico Fellini's *La Dolce Vita* (1961) gave its name to an era. Fellini's *Roma* (1972) is the director's exuberant paean to the city. Much of Pier Paolo Pasolini's work is set in the slums of Rome, including *Mamma Roma* (1962), and *Accattone* (1961). Nanni Moretti has earned a cult following here and across Europe with films such as *Caro Diario, Ecce Bombo,* and *Sogni D'Oro,* all of which are set wholly or partly in his native Rome. Peter Greenaway's *Belly of an Architect* (1987), Bernardo Bertolucci's *The Besieged* (1998), and Anthony Minghella's *The Talented Mr. Ripley* (1999) all benefited from Rome's incomparable cityscape.

ROME AT A GLANCE: A CHRONOLOGY

ca. 1000 BC Etruscans settle in central Italy.

753 Legendary founding of Rome by Romulus.

600 Latin script develops. Rome becomes urban center.

510 Last of the Etruscan kings—Tarquin the Proud—expelled from Rome; Republic founded, headed by two annually elected consuls. First Temple of Jupiter on the Capitol built.

471 First plebeian magistrate is elected.

390 Rome sacked by Celts.

380 Servian wall built to defend city.

312 Appius Claudius begins construction of the Via Appia and Acqua Appia, Rome's first aqueduct.

280–75 War against Pyrrhus, King of Epirus.

260–41 First Punic War: Rome struggles with Carthage in North Africa for control of central Mediterranean; gains Sicily.

250 Rome completes conquest of Italy.

220 Flaminian Way between Rome and Rimini completed.

219–02 Second Punic War: Hannibal invades Italy and destroys Roman army in 216; Scipio Africanus carries war back to Spain and to Carthage; in 206, Rome gains control of Spain; in 203, Hannibal defeated by Scipio.

168 Rome begins colonization of Greece and defeats Macedonia.

149–46 Third Punic War: Carthage is laid waste for good.

146 Rome completes conquest of Greece.

133 Rome rules entire Mediterranean basin except for Egypt.

102–01 Gaius Marius defeats Germanic tribes invading from north.

86 Civil war: Sulla defeats Marius.

82 Sulla becomes dictator of Rome.

71 Slaves revolt under Spartacus.

66–63 Pompey colonizes Syria and Palestine.

49 Gallic War: Julius Caesar defeats Gaul.

47–45 Civil War: Julius Caesar becomes ruler of Rome.

46 Julian calendar introduced.

44 Julius Caesar assassinated.

31 Octavian (later Augustus) defeats Antony and Cleopatra in the battle of Actium and becomes sole ruler of Rome.

27 Octavian becomes Emperor Augustus: Imperial Age begins. Augustan Age (31 BC–AD 14) is celebrated in the works of

Chronology

Virgil (70 BC–AD 19), Ovid (43 BC–AD 17), Livy (59 BC–AD 17), and Horace (65 BC–AD 27).

AD 42 Building of harbor at Ostia Antica begins.

43 Emperor Claudius (AD 41–54) invades Britain.

50 Population of Rome reaches 1 million; city is largest in world.

64 Rome burns; Nero (54–68) begins rebuilding city.

79 Emperor Titus (79–81) completes Colosseum.

90–120 Silver age of Latin literature: Tacitus (circa 55–120), Juvenal (circa 55–140), Martial (circa 38–102).

98–117 Emperor Trajan builds the Baths of Trajan and the Mercati Traianei.

100 Roman army reaches peak, with 300,000 soldiers.

116 Conquest of Mesopotamia.

117 Roman Empire at its apex.

125 Emperor Hadrian (117–138) rebuilds Pantheon and begins construction of his mausoleum (now Castel Sant'Angelo).

161–80 Rule of Marcus Aurelius, philosopher-emperor.

165 Smallpox ravages empire.

211–17 Rule of psychopath Caracalla; he begins Terme di Caracalla.

284–305 Rule of Diocletian; empire divided between West and East.

312–37 Rule of Constantine; reunites empire but transfers capital to Byzantium (later renamed Constantinople, today known as Istanbul).

313 Edict of Milan recognizes Christianity; Constantine begins construction of St. Peter's and San Giovanni in Laterano basilicas.

370 Huns appear in Europe.

380 Christianity made state religion.

406 Vandals lay waste to Gaul and Spain.

410 Visigoths under Alaric invade Italy and take Rome; Western Empire collapses.

452 Huns invade northern Italy.

455 Rome sacked by Vandals.

488 Ostrogoths invade Italy; in 493 Theodoric proclaimed ruler of Gothic Kingdom of Italy.

536–40 Justinian, Byzantine emperor, invades Italy.

553 Italy reincorporated into Roman Empire.

570 Lombards gain control of Rome.

590–604 Pope Gregory the Great reinforces power of papacy.

609 Pantheon consecrated as a church.

610 Eastern Empire separated from Rome for good and continues (until 1453) as Byzantine Empire.

800	Charlemagne crowned Holy Roman Emperor in Rome.
1073	Gregory VII elected pope; his rule sees start of struggle for supremacy between papacy and Germanic Holy Roman Empire. Rome sinks into stagnation and ruin for five centuries.
1309	Papacy moves to Avignon in southern France.
1347	Cola di Rienzo, adventurer and dreamer, tries to restore the Roman Republic; he is hanged six months later.
1377	Pope returns to Rome; Gregory XI makes Vatican the papal residence.
ca. 1500	Renaissance spreads to Rome—still little more than a malarial ruin—chiefly in persons of Bramante (1444–1514), Michelangelo (1475–1564), and Raphael (1483–1520).
1503–13	Reign of Pope Julius II; begins rebuilding St. Peter's and commissions Raphael to decorate his *stanze* (apartments) and Michelangelo to paint the Sistine Chapel.
1527	Sack of Rome: Confidence of High Renaissance evaporates as troops of Holy Roman Empire ravage city.
1534	Michelangelo begins *Last Judgment* in Sistine Chapel.
1546	Michelangelo commissioned to complete rebuilding of St. Peter's.
1568	Church of the Gesù begun.
1595	Annibale Carracci begins painting *salone* of Palazzo Farnese, ushering in Baroque Age. Architects Bernini (1598–1680) and Borromini (1599–1667) build churches, palaces, and fountains, largely under ecclesiastical patronage, transforming face of Rome. Leading painters include Caravaggio (1571–1610), Guido Reni (1575–1642), and Pietro da Cortona (1596–1669).
1626	St. Peter's completed.
1656–67	St. Peter's Square built.
1735	Spanish Steps laid out.
1797	Napoléon captures Rome and proclaims a new republic; Pope Pius VI expelled from city.
1808	Pope Pius VII prisoner in Quirinale.
1814	Pope Pius VII reinstated as ruler of Rome.
1870	Italian nationalists storm Rome and make it capital of united Italy; in protest, pope withdraws into voluntary confinement in Vatican.
1885	Monument to Vittorio Emanuele II begun (completed 1911).
1922	Fascists under Mussolini march on Rome.
1929	Lateran Treaty establishes formal relations between pope and state; Via dei Fiori Imperiali begun (completed 1933).
1936	Via della Conciliazione begun (completed 1950).
1944	Rome liberated from German occupation.
1957	Treaty of Rome establishes European Economic Community.

1960 Rome hosts Olympic Games.

1962 Pope John XXIII convenes the Second Vatican Council, culmination of his efforts to promote ecumenism and give new vitality to the Roman Catholic Church.

1978 Pope John Paul II, first Polish pope, elected. Extremist political activity in Italy reaches climax with kidnapping and murder of Premier Aldo Moro.

1981 Attempted assassination of Pope John Paul II. Cleaning of Michelangelo's frescoes on ceiling of Sistine Chapel in Vatican begins.

1990 Cleaning of Sistine Chapel ceiling completed. Work begins on cleaning Michelangelo's *Last Judgment* on wall over altar. Italian government passes so-called Law for Rome Capital, allotting funds and energy to a wave of major urban projects, including conservation and infrastructure.

1991 Rome's first mosque opens.

1997 Countdown toward replacement of the lira with the euro, the new European currency, begins, with the lira due to be phased out entirely by 2002. A copy of the statue of Roman emperor Marcus Aurelius is mounted on the pedestal of the original on the Campidoglio as a symbol of Rome's historic grandeur.

1998 Public works and restorations in preparation for the Jubilee year 2000 throughout Rome. Several 1st-century AD frescoes discovered in excavations of Nero's Domus Aurea on the Colle Oppio, including one cityscape that is the first of its kind ever found.

1999 Restoration work in the Sistine Chapel finally completed to universal acclaim.

2000 The Jubilee of the third millennium proclaimed by Pope John Paul II. Millions of pilgrims flock to the Eternal City.

2002 After more than 2,000 years Italy gives its up its monetary independence: the lira becomes obsolete and the new currency of all the European Community, the euro, is introduced.

WORDS AND PHRASES

English	Italian	Pronunciation
Basics		
Yes/no	Sí/No	see/no
Please	Per favore	pear fa-**vo**-ray
Yes, please	Sí grazie	see **grah**-tsee-ay
Thank you	Grazie	**grah**-tsee-ay
You're welcome	Prego	**pray**-go
Excuse me, sorry	Scusi	**skoo**-zee
Sorry!	Mi dispiace!	mee dis-spee-**ah**-chay
Good morning/ afternoon	Buon giorno	bwohn **jor**-no
Good evening	Buona serą	**bwoh**-na **say**-ra
Good bye	Arrivederci	a-ree-vah-**dare**-chee
Mr. (Sir)	Signore	see-**nyo**-ray
Mrs. (Ma'am)	Signora	see-**nyo**-ra
Miss	Signorina	see-nyo-**ree**-na
Pleased to meet you	Piacere	pee-ah-**chair**-ray
How are you?	Come sta?	**ko**-may **stah**
Very well, thanks	Bene, grazie	**ben**-ay **grah**-tsee-ay
And you?	E lei?	ay **lay**-ee
Hello (phone)	Pronto?	**proan**-to
Numbers		
one	uno	**oo**-no
two	due	**doo**-ay
three	tre	tray
four	quattro	**kwah**-tro
five	cinque	**cheen**-kway
six	sei	say
seven	sette	**set**-ay
eight	otto	**oh**-to
nine	nove	**no**-vay
ten	dieci	dee-**eh**-chee
eleven	undici	**oon**-dee-chee
twelve	dodici	**doe**-dee-chee
thirteen	tredici	**tray**-dee-chee
fourteen	quattordici	kwa-**tore**-dee-chee
fifteen	quindici	**kwin**-dee-chee
sixteen	sedici	**say**-dee-chee
seventeen	diciassette	dee-cha-**set**-ay

eighteen	diciotto	dee-**cho**-to
nineteen	diciannove	dee-cha-**no**-vay
twenty	venti	**vain**-tee
twenty-one	ventuno	vain-**too**-no
twenty-two	ventidue	vayn-tee-**doo**-ay
thirty	trenta	**train**-ta
forty	quaranta	kwa-**rahn**-ta
fifty	cinquanta	cheen-**kwahn**-ta
sixty	sessanta	seh-**sahn**-ta
seventy	settanta	seh-**tahn**-ta
eighty	ottanta	o-**tahn**-ta
ninety	novanta	no-**vahn**-ta
one hundred	cento	**chen**-to
ten thousand	diecimila	dee-eh-chee-**mee**-la
one hundred thousand	centomila	chen-to-mee-la

Useful Phrases

Do you speak English?	Parla inglese?	par-la een-**glay**-zay
I don't speak Italian	Non parlo italiano	non **par**-lo ee-tal-**yah**-no
I don't understand	Non capisco	non ka-**peess**-ko
Can you please repeat?	Può ripetere?	pwo ree-**pet**-ay-ray
Slowly!	Lentamente!	**len**-ta-men-tay
I don't know	Non lo so	noan lo **so**
I'm American/British	Sono americano(a)	**so**-no a-may-ree-**kah**-no(a)
	Sono inglese	**so**-no een-**glay**-zay
What's your name?	Come si chiama?	**ko**-may see kee-**ah**-ma
My name is . . .	Mi chiamo . . .	mee kee-**ah**-mo
What time is it?	Che ore sono?	kay **o**-ray **so**-no
How?	Come?	**ko**-may
When?	Quando?	**kwan**-doe
Yesterday/today/tomorrow	Ieri/oggi/domani	**yer**-ee/**o**-jee/do-**mah**-nee
This morning/afternoon	Stamattina/Oggi pomeriggio	sta-ma-**tee**-na/**o**-jee po-mer-**ee**-jo
Tonight	Stasera	sta-**ser**-a
What?	Che cosa?	kay **ko**-za
What is it?	Che cos'è?	kay ko-**zay**
Why?	Perché?	pear-**kay**
Who?	Chi?	kee
Where is . . .	Dov'è . . .	doe-**veh**
the bus stop?	la fermata dell'autobus?	la fer-**mah**-ta del ow-toe-**booss**
the train station?	la stazione?	la sta-tsee-**oh**-nay
the subway station?	la metropolitana?	la may-tro-po-lee-**tah**-na
the terminal?	il terminal?	eel ter-mee-**nahl**
the post office?	l'ufficio postale?	loo-**fee**-cho po-**stah**-lay

the bank?	la banca?	la **bahn**-ka
the . . . hotel?	l'hotel . . .?	lo-**tel**
the store?	il negozio?	ell nay-**go**-tsee-o
the cashier?	la cassa?	la **kah**-sa
the . . . museum?	il museo . . .?	eel moo-**zay**-o
the hospital?	l'ospedale?	lo-spay-**dah**-lay
the first aid station?	il pronto soccorso?	eel **pron**-to so-**kor**-so
the elevator?	l'ascensore?	la-shen-**so**-ray
a telephone?	un telefono?	oon tay-**lay**-fo-no
Where are the restrooms?	Dov'è il bagno?	do-**vay** eel **bahn**-yo
Here/there	Qui/là	kwee-la
Left/right	A sinistra/a destra	a see-**neess**-tra/ a **des**-tra
Straight ahead	Avanti dritto	a-**vahn**-tee **dree**-to
Is it near/far?	È vicino/lontano?	ay vee-**chee**-no/ lon-**tah**-no
I'd like . . .	Vorrei . . .	vo-**ray**
a room	una camera	**oo**-na **kah**-may-ra
the key	la chiave	la kee-**ah**-vay
a newspaper	un giornale	oon jor-**nah**-lay
a stamp	un francobollo	oon-frahn-ko-**bo**-lo
I'd like to buy . . .	Vorrei comprare . . .	vo-**ray** kom-**prah**-ray
a cigar	un sigaro	oon see-**gah**-ro
cigarettes	delle sigarette	day-lay see-ga-**ret**-ay
some matches	dei fiammiferi	day-ee fec-ah-**mea**-fer-ee
some soap	una saponetta	**oo**-na sa-po-**net**-a
a city plan	una pianta della città	**oo**-na **pyahn**-ta day-la chee-**tah**
a road map of . . .	una cara stradaleldi . . .	**oo**-na **cart**-a stra-**tah**-lay dee
a country map	una carta geografica	**oo**-na **cart**-a jay-o-**grah**-fee-ka
a magazine	una rivista	**oo**-na rec-**voess**-ta
envelopes	delle buste	**day**-lay **booss**-tay
writing paper	della carta da lettere	**day**-la **cart**-a da **let**-air-ay
a postcard	una cartolina	**oo**-na car-toe-**lee**-na
a guidebook	una guida turistica	**oo**-na **gwee**-da too-**reess**-tee-ka
How much is it?	Quanto costa?	**kwahn**-toe **coast**-a
It's expensive/ cheap	È caro/economico	ay **car**-o/ay-ko-**no**-mee-ko
A little/a lot	Poco/tanto	**po**-ko-**tahn**-to
More/less	Più/meno	pee-**oo**/**may**-no
Enough/too (much)	Abbastanza/troppo	a-bas-**tahn**-sa/**tro**-po
I am sick	Sto male	sto **mah**-lay
Please call a doctor	Chiami un dottore	kee-**ah**-mee oon doe-**toe**-ray

Italian Vocabulary

Help!	Aiuto!	a-**yoo**-toe
Stop!	Alt!	ahlt
Fire!	Al fuoco!	ahl **fwo**-ko
Caution/Look out!	Attenzione!	a-ten-**syon**-ay

Dining Out

A bottle of . . .	Una bottiglia di . . .	**oo**-na bo-**tee**-lee-ah dee
A cup of . . .	Una tazza di . . .	**oo**-na **tah**-tsa dee
A glass of . . .	Un bicchiere di . . .	oon bee-key-**air**-ay dee
Bill/check	Il conto	eel **cone**-toe
Bread	Il pane	eel **pah**-nay
Breakfast	La prima colazione	la **pree**-ma ko-la-**tsee**-oh-nay
Cocktail/aperitif	L'aperitivo	la-pay-ree-**tee**-vo
Dinner	La cena	la **chen**-a
Fixed-price menu	Menù a prezzo fisso	may-**noo** a **pret**-so **fee**-so
Fork	La forchetta	la for-**ket**-a
I am diabetic	Ho il diabete	o eel dee-a-**bay**-tay
I am vegetarian	Sono vegetariano/a	**so**-no vay-jay-ta-ree-**ah**-no/a
I'd like . . .	Vorrei . . .	vo-**ray**
I'd like to order	Vorrei ordinare	vo-**ay** or-dee-**nah**-ray
Is service included?	Il servizio è incluso?	eel ser-**vee**-tzee-o ay een-**kloo**-zo
It's good/bad	È buono/cattivo	ay **bwo**-no/ka-tee-vo
It's hot/cold	È caldo/freddo	ay **kahl**-doe/**fred**-o
Knife	Il coltello	eel kol-**tel**-o
Lunch	Il pranzo	eel **prahnt**-so
Menu	Il menù	eel may-**noo**
Napkin	Il tovagliolo	eel toe-va-lee-**oh**-lo
Please give me . . .	Mi dia . . .	mee **dee**-a
Salt	Il sale	eel **sah**-lay
Spoon	Il cucchiaio	eel koo-kee-**ah**-yo
Sugar	Lo zucchero	lo **tsoo**-ker-o
Waiter/Waitress	Cameriere/cameriera	ka-mare-**yer**-ay/ka-mare-**yer**-a
Wine list	La lista dei vini	la **lee**-sta **day**-ee **vee**-nee

INDEX

Icons and Symbols

★   Our special recommendations

✕   Restaurant

🏨   Lodging establishment

✕🏨   Lodging establishment whose restaurant warrants a special trip

🦆   Good for kids (rubber duck)

☞   Sends you to another section of the guide for more information

✉   Address

☎   Telephone number

🕓   Opening and closing times

💷   Admission prices

Numbers in white and black circles ③ ❸ that appear on the maps, in the margins, and within the tours correspond to one another.

FODOR'S ROME

EDITOR: Matthew Lombardi

Editorial Contributors: Jude Barrand, Bene Cipolla, Jon Eldan, Valerie Hamilton, Carla Lionello, Norman M. Roberson, Matt Small

Editorial Production: Stacey Kulig

Maps: David Lindroth, Inc., Mapping Specialists, cartographers; Rebecca Baer and Bob Blake, map editors

Design: Fabrizio La Rocca, creative director; Guido Caroti, art director; Jolie Novak, senior picture editor; Melanie Marin, photo editor

Cover Design: Pentagram

Production/Manufacturing: Yexenia Markland

COPYRIGHT

Copyright © 2002 by Fodors LLC

Fodor's is a registered trademark of Random House, Inc.

All rights reserved under International and Pan-American Copyright Conventions. Published in the United States by Fodors Travel Publications, a unit of Fodor's LLC, a subsidiary of Random House, Inc., and simultaneously in Canada by Random House of Canada Limited, Toronto. Distributed by Random House, Inc., New York.

No maps, illustrations, or other portions of this book may be reproduced in any form without written permission from the publisher.

Fourth Edition

ISBN 0–676–90124–7

ISSN 0276–2560

SPECIAL SALES

Fodor's Travel Publications are available at special discounts for bulk purchases for sales promotions or premiums. Special editions, including personalized covers, excerpts of existing guides, and corporate imprints, can be created in large quantities for special needs. For more information, contact your local bookseller or write to Special Markets, Fodor's Travel Publications, 280 Park Avenue, New York, NY 10017. Inquiries from Canada should be directed to your local Canadian bookseller or sent to Random House of Canada, Ltd., Marketing Department, 2775 Matheson Boulevard East, Mississauga, Ontario L4W 4P7. Inquiries from the United Kingdom should be sent to Fodor's Travel Publications, 20 Vauxhall Bridge Road, London SW1V 2SA, England.

PRINTED IN THE UNITED STATES OF AMERICA

10 9 8 7 6 5 4 3 2 1

IMPORTANT TIP

Although all prices, opening times, and other details are based on information supplied to us at press time, changes occur all the time in the travel world, and Fodor's cannot accept responsibility for facts that become outdated or for inadvertent errors or omissions. So always confirm information when it matters, especially if you're making a detour to visit a specific place.

PHOTOGRAPHY

Kindra Clineff, *cover. (Palatine Hill)*

Kindra Clineff, *11 top, 12C.*

Corbis: *2 bottom left, 2 bottom center, 3 to, 14D. Owen Franken, 13 top left. Araldo de , 9E. Ted Spiegel, 9C. Mark L. Stephenson, Michael S. Yamashita, 1.*

DIAF: *Langeland, 14E. Giovanni Simeone, 7B.*

Blaine Harrington III, *4–5, 10A, 12A.*

Hotel Eden, *13B.*

Italian Governnment Tourist Board, *2 top left, 2 top right, 3 bottom left, 14G.*

Myosotis, *14F.*

Network Aspen: *Jeffrey Aaronson, 13A.*

PhotoDisc, *2 bottom right, 3 top right, 3 bottom right, 14B.*

Andrea Pistolesi, *6A, 7C, 8B, 9D, 10B, 11D, 14C, 16.*

G. Rinaldi, *14A.*

Stone: *Robert Frerck, 8A. Sylvain Grandadam, 10C. A & L Sinibaldi, 12B.*

BOUT OUR WRITERS

he more you know before you go, the etter your trip will be. Rome's most ascinating small museum (or its chicest boutique or coziest trattoria) could be just around the corner from your hotel, but if you don't know it's there, it might as well be on the other side of the globe. That's where this book comes in. It's a great step toward making sure your next trip lives up to your expectations. As you plan, check out the Web as well. Guidebooks have been helping smart travelers find the special places for years; the Web is one more tool. Whatever reference you consult, be savvy about what you read, and always consider the source. Images and language can be massaged to make places appear better than they are. And one traveler's quaint is another's grimy. Here at Fodor's, and at our online arm, Fodors.com, our focus is on providing you with information that's not only useful but accurate and on target. Every day Fodor's editors put enormous effort into getting things right, beginning with the search for the right contributors—people who have objective judgment, broad travel experience, and the writing ability to put their insights into words. There's no substitute for advice from a like-minded friend who has just come back from where you're going, but our writers, having seen all corners of Italy, are the next best thing. They're the kind of people you'd poll for tips yourself if you knew them.

British-born journalist **Jude Barrand** has crossed the world, filing reports on developing nations for the U.N. and writing travel journalism. After writing for a ocal paper in the west of England, she made the leap to national television, working for ITN in London. She now resides Rome, where she works for Vatican adio when she's not out and about en-ing the best the eternal city has to er.

Eldan studied European history in eley, California, before packing his

bags in 1994 and going to see the real thing. After extensive travel up and down the Italian boot, he set up quarters in Rome, where he lived for five years, baking bread, and writing travel articles. He returned to his native country in 2001, but that won't prevent him from commuting to Rome several times a year.

In 1996 **Valerie Hamilton** turned in her surfboard and moved from San Francisco to Rome, where she works as a journalist, TV producer, and freelance bon vivant. She holds a degree in art history and archaeology, but her first love is travel; she has been covering Italy for Fodor's for the past three years.

Carla Lionello grew up in Venice, where she received a degree in English literature. In 1989 she traded Piazza San Marco for the Spanish Steps and moved to Rome, where she writes for food magazines and guidebooks. Carla also teaches Italian cooking workshops to culinary-inspired visitors.

Norman M. Roberson has lived in Rome for more than 18 years, spending a great deal of time walking in the area north of Rome known as Tuscia or southern Etruria. He is a freelance writer with more than 30 published articles, mostly about Etruscology and archaeology. He works at the American Academy in Rome and as a tour guide.

Don't Forget to Write

We love feedback—positive and negative—and follow up on all suggestions. So contact the Italy editor at editors@fodors.com or c/o Fodor's, 280 Park Avenue, New York, NY 10017. Have a wonderful trip!

Karen Cure
Editorial Director